WCN

Steps to Reading Proficiency

ANNE DYE PHILLIPS
(Formerly) Santa Monica College

PETER ELIAS SOTIRIOU
Los Angeles City College

WADSWORTH PUBLISHING COMPANY
Belmont, California
A Division of Wadsworth, Inc.

English Editor: Angela Gantner
Editorial Assistant: Lisa Ensign
Production: Del Mar Associates
Print Buyer: Randy Hurst
Text and Cover Designer: Vargas/Williams/Design
Copy Editor: Robin Witkin
Compositor: Thompson Type

This book is printed on acid-free paper that meets Environmental Protection Agency standards for recycled paper.

1   2   3   4   5   6   7   8   9   10 — 96   95   94   93   92

Library of Congress Cataloging in Publication Data

Phillips, Anne G.
    Steps to reading proficiency / Anne Dye Phillips, Peter Elias
Sotirious. — 3rd ed.
       p.   cm.
   ISBN 0-534-16518-4
    1. Reading—Aids and devices.   2. Reading (Higher education)
3. Rapid reading.   4. Reading comprehension.   I. Sotiriou, Peter
Elias.   II. Title.
LB2395.3.P48   1991
428.4'3—dc20   91-10974
                                                CIP

CONTENTS

. . . .

CHAPTER FIVE: OVERVIEW SKIMMING   185

. . . .

CHAPTER SIX: CRITICAL READING   267

. . . .

APPENDIX   329

PREFACE

This third edition of *Steps to Reading Proficiency* has kept what we think are the best features of the second edition and added some new features that respond to current research in reading theory. We have retained the overall organization of the book, moving from essential reading skills, to scanning, to study reading, to rapid reading, to overview skimming, and, finally, to critical reading. We have also attempted to make each of the reading selections of high interest and topical, replacing those readings that seemed dated.

The new features include a careful revision of all the introductions, making them more concise and including new information regarding current reading theory. Thirty percent of all the timed selections in rapid reading and overview skimming have been replaced, while half of the critical-reading and all study-reading selections are new. Further, many of the practices have been revised or replaced.

The major new feature of this third edition is the thematic approach that you will find in the study-reading and critical-reading chapters. All the study-reading selections treat some aspect of environmental pollution, and all the critical-reading selections treat the issue of crime. Reading theorists are now suggesting that introducing students to reading material on a related topic more efficiently improves their skills because they are reading with a focus rather than haphazardly from one topic to another. That is, their interest and familiarity with the content of the readings make the advanced reading skills easier to learn. To this end, we have provided preview questions for these two chapters as well as follow-up questions for students to discuss and write about.

We have also replaced several of the tests in the teacher's manual and revised many of the suggestions that we make regarding the teaching of various parts of the book.

We trust that these revisions and new features will make *Steps to Reading Proficiency*, as it enters its tenth year in print, an even more solid textbook for the advanced college reader.

ACKNOWLEDGMENTS

We would like to thank all of those who helped in producing this third edition. As always, the reviewers were very helpful. They include: Robert C. Andrews, Kean College; Cheryl Altman, Saddleback Community College; Jane DeSelm, University of California, Irvine; Barbara Tuntland, Illinois Valley Community

College; JoLynne Richter, Yavapi College; and Sylvia Wolff, Reading Area Community College.

Angie Gantner, our English editor, was again instrumental in moving this project through its various stages and made insightful suggestions about various parts of the book. Nancy Sjoberg, production editor, has cheerfully and professionally helped us through yet another project. Our spouses, Vasi and Bob, gave us needed expert advice about many computer and word-processing problems we encountered. They have lovingly and patiently stood by us during all three projects.

We are grateful for being able to work with all these lovely people.

HOW TO USE THIS BOOK

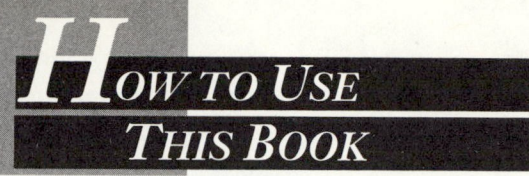

ORGANIZATION OF THE BOOK

This book divides reading proficiency into six areas: essential reading skills, scanning, study reading, rapid reading, overview skimming, and critical reading. Each reading skill builds on the previous skills, so we advise you to proceed through the book in the order we have established.

All chapters follow a similar organization: (1) Except for Chapter 1, each chapter opens with a Checklist of Symptoms, which enables you to assess your present strengths and weaknesses in that area. (2) The Checklist is followed by a thorough Introduction to the skill, which analyzes it and suggests practical ways to perfect it. (3) At intervals throughout the Introduction, you are directed to specific Practices (exercises) that reinforce the skill you have been studying. (4) Finally, a series of Timed Selections of increasing length and difficulty give you a chance to use the skill in sustained reading of actual college-level material.

HOW TO DO THE PRACTICES

Every chapter Introduction is followed by Practices that will prepare you for success in the Timed Selections. Some Practices are timed, some are not. They may be done as in-class warmups or as homework. In any case, always do them in the sequence established in the Introduction; never do them out of sequence, because they are carefully designed to reinforce each skill, step-by-step, as it is treated in the Introduction. After Chapter 1, your instructor will provide you with *all* answers to the Practices.

HOW TO DO THE TIMED SELECTIONS

1. Please do not—*ever*—read ahead in the Timed Selections. These are best done in class, under time pressure, and monitored by your instructor.
2. Follow all directions carefully. This includes accurate timing of each Selection in minutes and seconds. You may time yourself or have your instructor time you.

3. Score your quizzes using the Answer Key at the back of the book for all *odd-numbered* selections. Your instructor will provide answers for all *even-numbered* selections.
4. Check your comprehension score (%) against the target score, which is always preceded by an arrow (▶).
5. For Chapters 4, 5, and 6, record your rate (wpm) and comprehension score (%) on the Progress Chart at the end of each chapter. Be sure to keep accurate and complete records on these charts.

HOW TO DO THE QUESTIONS FOR DISCUSSION AND WRITING

After each Timed Selection in Chapters 3, 4, 5, and 6, you will see questions asking you to return to the Selection, reread more carefully, and prepare to discuss or write about the structure or meaning of the Selection. These questions are *not timed* and can be answered either in class or as homework, depending on your instructor's preference.

WHILE USING THIS TEXT

While you are working through these chapters, remember to use the skills you're learning here in all your outside reading—course work, magazines, newspapers, and pleasure reading. Your habits should change, not just in this book and course, but in everything you read.

AFTER FINISHING THIS TEXT

When you have finished the six chapters, you should be able to: read easy material rapidly with good comprehension, scan efficiently for specific information, comprehend and retain text material, skim for main ideas at high speed, and understand and analyze levels of meaning in difficult material. If you can master these skills, you will have developed true flexibility and proficiency that will serve you consistently in both your course work and your lifelong reading.

COMMON READING TERMS

CLOSURE: making complete meaning from incomplete stimuli. For example, in simple materials, we can comprehend close to 100 percent of the meaning of a page even if our eyes perceive only 80 percent of the print.

COMPREHENSION: understanding the meaning of a word, phrase, sentence, or passage. Many factors, possibly dozens or more, combine to make it possible for us to grasp the meaning of written language—that is, to "read."

EYE SPAN: the distance around a point of fixation, in which the eyes can recognize letters and words. For most readers, maximum eye span is a radius of two inches of print to left and right, above and below the point of fixation. This is about 29 letter spaces, 17 of which can be seen clearly.

FIXATION: concentrated, clear focus by the eyes on one spot. Fixation is possible only when the eyes are still, not moving.

FIXATION POINT: the point along a line of print where the eyes pause to focus sharply. Perception grows blurry away from the fixation point.

MAPPING: putting written material into a visual format. Mapping often helps us remember how main ideas and minor details are related.

PERCEPTION: an eye/brain activity in which the eyes see and recognize—and the brain comprehends—symbols such as familiar letters and words. Fast recognition of words and patterns is of course useful in better reading, and the speed and accuracy of perception can be increased through practice. But true comprehension of the meaning of a passage is a complex process that takes place in the brain, not in the eyes or through perception alone.

PERIPHERAL VISION: the ability of the eyes to see around a fixation point. Good peripheral vision aids in faster reading.

RATE: the speed at which we read, usually expressed in words per minute (wpm). Rate means little by itself, without some measure of our comprehension. Also, our eyes cannot perceive all the words on a printed page at rates higher than 800 to 900 wpm. At these high rates, we are skimming, or reading selectively.

RECITE: to reproduce, without referring to the material and preferably in our own words, the meaning of a passage we have read. Reciting is a way of self-testing to see if we have really comprehended the material.

REGRESSION: eye movement backward to a previous section of print. It is like a fixation in reverse. Regressions often are necessary for full comprehension of difficult material, but they are merely a poor reading habit in lighter material, slowing the reader down unnecessarily and garbling the writer's message.

RETURN SWEEP: the movement of the eyes from the end of a line back to the beginning of the next line. Skipping or repeating a line is common in beginning readers.

SUBVOCALIZING: "hearing the words" or "inner speech" when one is reading silently. This is common, even among fast readers with good comprehension. It especially occurs when one reads slowly, writes a composition, tries to comprehend difficult material, or reads literature (for example, poetry). During subvocalization, the throat muscles are tensed as if for speech. But at very rapid reading or skimming rates, the subvocalizing tends to drop out. Reading can then take place between eyes and brain only—one "reads the ideas" on the page rather than the individual, sounded words.

CHAPTER 1

Essential Reading Skills

*T*his opening chapter reviews many of the basic reading skills required to comprehend the literal, surface meaning of English prose. You will look for topic, main idea, and supporting details. Also part of literal comprehension, but not as basic, are recognizing writing patterns, summarizing, and preview skimming. In all this, we stress that reader and writer cooperate in the task of transferring meaning through the written word.

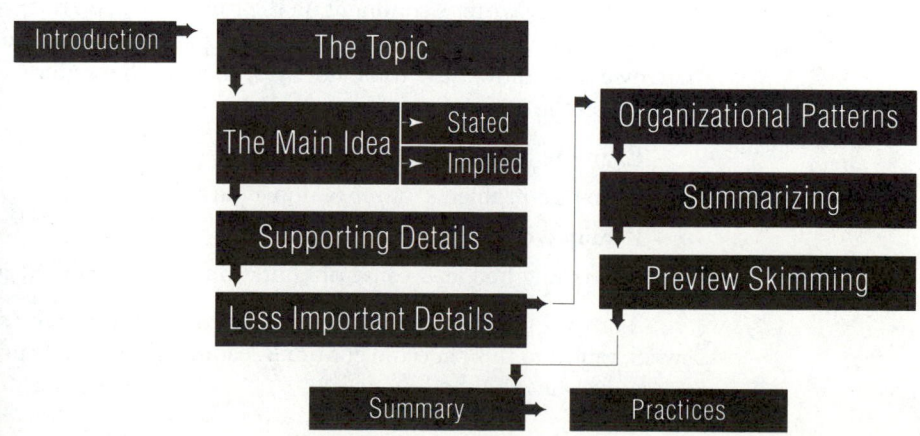

*I*NTRODUCTION TO *E*SSENTIAL READING SKILLS

To comprehend written material means to understand its meaning. To understand the meaning, the reader must retrace the writer's path. Luckily, trained writers of exposition—informational prose—present their ideas in a structured way. If you know the rules, you can unlock the meaning. You will grasp the literal content: who, what, when, where, and why. You will be able to discover the topic, the main idea about the topic, the support for the main idea, and how that support is arranged or organized. With a little more effort, you can go on to uncover the *inferences*—those unstated meanings that lie just under the surface of the literal content.

Let's review basic comprehension—how you comprehend the literal content of a written work.

THE TOPIC

First of all, the writer chooses, or is assigned, a topic to write about. (Another name for the topic is subject, or subject matter.) The topic can usually be expressed, by writer or reader, in a word or a phrase.

Examples of topics (subjects):

toads, African toads, African ridgeback toads, mating habits of African ridgeback toads

divorce, children of divorce, effects of divorce on children, effects of divorce on identical twins

our national parks, sanitation problems in our national parks

As you try to discover the writer's topic, avoid broadening it so much that you include the writer's comment on the topic. If you do this, you have really discovered what we call the main idea of the passage (see the next section). In its narrowest definition, the topic does not include the writer's comment or point of view on the topic.

Example of a topic alone:

sanitation problems in our national parks

Example of a topic plus comment:

a shrinking budget—cause of sanitation problems in our national parks

Turn to Practice 1.1 on page 18. After you do the exercise and check your answers, return to this page and continue reading. (Follow this procedure each time you move ahead to the Practices.)

THE MAIN IDEA—STATED

Writers not only choose, or are assigned, a topic or subject to write about. They must also have a focus, a main point to make about the topic. (The main idea may also be called the theme, or the comment on the topic.) A main idea may be expressed in a phrase or in a complete sentence.

Examples of main ideas:

why the African ridgeback toad is preferred for many lab studies

African ridgeback toads are preferred in development studies because their eggs hatch in only thirty-six hours

identical twins do not react identically to divorce

the recent budget cuts and their effect on our national parks

When the main idea of a single paragraph is stated in a complete sentence, it is called the topic sentence of the paragraph. When the main idea of a longer work—article, essay, term paper, editorial—is stated in a complete sentence, it is called the thesis statement. Look again at the four examples of main ideas just presented. Are any of these complete sentences that could function as topic sentences for paragraphs or as thesis statements for longer works?

How do you discover the main idea of a passage when the writer has stated it for you? Here are some tips to help you:

1. Recognize an umbrella idea, one that includes all the other, lesser ideas.
2. Know where writers are likely to state their main ideas, and direct your eyes (attention) to those places.
3. In longer works, notice any repetition of the main idea in the same or similar words.

Let's practice these three skills briefly here. (More Practices will be provided on pages 18–37.) Check your answers with your instructor.

1. *Recognize an umbrella idea.* In each of the following sets of terms, which term is broader than the others and includes the others? Underline the umbrella term.

   - toads, African ridgeback toads
   - German cars, Porsches, Volkswagens
   - interior, instrument panel, upholstery
   - park system, Yosemite, recreation, sanitation problems
   - visual system in goldfish, goldfish, how goldfish see colors

2. *Look at the likely places.* Main ideas can usually be found in the title, the subtitle (if any), the lead-in (if any), the introduction or first sentence or first paragraph, and the conclusion. You can be sure that no professional writer of exposition will bury his or her main idea—the whole point of the writing—in the middle of the material. In other words, the likely places are beginnings and endings.

Of course, not every title clearly indicates topic and main idea; for example, "Fame" or "My Cousin Gabriel" are too vague. But in the following four titles, see what you can tell about (1) the topic or subject matter and (2) the main point that will be made about each topic.

- "My Cousin Gabriel: Borrower Extraordinaire"
- "Why Your Child Must Have All His or Her Shots"
- "Cos Cob: From Indian Village to Giant Metropolis"
- "Walter Winnaker: Wizard of Woodworking"

Turn to Practice 1.2, starting on page 20, and try guessing the topic and main idea from actual titles and subtitles.

3. In a long paragraph or selection, *notice any repetition of the main idea in the same or similar words*. If a writer repeats a supporting detail, we may decide he is being repetitious and redundant. However, when a writer repeats the main idea once or several times, it is clear that he is trying to be emphatic. In fact, this is one of the best ways for you to recognize the main idea. It is often a general, umbrellalike statement that is stressed and repeated throughout a selection.

Example of a repeated main idea:

the main cause of the landslide—the single apparent cause—most evidence points to this reason for the slide—if it had not been for this one factor

For practice in spotting repetitions of a main idea, turn to Practice 1.3 on page 21.

Note: Writers of expository prose—textbooks, editorials, articles, essays, opinions, and the like—will usually present their main ideas clearly, stating them at least once, as in the preceding examples. Many other kinds of writing, however, do not contain direct statements of the main ideas. For these other reading situations, continue to the next section.

. . . .

THE MAIN IDEA—IMPLIED

If a writer does not state his or her main idea openly, we say that it is suggested, or *implied*. In this case, the reader must *infer* what the writer has implied.

This style, while not very common in objective, informational prose, is fairly common in writing of a more subjective or more literary nature. For example, you will often have to infer the main ideas in your reading of fiction (novel, short story, movie or play script), advertising, argument, and persuasion. These works do have main ideas or themes, as all clear writing must, but the writers may choose to convey their "messages" indirectly. Or perhaps their goal is to create suspense, a mood, a character, or a time period. When you read these writers, you must search for the deeper meaning. You may have to discuss, debate, and even disagree about the main ideas. (This kind of discussion is what makes inference and critical reading—skills you will be studying later in this book—so interesting, so much a part of "humane letters" or the humanities.)

In all later selections in this book, you will be asked to find the main idea if the writer has stated it. If it is implied—not stated—you will be asked to infer it and state it in your own words.

Turn to Practice 1.4 on page 22. You will look for main ideas in paragraphs when the writer has not stated them—when they are implied. Note: When you express an implied main idea in your own words, you are really condensing the passage or making your own umbrella statement for it. This is a large part of the skill of summarizing, which you will study later in this chapter on page 13.

. . . .

SUPPORTING DETAILS

So far, you have learned that a main idea may be expressed in a title, a phrase, or a sentence or two. Then what is the rest of a reading selection made up of? The answer is, support for the main idea. No writer can convince or inform you by simply stating and restating her main idea. If you think of the traditional three-part structure as beginning, middle, and end, and if you know that the beginning and the end are likely to contain the umbrella statement or theme, then you know that the middle (or body) contains the support. It is nearly always the largest part of the structure, too. It contains the details that support the short but general umbrella statement.

Students commonly mistake an interesting detail for a main idea. Here are some tests for supporting details: (1) A detail is different from the main idea; it does not simply restate it. (2) A detail is included within the main idea; it is under the umbrella idea. (3) Compared with the main idea statement, a supporting detail is more specific and less general, more concrete and less abstract, and often more factual. (4) A detail may be an example, a descriptive fact, a cause, an effect, an explanation, or an illustration—supporting or filling in the writer's main point about her topic.

Writers sometimes help you find separate sections or details by verbally "pointing" at them. These helpful words and phrases are called *transitions* or *signals*. Some obvious signal words are *first, second,* and *mainly*. Signal phrases include *on the other hand* and *the next step*. In longer works, signals or transitions may be as long as whole sentences or paragraphs.

Turn to Practices 1.5–1.6 on page 24. You will practice reading each paragraph for details that support the main idea and for the writer's transitions or signals. Once you have finished the exercises, return to this page and continue studying.

Note that you are learning step-by-step to underline, number, and mark in single paragraphs as an aid to comprehension. These same marking methods are a proven aid to better textbook reading; start using all of them in your other reading. (Chapter 3, Study Reading, will show you how to apply the methods to college-level textbooks.)

LESS IMPORTANT DETAILS

Not every detail in a passage is *significant* (important) in the support of the writer's main idea. Some writers and some fields are discursive—they discourse, or converse, rather than present only the facts and important ideas. Mathematics and most sciences tend to be written quite concisely; you overlook details at your peril. Some short fiction is nearly as concise. However, much of our lighter reading in newspapers and magazines, and even some social science materials, includes an abundance of detail, much of it interesting but not essential to a grasp of the main argument.

If you are reading just for main idea and main supporting details, you must learn to follow the thread of the presentation or argument, concentrating on key parts of the passage. You must recognize extra or less important details for what they are and, in some cases, skim through them lightly. (In Chapter 4, Rapid Reading, and especially in Chapter 5, Overview Skimming, you will really have to discriminate between important and unimportant details. There will not be enough time to read every little detail.)

Turn to Practice 1.7 on page 25. You will be reading quickly through main ideas and details, sorting out the important from the less important details.

ORGANIZATIONAL PATTERNS

So far, you are aware that as a reader you must retrace the writer's path. This means you must look for (1) stated main ideas and implied main ideas and (2) the support of those main ideas, especially the major supporting details. Does this sound pretty confusing to you? Luckily for readers, writers do not throw their details at us by the handful.

Instead, they nearly always organize the supporting material—the "body" of the work—in one or more recognizable ways. These are called *writing patterns* or *patterns of organization*. To further help us, writers often announce their pattern and guide the reader through it with certain "signal" words, phrases, or sentences. Another term for these signals is *transitions*. When you recognize these organizational patterns and their signals, you will comprehend the meaning more clearly and therefore faster. (Later on, in Chapters 4 and 5, you will even learn to skip some material, with no loss of basic literal comprehension.)

[margin handwritten note: certain type]

Note that although one pattern may be dominant, one or more other patterns may also be operating at the same time. Note also that fiction and other literature may employ patterns more subtly than informational prose does. In other words, the writer may not use any signals, but rather may *imply* the pattern or structure underlying his or her prose.

We present ten basic ways a writer may organize support for his or her main idea. As we said before, reader and writer follow the same path; so you have already used these patterns in your own speaking and writing. In this book, you will see them operating within a single paragraph; you will also see them operating over a several-paragraph unit or an entire article. Often, several writing patterns will be working at a time; usually, however, one of them is dominant.

Before you study these patterns, though, you should realize two things. First, you already know that every work has a focus or theme—a single controlling idea around which the writer organizes the support, or body, of the work. In longer, more formal works, this main idea is often called a thesis. The thesis naturally precedes the pattern. Recognizing this, some reading and writing experts call the "examples" pattern a "thesis-examples" pattern. You could mentally label each pattern that way: "thesis-reasons," "thesis-chronological," and so on.

Second, some of our ten patterns may be given slightly different labels by other experts in rhetoric or English; and they may add other patterns to their lists. But these ten are among the most commonly used patterns among writers, readers, and experts alike.

1. *Time sequence (sequence of events, chronological) pattern.* In this organizational pattern, the writer develops his or her thesis in time order, in a series, or step by step. It is probably the oldest and simplest of the patterns, going back to storytelling. Time sequence is the dominant pattern in any narrative, anecdote, story, plot of a movie or play, biography, or autobiography. In nonfiction prose, time sequence is also used in directions (how-to), process, the development or evolution of something, archaeology, history, and so on.

   - **Example:**
     The first sign any of the hikers had of the impending storm was a tall white cloud looming in an otherwise bright blue Sierra sky, far to the north. Late that day, the cloud had grown larger and had moved in closer. By sundown, the sky had turned uniformly gray; the temperature dropped ten degrees. They made camp hurriedly, ate a cold meal, and set up camp as snugly as possible.

   - **Common signals:**
     first, second, third, and so on; *now, later, next, soon, then, finally, afterward, before, after.* Times and dates are also common.

2. *Reasons (reasons why) pattern.* The writer gives one or more reasons why the thesis is a sound or valid one. This pattern is common in opinion, persuasion, and argumentation. Fields that commonly use the reasons pattern are medicine, history, the social sciences, and the natural sciences. The writer begins with an assumption that some belief or condition exists and then tries to show why it exists. Or the writer presents a conclusion, an outcome, and supports it with logical reasons. The reasons pattern is sometimes hard to distinguish from a cause-and-effect pattern. "Why did this happen?" is not very different from "What caused this to happen?"

   - **Example:**
     The hikers had no reason to expect anything but beautiful late-summer weather. Storms seldom moved in before late September. And this

weekend of September 5, the rangers assured them, would be three days of fair weather. So they were totally unprepared for the sudden blizzard that swept down on them Saturday night.

- **Signals:**
  so, reasons, why, because, hence, therefore, as a result. (And of course the ubiquitous *first, second, third.*)

3. *Examples pattern.* The writer lists two or more specific examples of his or her main idea or thesis. Examples are often facts or figures, or actual persons, places, dates, events, things, numbers, and so on.

   If the thesis is supported by only one example, and that one is developed in some detail, the pattern may be called a thesis-illustration pattern. (The illustration may consist of an anecdote, an episode, or an example discussed at some length.)

   Examples may be *typical* or *specific*. A typical example will not name specific individuals, dates, places, and so on but will support the idea with a general case. A specific example, on the other hand, does name one particular individual, date, place, and so on. You will learn to recognize both kinds of examples in the Practices.

- **Example (typical):**
  The kind of breakfast I most enjoy is one with the most calories and variety of foods. For example, an outstanding breakfast must have eggs, meat, pastries, pancakes, fruits, and coffee. Anything less is simply a businessman's breakfast.

- **Example (specific):**
  Our family enjoys getting together once a month for Sunday breakfast. For example, last Sunday we all met at 9 A.M. at Farmer Joe's, a family-style restaurant on the west side of town. We sat, all ten of us, around a big, round table and shared bacon and eggs, pancakes, and good conversation.

- **Signals:**
  for example, to illustrate, to give just one example of, for instance, specifically, in particular, especially, one example is, as in the case of, proof is found in

4. *Cause-and-effect pattern.* Here the writer tries to show a causal connection between two or more events (outcomes, situations, and so on). A is believed to lead to B, or B is the result of A. Since a cause can hardly occur simultaneously with an effect, this pattern often includes a strong chronological component as well. The writer must assemble proof, evidence, logical reasons, or data, or must appeal to shared experience, to convince the reader that A did indeed bring about B. This pattern is commonly used in the social sciences, the physical sciences, medicine, laboratory research, biography, and autobiography. We also see it used in English classes, when the teacher warns the student that missed work will lead to a low grade.

- **Example:**

  A large vocabulary is said, by some "pop" experts, to be closely correlated with a large income. It is no doubt true that high-salaried people
  in business and the professions have pretty fair-sized vocabularies, since
  they nearly always possess college and university degrees. Also, they must
  learn the specialized jargon of their fields. But how much more civilized
  to show a relationship between knowledge of one's language and ability
  to think. After all, words are thoughts. Without words, we could not have
  an abstract idea; we could only react and feel. Our high-salaried sample
  may simply be people who could learn and listen, could think and express themselves. Their big vocabularies did not lead directly to dollars
  but to an effective, civilized person—who might or might not choose to
  make a lot of money.

- **Signals:**

  *cause, effect, because, leads to, result, results in, brings about, ends in, traced
  back to, correlation, correlated with, link between, causal relationship, contributes
  to, proceeds toward, brings about, thereby, hence, since, if this . . . then that*

5. *Compare-contrast pattern.* The writer discusses two or more subjects and points
   out differences (contrast), similarities (comparison), or both differences and
   similarities (comparison). These are usually points or features or aspects of
   the two subjects. The passage may describe the features of one subject, then
   the features of the other subject(s), in separate sections. Or the writer may proceed one by one through the features, alternating between the two subjects.
   This pattern is useful in all writing—fiction, nonfiction, light reading or serious reading. We often learn what something is by noting how it is like or
   unlike something else.

   - **Example:**

     The demonstration in our city was similar to several others around the
     country that day, in numbers and makeup. However, the outcome was
     very different. Unlike the mass arrests in Boston and Atlanta, no one was
     arrested, and in fact the demonstration did not even make the television
     news.

   - **Signals (comparison):**

     *also, like, compared with, similarly, in the same way, as, just as, likewise, sim-
     ilar to, resemble*

   - **Signals (contrast):**

     *however, unlike, in contrast, whereas, but, on the contrary, opposite, opposing,
     on the other hand, unlike, differing from, contrary to, dissimilar, unique, un-
     usual*

At this point, try your hand at recognizing the five patterns you have just
studied in sample writings. Turn to Practice 1.8 on page 27. After you finish,
check your answers with your instructor. Then return to this page and study five
more writing patterns.

6. *Spatial or geographic pattern.* The writer organizes the details according to physical placement and spatial relationships. The details are often largely visual, structural, and quantitative; you read about amounts, distances, sizes, or outlines. This pattern asks you to visualize, imagine, or see relationships. Graphics such as photographs, sketches, diagrams, and maps may also be added to the text to help you "see" the writer's ideas.

   Like the other patterns, this pattern is found in all reading and in every field. But it is especially common in the natural and life sciences, medicine, mathematics, engineering, architecture, art, urban and ethnic studies, anthropology, history, population studies, and so on. These are fields in which parts, movement, proximities, and physical interrelations are paramount.

   • **Example:**
     The new mall is planned to be user-friendly. The ground floor will contain food shops, fountains, benches, and tables where people can stroll, eat, and chat. The second and third floors will contain the thirty or so shops—the business heart of the mall. The top floor will be open to the sun and sky, with small gardens and fine restaurants, and a 180-degree view of the bay.

   • **Signals:**
     left, right, up, down, in the rear, behind, in front; upper, lower, outward, inward; external, internal, dorsal, ventral, anterior, posterior; east, west, north, south; bordering, adjacent, next to

7. *Definition pattern.* The writer tries to explain or define a concept or object by delineating its qualities or aspects. Of course, a dictionary contains definitions of words—their *denotations*. Usually, the entry begins by assigning the general class of the word. Then it gives the particular features of the word that distinguish it from others in its class. (For example, "A horse is a large four-legged hoofed mammal which has been domesticated for riding and for carrying loads.") In our other reading, terms may be defined just as briefly, with one or two sentences, or the writer may expand on a word for a paragraph, a chapter, or even a book.

   Whether brief or lengthy, correct definitions of terms and concepts are essential if one is to learn anything in any field. In mathematics and the sciences, most terms lend themselves to clear and universally accepted definitions. In the social sciences, terms may not be so easy to define or may vary somewhat with the writer or with the context: aggression, adaptability, free elections, and so on. In the arts and in our daily lives, definition is even more difficult. What do you—or I—mean by a healthy mind? A romantic idea? Natural foods? Beauty? Success?

   A pure definition is usually fairly brief. If the writer goes on at length about the term, the pattern may verge on general description rather than being simple definition. This is especially true when connotations (the associations a word calls up) or specific examples and anecdotes are used to help explain the term. Most of us have had to write extended definitions in English composition classes; these become personal essays.

- **Example (denotation):**
  Depression is a mental condition of gloom or sadness; dejection.
- **Example (personal definition, connotations):**
  Depression is the conviction that nothing matters, nothing will work out. Depression is also the physical feeling of being twenty pounds heavier, twenty years older, than usual. You can hardly take a deep breath or move your large ungainly body. You can feel the sad droop of your eyes, each weighted down by puffiness.
- **Signals:**
  define, definition, describe accurately, explain exactly, mean, meaning, aspects of, discuss, analyze, is

8. *Process pattern.* The writer tells how something works or functions, or how something came about. (If the writer tells *you* how to do or make something, the process is informally called a how-to.) We often see this pattern in history, the physical and social sciences, and vocational courses. As we mentioned before, writing patterns often overlap or coexist. A process, a procedure, or a development by its nature occurs chronologically; it probably also involves some cause-and-effect pattern.

   - **Example:**
     How does a person grow up to be an Easy Reader? Usually the process starts soon after birth. The first necessity is loving parents who read to the child from earliest days on, holding him warmly and sharing the delight in the big picture books. Then the child notices that the home has books and magazines scattered about (good for playing with), and sometimes mother and father are sitting reading with evident enjoyment. The family sometimes give the child not just toys and money for presents, but wonderful books; they are his, to cherish as he does his computer and television set. The people in this thoughtful home read things to each other—sharing fun, facts, ideas. To this child, the whole world reads—so he reads—not well at first, but as naturally as he learns to ride a bicycle. By the time he is in his teens, he likes many activities, many ideas. Of course one of them is reading.
   - **Signals:**
     process, procedure; first, second, third; next, then, later, finally; happen; when, as, during; after, afterward, following; step(s); dates and times; interactions; leads to

9. *Classification pattern.* The writer discusses a subject by breaking it down into parts, which are then organized on the basis of traits, interrelationships, hierarchies, or some other system. Groups, classes, categories, types, flowcharts, family trees, chains of command in companies, job analyses—all these subjects lend themselves to the classification pattern. It is often the dominant pattern in these fields—botany, biology, and linguistics (language families)—as well as in popular articles about types of cars, travelers, students, colleges, fashions, and so on.

- **Example:**
We can all recognize the three dominant types of students at this college. First, we have the overachievers—they do everything twice as well as necessary, worry themselves sick over grades and exams, and usually get *A*'s. Then there are the remittance kids—their parents are paying to keep them in college and out of trouble. They do the minimum, ignore exams and grades, and try to get *D*'s just for showing up in class. The third type is the . . .

- **Signals:**
classify, group, type, sort out, analyze, order, arrange. This pattern often includes diagrams, flowcharts, "trees," and other graphics to show groupings.

10. *Description pattern.* The writer recreates a subject for you—a person, place, event, experience, mood, object, time, and so on—through many specific details. These details may be highly personal and imaginative, as in essays and stories, or they may be factual, as in a scientific or police report. The details are often sensory; that is, they involve the senses of sight, sound, taste, and touch. Writers add description anywhere. They insert it within other dominant patterns in order to enliven the content and make it vivid. Descriptive details can make a vague or abstract discussion more concrete. They help the reader see or experience the topic. As in all organizational patterns, a description may include a stated main idea or thesis. But sometimes the main idea—the focus for all those details—will only be implied, left for the reader to infer.

Descriptive passages are so common, and the pattern is so vague, that you may easily be tempted to label much of what you read *description.* However, outside of fiction, few long works are organized around description alone. Most description functions within some other dominant pattern. For example, a detailed description of a boat will form part of a chronological account of a prehistoric dig. So use the description label sparingly, as a last resort when no other pattern seems to be present.

The description pattern itself is sometimes broken down into kinds of description, or subpatterns: facts and statistics, spatial-geographic, and so on.

- **Example:**
This self-portrait by the Mexican painter Frida Kahlo is striking, even when reproduced in a textbook in black-and-white. She has set herself before a backdrop of lush tropical greenery; a small pet monkey peers enigmatically from behind her right shoulder. Like the monkey, she stares straight out of the canvas at the viewer, unsmiling, serious, self-aware, proud but not defiant. Her head and neck take up most of the frame; she has given herself an extremely long, straight, strong neck, almost like a pillar. Her face . . .

- **Signals:**
describe, description, the appearance, the look, in detail. (The writer may use no signals. He or she may simply begin to describe, filling in the broad statements with many specific details.)

Now that you have studied five more patterns, do Practices 1.9–1.11, starting on page 28. Practice 1.11 is a review of all ten patterns.

SUMMARIZING

Let's say that you have read an entire passage. You have become fairly competent in the essential reading skills: You can discover the main idea, the supporting details, and the dominant organizational patterns. You can infer the underlying or unstated meanings. All these skills are necessary before you can advance to the next skill: summarizing what you have read.

Summarizing means condensing the content of a passage into shorter form. (When you summarize a long work, such as an article, an essay, or a book, the summary is called a *précis*.) You must take care not to distort the main ideas and not to omit any significant supporting material. You obviously need to have an accurate and complete comprehension of the literal content of the passage, including important inferences the writer wishes you to make.

In a few cases, it may be almost impossible to summarize the contents without distortion or omission of essential details. Writing in which English is used very clearly and concisely is not common, but it can be found in mathematics, the sciences, straight news stories, directions, technical materials, or a very pared-down prose style.

Most written English is not so compact. In fact, much of what we read, even in textbooks, is wordier than it needs to be. Writers often include description or other details to amuse and entertain, or redundancy (unnecessary repetition) to "round out" their main ideas. Most of the time, main ideas clearly stand out from quantities of support, and we can summarize a passage in a fair and accurate way. We can condense, or squeeze into shorter form, without distortion and serious omission.

When you summarize another's writing, should you use the writer's own words? Ask your instructor's opinion about that. As long as you attribute your borrowing to the writer, you should not be guilty of plagiarism. Usually, however, you will write a much more accurate summary if you paraphrase (use synonyms) or, even better for condensing, use your own words to state the content without referring back to the original. The summary will flow in a natural way rather than sound like a patchwork of odd phrasings.

Summarizing is not easy. It is based on a total comprehension of the original work—not just the surface facts in it but also the relationship of major to minor ideas. Before you try to summarize another person's ideas, you must:

1. Read and reread the original several times. Remember, you are not commenting on or agreeing or disagreeing with the content. You are merely giving the gist of it as fairly as possible.
2. Underline or mark any stated main ideas. Mark or number the important supporting details (see Practice 1.5 on page 24).
3. Consider the organizational pattern; recognize important implied meanings as well as stated meanings.

4. Write your summary in your own words. Include exact words of the original only if they are essential and if your instructor permits you to quote them. Read your summary over; compare it with the original. Is it accurate—faithful to the original? Is it complete—all main ideas included? Is it short—no unimportant details included?

If the skill of summarizing still eludes you, try this: When you write a summary, imagine you are talking to someone, telling him or her the important points of what you have read. (And you don't have much time!)

To illustrate summarizing, we'll start with one paragraph:

> [1]*Slowly, we humans are learning the limits of our domination over nature.* [2]*Take the cheap, delicious hamburger.* [3]*At 49 cents or 99 cents, Americans and other citizens of "advanced" nations can eat a satisfying hunk of protein.* [4]*But how cheap is it, really?* [5]*These huge herbivores consume great quantities of water and plant life.* [6]*(It is reported that beef would cost $35 a pound if ranchers in the arid West were charged the true cost of their water.)* [7]*In pastures, their constant walking and cropping prevent small trees from growing; the common practice of overgrazing actually kills off grass to the point of desertification.* [8]*Agribusiness leaders in undeveloped countries destroy vital rain forests in order to reap huge profits by exporting beef, while their own people's needs for simpler foods go unmet.* [9]*The latest bad news about cattle sounds like science fiction: our tasty ruminants burp huge quantities of methane gas, one of the elements causing global warming.* [10]*The cheap hamburger is very expensive to everyone's environment.*

Read the paragraph several times. Underline the key words. Locate the topic sentence (it contains the main idea). Then write a summary of three to five sentences. Each reader's summary would vary, but here is ours:

> *We think we can easily dominate nature. But one example, the "cheap" hamburger, shows the hidden costs in our modern ways. Raising beef cattle is actually very destructive to land and water resources. In Third World countries, raising cattle for export means less food for the citizens. Lately it has been found that cattle produce a lot of methane.*

Notice that we moved the main idea from the end position to sentence 2. Your summary does not have to follow the same sequence as the original—just cover the main idea plus the main supporting ideas. In any case, our summary used 59 words to represent the 167 words of the original. You can also try summarizing into a short outline. (And did you note what organizational pattern the writer used to develop the main idea?)

Now turn to Practice 1.12 on page 33 and practice summarizing passages of more than one paragraph. This Practice is a review exercise for all the skills you have studied so far in this Introduction. (Later in this book, you will be asked to summarize even longer passages.)

PREVIEW SKIMMING

Like summarizing, the skill of preview skimming is considered rather advanced because it requires proficiency in all the previous skills. That is, you should be able to locate main ideas, important details, and basic writing patterns. If you can do these things when reading slowly and carefully, you are probably ready to do them more rapidly, under time pressure.

This book recognizes two kinds of skimming: preview and overview skimming. When we skim as a first step in the reading process—before reading the passage fully—we call it preview skimming. (It is also called reading prep, prereading, previewing, and—especially when we study read—surveying. You will learn to survey in Chapter 3, Study Reading.) Next to good basic comprehension, preview skimming is probably the most essential skill you must learn for every kind of reading.

Some students discover the usefulness of preview skimming through trial and error. Many others never discover it. For those unlucky people, the first step in reading is always to read every word slowly. But reading one word at a time, from the beginning, is very inefficient. It's like driving around in a strange city without a map. Of course, if you have unlimited time for driving, or reading, and if you like being surprised and confused, then you should not look at a map first, and you should not preview skim your reading first. But if you would like to read well, in the shortest time, make preview skimming your automatic first step for every reading task: letter, article, test, story, novel, or textbook chapter. "P E F!"— "Preview everything first!"

In this book, from now on, you will be directed to preview skim before doing anything else—rapid reading, overview skimming, study reading, and so on.

Specifically, what do you gain from preview skimming before reading? A good preview should:

1. Arouse your interest in the content.
2. Give you some minimum facts about it so that you do not begin reading it "cold."
3. Tell you the main ideas and organization and your best strategy for comprehension.
4. As a bonus, double your reading rate, with no loss of comprehension, when you return to read carefully.

The first value of preview skimming is that the reader gets a unified picture of the selection, a sense of the whole, well before plunging into the details, difficult vocabulary words, and so on. You see the forest before the trees. This view of a selection is necessary; otherwise, the individual trees do not add up to much.

How should you preview? First, time yourself. If you don't, you'll find yourself reading every word slowly and carefully, just as you've always done. Second, consciously direct your eyes to certain key areas only. This will be hard to do at first, but remember that you preview in order to comprehend better when you return and read. Previewing is not reading. Tell yourself to look only at the following:

1. Title; subtitle, if any; lead-in, if any (short summary at beginning)
2. Author, plus his or her credentials
3. Length: number of paragraphs or pages
4. Source; date published
5. Structure: major divisions, if any

That much constitutes a minimal preview skim, the very least you should know about a selection before you begin to read. For a more thorough preview, or if the material is difficult, add the following:

6. Headings, spacing, boldface subheads, other breaks in the text
7. Graphics: photos, graphs, maps, and the like
8. All of the summary or concluding paragraphs
9. First sentence or two of each fully developed paragraph

Do any of the preceding items sound familiar? They should! They are the same key parts you focus on when you discover a writer's main ideas (see page 3). In other words, a good preview skim gives the highlights of a reading selection. Do not worry about all the content you are missing; remind yourself that you will return in a moment to read carefully for every detail.

If you follow the steps—that is, preview skim first, then read—you will read the most important sections of the selection twice, an excellent reading and learning technique.

How much time must you spend on this first step? Students often fear they don't have time to both preview and read. However, previewing reduces total reading time, because it speeds up and improves full comprehension. Besides, it takes very little time (and less time the more you do it). Here are some suggestions:

Selection Length	*Preview Skim for*
up to one page	10–20 seconds
several pages; one chapter	½–2 minutes
entire book	15–20 minutes

A few seconds or minutes is not much time to invest for more thorough and efficient comprehension.

As with all the techniques in this book, practice during the school year will teach you to preview skim with more control and purpose and to gain more content from it.

We do not supply any Practices solely for preview skimming. Of course, to practice what we preach, we will always ask you to preview every selection you work on throughout this book, starting with Chapter 2, Scanning. Your real improvement will occur when you preview all your reading and studying materials outside this course. Don't forget to P E F—"Preview everything first!"

· · · · · · · · · · · · · · · · · ·

SUMMARY

This book began with a chapter on the Essential Reading Skills; they *are* essential—to any of the more advanced skills in later chapters. No reader can skim, scan, speed-read, study college textbooks, or read critically without a good grasp of basic literal comprehension. A reader must easily understand the topic, the main ideas, the supporting details, and the organization of anything he or she reads. Later the reader can move on to more difficult reading tasks.

Good reading means that one sees reading and writing as two sides of the same process: the giving and receiving of a written message. A writer takes a certain path, always with the reader in mind. The reader recognizes that path and follows it. Luckily, most informative writing (exposition) is structured according to certain basic patterns. Topic, thesis or main idea, and organizational pattern are located and developed in fairly predictable ways. This is where reading instruction can help a reader become proficient more rapidly than if he or she works alone.

Ideas are developed in writing through certain common patterns. This chapter has introduced ten of them; most written prose will be constructed along those lines or small variations of them.

One sign of true comprehension is the ability to summarize the writer's message. A reader who can only parrot the words on the page has not really comprehended them.

To make all our reading easier, we should try to "see the big picture first," or, to use another cliché, begin with a "map of the territory." We do this by previewing the material first, rapidly but alertly. Then when we go back and begin slower reading, we know something about the content and the organization. With practice, readers find they can nearly double their reading speed with no loss of—and often a gain in—comprehension, all by previewing first. So, except for mystery stories, P E F—"Preview everything first!"

PRACTICES:
ESSENTIAL READING SKILLS

Answers for the odd-numbered exercises are provided in the answer key. Ask your instructor for answers to the even-numbered exercises.

1.1 IDENTIFYING THE TOPIC (SUBJECT) OF A PARAGRAPH

In each of the following paragraphs, quickly find the topic and write it in the blank. Remember to use only a word or a phrase, not a complete sentence. Do not include the writer's opinion or comment about the topic, since this would constitute the main idea. When you are finished, check your answers on p. 334.

> **Sample topic (word or phrase, not a complete sentence):**
>
> relations between the USA and the USSR (*not:* relations between the USA and the USSR are at a low ebb)
>
> my father (*not:* my father always wanted to be a big-name comic)

1. [1]Anyone who has used our city parks recently can see that the sanitation problem in the parks is growing steadily worse. [2]Trash cans are inadequate, so litter spreads everywhere. [3]Drinking fountains are old and rusty; often they do not work at all. [4]Restrooms need paint, new doors, plumbing repairs, and better daily maintenance.

Topic (word or phrase): _____ sanitation in parks

2. [1]Divorce always has an effect on children in the family. [2]However, divorce does not affect every child the same way. [3]In fact, even identical twins, who often

share many similarities, do not necessarily react to their parents' divorce in identical ways. [4]Researchers have studied forty pairs of identical twins whose parents have divorced. [5]They found a surprising range of responses to the fact of divorce, from reasonably good acceptance to severe emotional disturbance.

Topic (word or phrase): Childrens reaction to divorce

3. [1]Serving on a jury can be boring, if you consider the hours and days you may sit in the Jurors Assembly Room, waiting to be called to a trial. [2]But it can be one of the most interesting things you'll ever do. [3]Consider it a chance to view, and take part in, one of the most cherished elements of modern democracy: the right to a fair trial. [4]You'll see how the American court system works—the judges, the opposing sets of attorneys, the witnesses, the accused. [5]You'll see how citizens act under the great responsibility of being jurors—of deciding the facts in a case. [6]You'll also find out about yourself—your ability to listen, take notes, use reason and logic, and arrive at a consensus with others from all walks of life.

Topic (word or phrase): Jury duty: both interesting und boring

4. [1]In many ways, a pure-bred Siamese cat is more like a dog than a typical cat. [2]A Siamese does not mind water as most cats do; some actually like to play in it. [3]Also, a Siamese cat does not stoop to making a tinny meow. [4]It speaks in a loud, deep, raspy voice. [5]Many Siamese become devoted to their owners, rather than to just their homes and dinner dishes. [6]I have known such cats to take walks with their owners in city or countryside. [7]Some day we may even read about a Siamese cat bringing in the newspaper, or attacking the postman!

Topic (word or phrase): Siamese vs Dogs

5. [1]The city council has a fight on its hands if it tries to carry out its threat to tear down the old Sunset Pier. [2]A Save-the-Pier group has formed and is publicizing the long and nostalgic history of the pier. [3]It dates back to the early 1800s, when the bay was a stop on the coastal route for furs and hides and the spot probably boasted only a small dock. [4]Later in the century, a small fishing fleet began to form, requiring a real pier of sorts. [5]By the 1880s, when the town had grown into a popular resort, the pier was extended. [6]Bathhouses, arcades, and a carousel were added. [7]Throughout the twentieth century, the Sunset Pier has been improved and updated. [8]After World War II, it became the "in" place for fine dining. [9]The disastrous typhoon of 1969 destroyed nearly half of the pier—will we ever forget the sight of those gourmet restaurants floating out to sea?—but thousands of people continued to flock to the remaining amusements. [10]In the 1980s, according to its many fans, the Sunset Pier is still an important tourist attraction, and should be kept as one of the few remaining links to the city's past.

Topic (word or phrase): history of old Sunset pier

Score, 1–5 _____%

▶   80%

Check answers on p. 334.

1.2 GUESSING TOPIC AND MAIN IDEA FROM TITLES AND SUBTITLES

Sometimes—not always—a writer uses a title that hints at or even clearly states the topic. Sometimes, the title even states the main idea (thesis) about that topic. Which one of the following titles gives the reader this kind of help? Put a checkmark [√] before the title(s), and fill in the topic (phrase) and main idea (complete sentence) in the space provided. Intelligent guessing and your own wording are both fine!

Sample: Title: "Women and Nontraditional Occupations"

Topic: *The kinds of jobs women choose*

Main idea: *Women seem to find success as truck drivers and railroad conductors.*

1. Title: "When the Juvenile System Becomes a Cure that Kills"

   Topic (phrase): *juvenile system*

   Main idea (sentence): *Sometimes* _____

2. Title: "Love Canal, New York" (famous toxic neighborhood)

   Topic: *Toxic Neighborhood*

   Main idea (can you tell?): *Victims of the neighborhood*

3. Title: "The Delights of Reading"

   Topic: *Delightful reading*

   Main idea: *How to enjoy reading*

4. Title: "Curtain Falling on Summer-Stock Theaters?"

   Topic: *End of Summer*

   Main Idea: *Closing of Summer stock theater.*

5. Title: "Iowa: More Than Corn and Hogs"

   Topic: *Iowa*

   Main idea: *There is more to Iowa than corn and hogs*

Score, 1–5 _____%

▶ 80%

Check answers with your instructor.

1.3 FINDING REPEATED STATEMENTS OF THE MAIN IDEA IN A PARAGRAPH (STATED IN THE SAME OR SIMILAR WORDS)

First, decide what the topic of each paragraph is, and write it as a word or a phrase in the blank. Then go back and reread the paragraph, underlining any phrase or sentence that expresses the main idea. It will be repeated at least once. In the second blank, write the numbers of the sentences that express the main idea.

1. [1]For several months, city engineers have studied the latest landslide in the Seaview area, which destroyed ten houses. [2]They have concluded that there was one main cause of the slide. [3]This was water seepage from the new housing tract on the mesa just above the cliff. [4]Ever since the tract was built, they say, the mesa has received abnormal amounts of water from cesspools and landscaping. [5]The water has seeped into the unstable cliff just below, causing it to gradually shift and sag. [6]Without this one factor, there would have been no landslide.

Topic (word or phrase): _Mudslides landslide_____

Main idea stated in sentence nos. _1_____

2. [1]The Mayor and the police credited ordinary citizens, alert and courageous, with the capture of a man who may be the most wanted criminal in the state. [2]It happened like this. [3]This morning the suspect went into a small Eastside store to buy a paper. [4]He saw his picture on page one, threw the paper down, and dashed out of the store. [5]The store owner, who had recognized him, phoned the police. [6]Meanwhile, the suspect ran to a parked car, pulled the young woman driver out, and brutally knocked her down. [7]Then he started up the car and began to drive away. [8]But the woman's husband had been watching from his apartment window. [9]Enraged, he ran out of the building, snatching up a metal stake on the way. [10]Some passersby immediately joined him. [11]They had no guns or other weapons, but all were angry and all were willing to become involved. [12]The husband managed to smash the windshield of the car and drag the suspect out. [13]Together, the residents held the suspect on the sidewalk until police arrived. [14]In this way a man suspected of being the infamous Night Killer was captured— by ordinary citizens who had no guns.

Topic (word or phrase): _heroes_____

Main idea stated in sentence nos. _1_____

3. [1]Skillful readers of expository (informational) prose should pay special attention to the first one or two sentences of each long paragraph they read. [2]In fact, "speed reading" or skimming consists in large part of reading *only* those sections of a prose work. [3]All readers should read these beginnings of paragraphs carefully. [4]Studies of prose style have shown that writers of textbooks and similar works state their main ideas in such "topic sentences" 70 percent to 90 percent of the time, depending upon the writer. [5]Main ideas are the essence of any selection. [6]Therefore, reading/study experts always urge students to slow down and absorb the beginnings of paragraphs, even if they skip other parts.

Topic (word or phrase): _finding main ideas_

Main idea stated in sentence nos. _1_

4. [1]"The Light in the Abyss," an article by Wayne Sage, describes the light emitted by organisms living deep within the oceans. [2]It illustrates the high literary quality of much of today's science writing designed for the general, college-educated public. [3]Sage enchants us with vivid images of this little-known area of the world. [4]For example, he writes: "A journey to the bottom of the ocean would be a journey into night." [5]Later in the same article, he says: "Cruising through the depths, *Leiognathus* might look like an aquatic UFO." [6]And as a final example: "To stand on the bottom of the ocean and look upwards would be not like staring into an inky void, but like gazing into the heavens. [7]Many creatures flicker like individual stars, identifiable solely by the character of their lights. [8]Others swarm in large groups like living galaxies in the darkness. [10]These excerpts illustrate the graphic images, the almost poetic quality, of the best science writers today.

Example

_No_

Topic (word or phrase): _The Abyss_

Main idea stated in sentence nos. _9_

5. [1]Linda stood in front of Hamilton Elementary School, for the first time since she was five and a kindergartner. [2]People told her, "Don't go back, everything will be changed." [3]But to her astonishment, it wasn't. [4]The brick facing had been cleaned, and the windows looked newer. [5]But the main entrance was still the worn double doors she remembered. [6]The steps leading up to it were not as wide or high—her perspective had changed. [7]She walked in hesitantly—surely the dread principal's office would have been moved. [8]No, it was still there; only the prints on the walls were different. [9]And instead of old Spellman, the principal was a smiling young woman in Guess? jeans. [10]But strangely, most of the rooms, hallways, grounds, and surrounding houses were just as she remembered them.

Compare-Contrast

Topic (word or phrase): _Memories and change_

Main idea stated in sentence nos. _10_

Score, 1–5 _____ %

▶   80%

Check answers on p. 334.

1.4 DISCOVERING THE IMPLIED MAIN IDEA OF A PARAGRAPH (INFERRING THE MAIN IDEA)

Read the following paragraphs carefully, more than once. In each one, notice that the writer does not directly state the main idea. You must infer what the main idea is from the content. In the first blank, write the topic of the paragraph. In the second blank, write a complete sentence of your own that expresses the main idea.

1. A large Hispanic population has settled in the city's south side, many of them new arrivals from Cuba and Central America. Just east of this area lies "Little Seoul," a Korean enclave which is rapidly sprouting new banks and shopping plazas. Just north of the Hispanic and Korean neighborhoods is the city's central business area. Here we see Anglo names on the older businesses and industries, interspersed with European and Asian newcomers. Finally the western edge of the city toward the river has been a European melting pot for generations. Recent arrivals include many from Mediterranean countries.

Topic (word or phrase): _____Immigration_____

Implied main idea (sentence): _____Many Immigrants are_____
_____now living in the south side_____

2. Long after the Segalla family sold the old house and the children grew up and scattered to their different destinies across the USA, they would always remember the house and land, talk about it when they gathered, dream of it in their individual dreams. And always the talk, the memories, the dreams were gentle, full of winter beauty and summer sweetness, of lamplight, of dearly loved voices talking low in the evenings. An oldtimer who lived a few miles away, the other side of Long Mountain, told them the meadows were natural, not cut out of the forest; the original Indian name for that side of the valley had been Chippewalla, or "Sunny Meadows." An old man once drove up in the 1940s, asked politely if he could visit his childhood home. Of course he could; and he told them stories of the house going back three generations, when it was a working farm. [6]Built in 1745, he said, and never a bad event or person connected with it that he knew of.

Topic (word or phrase): _____Childhood memories_____

Implied main idea (sentence): _____Looking back on their_____
_____childhood brought back many memories_____

3. On a typical charter tour, you have the reluctant ones, otherwise called the Moaners or Whiners. Nothing goes right for them. Their feet hurt; the food is awful; the tour is mismanaged. They wish they had never signed up for this tour. Then you have their opposites, the Sunshine Kids. These people enjoy every moment. They joke about their feet; they consider the food interesting; they admire the tour leader's expertise. Another typical subgroup are the Innocents Abroad. They are struck dumb by every sight and sound on the trip. [10]They listen avidly to every lecture, they gawk at every statue and rooftop exactly as they are told. Finally you have their opposites, the Knowitalls. These are the travelers who lag behind, yawning, who knew all these facts years ago, and who add to or correct their guide's speeches.

Topic (word or phrase): _Types of people on towns_

Implied main idea (sentence): _There are three types of people on guarded towns_

4. ⓐIt is extremely easy to fill your house or apartment with the magic of green plants.ⓑFirst, buy a number of inexpensive but healthy plants at a local nursery or variety store.ⓒSecond, place them attractively on windowsills and shelves. ⓓThird, water and fertilize lightly but lovingly, as directed by the seller, plant food labels, gardening books, or all those visitors who have definite ideas about plants. ⓔFourth, watch for signs of bugs or disease.ⓕYou will soon realize that your plants may suffer from too much light or too little, too much water and fertilizer or too little, too much advice or too little. . . .ⓖAfter you have disposed of your plants in the trash can, remember: it is extremely easy to fill your house or apartment with the magic of green plants—if they're made of silk.

Topic (word or phrase): _Plants as companions_

Implied main idea (sentence): _There are several steps to having healthy plants_

5.ⓐWhat exactly does the word _religion_ or _religious_ mean?ⓑSome people think a religious person is one who is a member of an established religion, believes its creed, and engages in formal worship.ⓒOthers would call "religious" anyone who consciously follows certain moral and ethical principles in his/her behavior, even if not a member of an established sect.ⓓTo still others, religion is a broader term, covering any set of beliefs that presupposes a force or spirit that is greater than man, that perhaps explains the universe, life, and death.ⓔFinally, it is even possible to call "religious" anyone whose life is ruled by a deep respect for nature, for all creatures including man, and for certain universally accepted higher values.

Topic (word or phrase): _Religion_

Implied main idea (sentence): _The definitions of religion vary from person to person_

Score, 1–5 _____%

▶ 80%

Check answers with your instructor.

1.5 FINDING THE MAIN SUPPORTING DETAILS OF A PARAGRAPH

Go back to Practice 1.3, pages 21–22. Read each paragraph again, this time for main details that support or develop the main idea. Number the details in order by writing a number inside a small circle at the beginning of each one (example: ①). Hint: Paragraph 1 has two main supporting details.

Score, 1–5 _____%

▶ 80%

Check numbering on p. 334.

Now turn to Practice 1.4, pages 22–24, and do the same thing: Number the main supporting details in order.

Score, 1–5 _____%

▶ 80%

Check numbering on p. 334.

1.6 RECOGNIZING SIGNALS, OR TRANSITIONAL WORDS AND PHRASES

Again, go back to Practice 1.3. This time, circle any signals or transitions you find.

Score, 1–5 _____%

▶ 80%

Check answers with your instructor.

Now turn to Practice 1.4. Circle any signals or transitions you find.

Score, 1–5 _____%

▶ 80%

Check answers with your instructor.

1.7 SORTING IMPORTANT FROM LESS IMPORTANT DETAILS

Each of the following is a main idea for an article, followed by various details that might be found within the article. For each group, read the main idea carefully and retain it mentally. Then as fast as possible, read through the list of details. Put a checkmark (√) next to each detail that pertains to or supports the topic. These are the significant details. The others may be interesting but do not need to be retained in most textbook or other informational reading. When you are finished, check answers on p. 335.

For practice in efficient reading, keep track of time by yourself, or in a group.

1. Why you should see Movie *X*:

   _____ a. Great acting

   _____ b. Fine cinematography (camera work)

_____ c. Was completed after many delays

_____ d. Important message

2. Why you should *not* see Movie *Z*:

_____ a. Poor casting

_____ b. Tasteless humor

_____ c. Script and characters are all clichés

_____ d. Introduces one very talented young actor

3. How burglary was foiled by next-door neighbor:

_____ a. Saw car parked, no headlights, grew suspicious

_____ b. City council has OK'd five extra patrols

_____ c. Kept lights turned off, phoned police quietly

_____ d. Owners were not home at the time

4. Causes of Linda's stammer when she saw Brad at Verdi's:

_____ a. She was there on date with Brad's brother Rocky

_____ b. She had told Brad she would be out of town that weekend

_____ c. She tends to stammer whenever she is upset

_____ d. Verdi's is the hot new singing-waiter restaurant

5. Do overweight Americans face unjustified discrimination?

_____ a. Hiring records of some schools, businesses may show discrimination

_____ b. Thin people are never told they are "too thin" for a job, task

_____ c. News item: 367-pound woman may lose her driver's license because her weight is "driving hazard"

_____ d. Many advertised diets are ineffective, even dangerous

6. Key steps in training your dog to obey you:

_____ a. Use only a few simple words

_____ b. Some breeds are more easily trained than others

_____ c. Realize that you, as well as your dog, are being trained

_____ d. Use love and rewards, not punishment

_____ e. Expect to spend half an hour a day for several weeks

_____ f. Cats do not seem to take well to obedience lessons

_____ g. Be firm—never let dog disobey a command

7. Dana's room shows he's a musician:

_____ a. The very latest in sound equipment

_____ b. Rock-artist posters on walls

_____ c. In separate building at rear of house

_____ d. Big expensive drum set in one corner

_____ e. He has lived there for two years

_____ f. Electric keyboard in center

_____ g. Clothes are messy; musical equipment is neat

8. Advantages of word processing over typewriter:

_____ a. May be combined with a printer

_____ b. Typos (errors) can be corrected immediately

_____ c. No spills of white-out liquid

_____ d. Both require knowledge of keyboard

_____ e. Extra functions, capacities of computer

_____ f. Some word-processing programs hard to learn

_____ g. Less wasted paper—rough drafts, cutting and pasting, etc.

_____ h. Some professional writers insist on typewriter

Time, 1–8 _____

Score _____ %

Check answers on p. 335.

1.8 RECOGNIZING ORGANIZATIONAL PATTERNS IN PARAGRAPHS

Remember that before you can recognize the dominant pattern in a passage, you must first follow the basic steps in comprehension. That is, you must first discover the topic or subject matter; discover the main idea, whether directly stated or clearly implied; note the signals and transitions, especially those that indicate the writing pattern; and note the important supporting details. *Then* you are ready to label the major writing pattern of the passage.

For this Practice, please return once again to the paragraphs in Practice 1.3, starting on page 21. You have already done the four basic steps listed above. Now you will reread each paragraph to determine which one of the patterns has been used. Remember that more than one pattern may be operating in a paragraph, but be able to argue for your choice as the *dominant* one.

Select from the five patterns you have studied so far in the Introduction to Chapter 1: chronological, reasons, examples or illustration, cause-and-effect, compare-contrast. (You may abbreviate.)

FROM PRACTICE 1.3

1. ("For several months")   Pattern: _Cause - effect_
2. ("The Mayor and")   Pattern: _chronological_
3. ("Skillful readers")   Pattern: _def._
4. ("The Light in")   Pattern: _example_
5. ("Linda stood")   Pattern: _compare contrast_

Score, 1–5 _____%

▶   80%

Check answers with your instructor.

1.9 MORE RECOGNIZING WRITING PATTERNS IN PARAGRAPHS

Follow the same steps as in Practice 1.8. This time, please return to Practice 1.4, starting on page 22. Again, you have already done the basic four steps: discovering the topic, main idea (you wrote the implied main idea in your own sentence), transitions, and important supporting details. Select from the next five patterns you have now studied in the Introduction to Chapter 1: spatial-geographic, definition, process, classification, and description. (You may abbreviate.) Remember to use description only as a last resort—if none of the other four seems to be dominant. Last, check your answers on p. 335.

FROM PRACTICE 1.4

1. ("A large Hispanic")   Pattern: _geographical_
2. ("Long after the")   Pattern: _description - example_
3. ("On a typical")   Pattern: _Classification_
4. ("It is extremely")   Pattern: _process_
5. ("What exactly")   Pattern: _def._ _Example_

Score, 1–5 _____%

▶   80%

Check answers on p. 335.

For extra practice, return to the paragraphs in Practice 1.1 on pages 18–19. Can you identify the dominant writing pattern in each? Check your answers on p. 334.

1.10 PREDICTING WRITING PATTERNS FROM TITLES

See if you can guess the dominant pattern a writer would use in each of these imaginary stories and articles, simply by reading the title. (Not all titles, of course, are as helpful as these.) Choose from all ten patterns you have studied: description, cause-effect, compare-contrast, chronological (time sequence), spatial-geographic, examples, reasons, process, classification, definition. Sometimes more than one pattern is possible; be able to argue for your choice. If you think a secondary pattern is very likely, add it in parentheses. And remember, choose description only if no other pattern clearly fits.

Sample: Title: "The Longest Day"

Pattern: _Chronological_

1. Title: "The Short Unhappy Life of Fudgely Willis"

Pattern: _chronological (description)_

2. Title: "The Last Virgin Forests in New England" (article with maps)

Pattern: _geographic_

3. Title: "Why the Unsinkable Ship *Dauntless* Sank"

Pattern: _reasons - cause + effect_

4. Title: "Installing a Garage Door Opener"

Pattern: _process + chronical order_

5. Title: "How to Survive Your Twenties"

Pattern: _process_

6. Title: "My Great-Aunt Penelope"

Pattern: _classification   description_

7. Title: "New Research into the Causes of AIDS"

Pattern: _description cause + effect_

8. Title: "The Olympics Need a Permanent Home"

Pattern: _geographic reasons_

9. Title: "Living with Multiple Sclerosis—Three Families"

Pattern: _cause effect Examples_

10. Title: "China in 1980 and 1990 — Ten Years of Change"

Pattern: _spatial compare + contrast_

Score, 1–5 _____%

▶   80%

Check answers with your instructor.

1.11 RECOGNIZING WRITING PATTERNS IN PARAGRAPHS: REVIEW EXERCISE

Follow the same procedure you have used throughout your paragraph reading so far. That is, begin with the four basic steps of comprehension. Discover the topic and the main idea. If the main idea is stated, underline the sentence and give the sentence number as your answer. If the main idea is not stated but implied, write it in a complete sentence. Circle important transitions; number important supporting details; and so on. Then reread to decide which one of the ten writing patterns is dominant.

This time, try to label the patterns from memory, without looking up the ten names. Be able to argue for the one you think is the dominant pattern; add any secondary pattern in parentheses.

1. ¹The barge industry has always been important to Ohio. ²For one thing, the state has many inland waterways; it has two big rivers, the Mississippi and the Missouri. ³Many towns and cities sprang up on those waterways. ⁴So a great deal of Ohio's commerce, plus many of its jobs, is dependent on barges and other water-type shipping. ⁵Also, Ohio has a long tradition of river life: Mark Twain's writings are an example. ⁶In general, the water is a big part of Ohio's heritage; and the barge industry is included in it.

Topic: _The barge industry in Ohio_____

Main idea (sentence no. or your own sentence): ___1_____

_____

Dominant pattern: _Reasons - Cause + effect_____

2. ¹Almost all of the known U.S. resources of geothermal energy are located within the western third of the country. ²California, Nevada, and Oregon have the highest concentration of known resource areas. ³Alaska, Idaho, Montana, New Mexico, Utah, and Washington have substantial potential. ⁴In fact, it is likely that the greatest geothermal resources will always be found in the Western region.*

Topic: _location of US geothermal resources_____

Main idea (sentence no. or your own sentence): ___1_____

_____

Dominant pattern: ~~spatial~~ ~~geographic~~ reasons example + cause effect

*This and the next three paragraphs are taken from Factsheet 8, "Geothermal Energy," U.S. Department of Energy, 1977.

3. [1]One of the strongest arguments for the increased exploitation of geothermal power is that there are very few environmental problems resulting from it. [2]The most serious potential problem is that boron and other chemicals (which are mixed in with the geothermal water and steam) can cause damage if they are released into nearby waters or allowed to escape into the atmosphere. [3]The other major hazard is that of land subsidence (slippage) from the withdrawal of large amounts of water. [4]But it is thought that both these problems can be managed.

Topic: _Environmental for problems with geothermal_

Main idea (sentence no. or your own sentence): _arguments of the exploitation of geothermal power_

Dominant pattern: _reasons_

4. [1]There is some worry that geothermal energy projects can trigger earthquakes, when water is re-injected under pressure. [2]A lesser problem is the odor of hydrogen sulfide which is released during exploration (the familiar rotten egg smell). [3]This can be a serious health hazard, particularly to drilling crews, if allowed to reach high concentrations. [4]There is also considerable noise involved as steam rushes out of the geothermal well at supersonic speeds, often exceeding 100 decibels when a well is vented. [5]Finally, large land areas are required—between 3,000 and 5,000 acres for a 1,000 megawatt plant.

Topic: _effects of geothermal energy_

Main idea (sentence no. or your own sentence): _drawback of_ _should be sentence_ _geothermal energy_

Dominant pattern: _cause - effect - examples_

5. [1]However, geothermal energy should be investigated more seriously for our future energy needs. [2]The geothermal generating plants appear to present less environmental threat than either nuclear or fossil fuel (gas, coal) plants. [3]Also, unlike those two types, their problems are highly localized, and seem to have available solutions.

Topic: _why we should support geothermal energy_

Main idea (sentence no. or your own sentence): _1_

Dominant pattern: _reasons_

6. [1]People often say, "Everything I eat, it seems, can cause cancer. [2]I don't care what the scientists say—I'm going to eat what I please." [3]These people are wrong. [4]Everything does *not* cause cancer. [5]For example, no amount of pure water will cause cancer in the body. [6]Thousands of substances are tested on laboratory animals every year, and only a small percentage of them cause cancer, even when consumed in large quantities. [7]But that small percentage is different. [8]These are toxic, dangerous substances—whether in tiny or in large amounts. [9]They alone can cause cancer—in lab animals and therefore in humans.

Topic: <u>Cancer causing substances</u>

Main idea (sentence no. or your own sentence): <u>4</u>

Dominant pattern: <u>Cause effect</u>

7. [1]There are at least two good reasons why we should consider setting up a permanent home for the Olympic Games. [2]First of all, it's very expensive for a nation to build facilities for thousands of athletes, officials, and spectators, use them for only a few weeks, and then tear most of them down again. [3]Permanent facilities could be paid for jointly by all the nations participating in the Games, and would require only occasional updating. [4]During off years they could be leased for other uses. [5]Second, a permanent home would put an end to much of the political wrangling that surrounds the Games, especially over the choice of a site every four years. [6]This would especially be true if the world could agree on a small neutral nation for the site, or if Greece—the original home of the Games—were chosen.

Topic: <u>Olympics need permanent site</u>

Main idea (sentence no. or your own sentence): <u>1</u>

Dominant pattern: <u>reasons</u>

8. [1]The world's population is increasing at an ever-faster rate, with severe consequences for the natural environment. [2]For example, in 1989 there were 5.3 billion people in the world, or 93 million more than in 1988. [3]At this rate, world population will double in less than forty years. [4]As one result, 100 acres of rain forest are being destroyed every minute. [5]Half of these forests are expected to be gone before the year 2000. [6]Yet at present, 70 percent of Third World families depend solely on wood for their heating/cooking fuel. [7]Other effects include rapid loss of species, which is well-documented, and a correlation with global warming, which is still being analyzed.

Topic: <u>possible overpopulation</u>

Main idea (sentence no. or your own sentence): <u>1</u>

Dominant pattern: <u>~~effect~~ cause effect</u>

9. [1]Philosophers distinguish between a fact and a value. [2]A *factual judgment* describes an empirical relationship or quality. [3]For example, "Washington, D.C., is the nation's capital" and "Water boils at 212 degrees Fahrenheit at sea level" are factual statements. [4]A value judgment, on the other hand, assesses the worth of objects, acts, feelings, attitudes, even people. [5]For example, "Beethoven was a good composer," "I should visit my sick brother," and "You were wrong in lying" are value judgments.*

Topic: *diff. b/w fact and # value*

Main idea (sentence no. or your own sentence): *1*

Dominant pattern: *definition*

10. [1]How do values arise? [2]Where do they come from? [3]Why does one person see beauty in an ocean, while another is unmoved? [4]Why does one person risk life and limb to ensure justice, while another stands detached and indifferent? [5]Our values are largely shaped and formed by experience. [6]Thus, the sea holds out little beauty for one who has watched a loved one die in it. [7]The person who has felt the sting of racial or sexual discrimination can understandably develop a hearty appetite for fair and just treatment, even at great personal risk. [8]In a word, the values we hold, as individuals and as groups, are inseparable from the endlessly changing experiences of our lives.†

Topic: *human values*

Main idea (sentence no. or your own sentence): *5*

Dominant pattern: *reasons*

Check your answers on p. 335. Each paragraph is worth 10 points, for a total of 100 points.

Score, 1–10 _____

80 points

Homework March 4th finish

1.12 RECOGNIZING WRITING PATTERNS IN LONGER PASSAGES (TWO OR MORE PARAGRAPHS). SUMMARIZING THE CONTENT.

As usual, follow the four basic steps to reading comprehension (topic, main idea, main supporting details, transitions). Then reread to find the dominant organizational pattern used.

---

*From Vincent Barry, *Philosophy: A Text with Readings* (Belmont, Calif.: Wadsworth, 1980), p. 93. Reprinted by permission.

†Barry, *Philosophy*, p. 93.

Since passages of two or more paragraphs are more complex than single paragraphs, you should use one of your more advanced techniques on each passage. For example, you should preview skim each passage before reading carefully. Also, we will ask you to practice your summarizing skills. Refer back to the discussion of summarizing on pages 13–14, if necessary, before writing your answers.

Sample: Topic: Learning to swim

Main idea of the passage: Paragraph 2, Sentence 4

(Or, if the main idea is implied, my own sentence):
It is much harder to learn to swim at 40 than at 5!

Dominant pattern: *Chronological (also some description and contrast)*

Summary, in your own words (2–3 sentences): *Mr. Smith signs up for a swim class. He compares his own slow progress with his daughter's — she's learning to swim in the next class.*

1. [1]In twentieth-century America, the median pay for women workers has ranged between 50 and 60 percent of the median pay for men workers. [2]Various reasons have been found for this disparity. [3]Women have been less educated, less unionized, more likely to be in "women's fields" (nursing, teaching, retail selling, clerical), more likely to begin working late in life, or to interrupt their working careers for family demands. [4]And of course, when all other factors are the same, women have often experienced gender discrimination. [5]Minority women, especially, have faced decades of low-paying work.

[6]Now, however, a recent Labor Department study has shown an improvement in the earnings ratio for women. [7]By 1987, women were earning 65 percent of the median pay for (white) male workers. [8]Researchers think the improvement results from the fact that women tend to get better educations than in the past, and are entering professions like business, engineering, and law. [9]Also, they start full-time work when they are younger, and stay in for years—the two-paycheck family is common now, even when women become mothers. [10]This in turn leads to more experience and seniority on the job.

[11]But even today, only a small percentage of women are employed in management positions or skilled trades, and few hold unionized jobs. [12]The new, young professionals still have some years to go before they can compete equally with older white males. [13]And the vast majority of women workers, as always, toil at the very lowest-paying jobs—clerical, household, nursery school, hospital aide,

and so on. [14]Most of these women have no job security or medical/retirement coverage. [15]The earnings ratio may have improved, but it is still only 67 percent.

Topic of the passage: _Pay for women workers_

Main idea (sentence no. or your own sentence): _6_

Dominant pattern: _Compare + contrast_

Summary of the passage, in your own words (2–3 sentences): _that womens pay have increased but men are still higher_

2. [1]A few decades ago an American family faced with a serious internal problem, such as addiction or spousal abuse, could find little community understanding or support. [2]Family members usually hid the problem from outsiders, or denied even to themselves that it existed. [3]As a result, neither the abuser nor the other members would reach out for professional help. [4]And the destructive behaviors did not go away; typically, they got worse.

[5]However, since the 1970s, researchers, therapists, and the media have begun to look at dysfunctional families more openly and realistically. [6]Today, individuals find that there is little stigma to acknowledging a problem or seeking professional help. [7]For long-term counseling, most communities offer a variety of support groups. [8]Troubled families are learning how to change destructive patterns, how to reverse the painful spirals of the past.

Topic of the passage: _Family on coping with abuse_

Main idea (sentence no. or your own sentence): _copying with the abuse_

Dominant pattern: _cause - effect - compare contrast_

Summary of the passage, in your own words (2–3 sentences): _____

3. [1]For years, scientists have been studying the relationship of stress to disease. [2]They have found increasing evidence of a strong connection between the two. [3]Early research focused on the physiological response to stress, beginning with Dr. Selye, who said it consisted of three stages.

[4]The first stage is alarm, an instinctive response pattern to supply energy. [5]The perceived threat excites the hypothalamus area of the brain to produce substances that stimulate the pituitary gland, discharging hormones into the bloodstream. [6]In turn, the adrenal glands produce sugar. [7]At the same time, the cardiovascular system increases the heart rate so that blood can be quickly pumped to the muscles in preparation for what is known as "fight or flight." [8]During the resistance period, the body attempts to return to normal, confronting or adapting to the stress. [9]Finally, there is the exhaustion phase, when adjustment has occurred and adaptive energy has been used up.[*]

Topic of the passage: _Stress + disease results_

Main idea (sentence no. or your own sentence): _The Di side_
causes on three stages of physiological stress

Dominant pattern: _Time Sequence_

Summary of the passage, in your own words (2–3 sentences): _____

_____

_____

4. [1]Socialist countries belong to three general categories, depending on their origins and intentions:

(1) [2]So-called "communist" countries like the People's Republic of China or the Soviet Union (USSR.) and its satellites. [3]These countries claim to have abolished private property. [4]They have nationalized the means of production—in most cases by revolutionary means, and their governments often urge others to do the same. [5]However, as we shall see, elements of the market-price system are surviving and in some cases growing even in these countries.

(2) [6]So-called "market-socialist" countries like Germany, Great Britain, most countries of Western Europe, and Japan. [7]Note that socialism does not necessarily imply authoritarian government. [8]The market-socialist countries have democratic governments.

(3) [9]So-called "Third World" countries like Algeria, Libya, Syria, Iraq, Tanzania, and Guyana. [10]Despite their great differences, these countries have two attributes in common: (1) They are all former colonies and are anxious to rid themselves of the colonial practices that exploited them, and (2) they are pursuing policies aimed at reducing the importance of private property.[†]

---

[*]From Robin Heffler, "Stress on the Job," *The UCLA Monthly*, May–June 1984. Reprinted by permission.

[†]From Philip C. Starr, *Economics: Principles in Action* (Belmont, Calif.: Wadsworth, 1984), p. 38.

Topic of the passage: _Sciolists/kinds + types of countries_

Main idea (sentence no. or your own sentence): _1_ _____

_____

Dominant pattern: _Classification_ _____

Summary of the passage, in your own words (2–3 sentences): _____

_____

_____

_____

5. [1]By the mid-1960s, the industrial countries that had been involved in World War II demonstrated full recovery from the damage they had suffered, and in the early 1970s most of these countries enjoyed a business boom. [2]This post-war recovery led to enormous increases in demand for resources (like oil) that often were not available in sufficient quantities. [3]In addition, widespread drought and two oil crises (1973 and 1979) helped to aggravate shortages and to accelerate price increases.

[4]Total world production of all goods and services exploded between World War II and the early 1980s—from $1 trillion worth to about $10 trillion in 1982. [5]By the late 1960s, signs of stress appeared: pollution became a front-page concern, and food-production capacity was strained as demand for food grew by 30 million tons per year.*

Topic of the passage: _Recovery of the industrial countries after World War II_

Main idea (sentence no. or your own sentence): _the problem from World War II_

Dominant pattern: _Cause + effect_

_____

Summary of the passage, in your own words (2–3 sentences): _____

_____

_____

_____

Each passage has 4 points, for a total of 20 points.

Score, 1–5 _____

▶ 16 points

Check answers with instructor.

_____

*Starr, *Economics*, p. 6.

Scanning

*S*canning is not reading. It is a semireading skill whereby we search rapidly through print for specific information. We rely on scanning ability every day, on every level from simple to complex. Since scanning must be done both accurately and quickly to be of any use, this chapter is designed to make you more self-aware when you scan, and more efficient.

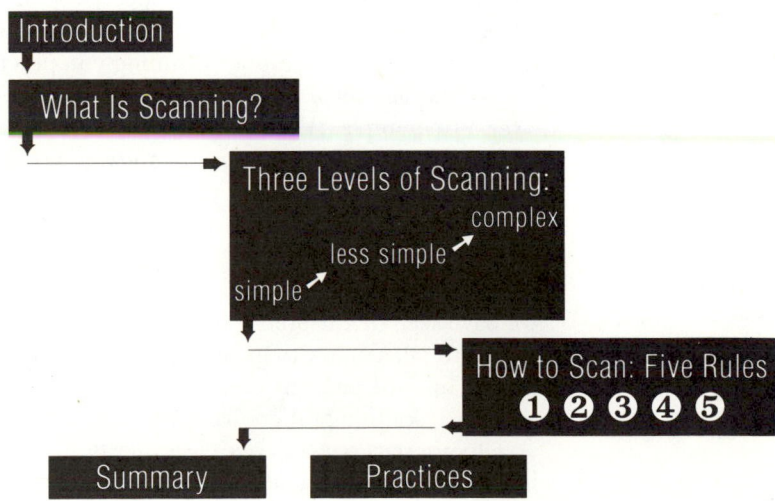

Introduction

What Is Scanning?

Three Levels of Scanning: simple, less simple, complex

How to Scan: Five Rules ①②③④⑤

Summary   Practices

INTRODUCTION TO SCANNING

CHECKLIST OF SYMPTOMS

Do you often:

_____√____ 1. avoid looking things up in reference books because it takes too long?

_____ 2. fail to find the answer to a question, only to have others find it for you?

Sometimes ← _____√____ 3. waste time looking for an answer in the wrong places?

_____ 4. find the answer much more slowly than others do?

_____ 5. get lured away from your search and end up reading irrelevant things?

If you checked one or more of these symptoms, don't feel defeated; feel normal. You may very likely be a good, careful reader, one who likes to "read it all and not miss anything" regardless of time. But if these traits become problems, this chapter can help.

WHAT IS SCANNING?

To reading experts, scanning is a specific skill. Some call it "semireading"; others call it "selective reading." It is very different from both the basic reading comprehension and the preview skimming you practiced in Chapter 1.

When you scan print, you begin with a specific question, which has a specific answer. For example, "Who won the Plush-Green Open yesterday?" Then you look, or scan, through the print for the answer. You ignore or mentally discard material that does not pertain to your question. When you find the part that probably contains the answer, you slow down and read carefully. "So Joe Tschopper won!" You then experience, in a minor way, the famous "Aha!" reaction.

Scanning differs from literal comprehension in purpose and technique. As we have seen in Chapter 1, to comprehend a writer's message fully, you read *all* the material. You try to grasp the subject matter, the main ideas, the supporting details, and the patterns of organization.

Also, scanning differs from preview skimming. When you preview a work, you do not start out with one clear question in your mind. Rather, you are preparing for a full reading and comprehension of the material by reading the key parts carefully and thoughtfully.

In contrast, scanning—at least the simplest kind—requires little basic comprehension. In fact, when you scan, you read even less of the material than when you preview. Because the information you are searching for is very limited, scanning is the fastest way you will ever process print.

As you may have guessed by now, scanning skills are often used in reference, research, business, and all office work. We also use them in daily life. For example, we scan print whenever we look up a phone number, check on directions, or distinguish among road signs. In reading and studying, we scan when we reread to find a fact, a quote, or a salient point.

Of the six special skills presented in this book—previewing, study reading, rapid reading, overview skimming, and critical reading—scanning involves the least actual reading of continuous prose. Yet as readers we must agree that scanning often occurs in ordinary sustained reading. Some of our regressions are really a "scanning backward" to check a specific word or detail. These regressions occur so fast—in hundredths of a second—that we usually don't sense we are making them. But they provide valuable feedback to the brain, clearing up ambiguous messages and inaccuracies.

Besides occurring *during* our ordinary reading, scanning may sometimes (1) *precede*, (2) *follow*, or (3) *substitute for* reading. For example, you might first scan through a news story about food poisoning to see what cities were involved in the reports. If your city was mentioned, you would return to the beginning of the story and read very carefully (and no doubt anxiously!).

As an example of scanning that follows reading, let's say that your sociology professor makes a statement in class that seems to contradict the textbook. You scan back into the chapter to find the exact point in question, before you raise your hand.

And finally, as an example of scanning that substitutes for reading, you might scan a popular magazine to see if there is an article on Madonna's newest hairstyle. Seeing none, you toss the magazine back on the shelf. Why spend time reading something that will not answer your specific question?

In each of these three examples, you began with a specific question and then read selectively—only enough to answer your question.

The examples also show that scanning tasks can vary tremendously, depending on just how simple your question is. We will try to deal with this variety by dividing your scanning tips and practice into "simple," "less simple," and "complex."

In every situation, however, scanning will be of little practical use unless you can scan accurately and quickly. One wrong number in a telephone call means you must dial again. Reading "Eastern Highway" as "Western Highway" may lead you 50 miles off course. If you read $100 in your checkbook as $1,000, your bank will be the one saying "Aha!" rather than you. So, unless your accuracy is 100 percent, you should not try to scan more quickly.

But if you *are* accurate, then work to increase your speed. A person who uses the dictionary and other references very slowly tends to use them very seldom. A person who can't find a direction on a map quickly enough may make a wrong turn. A slow office or clerical worker is an exasperation to us all. Therefore, we must use our eyes—our vision—quickly. We must learn to recognize what we need really fast. (This ability to see and discriminate among stimuli around us is called *perception*.)

Luckily, both accuracy and speed of scanning improve rapidly with practice. Many of us have become superscanners through the pressures of study or a job. Also, a few tips from the experts can help. Remember the "P E F" motto: "Preview everything first!" Knowing the organization of the classified ads, the telephone book, or the reference work or article *before* you begin scanning for a specific answer will do wonders for your speed. On the other hand, success with more complicated kinds of scanning will require you to know a good deal about how writers write, and how printers print what they write.

Simple Scanning

On this level of scanning, you are looking for a factual answer, sometimes only a single number or word. For example, a child can scan two doors and distinguish the word *In* from *Out*. On the same level, we scan phone directories, dictionaries, TV and movie guides, classified ads, and perception drills in reading classes. We check lists, names, and numbers. We distinguish among highway signs.

How do the eyes and brain work during this kind of scanning? Apparently we make a mental image of the number or fact we are searching for. Then we cue our eyes to perceive it when it appears. We skip over or ignore any other images. It is essentially a matching or recognition process.

If you suspect that your perceptual abilities—speed of recognition, eye–brain coordination—may need polishing, you should start with a few perception drills. Your instructor is a good source. Otherwise, turn to page 44 and study "How to Scan: Five Rules." You should occasionally reread this section as you work through all the levels of scanning practices.

Turn to page 47 for Practices 2.1–2.6, Simple Scanning, and practice finding specific answers accurately and quickly in a dictionary, contents page, and textbook chapter. You should have a paperback or desk-size dictionary handy for the first four Practices.

Less-Simple Scanning

On this level, you are still looking for specific information. But the answer may not be found merely by matching a mental cue to the same number or word on the printed page, as was true in simple scanning. You may have to be flexible about mental cues—to think of synonyms for your question, to "translate" into other terms. A good vocabulary and ability to paraphrase are big assets at this point. You will probably want to go a step further and use what you know of writing patterns to speed your search.

For example, suppose you are considering enrolling in a health-care program leading to a license or degree. Naturally you want to know your chances for a future job in this kind of work, especially in your city or state. You notice a long feature article in the paper about the nation's hospitals and clinics. Do you have to read the entire article? No—ideally, you scan only for the answers to your question. You would look through the pages for proper names such as your city and state (simple scanning) and for words like *future jobs*. But the writer may not have used these exact words. So you keep your mind flexible; you also look for *outlook*, *funding problems*, *expansion*, *demand*, *population centers*, *glut of qualified workers*, and so on. You pay special attention to beginnings of paragraphs and sections; they will contain transitions such as *Experts think that the trend . . . , A major new direction, Training programs in the field are expected to. . .* , and so on.

For another example of less-simple scanning: suppose you scan the directory Yellow Pages for "Weight Training Classes." Alas! You find no such listing in the *W*'s. So you must mentally substitute the cue words *Gym, Health Spa, Physical Fitness*, and so on until you hit on the right entry. Of course, if you are lucky, your directory will tell you to "See Gym, Health Spa, Fitness," and so on, but don't count on it. Cross-referencing is not as common as it should be.

Here is a third example of less-simple scanning, requiring you to do more than just recognize identical terms. Let's say you wonder where a certain actress was born. You find a five-page article about her life in a magazine. Of course you consider synonyms for *was born*, such as *came from, began life in, first saw the light of day*, and even cuter translations. But why scan all five pages for these cues to your answer? In your first step, a preview skim, you saw that the piece is organized like most life stories (biographies): in a time-sequence or chronological pattern. So where do you look for your answer? (Reply here: _____.)Poorer readers would no doubt waste time reading irrelevant parts of the article. They might even become mired in word-by-word reading rather than scanning and eventually forget the question. But a person who knows writing patterns and their signals will know where to look and so will find the answer faster and more accurately.

Turn to Practices 2.7–2.9, beginning on page 53, for practice in less-simple scanning (table of contents, rephrasing your question, and transitions and signals).

Complex Scanning

Even more advanced mental processes are required when you scan for answers to less specific questions in material that is organized less obviously. Here, you need all your big guns: perceptual speed and accuracy, synonyms and other "translations" of your question, thorough prior knowledge of your material, and a knowledge of "the writer's path" or writing patterns. But that is not all.

For example, you may decide you do not like a short story you just read. The question is, why not? Not a very specific question, is it? What exactly didn't you like about the story? Were you bored, frustrated, too baffled, unmoved, disgusted? Then it occurs to you, before you begin to scan for reasons, that you will have to start somewhere else, maybe with ideas and ideals of style, of "good" plot and characterization. And then you will have to find evidence, examples, and passages to quote to establish some cause-effect relationship. ("The characters were so stereotyped, I did not care what happened to them. For instance, the protagonist . . .") And then you will have to compare this story with your ideal, or with other stories and other writers.

Suppose you are gathering material for a persuasive paper or speech. Or just browsing in the library to help you decide some issue in your own mind, such as, Was it necessary for the United States to drop nuclear bombs on Hiroshima and Nagasaki? Scanning library materials on such topics will also demand a flexible mind and a knack for paraphrase. When you begin to read some of the materials, you will do even more complex scanning as you try to sift for relevant facts and ideas.

The same sophisticated mental processes are necessary when you scan an editorial for bias or omitted information, or evaluate a *Consumers Report* article comparing various products, or—in a literature class—study a play or novel for certain motifs or symbols. For example, you might analyze the motion picture *The Godfather* or the novel *The Scarlet Letter* for the symbolic meanings of light versus darkness. How would you go about this? You would have to look for all possible descriptions of light, sunlight, dark, blackness, weather, and so on. Then you would read the context surrounding each use of this motif, analyze what is happening at the time, and compare it with other parts of the story that take place in the light or dark.

Complex scanning is a part of advanced reading, which we call interpretation or critical reading. It often involves long passages of continuous prose—books, articles, essays, stories, documents—where you search for evidence, examples, logic, style, influences, and so on. Complex scanning requires intelligence and good comprehension to start with, and patience! But it is a skill that thinking, educated people must use if they are to avoid a common error: baseless assumptions and uncritical acceptance of the printed word.

Now turn to page 55 for Practices 2.10–2.12 in Complex Scanning. These Practices are of course only an introduction to the skill of complex scanning. We will offer more exercises like these later in this book.

. . . .

HOW TO SCAN: FIVE RULES

Recall that scanning requires you to begin with a specific question, to be 100 percent accurate, and to find the answer quickly. The following rules seem obvious, but we all have made enough scanning mistakes that these rules bear repeating here.

1. *Preview everything first.* Like all reading tasks, all scanning tasks should begin with the same first step—preview skimming. Before you search for specific information, you must have a map of the territory to be scanned. "What are the boundaries of my source material? How is it organized? Where am I most likely to find my answer?" Armed with this map, you scan only in the likely areas. (But note that in a complex scanning job, such as discovering the symbolic meaning of sunlight in a novel, your first step is a complete reading of the novel, not just a skimming.)

2. *Know your question*—whether it is yours, or posed by someone else. Be very clear about what it is you are scanning for. Otherwise, you will waste time

and may even come up with the wrong answer. For example, when you are writing a history of the suffragette movement from 1910 to 1919, it will not help you to amass facts about the feminist movement of the 1960s. Scan to answer the right question—only.

3. *Keep a one-track mind.* You must constantly repeat the question and the possible verbal cues in your mind. Do not begin to read unrelated material. Good scanners usually use their fingers or pencils to run down pages and columns rapidly and have been heard to mutter their question over and over. Your mind-set must be: "Only the answer, please." (If the answer eludes you for some time, you are forgiven if you phrase your request less politely.)

4. *Search aggressively.* Be alert—mentally, physically, and visually. Time yourself. Sometimes it helps to stand up as you scan, rather than sit. This is especially true if you are a readaholic who is easily seduced into slowing down and reading irrelevant material. (You may even forget what you set out to look for!) Remember that the goal in scanning is never sustained reading—only enough reading to locate your answer. Scanning is only a tool for something else.

5. *Be prodigal with synonyms, with "translations" and rephrasings of your question into other possible terms* if your first cue does not work. This is especially necessary in less-simple or in complex scanning. Also, follow the writer's path. *Use your knowledge of organizational patterns and signals to direct you to likely areas for close reading.*

. . . .

SUMMARY

Scanning is a highly directed way of searching print for answers to questions. In it, we process print faster than any other kind of reading or skimming, at speeds well over 1,000 words per minute (wpm). However, most of these words will not be read, only discarded; the scanner reads only the part that contains his or her answer. Scanning tasks range from the very simple, such as the perception and recognition of identical elements, to the less simple, where the question must be "translated" into various terms, to the very complex, such as collecting evidence or tracing an idea.

All scanning improves gratifyingly with practice. For best performance, follow these five rules:

1. Know your question.
2. Preview skim your source material.
3. Keep a one-track mind.
4. Search aggressively.
5. For more complex scanning: know the material well, know writing patterns, and be flexible in your choice of mental cues.

Note: If you set out to scan the classifieds in the evening newspaper and soon find yourself reading the latest discoveries about Mars, you have violated all our rules. But all is not lost. A lot of good reading gets done that way!

SUMMARY BOX: SCANNING

What?	Why?	Acceptable Comprehension	Acceptable Rates
Simple: lists, perception drills, dictionary, White Pages, tables, signs, classified ads	To find particular facts, words, names, numbers, specific information	100%	1,000 wpm and up
Less-simple: Yellow Pages, reference words, tables of contents, indexes, card catalog	To find services, data, resources, when exact wording not available	100%	
Complex: in continuous prose—documents, articles, books, long descriptions	To follow an argument, evidence of logic, propaganda, style, reasons, motifs, patterns, support for inference	100%	

PRACTICES: SCANNING

Answers to odd-numbered exercises are provided in the answer key. Ask your instructor for answers to even-numbered exercises.

Simple Scanning

2.1 PARTS OF A DICTIONARY
2.2 FINDING SPECIFIC WORDS IN THE DICTIONARY
2.3 USING THE DICTIONARY—MISCELLANEOUS INFORMATION
2.4 USING THE DICTIONARY—MORE MISCELLANEOUS INFORMATION
2.5 USING THE CONTENTS PAGES OF A BOOK
2.6 SCANNING FOR SPECIFIC ITEMS IN A TEXTBOOK

Less-Simple Scanning

2.7 FINDING TOPICS IN A TABLE OF CONTENTS
2.8 REPHRASING YOUR QUESTION
2.9 LOCATING CLUES: TRANSITIONS, SIGNAL WORDS, AND PHRASES

Complex Scanning

2.10 LIBRARY RESEARCH
2.11 FINDING ANSWERS WITHIN CONTINUOUS PROSE
2.12 MORE PRACTICE WITHIN CONTINUOUS PROSE

Simple Scanning

For Practices 2.1–2.4, you need a paperback or desk copy of a dictionary. First, write down the title and the publication year of the dictionary you are using. We are assuming that you have already done at least a preview skim on your dictionary—that is, you know how it is organized.

Title: _____

Year published: _____

2.1 PARTS OF A DICTIONARY

Work as fast, yet as accurately, as you can. Do the items in order. If you cannot find an item, go on to the next item after a reasonable search. If your dictionary does not seem to contain the answer, write the page number where it *would* be located and add, "Not in my dictionary." Time yourself, preferably against others.

1. Where does your dictionary list abbreviations? Check the correct answer.

    __X__ a. with regular entries

    _____ b. in a separate list (give beginning page number)

    Note: If you don't know, try looking up the abbreviation *lb*.

    __X__ a.

    _____ b. (beginning with page _____)

2. Answer the same question for biographical names. If you don't know, try looking up *Frederick Douglass*.

    __X__ a.

    _____ b. (beginning with page _____)

3. Answer the same question for geographical names. If you don't know, try looking up the word *Greece*.

    _____ a.

    __X__ b. (beginning with page 646)

4. Find the page(s) where the full phonetic key (pronunciation key) is found. Page(s) _____

5. Find a shorter, more practical version of the phonetic key. Page _____

6. How many words are included in your dictionary? (See the cover or the beginning pages.) Remember that the English language contains about 500,000 words! _____ words

7. How many total pages make up the introduction to your dictionary (before the letter *A* of the regular entries begins)? _____ pages

8. Is there a table of contents? _____ If yes, on what page? _____ Is there an index? _____ If yes, on what page? _____

9. Is there an appendix? _____ More than one? _____ If yes, what does each one contain? _____
_____

10. Look up the word *habitat*. Copy the mark(s) your dictionary uses to show:

    a stressed syllable: _____

    separate syllables: _____

    pronunciation: _____

    etymology (origin): _____

Total time, 1–10 _____ : _____

Accuracy _____%

Check answers on p. 336.

2.2 FINDING SPECIFIC WORDS IN THE DICTIONARY

As fast and as accurately as possible, look up the following bits of information. Time yourself, preferably against others.

1. On what page does each of these letters begin?

   A Page __1__   *B* Page __40__

   Z Page __634__   *L* Page __331__

   O Page __408__

2. Find the guide words or catchwords at the top of the page on which each of the following words is listed. (You don't need to find the word, yet.)

   adore Guide words:_____

   zone Guide words:_____

   laugh Guide words:_____

3. Use the guide words to find the page on which each word is found. Then find the word on the page. (For speed, use a pencil or your finger.)

   piranha Page _____   *mosquito* Page _____

   eel   Page _____   *cockroach* Page _____

   scorpion Page _____

   Time, 1–3 _____ : _____

   Check answers with your instructor.

2.3 USING THE DICTIONARY: MISCELLANEOUS INFORMATION

Scan for the answers to these questions as fast and as accurately as possible. If your dictionary does not contain the item, write the page number where it *would* be found. Spell out the names of all languages—do not use abbreviations. (You may first have to find the dictionary page listing the abbreviations for languages.) Time yourself, preferably against others.

1. Page _____ What is an informal or slang meaning for the verb *to beef*?

   _____

   Give the entire etymology (origin) of the word: _____

   _____

   What is the plural of the noun *beef*? _____

2. Page _____ How many different meanings (definitions) are listed for the noun *fast*? _____ For the verb? _____

3. Page _____ From what language did English borrow its word *comet*? _____ What was the original meaning of the word? _____

4. Page _____ We use the English word *pile* in many different ways today. The word is actually three different words, as we find when we look it up (note the superscript numbers). From what language did all three come? _____ They were all clearly different then; what were the three forms? _____ _____ _____

5. Page_____ The word *treacle* is used in mainly what country today? _____What is its literal meaning? _____ Less literally, what does it mean? _____

_____

6. Page _____ How does one pronounce *Graz* (a city in Austria)? _____

7. Page _____ The abbreviation *dep.* (exactly like that) can stand for how many different words? _____

8. Page _____ The abbreviation or symbol *X* can stand for how many different things? _____

9. Page _____ Who killed Abel? _____

10. Page _____ When was the battle of Thermopylae fought? _____

Speed demons may continue and do items 11–15.

11. Page _____ Who was Bertolt Brecht, and when did he die? _____

_____

12. Page _____ How many syllables are there in *lineage:* 2 or 3? _____

13. Page _____ If someone has recently been *lionized*, does it mean he has been eaten up? _____ If not, what does it mean? _____

_____

14. Page _____ In the word *derringer*, the *g* is pronounced like a _____. Where did this name come from? _____

15. Page _____ Give the number of the adjective definition that explains what someone means when she says you're singing *flat*. What is the special usage label on this meaning? _____

_____

Time, 1–10 _____ : _____

Accuracy, 1–10 _____%

Check answers on p. 336.

2.4 USING THE DICTIONARY: MORE MISCELLANEOUS INFORMATION

Do this Practice exactly as you did the previous one. If necessary, reread directions to Practice 2.3 first.

1. Page_____Where did the name *soccer* come from? _____

_____

2. Page _____ Linguists don't always know where a word comes from. How does the dictionary show this with the word *surf*? _____

_____

3. Page _____ From what language did English get the words *magi* and *magic*?

_____

4. Page _____ People sometimes pronounce the word *zoology* as if the first syllable were our word *zoo*. Show here how it *should* be pronounced. _____ _____The first syllable should rhyme with (a) cue (b) two (c) hoe. _____

5. Page _____ How many different ways may the word *banal* be pronounced? _____ Copy all the ways here. Can you pronounce each one?

_____

_____

6. Page _____ Which definition of the verb *to tax* fits this context? Give the number and quote the definition. "Moving the king-size waterbed by himself, when it was still full of water, really taxed the muscle-man's strength." Verb number _____ Definition: _____ _____

_____

_____

7. Page _____ Copy out the etymologies of the two different words *tear*.
   Tear 1: _____
   Tear 2: _____
   Copy the two pronunciations and give a rhyming word. *Tear* 1 (_____) rhymes with _____. *Tear* 2 (_____) rhymes with _____.

8. Page _____ How should we pronounce the first syllable of *bayou*? Copy out the pronunciation, and add a rhyming word: _____ like _____. Where did we get the word? _____

9. Page _____ How should we pronounce the word *chutzpah*? Copy out the dictionary's "sound spelling" (pronunciation): _____
   From where did English borrow the word? _____

10. Page _____What is the capital city of Jamaica? _____
    What is its population? _____

Speed demons may continue and do items 11–15.

11. Page _____ Does the ancient country of Armenia still exist? If not, what happened to it? _____

12. Page _____ Is a *claque* a group of devoted fans? If not, what is it or what are they? _____

_____

13. Page _____ Can you pronounce *cirrhosis*? If you are unfortunate enough to contract it, can you recover?
    a. Pronounced _____
    b. (Yes or No) _____

14. Page _____ How many English kings were named Henry?_____

15. Page _____ Find one amazing fact in your dictionary not appearing above, and write it here: _____

_____

Time, 1–10 _____ : _____

Accuracy, 1–10 _____ %

Check answers with your instructor.

2.5 Using the Contents Pages of a Book

Turn to the Contents pages of this textbook. Then, as fast as possible, find the answers to the following questions.

1. Which chapter has the most pages? _5_
2. Which chapter has the fewest pages? _2_
3. What answers will *not* be found in the answer key? _Even_
4. Is there a chapter called "Speed Reading"? _yes_
5. Every chapter begins with an identical feature; what is it? _Introduction_
6. Are there five "Checklists of Symptoms"? Or six? _5_
7. How many chapters provide Practices? _6_
8. How many Progress Charts are offered for record-keeping? _3_
9. Which of the six chapters focuses on the subject of crime? _6_
10. To find your rate, or words per minute, you would turn to page _330_. _-333_

Time, 1–10 _____ : _____   _8/10_
Accuracy _80_%
Check answers on p. 336.

2.6 Scanning for Specific Items in a Textbook

As fast and as accurately as possible, scan for the exact answers to the following questions. All answers will be located in the Introduction to this chapter, pages 40–45. In some cases we provide the page number for you. If you cannot find an answer in a reasonable time, move on to the next question.

1. On what page do you find the "Checklist of Symptoms"? If on more than one page, write "pp. _____ to _____." Page _40_
2. On what page do you find a four- or five-line definition of scanning? Page _45_
3. How many paragraphs do you see on page 41? _9_ (Remember to count indenting only.)
4. Where on page 42 is the abbreviation "P E F" mentioned? Give the number of the paragraph. _1_
5. On what page of this Introduction do you find one paragraph describing how the eyes and the brain work when we do simple scanning? Page _42_
6. Page 43. The example of the actress's birthplace illustrates which kind of scanning: simple, less-simple, or complex? _Less Simple_ _track mind_
7. Page 45. What is the third rule of scanning? _keep a on_ Are you following it? _yes_
8. The Summary of the Introduction begins on what page? Page _45_
9. Page _45_ The last paragraph of the Summary ends with what punctuation mark? _exclamation_
10. Page _30_ The Introduction consists of how many major sections? _5_

Time, 1–10 _____ : _____

Accuracy 10 %

Check answers with your instructor.

Less-Simple Scanning

Practices 2.7–2.9 require you to think of synonyms and other translations rather than just looking for identical words.

2.7 · FINDING TOPICS IN A TABLE OF CONTENTS

Scan through the Contents pages of this book for the answers to the following questions. Work as fast and accurately as possible. As usual, if you can't find an answer after a reasonable search, move on to the next item. Also as usual, time yourself for greater efficiency, preferably against others.

Use selection numbers for long titles. We indicate the chapter in all items except the last.

1. Chapter 4: Which selection is most likely to be about religious studies? Clue word is _Summonewew_ in selection number _3_, which begins on page _148_.
2. Chapter 4: Which selection is most likely to discuss modern medicine? Clue words are _Patients Pain_ in selection number _4_, which begins on page _52_.
3. Chapter 5: How many selection titles clearly indicate content relating to personal psychology? _3_ Selection numbers _5, 8, 9_
4. Chapter 5: Which selection would likely address the issue of environmental pollution? Selection number _6_ Title: _Artificial Paradise_
5. Chapter 3: Which selection seems to treat the philosophical concerns relating to the environment? Selection number _4_
6. Chapter 3: Which selection seems to treat the political concerns relating to the environment? Selection number _3_
7. Chapter 3: Which selection will likely discuss pollution and its relationship to the ozone layer? Selection number _2_
8. Chapter 6: Which selection seems to be against the current system of treating offenders? Selection number _1_
9. Chapter 6: Which selection seems to assume that crime is a disease? Selection number _1_
10. Scan through all six chapters for this answer: Which title hints that it's probably about an early-model car? Chapter _____ Selection number _____ Title: _____

Time, 1–10 _____ : _____

Accuracy _____%

Check answers on p. 336.

2.8 REPHRASING YOUR QUESTION

When you use a reference work, directory, almanac, or similar source to answer a question, you must usually keep a flexible mind; that is, you must think of synonyms or other rephrasings of your question or topic. Read the following topic, then scan through the list and check [√] any likely synonyms. Leave the others blank.

Example: Gyms

√ a. Spas
____ b. Elementary schools
____ c. Nutrition specialists
√ d. Health spas
____ e. Resorts
√ f. Clubs, health
√ g. Exercise clubs
√ h. Fitness

Check your answers with your instructor and the group, and discuss any questions you may have. Now do the next three drills as one unit. Accuracy is important, but also work as fast as you can!

1. My congressional representative
    √ a. Federal offices
    ____ b. County government
    ____ c. Government, city
    ____ d. Voter registration
    √ e. Elections, Board of
2. U.S. population, 20th century
    ____ a. American colonies, 1630–1780
    √ b. Demographics, American
    √ c. Census, statistics
    √ d. U.S. census figures
    √ e. Population by states, 1900–1990
3. City trash pickup
    √ a. City services
    √ b. Waste removal, local
    √ c. Municipal garbage department
    √ d. Government offices, city
    √ e. Information, City Hall
4. Family problems
    √ a. Counseling, family
    √ b. Therapists—children, family, marital
    √ c. Referral service, psychological
    ____ d. Family fun parks
    √ e. Agencies, city and county

Time, _____ : _____

Accuracy _____ correct of 20 = **15** %

Check answers with your instructor.

2.9 LOCATING CLUES: TRANSITIONS, SIGNAL WORDS, AND PHRASES

Scan the following lists of signals for those that point to the content you want. As an example, the first answer is provided for you.

If you are scanning for:		Look for words like:
1. Spatial relations	*e*	a. First, second, next, last
2. In opposition	D	b. And, also, plus, besides
3. An additional or similar point	B	c. For example, for instance, to illustrate
4. A comparison	G	d. However, but, on the other hand
5. A cause-effect relationship	H	e. Here, there, on the left, in the foreground, above
6. Special emphasis	K	f. Soon, next, then, later
7. A time sequence	F	g. Like, as, resembling
8. A conclusion	J	h. Because, since, as a result
9. A step-by-step process	A	i. Again, i.e., in other words, to repeat
10. A repetition	I	j. Finally, to sum up, in other words
11. A specific case	C	k. Especially, most of all, above all

Time, 1–10 _____ : _____

Accuracy _____ %

Check answers on p. 336.

Complex Scanning

For these last two sets of scanning exercises, you will have to go beyond synonyms and paraphrasing. You will have to evaluate ideas and their relevance to one another.

2.10 LIBRARY RESEARCH

Read the research area or question heading each list. Then scan through the list of topics, putting a checkmark [√] next to those that relate to that area. Leave the unlikely topics blank. (For the sake of speed, you are allowed to write a question mark by the truly ambiguous items—but you'll get credit only for checkmarks or blanks!) As usual with scanning ability, accuracy comes first; speed is a close second. So for greater efficiency, time yourself.

Example: Recent effects of acid rain on Eastern U.S.

_____ a. Decline in frog populations
_____ b. Ph levels in Idaho lakes
_____ c. Needle drop in conifer forests, Maine to Virginia
_____ d. Scientists disagree over effects
_____ e. Fish die-off in some New York lakes—related?
_____ f. Comparisons, air pollution, 1960s vs. 1980s

Time in seconds, a–f _____

Accuracy, number correct of 6 _____

Check answers with your instructor. Discuss any questions you may have. Now go on and time the next three drills as one unit.

1. New developments in adoption procedures
_____ a. "Open" adoptions
_____ b. Case histories, 1985–1990
_____ c. Comparative study, older "secret" style vs. modern
_____ d. Public agencies vs. private contracts, 1970s
_____ e. Changes in adoption laws, state/federal, 1980 to present
_____ f. Famous Adoptees Through History

2. Who's legally responsible for alcohol-related auto accident?
_____ a. "Dramshop" laws, several states (alcohol seller)
_____ b. Auto accident rates, graphs, 1930–1980
_____ c. Position of MADD, other organizations
_____ d. Recent history, changes—state DUI or DWI laws
_____ e. Effect of marijuana on driving ability
_____ f. Determining liability: provider or drinker?

3. Alternatives to fossil fuels
_____ a. Great future predicted for Alaskan oil reserves
_____ b. Wind farms: advantages, disadvantages
_____ c. Government subsidies—encourage alternate energy sources?
_____ d. History of coal mining in Appalachia
_____ e. Trends in solar devices for homes
_____ f. Nuclear plants—pros and cons
_____ g. Alternative lifestyles today
_____ h. More electricity from fewer rivers?

Time _____ : _____

Accuracy, number correct of 20 _____

Check answers with your instructor.

2.11 FINDING ANSWERS WITHIN CONTINUOUS PROSE

Answers to the following questions will be found in the Introduction to this chapter, pages 40–45. We assume you have already done the required first step, preview skimming—in fact you've done more, you've read the Introduction carefully! Before you begin timing, pause here and skim back over the Introduction to remind yourself how it is organized.

In items 1–5, we tell you the pages to scan for the answers. In items 6–10, the answers may be located anywhere in the Introduction. Read each question carefully to know exactly what question you are trying to answer. Then scan back to the earlier pages as fast as possible.

Remember, be flexible about possible synonyms, "translate" into other words, and use all you know about how a writer writes—paragraphing, signal words and phrases, writing patterns and sequences. Time yourself, preferably against others. If you cannot find an item after a reasonable search, go on to the next item.

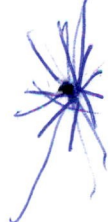

1. Page 40 The writer describes scanning here by comparing it with what two previously learned skills? _Semi Reading_ and _Selective Reading_

2. Page 40 What sport is the imaginary reader interested in, in paragraph 2 of "What Is Scanning?" _plush Green open_

3. Page 41 Which one of the three examples illustrates scanning that might *precede* a careful reading? _Seeing Madonna frankewrda_ _____

4. Page 42 Which paragraph tries to explain how one's eyes and brain work together to scan? par. 1 _____ 2 _✓_ 3 _____

5. Page 42 In what order are scanning levels discussed in this Introduction? From simple to complex _✓_ From complex to simple _____

In items 6–10, find the page that contains the answer, and write the page number in the blank.

6. When presenting the five rules, does the writer follow the same order you noted in item 5? Yes _✓_ No _____

7. Page _43_ Under the section "Complex Scanning," look for evidence that the authors of this book agree or disagree with the common notion, "If it's in print, it must be true." _disagree_ _____

8. Page _43_ On what page does the writer describe the kind of scanning you must do when you explain your reaction to a short story? Label the type or "level" of scanning: _Complex_

9. Page _41_, paragraph _7_ On what page, and in what paragraph, does the writer *first* list the three levels of scanning (in a sentence)? Tip: they're in quotation marks!

10. Page _45_ On what kind of note or tone does the body of the Introduction end (just before the Summary Box)? _tolerant everything_

Time, 1–10 _____ : _____

Accuracy _____ %

Check answers on p. 336.

2.12 More Practice Within Continuous Prose

The answers to the following questions will be found in the Introduction to Chapter 1, Essential Reading Skills. Scan as fast and yet as accurately as you can.

1. Which subtopic is given more space, stated main idea or implied main idea? _____ Number of pages: _____

2. Does a reader imply or infer meaning from the printed page? _____ Does the writer imply or infer meaning to the reader? _____

3. How many pages are spent on explaining how to read for details? _____

4. Page 6: Under the section "Organizational Patterns," find the paragraph that illustrates the Reasons (Reasons Why) pattern. How many reasons are given for the hikers' lack of precautions? _____

5. Page 10: What is a synonym for *dictionary definition*? _____
_____

6. Under "Organizational Patterns," find the page and the paragraph that states that names or labels for writing patterns may differ somewhat, according to the textbook or expert. Page _____, paragraph _____

7. In the paragraph illustrating the cause-effect pattern, does the writer believe that a large vocabulary directly causes a large salary? Or are the dollars incidental? _____
_____

8. On page 11, under the heading "Process Pattern," the writer makes an allusion to the movie title *Easy Rider*. What is the exact term used here?
_____

9. Under "Description Pattern," what reason does the writer give for labeling a written passage *description* only as a last resort? _____
_____
_____

10. Under the heading "Summarizing," do we state that you may always quote the original wording if you feel it is best? Cite the page and the paragraph number, and give a brief answer. Page _____, paragraph _____.
_____
_____

Time, 1–10 _____ : _____

Accuracy _____ %

Check answers with your instructor.

Study Reading

3.1, 3.3, 3.4
homework

*T*his chapter may well be crucial to your success in college. You will learn here the SQ3R study system, which helps you understand and remember textbook material. We will also introduce a popular new visual approach to learning, called mapping. You can begin applying both methods immediately to all your college textbook reading.

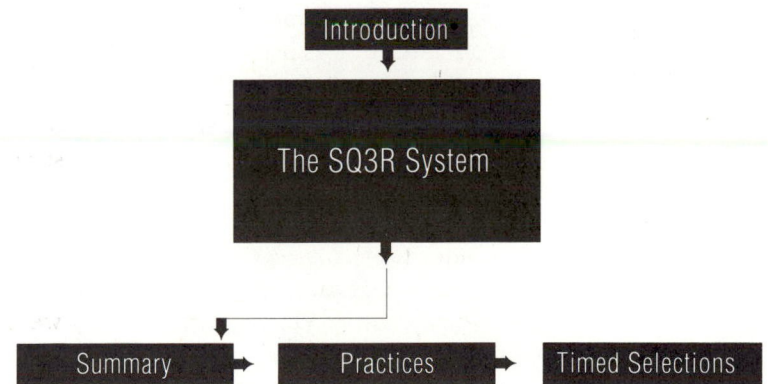

*I*NTRODUCTION TO STUDY READING

CHECKLIST OF SYMPTOMS

Do you often:

_____ 1. get bored or fall asleep when reading a textbook chapter?

_____ 2. feel that you haven't remembered a thing after you finish reading a chapter?

_____ 3. get poor grades in courses that require reading textbook material?

_____ 4. get poor grades on chapter tests when you think that you knew the material?

_____ 5. spend several hours rereading a chapter in a textbook?

If you checked one or more of these symptoms, you need to read this introduction carefully. If you learn to effectively use the system that we present, you can help improve your reading of textbook material.

A large amount of your college reading consists of reading and learning the information in textbooks. They are not the most interesting books to read, but they are often the most predictable. Sections are clearly divided and subdivided into boldface print and italics; study questions often come at the end of the chapter; charts and illustrations usually represent the most important facts and concepts discussed in the chapter; and usually the style of textbook material is straightforward. With the right system, reading textbook material can prove to be a worthwhile study experience.

THE SQ3R STUDY SYSTEM

One consistently successful program that learning experts have developed for reading textbooks is called SQ3R. The initials stand for: Survey, Question, Read, Recite, and Review. You need to understand each step of this reading system before you can successfully apply it to your study reading. So read and, if necessary, reread the following steps until you understand how the SQ3R works.

Step 1: Survey

This first step is similar to the preview skimming that you were introduced to in Chapter 1. Surveying is a major study-reading step, because, like preview skimming, it prepares you for what you are to read. Educational studies consistently show that a survey of a textbook improves your comprehension.

Surveying the Entire Text.   If you are reading a textbook for the first time, get to know the book by:

1. Reading the preface. It gives the author's reasons for writing the book, the topics covered, and the audience that the textbook is written for—items that will help you read the chapters efficiently.
2. Studying the table of contents to see how it is organized. Look at its divisions and subdivisions. The textbook's overall organization will help you understand how the author thinks about the material that he or she is presenting.
3. Thumbing through the index to see the number and types of words listed.
4. Looking to see if there is a glossary or appendix. See whether you will need to refer to charts or graphs as you read various chapters of the textbook.
5. Noting if there is an answer key at the end of the book or at the end of each chapter. Are answers given to all problems, or only to odd- or even-numbered problems?
6. Reading through a few pages at the beginning, middle, and end of the textbook to get a sense of the author's style and the difficulty level of the textbook. Does the author use a difficult vocabulary? Are the sentences complicated and hard to follow?

Surveying a Specific Chapter.   Once you have surveyed the entire textbook, you are ready to survey a specific chapter. Assume that you are reading an environmental science textbook chapter titled "Ecosystems: What Are They and How Do They Work?" In your survey, you should:

1. Study the title. Do you know what an *ecosystem* is? If not, look it up in the glossary, if the textbook provides one, or in a dictionary.
2. Read the general objectives to the chapter. This section will provide you with the major questions that this chapter will attempt to answer.
3. Read over the subdivisions; note words and phrases in boldface and italics. These are the terms that you will need to learn once you finish the chapter.
4. Glance at any illustrations and charts. How do these visual statements help explain the ecosystem and answer the questions posed in the general objectives?
5. Skim over the chapter summary and discussion questions at the end of the chapter to see what the author considers the most important issues for you to learn.

Step 2: Question

The second step—formulating questions from the chapter survey—is crucial. If you have questions to answer, then your reading is more directed. In most textbooks, the questioning step is simple because questions are provided either at the beginning or end of the chapter. If this is the case, read the questions over carefully, and choose four or five that seem most important to you and that you intend to answer as you study read.

If there are no questions at the beginning or end of the chapter, review the boldface or italicized words and phrases, and make up your own questions from them. In a subdivision titled "The Biosphere and Ecosystems," for example, you can formulate two questions: What is the biosphere? What are ecosystems?

Asking the right kinds of questions is one of the most important skills that an educated reader can develop. As you continue to read your textbook, the quality of your questions will improve, and so will your understanding of the material. You may soon find that the questions you ask are the same ones that your professor asks in class and on examinations.

Step 3: Read

Finally, you are ready to read, but now you are reading with a purpose because you know the chapter's organization and you have asked your own key questions. Read with concentration. Find a quiet area and choose the time of day when you are most alert. This may be in the morning or the evening. Always schedule your study-reading time when your mind is freshest.

As you read, mark your textbook. Underline only main ideas and supporting details in each paragraph so that the page is not filled with too many markings. You may choose to highlight main ideas and supporting details with a felt marker. Make marginal notes when a phrase or sentence is confusing; when you want to identify a definition, step, cause, or effect; and when you come across an insight that is not treated directly in the textbook. If you cannot understand a phrase or sentence in the first reading, reread it as well as the sentence before and after it. Finally, keep your questions in mind, and answer them as you move through the chapter.

Be diligent. Do whatever you have to do to make sense of the chapter—read silently, read aloud, reread passages, jot down notes—and to make the subject matter understandable to you.

Reading Tips.   Here are ten tips that should help you in marking and underlining textbook material.

1. Mark main ideas with a double line or a curved line, or use a marker to highlight the main idea. Underline only the key parts of the main idea, not the entire sentence. If you find that main ideas are related, number them 1, 2, 3, and so on to underscore this relationship.
2. Mark the major detail with a single line, or use a marker to highlight it. Only mark the important details in each paragraph and, like main ideas, only mark the important parts. If these details are related, use a numbering system similar to the one you used in relating the main ideas.
3. Place an asterisk (*) in the margin to emphasize a very important point. The asterisk will help you study this important point when you review the material.
4. When you think it is important, identify the detail as an example, step, cause, effect, or characteristic. Write the appropriate abbreviation in the margin to

alert you to the kind of detail that you are studying. By identifying the kind of detail that you are reading, you will have a better chance of remembering this detail and relating it to the main idea.

5. Mark especially carefully sections that define terms. Definitions are essential in learning any subject. You may want to circle the key parts of a definition so that they will stand out from the main ideas and major details that you have underlined.

6. When you cannot understand a particularly difficult passage after rereading it, place a question mark (?) in the margin. When you return to study this material, the question mark will alert you to those sections that you did not understand.

7. As you read, write a few comments in the margins. Place them anywhere in the margins: right or left, top or bottom. These comments could be summaries, rewordings of difficult sentences, or original insights.

8. Do not begin marking your textbook until you have read through several paragraphs. Remember that if your markings are incorrect, you will have difficulty erasing them. Some students quickly read through the entire chapter without marking anything. Then, in their second reading, they begin to mark the chapter. See your textbook marking as an in-process assignment that you continue to reshape as you reread and study the chapter.

9. Be consistent with your underlinings. You may use the system we have suggested, or you may design your own. Just be sure that when you study your markings, you can easily separate main ideas from major details, you can identify particular organizational patterns, and you can read your comments and easily see how they relate to the chapter.

10. These suggestions clearly show how study reading is an active process. After study reading effectively, you can demonstrate that you understand the main points and major details of a chapter, that you can follow the organization and logic of the chapter, and that you can make appropriate inferences about the chapter. Passively underlining pages of a chapter is not study reading.

Figure 3-1 (pp. 64–65) provides an example of a successfully marked page from an environmental science textbook. Study it to see how it effectively incorporates many of the ten suggestions that we have just explained.

Turn to Practice 3.1 on p. 72. Then do Practice 3.3 on p. 74.

Step 4: Recite

By itself, careful reading will not ensure that you have mastered a chapter of your textbook. If you cannot remember what you have read, if you cannot recite the material that you have studied, you have not learned the material. In the beginning of the recite step, close your textbook after ten minutes of study reading; open your notebook, and in your own words, write down the main points that you have learned. If you are unhappy with what you have written, return to the material that you have read and review your marginal notes and underlinings. As you continue to recite, extend your concentrated reading to fifteen, then twenty

Notes written from memory.
Notes reflect, main idea - topic, major support

Figure 3-1. *Example of a Well-Marked Page of Text*

Ecological Questions {
What plants and animals live in a forest or a pond? How do they get the matter and energy resources needed to stay alive? How do these plants and animals interact with one another and with their physical environment? What changes will this forest or pond undergo through time?

Questions of <u>Ecology is the science that attempts to answer such questions.</u> In 1866 German biologist Ernst Haeckel coined the term *ecology* from two Greek words: *oikos*, meaning "house" or "place to live," and *logos*, meaning "study of." Literally, then *ecology is the study of living things or organisms in their home.* In more formal terms, **ecology** is the study of interactions among organisms and between organisms and the physical and chemical factors making up their environment. This study is usually carried out as the examination of **ecosystems:** forests, deserts, ponds, oceans, or any self-regulating set of plants and animals interacting with one another and with their nonliving environment. This chapter will consider the major nonliving and living components of ecosystems and how they interact. The next two chapters will consider major types of ecosystems, and the changes they can undergo as a result of natural events and human activities.

Def.

Def.

Def.

THE BIOSPHERE AND ECOSYSTEMS
The Earth's Life-Support System What keeps plants and animals alive on this tiny planet as it hurtles through space at a speed of 66,000 miles per hour? The general answer to this question is that life on earth depends on <u>two fundamental processes:</u> *matter cycling* and the *one-way flow of high-quality energy* <u>from the sun,</u> through materials and living things on or near the earth's surface, and into space as low-quality heat (Figure 4-1).

All forms of life depend for their existence on the multitude of materials that compose the **(1)** solid **lithosphere,** consisting of the upper surface or crust of the earth, containing soil and deposits of matter and energy resources, and an inner mantle and core. **(2)** the gaseous **atmosphere** extending above the earth's surface **(3)** the **hydrosphere,** containing all of the earth's moisture as liquid water, ice, and small amounts of water vapor in the atmosphere and **(4)** the **biosphere,** consisting of parts of the lithosphere, atmosphere, and hydrosphere in which living organisms can be found.

Def. 1

Def. 2
Def. 3

Def. 4

Human life and other forms of life whose existence we can threaten also depend on the **culturesphere:** the use of human ingenuity and knowledge based on past experience to extract, produce, and manage the use of matter, energy, and biological resources to enhance human survival and life quality. A <u>major input of ecology</u> into the culturesphere is that <u>all forms of life on earth are directly or indirectly interconnected.</u> This means that to enhance long-term human survival and life quality, we must not blindly destroy other forms of plant and animal life—we must learn to work with, not against, nature.

Def.

Imp. pt.

The biosphere contains all the water, minerals, oxygen, nitrogen, phosphorus, and other nutrients that living things need. For example, your body consists of about 70% water obtained from the hydrosphere, small amounts of nitrogen and oxygen gases continually breathed in from the atmosphere,

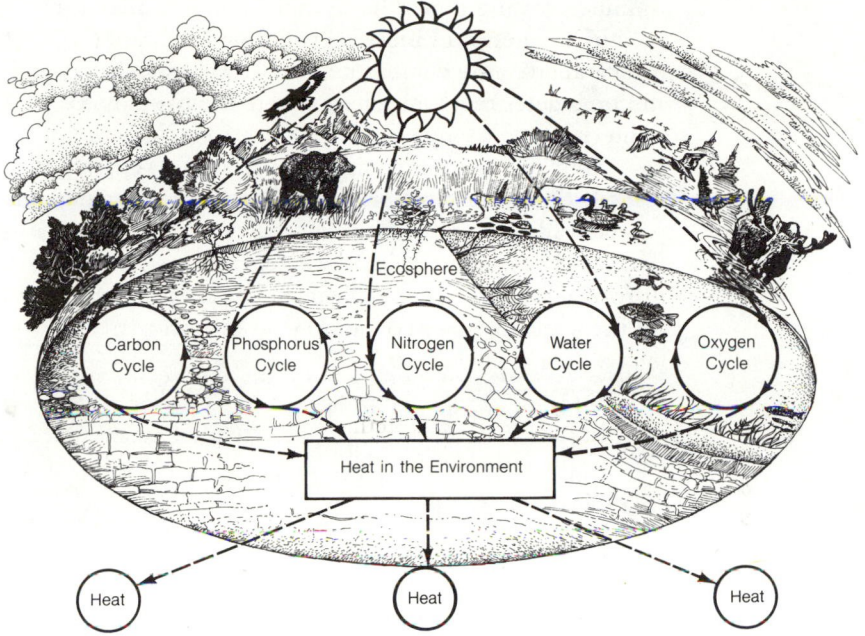

Figure 4-1 *Life on earth depends on the cycling of critical chemicals (solid lines) and the one-way flow of energy through the biosphere (dashed lines).*

and various chemicals whose building blocks come mostly from the lithosphere. If the earth were an apple, the biosphere would be no thicker than the apple's skin. Everything in this "skin of life" is interdependent: air helps purify water and keeps plants and animals alive, water keeps plants and animals alive, plants keep animals alive and help renew the air and soil, and the soil keeps plants and many animals alive and helps purify water. *The goal of ecology is to find out how everything in the biosphere is related.*

The Realm of Ecology

Ecology is primarily concerned with interactions among five of the levels of organization of matter, organisms, populations, communities, ecosystems, and the biosphere. An **organism** is any form of life. Although biologists classify the earth's organisms in anywhere from 5 to 20 categories, in this book it is only necessary to classify organisms as plants or animals. Plants range from microscopic, one-celled, floating and drifting plants known as phytoplankton to the largest of all living things—the giant sequoia trees of western North America. Animals range in size from floating and drifting zooplankton (which feed on phytoplankton) to the 14-foot-high, male African elephant and the 100-foot-long blue whale.

Def.

G. Tyler Miller, Jr., *Living in the Environment*, Fifth ed., pp. 68–69. ©1988 by Wadsworth, Inc. Reprinted by permission of the publishers.

minutes, jotting down the significant points after each reading session. By the end of a semester of practice, you should be able to read for an hour at one sitting and give an accurate summary of what you have read. These summaries can become notes that you will be able to use to study for your examinations on this material.

Your recite notes should be placed in a separate section of your notebook called "Study Reading." Each course that you are taking should have a separate study-reading section. Title each entry with the chapter title or subtitle (if there is one), the pages read, and the date. Here is a sample entry: "Human Population Growth," pp. 2–8, 1/2/92. By including these entries, you will know which pages of the textbook you have put in your own words.

Note Taking.   You may write these notes in any style that seems easier for you. The two most common note-taking formats are numeral-letter and indenting. In the numeral-letter system, you use Roman numerals and capital letters—the Roman numerals to indicate main ideas, the capital letters major details. Study the following example:

> *I. Two types of countries*
>   *A. More developed countries (MDCs)*
>   *B. Less developed countries (LDCs)*

The main ideas and major details can either be in phrases or sentences. The main idea, indicated by the Roman numeral I, is to the left; the major details, A and B, are to the right of the main idea.

The indenting format follows the same left-to-right pattern. Main ideas are to the left, major details to the right. This outline can be easily transferred into the indenting format:

> *Two types of countries*
>   *More developed countries (MDCs)*
>   *Less developed countries (LDCs)*

With both formats, it is wise to skip a line between main ideas so that in your review you can easily distinguish different types of information.

A third technique that some students find effective is to write short paragraphs. These outlines can be translated into three short sentences:

> *There are two types of countries. The first is the more developed countries (MDCs). The second is the less developed countries (LDCs).*

What all three systems share is that only main ideas and significant details are noted. As in all effective summaries, the minor details have been omitted in favor of the important general and specific statements.

Advanced Organizers.   Once you have read an entire chapter or several chapters and you begin to study the material for a midterm or final examination, you may want to tie all of the information into clear visual representations. Known as study maps or advanced organizers, these visual representations should be used

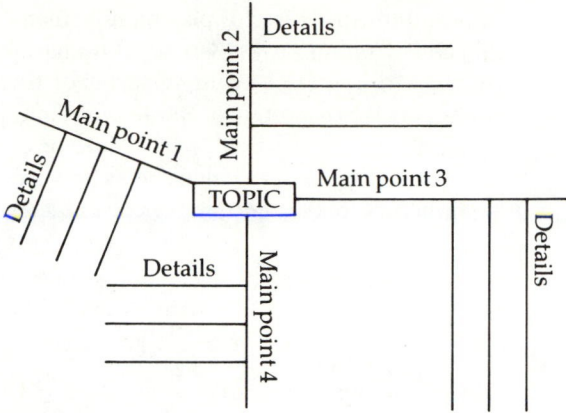

Figure 3-2 *Diagram of a Study Map.*

when you have had time to restudy or rethink a chapter or chapters and organize the material in the most economical way you can.

Study maps often use geometric shapes like circles, squares, rectangles, triangles, radiating lines, and arrows to place information in correct order. Each study map should be placed on a separate sheet of paper and should emanate from the center of the page. Many learning theorists contend that the brain remembers much more if material is placed in the center with additional information moving outward rather than if material is placed to the left or right.

Three geometric structures are commonly used as the basis for advanced organizers. In the first structure, the topic is boxed in the center. The main points then radiate from the center as lines, and details are added to each radiating line. See Figure 3-2.

A variation of this advanced organizer is known as the tree study map. The topic comes first. Branching from the topic are main ideas, and branching from these main ideas are major details. See Figure 3-3.

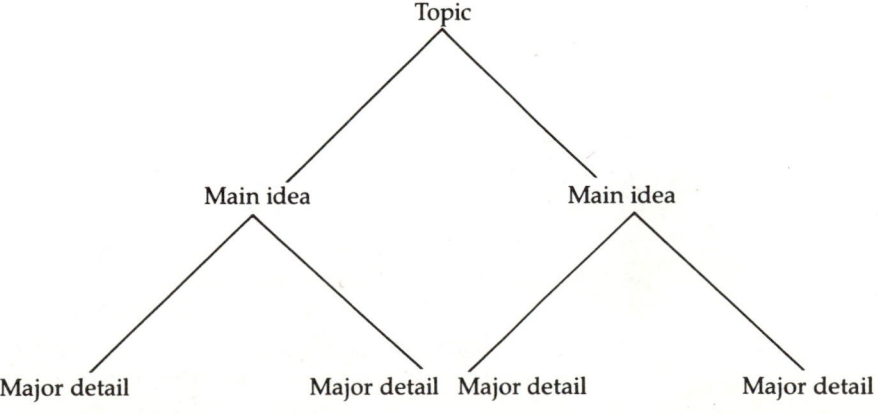

Figure 3-3 *Tree Study Map.*

A third structure for placing information into a visual pattern is more complicated. Commonly known as a flowchart, this advanced organizer works effectively with material having a series of time sequences or procedures. In the flowchart, arrows often go left or right and up or down. These arrows show the correct steps in a particular procedure or event.

Study Figure 3-4, which shows how poverty, malnutrition, and disease work together. Note how certain processes like malnutrition and decreased resistance

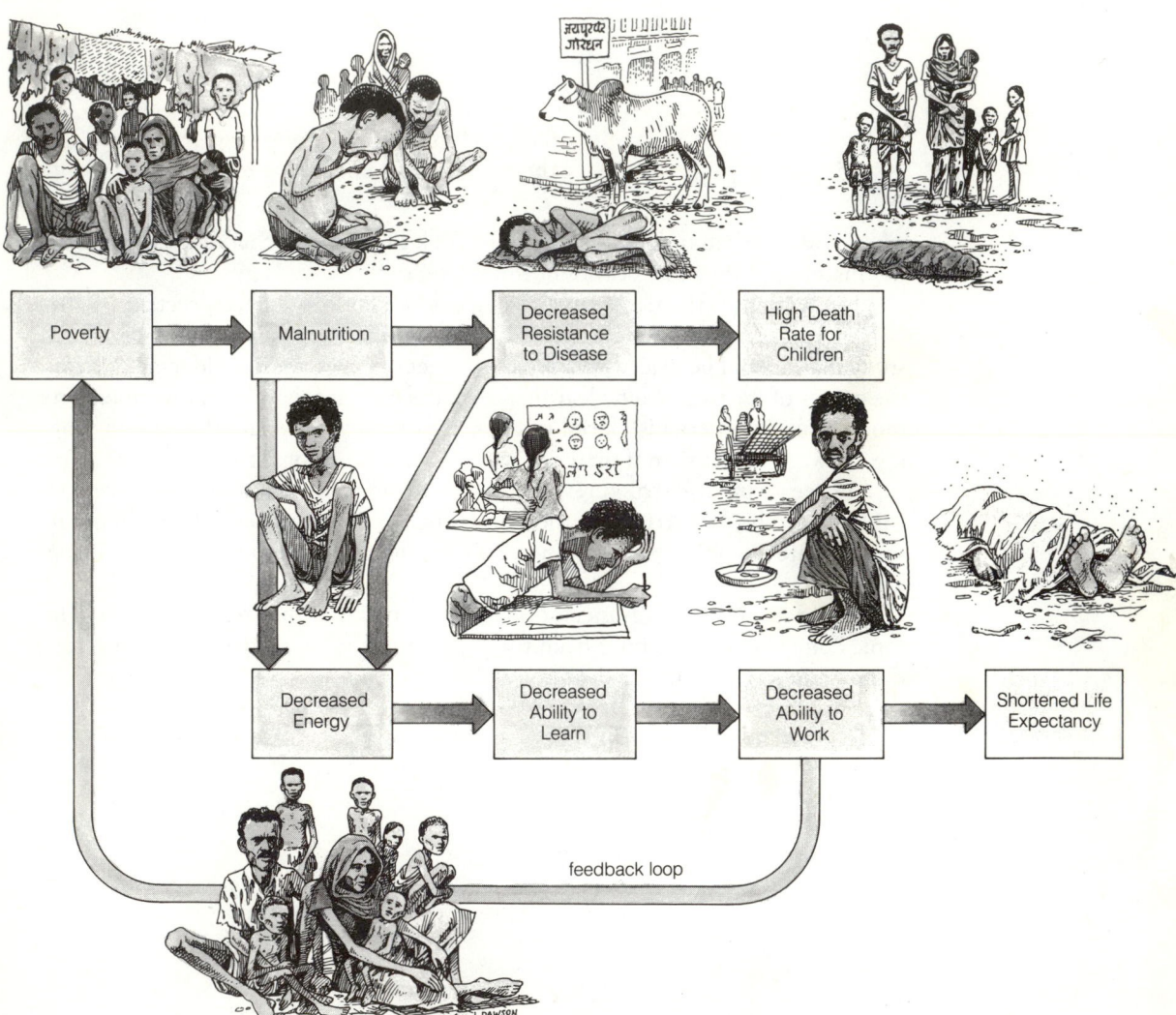

Figure 3-4 *Interactions among poverty, malnutrition, and disease form a tragic cycle that perpetuates such conditions in succeeding generations of families.*

G. Tyler Miller, Jr., *Living in the Environment*, Fifth ed., p. 243. ©1988 by Wadsworth, Inc. Reprinted by permission of the publishers.

to disease move from left to right and down, showing that they affect two processes simultaneously. Also, note how the decreased ability to work moves from right to left, affecting the original cause of poverty. Finally, note how much information, how many cause-effect relationships, are economically portrayed in this flowchart. A student studying from this advanced organizer would likely remember a lot of rather complicated information because it is expressed economically on one page.

Often students come on small bits of information that can be efficiently expressed in a visual manner. The students often use small advanced organizers—radiating lines, arrows, or intersecting circles—as they attempt to learn study-reading material. Let's say that an environmental science textbook mentions three disciplines that are concerned with the environment: chemistry, biology, and physics. A student's recite notes could look like the study map shown in Figure 3-5. This study map expresses the relationship among the four disciplines more effectively than would a sentence in a notebook.

In another example from environmental science, see how the statement "Environmental science often relies on studies in biochemistry or experts in biology and chemistry" is nicely expressed in a study map using intersecting circles (Figure 3-6).

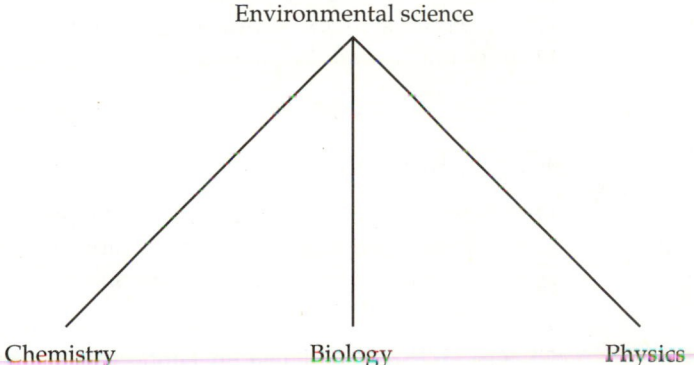

Figure 3-5   *Student Study Map.*

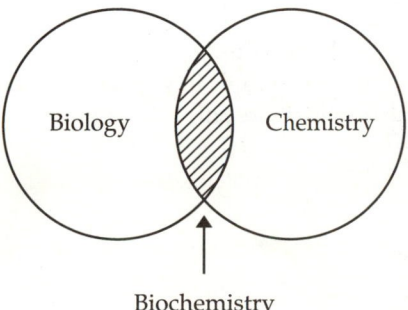

Figure 3-6   *Small Study Map.*

Finally, cause-effect statements can be expressed in recite notes via arrows. See how the following information about the use of carbon dioxide is easily represented with arrows that indicate a cause-effect relationship: "Carbon dioxide in the atmosphere is used by plants in the photosynthesis process, which in turn creates stored chemical energy for the plants to use."

Carbon dioxide

↓

Photosynthesis

↓

Stored chemical energy

In summary, your recite notes from textbook material can be expressed in several ways: (1) through traditional note-taking techniques, (2) through summaries written in paragraph form, and (3) through study maps expressing minor or major concepts in a chapter or chapters of the textbook. No matter what note-taking styles you choose, keep in mind that recite notes are very important because they place textbook information into your own voice or point of view. Only when you have translated textbook material into your own, accurate summaries can you begin to understand the material that you have read.

Step 5: Review

Once you have successfully completed the previous four steps in the SQ3R system—Survey, Question, Read, and Recite—you are ready for the last step. You now know what to review for your examination on ecosystems.

1. Review your underlinings: main ideas and supporting details.
2. Carefully review all marginal notes—your inferences and questions about the textbook material.
3. Study your recites carefully so that on your examination you will be able to recall most of what you have written in your notes.
4. Give yourself several days before the examination date to review your notes and underlinings. In some cases, you may need to review a page in the textbook or a topic in your notes several times before it becomes material that you can easily recall. Like study reading, reviewing is an active process.

• • • • • • • • • • • • • • • • • • • •

SUMMARY

You can now see why efficient learning requires much concentration and planning. Textbooks are dense; they present a lot of information concisely. The passive reader cannot expect to master textbook material. The active reader of textbooks:

1. Knows when to reread.
2. Knows how to summarize.
3. Is able to make appropriate inferences from the material he or she reads.
4. Can take accurate, concise, and easy-to-read notes.

To study read textbooks efficiently, you must learn to effortlessly use the following steps: Survey, Question, Read, Recite, and Review.

Apply this SQ3R system to the practices and study selections that follow.

SUMMARY BOX: CRITICAL READING

What?	Why?	Acceptable Comprehension	Acceptable Rates
Textbooks in all fields	To understand the recall material for exams and job-related tasks, get better grades, save time in studying	80–90%	100–300 wpm

PRACTICES: STUDY READING

Answers for these questions are not provided in the answer key. Check your work with your instructor.

3.1 UNDERLINING A TEXTBOOK EXCERPT
3.2 MAPPING SHORT STATEMENTS
3.3 UNDERLINING AND MARKING A TEXTBOOK EXCERPT
3.4 UNDERLINING, MARKING, AND MAPPING A TEXTBOOK EXCERPT

3.1 UNDERLINING A TEXTBOOK EXCERPT

Following is a four-paragraph excerpt, titled "Life in the Poorest Countries," taken from an environmental science textbook. Read the four paragraphs through carefully; then go back to underline the main ideas twice and the major details once. Remember to underline only important parts of the main ideas and major details. If any main ideas or details are particularly important, place an asterisk in the margins.

LIFE IN THE POOREST COUNTRIES

Life for the poor people who comprise at least half the population of the 79 LDCs with low and very low average GNPs per person consists of a harsh daily struggle for survival. In typical rural villages or urban slums, groups of malnourished children sit around wood or dung fires eating breakfasts of bread and coffee. The air is filled with the stench of refuse and open sewers. Children and women carry heavy jars or cans of water, often for long distances, from a muddy, microbe-infested river, canal, or village water faucet. At night people sleep on the street in the open, under makeshift canopies, or on dirt floors in crowded single-room shacks, often made from straw, cardboard, rusting metal, or abandoned sections of drainage pipes. Families consisting of a father, mother, and from seven to nine children consider themselves fortunate to have an annual income of $300—an average of 82 cents a day. The parents, who themselves may die by age 45, know that three or four of their children will probably die from hunger or childhood diseases, such as diarrhea or measles, that rarely kill in affluent countries.

When citizens of affluent countries see such conditions in person or on television, they often try to blot these grim pictures out of their minds. Some consider poor people ignorant for having so many children. To most poor parents, however, having a large number of children, especially boys, makes good sense. It gives them much needed help for work in the fields or begging in the streets and provides a form of social security to help them survive when they reach old age (typically in their forties). For people living near the edge of survival, having too many children may cause problems, but having too few can contribute to premature death.

Although the world is feeding more people than ever before, there are an estimated 750 million desperately poor people—one out of every six people on earth—living mostly in low- and very low income countries. These people do not have enough fertile land or money to grow their own food in rural areas or enough money to buy the food they need in cities. As a result, between 12 million and 20 million die prematurely each year from starvation, malnutrition (lack of sufficient protein and other nutrients needed for good health), or normally nonfatal diseases such as diarrhea brought on by contaminated drinking water, which, for people weakened by malnutrition, becomes deadly.

This means that during your lunch hour 1,400 to 2,300 people died of such causes; by the time you eat lunch tomorrow 33,000 to 55,000 more will have died; and by this time next week, 231,000 to 385,000. Half are children under the age of 5. This starvation and malnutrition is not classified as famine by most officials because it is spread throughout much of the world (especially rural Africa and Asia) and not confined to one country.

G. Tyler Miller, Jr., *Living in the Environment*, Fifth ed., p. 5. © 1988 by Wadsworth, Inc. Reprinted by permission of the publisher.

• •

Score: Underlinings will vary.

Ask instructor for sample underlinings.

3.2 MAPPING SHORT STATEMENTS

Use any mapping system that seems appropriate to visually represent the following statements. Your maps may vary from those that your instructor shows you.

1. There are three types of resources in our environment: (a) a renewable resource, one that is depleted but can be replaced; (b) a perpetual resource, one that will always be available; and (c) a nonrenewable resource, one that exists in fixed amounts.
2. Examples of nonrenewable resources include (a) fossil fuels, (b) metallic minerals, and (c) nonmetallic minerals.
3. There seem to be three major causes of environmental pollutions: (a) development of technology, (b) overpopulation, and (c) natural occurrences like fires and volcanic eruptions.
4. The world can be divided up into two types of countries: (a) less developed countries (LDCs) and (b) more developed countries (MDCs).
5. Overpopulation has created many problems. First, it has led to the overuse and depletion of many natural resources. Also, in some parts of the world it has led to famine and the spread of communicable diseases. These diseases have caused the deaths of millions. Occasionally, famine has caused disputes among organizations in more powerful countries over decisions to help or ignore the starving countries. Finally, the increase in human population has led to habitat loss for other species; as a result, many plant and animal species face extinction in the coming years.

Score: Answers will vary.

Ask instructor for sample maps.

3.3 UNDERLINING AND MARKING A TEXTBOOK EXCERPT

The following is an excerpt on natural resources from an environmental science textbook. As in Practice 3.1, read through the excerpt carefully; then underline main ideas twice and major details once. Be sure that you underline only important parts of these sentences. Make marginal comments regarding organizational patterns and write any insights that you have while reading. Remember not to make too many marginal comments. As review, you may want to turn to pp. 64–65 in the Introduction, for an example of a marked text.

• • • • • • • • • • • • • • • • • • • •

RESOURCES AND ENVIRONMENTAL DEGRADATION

WHAT IS A NATURAL RESOURCE?

A **natural resource** or **resource** is usually defined as anything obtained from the physical environment to meet human needs. Some resources are available for use directly from the environment. Examples include solar energy, fresh air, rainwater, fresh water in a river or stream, and naturally growing edible plants. Other resources, such as oil, iron, groundwater, fish, and game animals, are not directly available for our use. Whether these and other materials in the environment are considered to be human resources depends on a combination of human ingenuity, economics, and cultural beliefs.

Human ingenuity enables us to develop scientific and technological methods for finding, extracting, and processing many of the earth's natural substances and converting them to usable forms. Groundwater found deep below the earth's surface was not a resource until we developed the technology for drilling a well and installing pumps and other equipment to bring it to the surface. Fish and game animals are not a resource unless we have some way of catching and (in most cases) cooking them. Petroleum was a mysterious fluid until humans learned how to locate it, extract it, and refine it into gasoline, home heating oil, road tar, and other products. Cars, television sets, tractors, and other manufactured objects are available only because humans developed methods for converting an array

of once-useless raw materials from the earth's crust into useful forms.

Economics also determines whether something is classified as a resource or a potential resource. Some known deposits of oil, coal, copper, and other potentially useful materials are located so far beneath the earth's surface or in such low concentrations that they would cost more to find, extract, and process than they are worth. In the future, however, their prices may rise due to their scarcity, or cheaper, more efficient mining and processing technologies may be developed, converting these potential resources to actual resources.

Cultural beliefs can also determine whether something is considered a resource. For example, protein-rich grasshoppers and other insects are considered food resources in some parts of Africa, but are viewed with disgust as sources of food in the United States and in most MDCs. In some cultures, religious beliefs prohibit the use of pork or other types of food resources. The perceived or actual degree of risk involved in using a resource such as nuclear power can also play a role in whether or how widely it is used.

NONRENEWABLE RESOURCES

Resources can be classified as nonrenewable, renewable, and perpetual. A **nonrenewable resource** is one that exists in a fixed amount (stock) in various places in the earth's crust and either is not replenished by natural processes or is replenished more slowly than it is used. Examples include **(1) fossil fuels**—buried deposits of decayed plants and animals that have been converted to materials such as oil, coal, and natural gas by heat and pressure in the earth's crust over hundreds of millions of years; **(2) metallic minerals** such as uranium, iron, and aluminum; and **(3) nonmetallic minerals** such as phosphates and potassium used as plant nutrients in commercial fertilizers.

The easily available deposits of nonrenewable minerals and fossil fuels are usually found in high concentrations near the earth's surface in nonhostile environments; once they are depleted, extraction costs rise. Increasing scarcity can raise the prices paid for such resources, stimulating a search for new deposits or making the mining and processing of lower grade deposits more feasible. Eventually, however, the cost of finding, extracting, and concentrating increasingly lower grade or difficult-to-extract deposits may become so high that these substances are no longer considered resources even though some supplies remain. *Typically, a nonrenewable resource such as oil or copper is considered depleted from an economic standpoint when 80% of its total estimated supply has been removed and used.*

Some nonrenewable resources can be recycled or reused to stretch supplies—copper, aluminum, iron, and glass, for example—and others, such as fossil fuels, cannot. **Recycling** involves collecting and remelting or reprocessing a resource (aluminum beverage cans), whereas **reuse** involves using a resource over and over in the same form (refillable beverage bottles). But discarded aluminum cans, refillable bottles, and abandoned car hulks can be dispersed so widely that it becomes too costly to collect them for reuse or recycling.

We live in a brief **fossil fuel era** in which deposits of solar energy captured by plants and converted to nonrenewable deposits of crude oil, coal, and natural gas over hundreds of millions of years are being used up in several hundred years. During 1986 these one-time deposits of fossil fuels, which cannot be recycled or reused, provided about 82% of the energy used in the world for electricity, heating, cooling, transportation, and manufacturing. The largest fraction of this energy (36%) was provided by oil. Affordable supplies of oil are projected to last for only a few more decades.

Sometimes a substitute or replacement for a nonrenewable resource that is scarce or too expensive can be found. Although some resource economists argue that we can use human ingenuity to find a substitute for any nonrenewable resource, this is not always the case at a particular time or for a particular purpose. Some materials have such unique properties that they cannot easily be replaced; the would-be replacements are inferior, too costly, or otherwise unsatisfactory. For example, nothing now known can replace steel and concrete in skyscrapers, nuclear power plants, and dams.

G. Tyler Miller, Jr., *Living in the Environment*, Fifth ed., pp. 8–10. © 1988 by Wadsworth, Inc. Reprinted by permission of the publisher.

• •

Score: Underlining and marking will vary.

Ask instructor for sample underlinings and markings.

3.4 Underlining, Marking, and Mapping a Textbook Excerpt

Read the following textbook excerpt on pollution. Reread, then underline main ideas and major details. Make marginal comments on (1) organizational patterns and (2) points that you consider important.

When you have finished marking and underlining the passage, use the numeral-letter format to summarize the key points in the excerpt. Finally, from these recite notes, make up a study map that visually represents these points.

▪▪▪▪▪▪▪▪▪▪▪▪▪▪▪▪▪ ▪
POLLUTION

WHAT IS POLLUTION?

Any change in the physical, chemical, or biological characteristics of the air, water, or soil that can affect the health, survival, or activities of humans or other forms of life in an undesirable way is called **pollution**. Pollution does not have to cause physical harm; pollutants such as noise and heat may cause injury but more often cause psychological distress, and aesthetic pollution such as foul odors and unpleasant sights offend the senses.

People, however, may differ in what they consider to be a pollutant, on the basis of their assessment of benefits and risks to their health and economic well-being. For example, visible and invisible chemicals spewed into the air or water from an industrial plant might be harmful to humans and other forms of life living nearby. However, if the installation of expensive pollution controls forces the plant to shut down, workers who would lose their jobs might feel that the risks from polluted air and water are minor weighed against the benefits of profitable employment. The same level of pollution can also affect two people quite differently—some forms of air pollution might be a slight annoyance to a healthy person but life threatening to someone with emphysema or another respiratory disorder.

Such risk-benefit analysis enters into most environmental decisions and leads to economic, political, and ethical trade-offs. . . . As the philosopher Georg Hegel pointed out, the nature of tragedy is not the conflict between right and wrong but between right and right.

TYPES, SOURCES, AND EFFECTS OF POLLUTANTS

As long as they are not overloaded, natural processes or human-engineered systems (such as sewage treatment plants) can biodegrade or break down some types of pollutants to an acceptable level or form. Depending on their biodegradability, pollutants can be classified as being **rapidly biodegradable** (such as human sewage and livestock wastes), **slowly biodegradable** (such as DDT and other chemical pesticides), and **nonbiodegradable** (such as toxic mercury and lead compounds and some radioactive substances).

Polluting substances can enter the environment naturally or through human activities. Most natural pollution is dispersed over a large area and is often diluted or degraded to harmless levels by natural processes. In contrast, the most serious human pollution problems occur in or near urban and industrial areas, where large amounts of pollutants are concentrated in relatively small volumes of air, water, and soil. Furthermore, many pollutants from human activities are synthetic (human-made) chemicals that are slowly biodegradable or nonbiodegradable.

Often, pollutants released into one part of the environment don't remain there and can affect people and other forms of life at the local, regional, and in some cases the global levels. Sulfur dioxide gas released into the atmosphere by coal-burning industrial and electric power plants in the midwestern United States is converted to acidic droplets and solid particles that fall to the earth's surface and kill some species of trees in mountain forests and fish and other aquatic life in lakes in

definitions

the northeastern United States and southeastern Canada.

Complicating matters further, pollutants can have both acute and chronic effects on human health. An **acute effect**, such as a burn, illness, or death, occurs shortly after exposure, often in response to fairly high concentrations of a pollutant. A **chronic effect** is a condition that lasts a long time and usually takes a long time to appear, often due to exposure to low concentrations of a pollutant. For example, people exposed to a large dose of radiation may die within a few days. However, people receiving the same total dose in small amounts over a long period may develop various types of cancer 10 to 20 years later or may transmit genetic defects to their children.

During a lifetime an individual is exposed to many different types and concentrations of potentially harmful pollutants. The scientific evidence correlating a particular harmful effect to a particular pollutant is usually statistical or circumstantial—as is most scientific evidence. For example, so far no one has been able to show what specific chemicals in cigarette smoke cause lung cancer; however, smoking and lung cancer are causally linked by an overwhelming amount of statistical evidence from more than 32,000 studies.

Another complication is that certain pollutants acting together can cause a harmful effect greater than the sum of their individual effects. This phenomenon is called a **synergistic effect**. For example, asbestos workers, already at higher-than-average risk of lung cancer, greatly increase that risk if they smoke because of an apparent synergistic effect between tobacco smoke and tiny particles of asbestos inhaled into the lungs.

Testing all the possible synergistic interactions among the thousands of possible pollutants in the environment is prohibitively expensive and time-consuming, even for their effects on just one type of plant or animal.

POLLUTION CONTROL

Some countries, especially MDCs such as the United States, are making progress in controlling some types of pollution; others are not. There are two fundamentally different approaches to pollution control. **Input pollution control** prevents potential pollutants from entering the environment or sharply reduces the amount emitted or discharged. In this preventive approach taxes, incentives, or other economic devices are used to make the resource inputs of a process so expensive that these resources will be used more efficiently, thus decreasing the output of waste material.

The other is a "treat-the-disease" or **output pollution control** approach that deals with wastes after they have been produced. The three major methods of output control are (1) cleaning up polluted air, water, or land by reducing pollutants to harmless levels or by converting them to harmless or less harmful substances, (2) disposing of harmful wastes by burning them, dumping them in the air or water in the hope that they will be diluted to harmless levels, or burying them in the ground and hoping they will remain there, and (3) recycling or reusing matter output from human activities.

ways to deal with pollution

. . . .

Score: Answers for underlinings, mapping, and summary will vary.

Ask your instructor for sample responses.

SELECTIONS: STUDY READING — ENVIRONMENTAL POLLUTION

The four selections in this chapter may be done in class or outside of class on your own. In either case, be sure to follow the step-by-step directions carefully. Please do not skip any step or change the order.

In this set of selections—all on the issue of environmental pollution—you will practice reading text material using the SQ3R system. You will begin by surveying each one. This is followed by a five-item survey quiz. Next you will write five questions of your own that will direct your study reading. With these in mind, you will read, underline, mark, and recite as part of the process of understanding what you have read. Then you will take a ten-item study quiz, testing your understanding of what you have read. Next you will work on five questions for discussion and writing; here you will return to reread and rethink the selection. The last exercise consists of five scanning questions—locating exact information in the selection. The survey and scanning exercises are timed; the rest are not.

Each selection concludes with a self-evaluation. Here you rate your success in the various exercises and read some additional suggestions about how to study read in that particular discipline. Any unusual, important words will be defined at the beginning of the selection. Answers to odd-numbered selection quizzes (1 and 3) will be found on p. 337. Answers to even-numbered selection quizzes (2 and 4) will be provided by your instructor.

Before you begin study reading these four selections, consider the following questions on environmental pollution. Since all of the selections will deal with some aspect of this issue, answering these questions will help uncover what you and your class already know about this important social topic. You may want to respond to these questions individually or discuss them in small or large groups in class:

1. How would you define the word *environment*?
2. How would you define the word *pollution*?
3. How do you think pollution affects the environment?
4. How do you think society is responding to the pollution problem?
5. Do you think the pollution problem is a serious one? Why? Why not?

STUDY READING SELECTIONS

1. "The Roots of Environmental Degradation" 1,789 words
2. "Changes in the Atmosphere" 1,578 words
3. "Government Efforts to Protect the Environment" 2,611 words
4. "The Environment and Ethical Theories" 2,689 words

SELECTION 1

"The Roots of Environmental Degradation" *by G. Tyler Miller, Jr.*
1,789 words

Vocabulary

degradation: a breaking down; "The Roots of Environmental Degradation"

nonrenewable resource: resource available in a fixed amount; "people . . . are using nonrenewable and renewable resources"

renewable resource: resource that can be replaced through natural processes; "people . . . are using nonrenewable and renewable resources"

LDCs: abbreviation for less developed countries; "In the world's poorest LDCs . . ."

biodegraded: material broken into simpler substances; "either slowly biodegraded or not biodegraded by natural processes"

phosphate: a salt containing phosphorus; "such as the automobile and phosphate detergents"

nurtured: referring to promoting the development of; "a trend that should be nurtured"

exponentially: a mathematical formula of increase through multiplication; "human population growing exponentially"

This excerpt comes from an environmental science textbook. Like most environmental science material, it relies heavily on the organizational patterns of definition and cause-effect. The sentence structure and style are fairly easy to follow. You may have some difficulty, however, in keeping track of and using the several definitions that you come across. Be sure that you reread any definitions that are not immediately clear to you and make appropriate marginal notes.

This excerpt will provide you with an important introduction to the general issues that concern environmental pollution. As such, it will help make the next three selections easier to understand. Basically, you will be introduced to the major causes of environmental pollution, and you will learn about the positions that various people have regarding pollution.

Reading Strategies.   To effectively read this excerpt, use the following strategies:

1.   Circle the key parts of the definitions, or highlight them in such a way that you separate them from the rest of the material.
2.   See how the various definitions relate to each other, such as people overpopulation and consumption overpopulation; less developed country and overdeveloped country; neo-Malthusians and cornucopians.
3.   Note in the margins the important cause-effect patterns, particularly the factors influencing environmental problems.

A. Survey

Take 2 minutes to survey the excerpt. Read the chapter title, the subtitles, the terms in boldface print, the words and phrases in italics, and the figures. If time permits, begin reading the first paragraph or two.

When your time is up, answer the five questions without looking back at the excerpt. Place all answers in the answer box.

- -

THE ROOTS OF ENVIRONMENTAL DEGRADATION

by G. Tyler Miller, Jr.

RELATIONSHIPS AMONG POPULATION, RESOURCE USE, TECHNOLOGY, ENVIRONMENTAL DEGRADATION, AND POLLUTION

[1] The Roots of Environmental Degradation and Pollution

What causes most environmental degradation and pollution? The obvious answer is people trying either to survive or to make short-term profits. We could conclude that most forms of pollution and environmental degradation tend to increase with population growth, but the real situation is not that simple because pollution and environmental degradation vary with the technological methods and the types of resources people use. According to one simple model, the total environmental degradation and pollution or environmental impact of population in a given area depends upon three factors: **(1)** the number of people, **(2)** the amount of resources each person uses, and **(3)** the environmental degradation and pollution resulting from each unit of resource used (Figure 1).

[2] Two Types of Overpopulation

In general, **overpopulation** occurs when the people in a country, a region, or the world are using nonrenewable and renewable resources to such an extent that the resulting degradation or depletion of the resource base and pollution of the air, water, and soil are impairing their life-support systems. Differences in the relative importance of each factor in the model in Figure 2 have been used to distinguish between two types of overpopulation.

[3] The type known as **people overpopulation** exists where there are more people than the available supplies of food, water, and other vital resources can support, or where the rate of population growth so exceeds the rate of economic growth that an increasing number of people are too poor to grow or buy sufficient food, fuel, and other vital resources. In this type of overpopulation, population size and the resulting environmental degradation of potentially renewable soil, grasslands, forests, and fisheries tend to be the most important factors determining the total environmental impact. In the world's poorest LDCs, people overpopulation results in premature death for 12 million to 20 million human beings each year and bare subsistence for hundreds of millions more—a situation that many fear will worsen unless population growth is brought under control and improved resource management is used to restore degraded renewable resource bases.

[4] Affluent and technologically advanced countries such as the United States, the Soviet

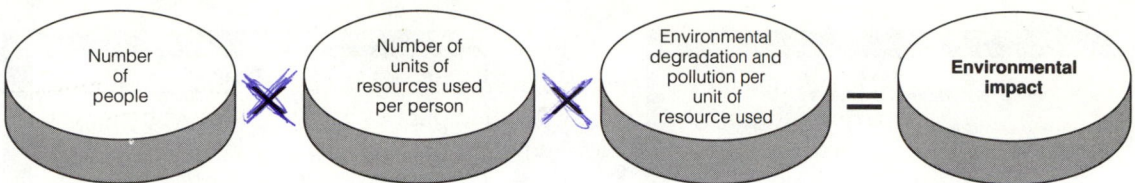

Figure 1   *Simplified model of how three factors affect overall environmental degradation and pollution or environmental impact.*

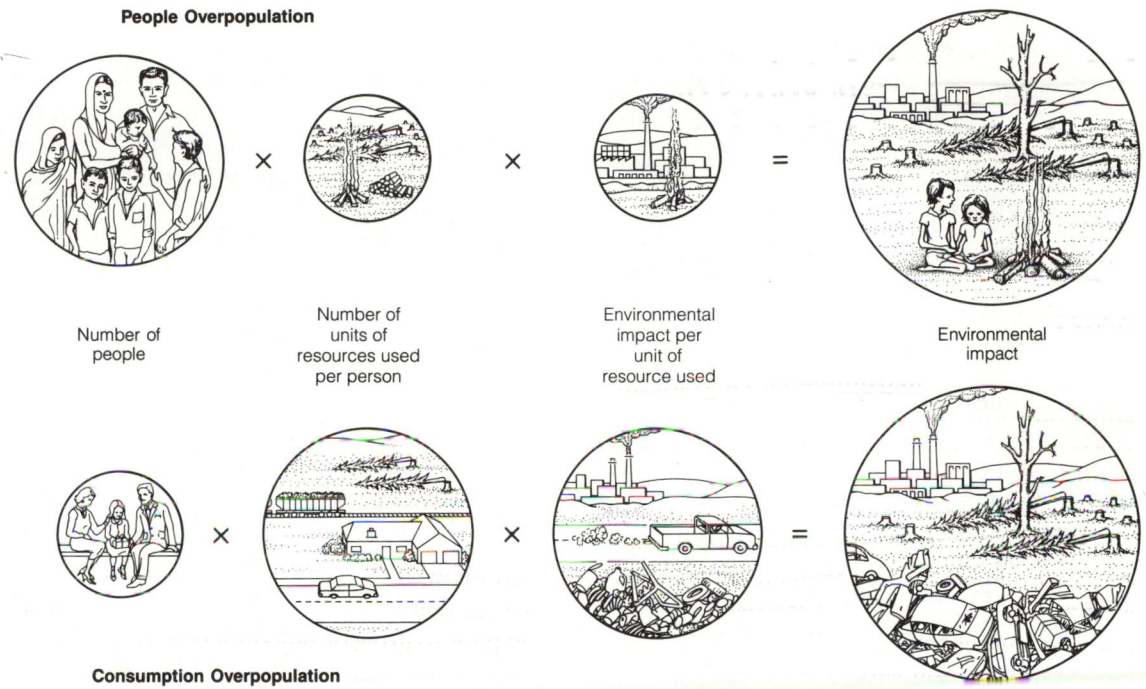

Figure 2   *Two types of overpopulation based on the relative importance of the factors in the model shown in Figure 1.*

Union, and Japan are said by some to have a second type of overpopulation, known as **consumption overpopulation**. It is based on the fact that without adequate pollution and land use controls, a small number of people using resources at a high rate produces more pollution and environmental degradation than a much larger number of people using resources at a much lower rate. With this type of overpopulation, high rates of resource use per person and the resulting high levels of pollution per person tend to be the most important factors determining overall environmental impact.

5   In countries said to have consumption overpopulation, relatively few people face starvation. Instead, unless such countries devote a growing fraction of their GNP to pollution and land use control, many people face illness or premature death over the *long-term* from contaminated air and water and increasingly degraded croplands, grazing lands, and forests. Such countries,

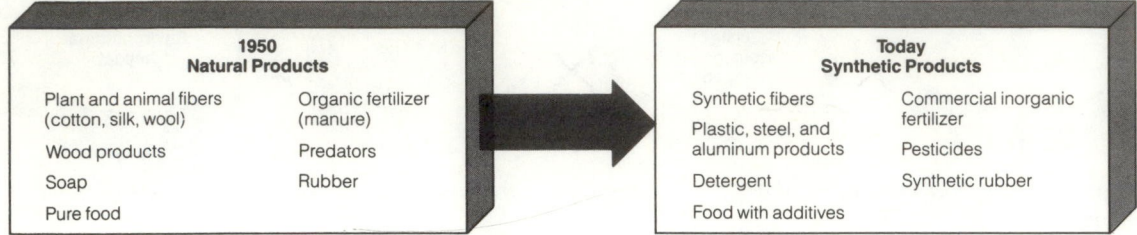

Figure 3   *Some synthetic products substituted for natural products in industrialized countries since 1950.*

sometimes referred to as **overdeveloped countries** or **ODCs**, are accused of hastening the depletion of many of the world's vital resources through a throwaway lifestyle based on unnecessary resource waste—thus helping make many of today's LDCs *never-to-be-developed countries.*

6   There is disagreement, however, over whether LDCs are really overpopulated—especially over whether the MDCs should be considered as being overpopulated.

7 Is Technology the Culprit?

Some analysts argue that the most important factor in the model presented in Figure 2 is the pollution per unit of resource used. They suggest that the introduction of environmentally harmful technologies since World War II has become the major cause of pollution in industrialized affluent countries. These countries have shifted much of their production and consumption from natural materials that can be broken down, diluted, or absorbed by natural processes to synthetic products that are either slowly biodegraded or not biodegraded by natural processes (Figure 3).

8   Others argue that this is an oversimplification. While technological developments such as the automobile and phosphate detergents create new environmental problems or aggravate existing ones, other technological developments can help solve various environmental and resource problems. For example, substitutes have been developed for many scarce resources (light bulbs have replaced whale oil in lamps, thus helping protect the world's rapidly diminishing supply of whales from extinction). Unnecessary resource waste has been reduced. For example, more of the branches, trunks, and other woody parts of trees are now used, and more energy is recovered from a ton of coal than in the past. Processes to control and clean up many forms of pollution have been developed.

9   Most analysts agree that *our problem and challenge is not to eliminate technology but to decide how to use it more carefully and humanely.* One major attempt to use technology wisely is the increased global emphasis on using appropriate technology. **Appropriate technology** is usually small, simple, decentralized, and inexpensive to build and maintain, and it usually utilizes locally available materials and labor. The use of huge tractors to plow fields in a poor rural village in India is often cited as an example of inappropriate and destructive technology. In such villages the most plentiful resource is people—willing and needing to work on farms. The tractor deprives these people of their only means of survival and forces them to migrate to already overpopulated cities, looking for nonexistent jobs. The wealthier farmers who remain become dependent on industrialized countries for expensive gasoline and parts and find the tractor too complex to be repaired by untrained local people. Instead of a large tractor, an appropriate technology would be a well-designed metal plow, made and repaired by a local blacksmith and pulled by locally available draft animals such as oxen or water buffaloes.

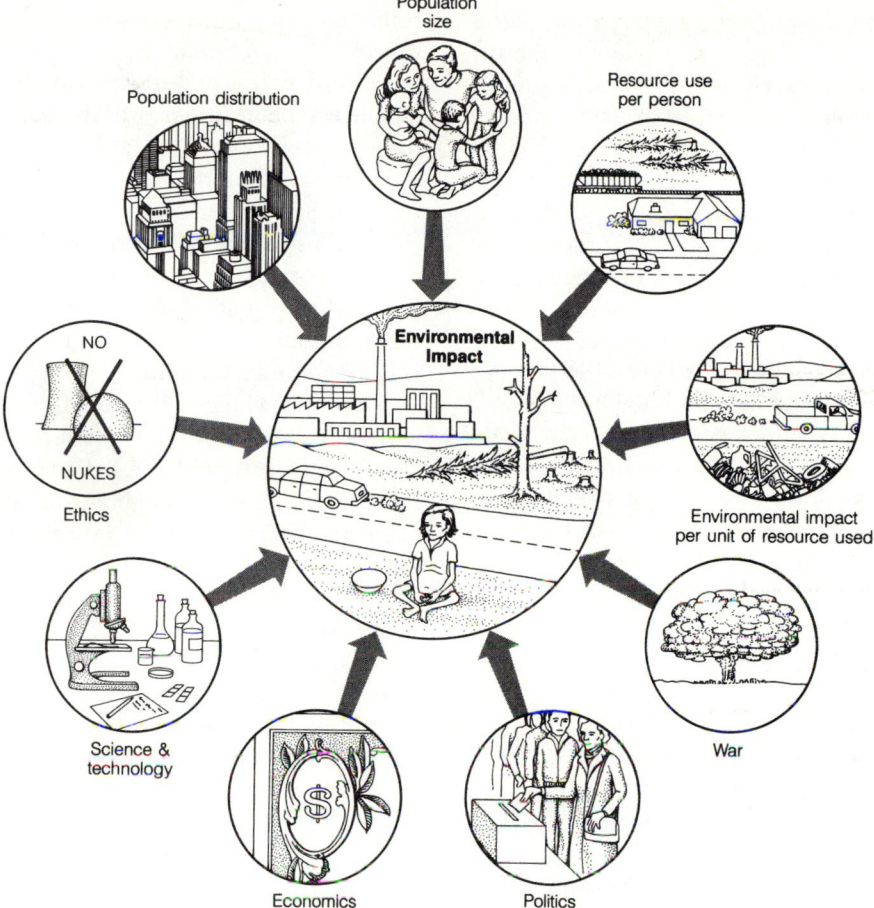

Figure 4   *Environmental problems are caused by a complex, poorly understood mix of interacting factors, as illustrated by this greatly simplified multiple-factor model.*

Supporters of appropriate technology recognize that it is not a cure for all our environmental problems but believe that its increasing use is an encouraging trend that should be nurtured.

10 **Other Factors**

The four-factor model shown in Figure 1, though useful, is far too simple. The actual situation is much more complex: an interacting mix of problems and contributing factors shown in simplified form in Figure 4. For example, pollution and en-vironmental degradation are intensified not only by population size but also by population distri-bution. The most severe air and water pollution problems usually occur when large numbers of people are concentrated in urban areas. Conversely, spreading people out can have a dev-astating effect on potentially renewable soil, for-est, grassland, and recreational resources. War also has a devastating environmental impact.

11   Economic, political, and ethical factors are also involved. We can manipulate the economic

system to control pollution, environmental degradation, and resource waste by making it unprofitable (in free-market economies) or illegal (in centrally controlled economies) to engage in such practices. We can use the political process to enact and enforce pollution control and land use control laws. However, such economic and political efforts will not be undertaken until an informed and politically active segment of the population (probably 5% to 10%) in countries with free elections and the leaders in other countries realize that it is both unwise and unethical to abuse the world's life-support systems for short-term economic gain. Finally, as pointed out earlier, science and technology can be applied to pollution control and efficient resource use, but they often lead to products and processes that have detrimental environmental effects.

WHAT SHOULD BE DONE? NEO-MALTHUSIANS VERSUS CORNUCOPIANS

12   There are two fundamentally different, opposing schools of thought about what the role of humans in the world should be, how serious the world's present and projected future environmental problems really are, and what should be done to deal with them. **Neo-Malthusians** (called "gloom-and-doom pessimists" by their opponents) believe that if present trends continue, the world will become more crowded and more polluted, leading to greater political and economic instability and increasing the threat of nuclear war as the rich get richer and the poor get poorer. The term *neo-Malthusian* refers to an updated and greatly expanded version of the hypothesis proposed in 1789 by Thomas Robert Malthus, an English clergyman and economist, that human population growing exponentially will eventually outgrow food supplies and will be reduced in size by starvation, disease, and war.

13   The opposing group, called **cornucopians** (or unrealistic "technological optimists" by their opponents), believes that if present trends continue, economic growth and technological advances based on human ingenuity will produce a less crowded, less polluted world, in which most people will be healthier, will live longer, and will have greater material wealth. The term *cornucopian* comes from *cornucopia*, the horn of plenty, which symbolizes an abundance.

14   This debate between cornucopians (most of whom are economists) and neo-Malthusians (most of whom are environmentalists and conservationists) has been going on for decades. But it is much more than an intellectual debate between people who generally use the same data and general trends to reach quite different conclusions. At a more fundamental level it represents radically different views of how the world works— one's *worldview*— and thus how we should operate in the world.

15   Cornucopians generally have a **frontier** or **throwaway worldview**. They see the earth as a place of unlimited resources where any type of conservation that hampers short-term economic growth is unnecessary. If we pollute or deplete the resources in one area, we will find resource substitutes, control the pollution through technology, and if necessary obtain additional resources from the moon and asteroids in the "new frontier" of space.

16   In contrast, neo-Malthusians generally have a **sustainable-earth worldview**.* Seeing the earth as a place with finite room and resources, they believe that ever-increasing production and consumption inevitably put severe stress on the complex, poorly understood natural processes that renew and maintain the air, water, and soil. Some neo-Malthusians have used the term *Spaceship Earth* to help people see the need to protect the earth's life-support systems.

---

*Others have used the terms *sustainable society* and *conserver society* to describe this view. I use the word *earth* to make clear that it is the entire earth system, not just the subsystem of humans and their societies, that must be sustained.

However, other neo-Malthusians have criticized this image, believing the spaceship analogy subtly reinforces the arrogant idea that the role of humans is to dominate and control nature; it encourages us to view the earth merely as a machine that we can manipulate at will and to think that we have essentially complete understanding of how nature works.

17 As we examine major environmental problems and their possible solutions throughout this book, we should be guided by the motto of philosopher and mathematician Alfred North Whitehead (1861–1947): "Seek simplicity and distrust it," and by writer and social critic H. L. Mencken (1880–1956), who warned: "For every problem there is a solution—simple, neat, and wrong."

What is the use of a house if you don't have a decent planet to put it on?

Henry David Thoreau (1817–1862)

G. Tyler Miller, Jr., *Living in the Environment*, Fifth ed., pp. 13–17. © 1988 by Wadsworth, Inc. Reprinted by permission of the publisher.

• •

1. This excerpt seems to concern:
   a. pollution.
   b. how population affects pollution.
   c. how technology and the use of natural resources affect pollution.
   d. all of these.

2. The author divides overpopulation into:
   a. two types.
   b. three types.
   c. four types.
   d. five types.

3. This excerpt includes several figures and illustrations.
   a. true
   b. false

4. To highlight key terms and concepts, this excerpt uses:
   a. italics.
   b. terms in boldface.
   c. underlining.
   d. both *a* and *b*.

5. This excerpt ends with:
   a. an illustration.
   b. a question from Thoreau.
   c. a bibliography.
   d. a summary of the excerpt.

Sel. 1 Sur	1. _____
Score _____ %	2. _____
▶ 80%	3. _____
Score = number correct x 20	4. _____
	5. _____
	Check answers on p. 337.

B. Question

Having surveyed the excerpt, make up five questions that you intend to answer when you study read. Make up questions from the title, the subtitles, and the words and phrases in italics. Write the questions in the spaces below:

1. _____
2. _____
3. _____
4. _____
5. _____

See sample questions on p. 337.

C. Read

With these questions in mind, read the selection carefully. You may want to read it through once before you begin marking. When you do begin to mark, remember, whenever possible, to underline parts of sentences only and to write sparingly.

D. Recite

Without looking back at the excerpt, write down in note-taking or paragraph form the important points made in the excerpt. When you have finished your summary, compare its accuracy with the statements made in the excerpt.

E. Review

Now review all of your material: your underlinings, your marginal comments, and your recite notes. You may now want to organize this information into one or more study maps.

F. Study-Reading Questions

When you have carefully studied the information in the excerpt and in your notes, answer the following ten questions without looking back. Place all answers in the answer box.

1. Pollution seems to always be a result of increased population.
   - a.   true
   - b.   false

2. Overpopulation affects:
   - a.   renewable resources.
   - b.   nonrenewable resources.
   - c.   life-support systems.
   - d.   all of these.

3. Which country would likely *not* have a consumption overpopulation problem?
   - a.   Venezuela
   - b.   Japan
   - c.   the USSR
   - d.   the United States

4. Which country would likely *not* qualify as an overdeveloped country (ODC)?
   - a.   Venezuela
   - b.   Japan
   - c.   the USSR
   - d.   the United States

5. Appropriate technology is *not*:
   - a.   large.
   - b.   expensive.
   - c.   complicated.
   - d.   all of these.

6. Neo-Malthusians believe that:
   - a.   the world has limited resources.
   - b.   overpopulation will lead to human suffering and death.
   - c.   both *a* and *b*.
   - d.   none of these.

7. The cornucopians believe that:
   - a.   the neo-Malthusians are correct.
   - b.   technology will resolve human overpopulation and pollution.
   - c.   the planet has limited resources.
   - d.   both *a* and *c*.

8. Henry David Thoreau's question "What is the use of a house if you don't have a decent planet to put it on?" would agree with:
   - a.   the cornucopians.
   - b.   the neo-Malthusians.
   - c.   the frontier worldview.
   - d.   none of these.

9. To see the earth as a spaceship suggests that the earth:
   a.   is a natural object.
   b   is out of human control.
   c.   can be dominated by the human being.
   d.   will never disintegrate.

10. The excerpt repeats the notion that:
   a.   the pollution issue is made up of a few identifiable causes.
   b.   the pollution issue is made up of a series of interconnected causes.
   c.   there is a clear solution to the pollution problem.
   d.   only industrial countries produce pollution.

Sel. 1 S-Read	1. _____
Score _____ %	2. _____
▶ **80%**	3. _____
Score = number correct x 10	4. _____
	5. _____
	6. _____
	7. _____
	8. _____
	9. _____
	10. _____
	Check answers on p. 337.

G. Questions for Discussion and Writing

1. In your own words, define overpopulation.

2. In your own words, define people overpopulation and consumption overpopulation. Then compare and contrast these concepts.

3. What is appropriate technology? Give examples of this kind of technology, and show how its use affects the environment.

4. How does the H. L. Mencken quotation relate to what the excerpt is saying about environmental pollution? "For every problem there is a solution—simple, neat, and wrong."

5. What perspective on the environment seems more accurate to you: the neo-Malthusian or the cornucopian? Give evidence from this excerpt to support your choice.

H. Scanning

Assume that you are reviewing for a test on this excerpt. You need to know the answers to the following questions to complete your studying.

Take no more than 3 minutes to scan for the answers. Record your finishing time in the answer box.

1. According to the excerpt, how many factors influence pollution?
2. How many deaths are caused by overpopulation?
3. What percentage of people does the excerpt say need to be educated before the pollution problem is put under control?
4. What were Malthus's two professions?
5. How does the author of the excerpt define the earth?

Sel. 1 Sc   1. _____

Time _____ : _____   2. _____

      min   sec   3. _____

Score _____ %   4. _____

   ▶ **100%**   5. _____

Score = number correct x 20

Self-Evaluation Environmental Science

Answer the following questions by circling yes or no. Your responses will help you assess your study-reading abilities in environmental science.

1. yes   no   Was your score in Section F, Study-Reading Questions, below 80 percent?

2. yes   no   Did you miss questions 5, 6, or 7, dealing with the organizational pattern of definition?

3. yes   no   Did you miss question 2, dealing with the organizational pattern of cause-effect?

4. yes   no   Did you have difficulty recalling the definitions of key terms presented in this excerpt?

5. yes   no   Did you have difficulty understanding any of the figures used in the excerpt?

Scoring: If you answered yes to two or more of these questions, you probably need more practice reading environmental science material.

Follow-up: To improve the strategies that you use in reading environmental science material, consider these suggestions:

1. When you come across a definition in your study reading, circle or underline the key elements in the definition and write *def.* in the margin. Understanding definitions is central to understanding environmental science material.

2. Realize that the cause-effect organizational pattern is central to the structure of most environmental science material. In your reading, carefully separate cause from effect. Also determine if there are several causes related to a particular effect. Identify each and see how they relate to each other and to the effect.

. . . .

SELECTION 2

"Changes in the Atmosphere" *by Cecie Starr and Ralph Taggart 1,578 words*

Vocabulary

topography: the physical features of a geographical area; "depends on local climate and topography"

lethal: causing death; "may reach lethal concentrations"

alkaline: pertaining to strong, water-soluble substances that neutralize acid; "highly alkaline soils"

stratosphere: the region of the upper atmosphere extending from 7 to 15 miles above the earth; "the ozone layer in the lower stratosphere"

cataracts: an eye abnormality; "cataracts may be more common"

photosynthesizers: substances in plant life that aid in the process of photosynthesis, or the making of carbohydrates through the conversion of carbon dioxide and water; "these microbial photosynthesizers"

"Changes in the Atmosphere" is an excerpt from a biology text devoted to the biosphere. Like most biology material, this excerpt relies heavily on three organizational patterns: definition, cause-effect, and sequence of events. As you study read this excerpt, be sure to reread the material that is structured around these three patterns.

Where the previous excerpt has treated the causes of pollution generally, "Changes in the Atmosphere" focuses specifically on how pollution affects the air we breathe and the water we drink.

Reading Strategies.   For successful reading of this material, consider the following strategies:

1. Circle the key parts of a definition, or highlight them in such a way that you separate them from the rest of the material. Make appropriate marginal notes.

2. See how the various definitions relate to each other—for example, dry acid depositions and wet acid depositions, industrial smog and photochemical smog.

[handwritten margin notes:]
Key
1. Main Idea —
2. Supporting details —
3. defination
4. Margin notes
5. ? Questions

3. Note in the margins the major cause-effect patterns that you find, especially the chemical changes of nitric acid in paragraph 7 and the causes of ozone reduction in paragraphs 14–16. Whenever there are multiple causes and effects, number these sequences in order. In this way you can remember the chemical processes more easily.

A. Survey

Take 2 minutes to survey the excerpt. Read the chapter title, the subtitles, the terms in boldface print, the words and phrases in italics, and the figures. If time permits, begin reading the first paragraph or two. When your time is up, answer the five questions without looking back at the excerpt. Place all answers in the answer box.

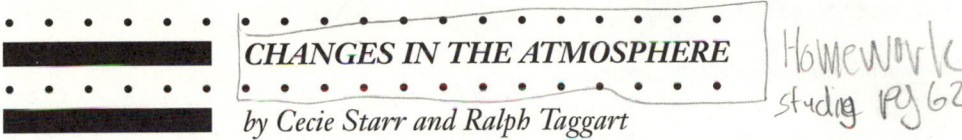

CHANGES IN THE ATMOSPHERE

by Cecie Starr and Ralph Taggart

[handwritten note: Homework studing pg 62]

1   If you were to compare the earth with an apple from the supermarket, the atmosphere would be no thicker than the layer of shiny wax applied to it. Yet this thin, finite wrapping of air around the planet receives more than 700,000 metric tons of pollutants each day in the United States alone. **Pollutants** are substances with which ecosystems have had no prior evolutionary experience, in terms of kinds or amounts, and so have no mechanisms for dealing with them. From the human perspective, pollutants are substances that adversely affect our health, activities, or survival.

2   Table 1 lists the major air pollutants. They are carbon dioxides, sulfur oxides, nitrogen oxides, chlorofluorocarbons (CFCs), and photochemical oxidants.

LOCAL AIR POLLUTION

3   Whether air pollutants are dispersed throughout the atmosphere or concentrated at their source in a given time period depends on local climate and topography. Consider what happens during a **thermal inversion**, when a layer of dense, cool air becomes trapped beneath a layer of warm air (Figure 1). The pollutants cannot be dispersed by winds or rise higher in the atmosphere, so they accumulate to dangerous levels close to the ground. By intensifying a phenomenon known as smog, thermal inversions have contributed to some of the worst local air pollution disasters.

4   There are two types of smog (gray air and brown air), both of which occur in major cities.

Table 1   *Major Classes of Air Pollutants*

Carbon oxides:	Carbon monoxide (CO), carbon dioxide (CO_2)
Sulfur oxides:	Sulfur dioxide (SO_2) sulfur trioxide (SO_3)
Nitrogen oxides:	Nitric oxide (NO), nitrogen dioxide (NO_2) nitrous oxide (N_2O)
Volatile organic compounds:	Methane (CH_4), benzene (C_6H_6), chlorofluorocarbons (CFCs)
Photochemical oxidants:	Ozone (O_3), peroxyacyl nitrates (PANs), hydrogen peroxide (H_2O_2)
Suspended particles:	Solid particles (dust, soot, asbestos, lead, etc.), liquid droplets (sulfuric acid, oils, dioxins, pesticides)

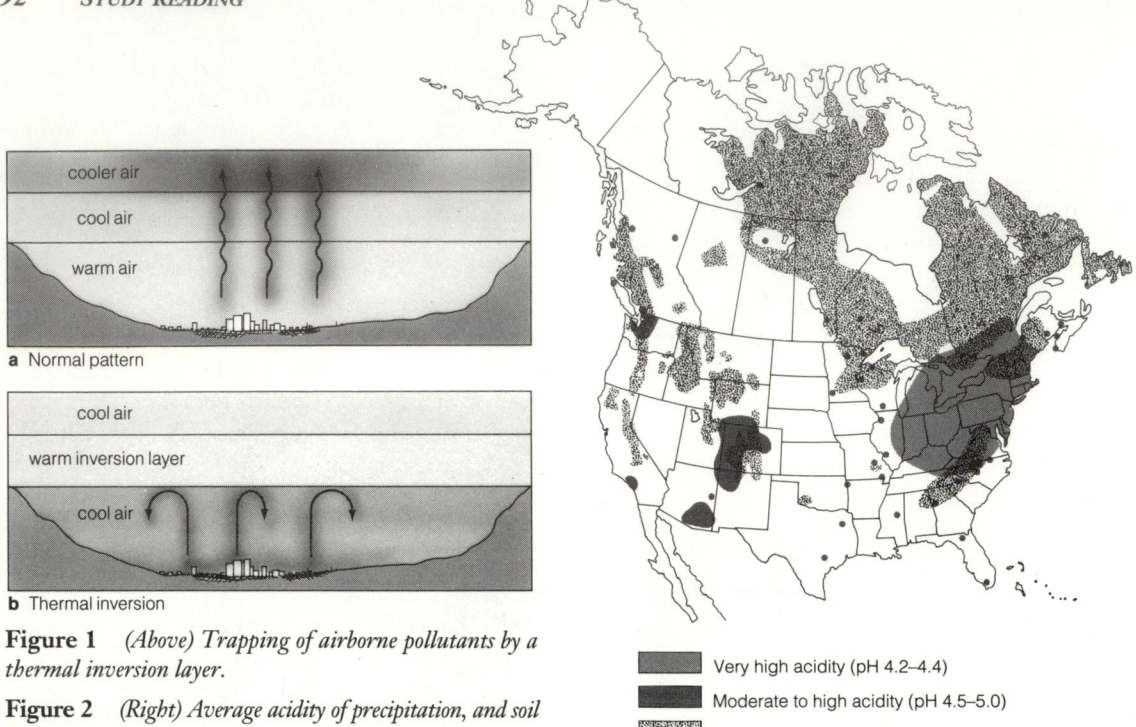

a Normal pattern

b Thermal inversion

Figure 1 *(Above) Trapping of airborne pollutants by a thermal inversion layer.*

Figure 2 *(Right) Average acidity of precipitation, and soil sensitivity to acid deposition for regions of North America (1984).*

Very high acidity (pH 4.2–4.4)

Moderate to high acidity (pH 4.5–5.0)

Areas sensitive to acid deposition

Industrial smog is gray air that predominates in industrialized cities with cold, wet winters. London, New York, Pittsburgh, and Chicago are examples. These cities use fossil fuel for heating, manufacturing, and producing electric power. The burning fuel releases airborne pollutants, including dust, smoke, ashes, soot, asbestos, oil, bits of heavy metals, and sulfur oxides. The pollutants may reach lethal concentrations when winds and rain do not disperse them. Industrial smog was the cause of London's 1952 air pollution disaster, in which 4,000 people died.

5   **Photochemical smog** is a brown and smelly trademark of large cities found in warm climates. When the surrounding land forms a natural basin, as it does around Los Angeles and Mexico City, photochemical smog can reach harmful concentrations. The main culprit is nitric oxide, which is produced chiefly by cars and other vehicles with internal combustion engines. Nitric oxide reacts with oxygen in the air to form nitrogen dioxide. When exposed to sunlight, nitrogen dioxide can react with hydrocarbons (spilled or partly burned gasoline, most often) to form photochemical oxidants. Other components of smog are ozone and PANs (short for *peroxyacyl nitrates*). PANs are similar to tear gas; even traces can sting the eyes and irritate the lungs.

ACID DEPOSITION

6   Oxides of sulfur and nitrogen are among the most dangerous air pollutants. Coal-burning power plants, factories, and metal smelters are the main sources of sulfur dioxides. Vehicles, power plants that burn fossil fuels, and nitrogen fertilizers are sources of nitrogen oxides.

7   Depending on climatic conditions, tiny particles of these substances may be airborne for a while and then fall to earth as **dry acid deposition**. Most sulfur and nitrogen dioxides dissolve in atmospheric water to form weak solutions of sulfuric acid and nitric acid. Winds can distribute

them over great distances before they fall to earth in rain and snow; this is called **wet acid deposition**. Acid rain can be four to forty times more acidic than normal rainwater, sometimes as much as lemon juice. The acids attack marble, metals, mortar, rubber, plastic, even nylon stockings. And they are disrupting ecosystems.

8   Because soils and vegetation are not identical in all watersheds, some regions are more sensitive to acid deposition than others (Figure 2). Highly alkaline soils neutralize some of the acids before runoff carries them into lakes, streams, and rivers. Water with high concentrations of carbonates also will help neutralize the acids. However, in watersheds throughout much of northern Europe, southeastern Canada, and scattered regions of the United States, thin soils overlie solid granite—and such soils provide little buffer against the acids.

9   The precipitation in much of eastern North America is thirty to forty times more acidic than it was several decades ago, and croplands and forests are suffering. All fish populations have been wiped out in 300 lakes of the Adirondack Mountains of New York. Some Canadian biologists predict that within the next two decades, fish will disappear from 48,000 lakes in Ontario. Acidic pollutants originating in industrial regions of England and West Germany are acidifying lakes and streams, and damaging large tracts of forests in northern Europe. They also are emerging as a serious problem in heavily industrialized parts of Asia, Latin America, and Africa.

10   Researchers confirmed years ago that power plants, factories, and vehicles are the main sources of acid depositions, and that the depositions are indeed damaging the environment. Not much has been done about it. Also, some of the responses to local air pollution standards have contributed to the problem, as when very tall smokestacks are added to power plants and smelting plants. The idea is to dump acid-laden smoke high in the atmosphere so winds can distribute it elsewhere—which winds readily do. The world's tallest smokestack, in Sudbury, Ontario, accounts for about one percent of the annual worldwide emissions of sulfur dioxide.

11   But Canada cannot be singled out in this issue. Canada presently receives more acid depositions from industrialized regions of the northeastern United States than it sends across its southern border. Most of the acidic pollutants in Finland, Norway, Sweden, the Netherlands, Austria, and Switzerland are blown there from industrialized regions of western and eastern Europe. Prevailing winds do not stop at national boundaries; the problem is of global concern.

DAMAGE TO THE OZONE LAYER

12   The ozone layer in the lower stratosphere absorbs most of the ultraviolet wavelengths from the sun—a form of radiation that is harmful to organisms. Yet this layer has been thinning since 1976. Each spring, an ozone "hole" appears over the Antarctic; it extends over an area about the size of the continental United States. Less pronounced thinning also occurs all the way into the midlatitudes.

13   Satellites and high-altitude planes have been monitoring the ozone hole since 1978. . . . By 1987, ozone levels above Antarctica had declined by fifty percent—this compared to the previous worst case of forty percent in 1985.

14   The reduction in the ozone layer is allowing more ultraviolet radiation to reach the earth's surface, with potentially serious and wide-ranging consequences. Already there has been a dramatic increase in skin cancers, which almost certainly are related to increases in ultraviolet radiation. Cataracts may become more common, and it appears that ultraviolet radiation also can weaken the immune system, making individuals more vulnerable to some viral and parasitic infections. Reduction in the ozone layer also may adversely affect the world's populations of phytoplankton—the basis of food webs in freshwater and marine ecosystems and a factor in maintaining the composition of the atmosphere. (Collectively, these microbial photosynthesizers serve as a sink for carbon dioxide and a source for oxygen.)

15 The causes of ozone reduction are hotly debated in the scientific community. To be sure, large volcanic eruptions and cyclic changes in solar activity have some effects. But the prime suspects are chlorofluorocarbons (CFCs), which are compounds of chlorine, fluorine, and carbon. These odorless, invisible, and otherwise harmless compounds are widely used as propellants in aerosol spray cans, coolants in refrigerators and air conditioners, and industrial solvents; and they also are used in making plastic foams, including the Styrofoam cups and cartons used for packaging foods, drinks, and other consumer goods. CFCs enter the atmosphere slowly and resist breakdown. By some estimates, about ninety-five percent of the CFCs released between 1955 and 1987 are still making their way up to the stratosphere.

16 When a CFC molecule absorbs ultraviolet light, it gives up a chlorine atom. The chlorine can react with ozone to form an oxygen molecule and a chlorine monoxide molecule. When the chlorine monoxide reacts with a free oxygen atom, another chlorine atom is released that can attack another ozone molecule. Each chlorine atom released in the reactions can convert as many as 10,000 molecules of ozone to oxygen!

17 Recent studies show that chlorine monoxide levels above Antarctica are 100 to 500 times higher than at midlatitudes. Why? High-altitude clouds of ice form there during the frigid winters, and they are isolated from other latitudes by winds that rotate around the South Pole for most of the winter months. The ice provides a surface that facilitates the breakdown of chlorine compounds, so that chlorine is free to destroy ozone when the Antarctic air warms somewhat in the spring. (Hence the ozone hole.)

18 Since 1978, the United States, Canada, and most Scandinavian countries have banned the use of CFCs in aerosol spray cans. Aerosol uses have risen sharply in western Europe, however, as have nonaerosol uses of CFCs throughout the world. In late 1987, an international group assembled by the United Nations Environment Program agreed to a draft treaty to halve CFC emissions by the year 1999. Most nations seem certain to ratify its provisions. The treaty is a step in the right direction, although some feel that it is too little and too late. CFCs already in the air will be there for over a century, before natural processes neutralize them. You, your children, and your grandchildren will be living with their destructive effects. Think about that, the next time you carry a Styrofoam container out of a fast-food restaurant.

Biology: The Unity and Diversity of Life, Fifth ed., by Cecie Starr and Ralph Taggart, pp. 794–797. ©1989 by Wadsworth, Inc. Reprinted by permission of the publisher.

• •

1. The excerpt begins by defining:
   a. acid rain.
   b. ozone.
   c. pollutants.
   d. the CFC molecule.

2. Which of the following topics is *not* covered in the excerpt?
   a. air pollution
   b. photochemical smog
   c. acid deposition
   d. population growth

3. In this excerpt, terms are:
   a. underlined.
   b. placed at the top of each page.
   c. put in quotation marks.
   d. put in boldface print.

4. The figures treat:
   a. thermal inversion.
   b. acid deposition.
   c. ozone layers.
   d. both *a* and *b*.

5. The excerpt presents several mathematical equations.
   a. true
   b. false

Sel. 2 Sur	1. _____
Score _____ %	2. _____
▶ **80%**	3. _____
Score = number correct x 20	4. _____
	5. _____
	Check answers with your instructor.

B. Question

Having surveyed the excerpt, make up five questions that you intend to answer when you study read. Make up questions from the title and subtitles. Write the questions in the spaces below.

1. _____
2. _____
3. _____
4. _____
5. _____

Ask your instructor for sample questions.

C. Read

With these questions in mind, read the selection carefully. You may want to read it through once you begin marking. When you do begin to mark, remember to underline parts of sentences only, where possible, and to write sparingly.

D. Recite

Without looking back at the excerpt, write down in note-taking or paragraph form the important points made in the excerpt. When you have finished your summary, compare its accuracy with the statements made in the excerpt.

E. Review

Now review all of your material: your underlinings, your marginal comments, and your recite notes. You may want to organize this information into one or more study maps.

F. Study-Reading Questions

When you have carefully studied the information in the excerpt and in your notes, answer the following ten questions without looking back. Place all answers in the answer box.

1. In the definition of pollutants, this excerpt mentions that:
   a.   they hurt human health.
   b.   they can even interfere with human survival.
   c.   the environment is not equipped to respond to them.
   d.   all of these.

2. A thermal inversion is caused by cool air:
   a.   being trapped by warm air below it.
   b.   being trapped by warm air above it.
   c.   becoming industrial smog.
   d.   becoming photochemical smog.

3. Which statement does *not* describe industrial smog?
   a.   It is brown.
   b.   It is gray.
   c.   It occurs in wet climates.
   d.   It is found in New York.

4. What statement does *not* describe photochemical smog?
   a.   It is brown.
   b.   It occurs in cities with wet climates.
   c.   It occurs in cities with dry climates.
   d.   It is found in Denver.

5. Dry acid deposition dissolves in water and becomes:
   a.   sulfuric acid.
   b.   nitric acid.
   c.   ozone.
   d.   both *a* and *b*.

6. Ozone helps to:
   a.   neutralize smog.
   b.   capture the sun's ultraviolet waves.
   c.   create acid rain.
   d.   neutralize acid rain.

7. A reduction in the ozone layer seems to be responsible for:
   a.   skin cancer.
   b.   a decrease in certain viral infections.
   c.   reducing the amount of phytoplankton produced.
   d.   both *a* and *c*.

8. Chlorofluorocarbons (CFCs) are used in:
   a. aerosol cans.
   b. Styrofoam cups.
   c. diesel fuel.
   d. both *a* and *b*.

9. When they react to free oxygen atoms, chlorine atoms seem to:
   a. create more ozone.
   b. create more oxygen.
   c. create more carbon dioxide.
   d. create more acid rain.

10. The ozone hole is largest in Antarctica because:
    a. icy clouds there allow for more ozone to be destroyed.
    b. freezing weather keeps ozone away.
    c. it has more refuse dumps than anywhere else in the world.
    d. all of these.

Sel. 2   S-Read

Score _____ %

▶ **80%**

Score = number correct **x** 10

1. _____
2. _____
3. _____
4. _____
5. _____
6. _____
7. _____
8. _____
9. _____
10. _____

Check answers with your instructor.

G. Questions for Discussion and Writing

1. Using your own words, define pollutants and describe the damage they cause.
2. In your own words, define industrial smog and photochemical smog; then explain ways in which they differ.
3. Explain how smog is trapped in thermal inversions.
4. In your own words, define dry acid depositions and wet acid depositions; then explain how they differ.
5. Carefully explain why the ozone hole is so large in Antarctica.

H. Scanning

Assume that you are studying for a unit test on atmospheric changes caused by pollution, and you need to know the answers to the following five questions to complete your studying.

Take no more than 3 minutes to scan for the correct answers. Record your finishing time in the answer box.

1. How much pollution does the atmosphere of the United States receive in one day?
2. In what part of Europe are forests being damaged by acid rain?
3. How many lakes in Upstate New York have had all their fish killed due to acid rain?
4. What is Sudbury, Ontario, famous for?
5. What does PANs stand for?

Sel. 2 Sc   1. _____

Time _____ : _____   2. _____

       min   sec   3. _____

Score _____ %   4. _____

▶ **80%**   5. _____

Score = number correct x 20   **Check answers with your instructor.**

Self-Evaluation Biology

Answer the following questions by circling yes or no. Your responses will help you assess your study-reading abilities in biology.

1. yes   no   Was your score in Section F, Study-Reading Questions, below 80 percent?

2. yes   no   Did you miss questions 2, 5, 6, 7, or 9, dealing with the organizational pattern of cause-effect?

3. yes   no   Did you miss questions 1, 3, or 4, dealing with the organizational pattern of definition?

4. yes   no   Did you have difficulty recalling the definitions of key terms presented in this excerpt?

5. yes   no   Did you have difficulty remembering the sequence of events related to the chemical processes involved in air pollution?

6. yes   no   Did you have difficulty understanding the figures and chart used in this excerpt?

Scoring: If you answered yes to three or more of these questions, you probably need more practice reading biology material.

Follow-up: To improve your skills in reading biology, follow these suggestions:

1. When you come across a definition in your study reading, circle or underline the key elements of the definition and write *def.* in the margin. Understanding definitions is crucial to understanding biology.

2. Make careful marginal notes listing the sequence of events in a biological process. Have the correct sequence clearly in mind before you take an examination—objective or essay.

3. Whenever possible, try to visualize the biological or physical processes discussed in your reading, such as the "thermal conversion layer" in this excerpt. Visualizing is an important aid to remembering biology material.

4. Realize that the cause-effect organizational pattern is a key structure in biology. Carefully separate cause from effect. Also determine if there are several causes influencing an effect, like the various effects of acid rain or the various results of the diminution of the ozone layer.

. . . .

SELECTION 3

"Government Efforts to Protect the Environment" *by Philip C. Starr*
2,611 words

Vocabulary

Chernobyl: a very serious nuclear power plant accident occurring in the USSR in the mid-1980s; "by-products of the Chernobyl accident"

jurisprudence: the formal study of the law; "used in the field of jurisprudence"

Adam Smith: eighteenth-century Scottish economist who believed that the government should not interfere with the economy; "in an Adam Smithian, self-interested world"

entrepreneurs: persons who organize or manage business operations; "what may be sensible for entrepreneurs"

license: excessive freedom; "an inexpensive license to pollute"

allocation: an allowance, allotment, or apportionment; "such an allocation of resources"

This excerpt comes from an introductory economics textbook called *Economics: Principles in Action*. In this excerpt, Starr analyzes the ways that the government discourages industry from polluting the environment. Unlike the previous two selections which treat the scientific responses to environmental pollution, this excerpt considers pollution from its social perspective: How are government and industry involved in environmental pollution, and how does this involvement affect the economy?

Starr's style is characterized by short sentences, yet these short sentences present complex economic principles. Like most readings in economics, this excerpt is structured around three organizational patterns: definition, cause-effect, and sequence of events. These are patterns that you have already used in the previous two selections. Of these three patterns, cause-effect is the most frequently employed to explain the economy's response to environmental pollution.

Reading Strategies.   For successful reading of this excerpt, consider the following strategies:

1.   When you come across a definition printed in boldface, circle or highlight its key parts. Write the abbreviation *def.* in the margin next to the term. As you continue reading, try to see how one definition is related to a subsequent definition. After completing the excerpt, be sure you have marked the following terms: *private costs*, *direct approach*, *charging-polluters-for-their-pollution approach*, *bubble plan approach*, and *allocative efficiency*.

2.   Note the several cause-effect patterns by identifying them in the margin. You may even want to include marginal comments at the top or bottom of the page, showing the cause-effect pattern by means of an arrow: X (cause) $\rightarrow Y$ (effect). This should be part of your marking for the following terms: *direct approach*, *charging-polluters-for-their-pollution approach*, *bubble plan approach*, and *allocative efficiency*.

3.   See if you can understand the cause-effect relationships suggested in the figure relating supply and demand to antipollution equipment. You may want to write out the various supply and demand relationships suggested in this figure.

4.   Before reciting this information, see whether you can orally define the key terms that you have studied.

A. Survey

Take 3 minutes to survey the excerpt. Read the chapter title, the subtitles, the terms in boldface print, the sections in italics, and the figure. If time permits, begin reading the first paragraph or two. Place all answers in the answer box.

GOVERNMENT EFFORTS TO PROTECT THE ENVIRONMENT

by Philip C. Starr

[1]   One of the many public goods we ask the government to provide is the protection of a clean and beautiful environment. The balance of this chapter is about that area of government intervention in our market-price system.

[2]   Government intervention to protect the environment is necessary for an unusual reason. Chemists and physicists call the reason "the conservation of matter." By this, they mean that during combustion, for example, matter changes

form, but matter is not destroyed. Thus, the by-products of the Chernobyl accident or of acid rain or from the air or water pollution in any large city are likely to remain in the earth's atmosphere, sometimes for thousands of years. Wherever you may be living, you may be exposed to the by-products of combustion that took place hundreds of miles away and decades ago. A market-price system cannot deal with situations of this sort, where the connection between buyers and sellers is either nonexistent or extremely remote. That is why government intervention is necessary. Protection of the environment is not only a national (macro) problem; it is a global issue.

THE PROPERTY-RIGHTS BASIS FOR POLLUTION CONTROL

3 Protection of the environment is based on a principle that is beginning to be used in the field of jurisprudence. The principle has to do with property rights. The idea is that we all have a property right in the air and water around us. If a business firm pollutes that air or water, their act in so doing constitutes damage to something we *own*—just as if the firm had dropped a smoke bomb down our chimney. Our legal case against such a firm is then based on the complaint that we deserve compensation for an infringement of our right to use our private property as we please (provided we don't interfere with the same rights of a neighbor). Assuming we win the case, the offending firm then has to pay us for damaging our property—the air or water we "own."

4 And so protection of the environment, specifically the control of pollution, now rests on the idea that we, as members of the public, share a right to clean air and water and to the good health that clean air and water quality can give us. But, as always, costs and benefits are involved in any decision to improve the environment. The next section helps to explain these costs and benefits.

5 In an Adam Smithian, self-interested world, entrepreneurs are expected to increase their profits as much as possible. The natural way to do this is to produce at the lowest possible cost. But at whose cost? It is obviously cheaper for entrepreneurs to dump waste into the nearest stream or into the atmosphere than to truck it to some waste disposal facility or to filter it as it comes out of smokestacks. Therefore, what may be sensible for entrepreneurs may not be desirable for the community.

6 Here is a classic trade-off: When the government intervenes to force entrepreneurs to stop polluting, entrepreneurs have to adopt more expensive means of production or waste disposal. Inevitably, they will charge higher prices, and, given no change in demand, the quantity demanded will drop and workers will be laid off. The trade-off is therefore cleaner air and water *or* more unemployment. Here is how economists view this problem.

PRIVATE COSTS + EXTERNAL COSTS = SOCIAL COSTS

7 The costs associated with the manufacturer's production or buyer's use of any product are called **private (internal) costs**. They are borne by the seller and the buyer and are included in the market price or in the costs of using the product after purchase.

8 Normally, transactions involve only a buyer and a seller. When a seller sells a pad of paper to a buyer, only two people are apparently involved in the transaction. But if the factory that makes the paper contributes to air or water pollution, economists say that people outside the transaction are affected or that the transaction has **external effects**. Because paper production in this instance is harmful to people unconnected with the production or purchase of paper, **external costs** are involved. The term **social costs** refers to the total impact on society of the production, distribution, and use of whatever is produced. Thus, social costs are the sum of private (internal) costs plus external costs.

9 The problem is that in a market-price system prices usually reflect only private (internal) costs and benefits. If buyers and sellers don't have to consider environmental regulations, the equilibrium price will be below what is necessary to

cover external costs. And if the equilibrium price is below what is necessary to cover external costs, we can conclude that such industries will sell more of their products and hire and use more resources than if their product prices *did* reflect external costs.

10   At this point we are confronted with the failure of the market-price system to allocate resources so as to best serve the interests of society. Some nonmarket mechanism will have to decide what to do; that is, voters will have to decide whether or not to turn some control of the offending industry over to a government agency.

11   To simplify this discussion we overlook the possibility that the voters might instruct their government to do nothing directly to the industry but to clean up the community as best it can through trash collection or whatever. In such a case the voters would have to pay the external costs themselves through higher taxes. In the example of government control that follows, we assume that the voters have found some way through the regulatory powers of a government agency to force or persuade the offending industry to clean up its own act.

12   The government agency has three methods of control at its disposal: (1) It can order the offending industry to stop polluting by installing filters to prevent pollution of the air or water in some acceptable (to voters) degree; (2) it can charge the polluter some amount per pound of the toxic material that leaves the factory; or (3) it can require acceptance of a "bubble plan." The next section discusses these three options using the example of a steel mill that has been spewing toxic soot into the air.

METHODS OF POLLUTION CONTROL

13 The Direct Approach

Economic theory can examine what happens when environmental regulations are enforced. If, say, a steel mill is forced to put in antipollution equipment, the company's product costs will rise. Its supply curve will shift to the left because a

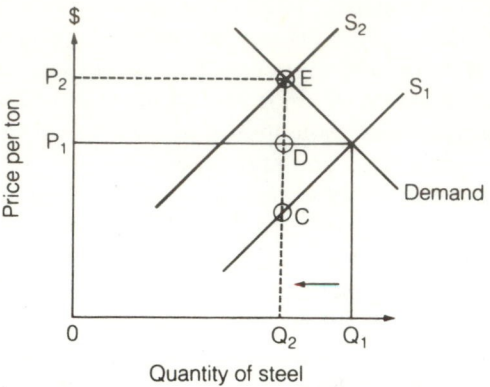

Figure 1   *Example of demand and supply when antipollution equipment is installed in a steel mill.*

higher market price is now necessary to induce the mill to produce any given quantity. Assuming no change in demand, the shift in supply will cause the product price to rise and the quantity demanded to fall. Figure 1 shows what happens. Higher production costs are shown by the shift of the supply curve from S_1 to S_2. The price rises from P_1 to P_2, causing the quantity demanded to decrease from Q_1 to Q_2. As the quantity demanded falls, the steel mill will buy fewer resources, among them labor. Employees will be laid off. Note also that the higher price that buyers must pay may or may not be socially desirable, depending on how different income groups are affected.

14   Ideally, the vertical distance between the two supply curves (the distance CE in Figure 1) reflects the external cost of producing the steel. We have to say "ideally" because external costs may be extremely difficult to measure. (We can never be sure, for example, if the incidence of lung cancer in the local community has been caused by emissions from the steel mill's stacks or by excessive smoking.)

15   Nevertheless, we shall assume that an estimate of external costs can be made and that we can force the steel company to absorb all external costs by installing a filtration system for its chimneys at an average cost of CE per ton of steel.

Figure 1 now tells how this cost will be split between the mill and the buyer. At the new quantity (Q_2), CE is the vertical distance between the supply curves or the additional cost of producing each unit at Q_2. We notice that the price rises from P_1 to P_2, the same as from point D to point E, or only about half the full distance CE. It is apparent, therefore, that the additional costs of production are *shared* by the buyer (who absorbs part of the cost in the form of higher prices) and by the steel mill (that is, by its stockholders).

16 The Charging-Polluters-for-Their-Pollution Approach

Most economists prefer another approach to pollution control. They reason that no one understands better how to control pollution than the polluting business itself. Given the right incentives, the polluting firm is in the best position to determine the cheapest way of solving the problem.

17   For example, many economists prefer to charge polluting firms so much a pound for the waste they spew into the air or water. Such charges are called **effluent charges**. They are based on the legal principle that the firms are trespassing on property rights all of us share—the rights to clean air and water—and should pay for doing so. Economists prefer the effluent charge because business firms are given the freedom to find their own best solution to the problem—or pay the charge. Environmentalists are not supportive of the effluent charge unless the charge is commensurate with actual social cost. In the Los Angeles area, the social cost of all air pollutants is estimated at $10,000 per ton. This large figure is the sum of the negative effects of air pollution on property values, on health, on lost work time, on crops, on materials like rubber (tires), on acid rain, and on tourism. In those cases where business firms do pay an effluent charge, the charge is typically $30 per ton, a far cry from the total social cost. Consequently, business firms find the effluent charge very attractive. But at present, environmentalists argue that the effluent charge approach is simply an inexpensive license to pollute.

18 The Bubble Plan Approach

A third approach is the **bubble plan**. The Environmental Protection Agency (EPA) pretends there is a glass bubble, or lid, covering or surrounding all the chimneys and sewage outlets of a factory or group of factories. The waste materials coming out of the factory are weighed annually. If the factory succeeds in reducing this quantity, it is given a "credit," stated in number of tons of waste, equal to a certain percentage (say, 70 percent) of the reduction the factory achieved during the year. This credit is put into a "bank account" kept with the EPA.

19   The only way a factory can expand and increase the waste it produces is to withdraw its own credits from its bank account. Or, it may buy credits from another firm. In this way, the EPA prevents total emissions in the area from exceeding the starting figure. Even new firms, when they come to the area, have to obtain credits from existing firms. Over the long term, total emissions in the area will decrease because the credits given are always some fraction (like 70 percent) of actual waste reductions. The plan has a provision to satisfy those worried about lack of growth in industrial output, employment opportunities, payrolls, and tax receipts. If not used within, for example, eight years, all credits have to be sold to other firms to permit *them* to expand. The eight-year limit prevents participating firms from "banking" the credits for indefinite periods. The credits must either be used to make additional expansion possible or sold to enhance the firm's profits.

20   Bubble plans are now in widespread use throughout the United States. Like effluent charges, they are popular because they give business firms several options. But again, environmentalists are not enthusiastic. Within the bubble, environmentalists argue, average pollution may come down, but any one factory can still exceed tolerable limits. Driving at an excessive speed is a possible analogy. Suppose the average speed

of two drivers is 60 miles per hour. But one of them drives 80, the other 40. Shouldn't we still do something to restrict the driver who goes 80?

21 The possible uses of the credits, often called **emission transfers**, are what put the bubble plan into the framework of a market-price system. However the firm uses the transfers, it has a strong incentive to earn lots of them in order to increase its options for the future. The more the firm reduces pollution, the more transfers it receives.

22 The effluent charge and the bubble plan are efforts to reduce pollution with market-price methods. Whereas free markets, operating within the limits set by laws and court decisions, once permitted uncontrolled pollution, now market tactics are proposed for reducing it. The success or failure of the two plans is still in doubt. Many business firms resent the limits placed on their own growth, and many communities worry about unemployment.

23 It's easy to place a value on private goods. Our willingness to pay the price of a television set measures the set's private benefit. It's much harder to measure the private benefit of a good held in common like air, or water in the local river, or to *agree* with other members of our community on how much it's worth to keep the air and water clean.

24 The analysis of pollution highlights a typical economic problem. Government measures to correct pollution will raise the prices of those products whose production, use, or disposal pollutes the environment. The increased prices of these products will cause a decrease in the quantity demanded (assuming no change in demand), a move upward along the demand curve. At higher prices, more people will be excluded from buying, and less of the product will be sold. The drop in sales will cause an increase in unemployment in that industry.

25 With government prodding, we can hope that eventually prices will reflect the total social cost of production, distribution, use, and disposal of all goods and services and that therefore consumer choice will be based on prices that include all of these costs. Eventually, but after difficult periods of adjustment, the unemployment effects of pollution control will diminish as those who become unemployed as a result of the controls find jobs in nonpolluting industries or perhaps with businesses that manufacture pollution-control devices.

WHAT IS THE IDEAL ALLOCATION OF RESOURCES?

26 The pollution example highlights the importance of the question of resource allocation. If entrepreneurs can forget about pollution, their costs of production will be lower, their selling prices will be lower, they will sell more of their products, and as a result they will produce more, hire more people, and use more resources. Consequently, firms that pollute will use larger quantities of resources than if they were prevented from polluting.

27 But society would probably be better off if these resources were used in industries where production is cleaner. Society might also be better off if more resources went to industries that produced products with widespread social benefit. We could expect the public to vote for subsidies that would help those industries attract more resources and sell their products or services at lower prices (just the way we subsidize education and health care). Either way, free, unregulated market prices may not bring about an allocation of resources that best serves society. Economists will generally agree that *resources are allocated to their best uses when the selling price includes all external costs and/or benefits, and when this price causes all industries to buy and use resources up to the point where the social benefit conferred by the last unit produced is equal to or exceeds the social cost of producing it.* At this price, economists like to say, firms are "internalizing all the externalities" of their production. Such an allocation of resources is what economists mean by **allocative efficiency**.

1. This excerpt focuses on:
    a. the environment.
    b. the government.
    c. how the government attempts to protect the environment.
    d. pollution.

2. The figure focuses on:
    a. the amount of pollution in the United States.
    b. money lost by industries that pollute.
    c. supply and demand as it is affected by antipollution equipment.
    d. the number of industries that do not pollute.

3. This excerpt is broken up into:
    a. two sections.
    b. three sections.
    c. four sections.
    d. more than four sections.

4. Subsections are divided up by:
    a. italics.
    b. capital letters.
    c. boldface print.
    d. both *c* and *d*.

5. This excerpt will likely *not* discuss:
    a. how government is involved in preventing industries from polluting.
    b. ways to prevent industries from polluting.
    c. property rights and its relationship to pollution.
    d. how automobiles pollute.

Sel. 3 Sur	1. _____
Score _____ %	2. _____
▶ **80%**	3. _____
Score = number correct x 20	4. _____
	5. _____
	Check answers on p. 337.

B. Question

Having surveyed the excerpt, list five questions that you intend to answer when you study read. Make them up from the title, the subtitles, and the words and phrases in italics that you surveyed.

1. _____
2. _____
3. _____
4. _____
5. _____

Find sample questions on p. 337.

C. Read

With these questions in mind, read the excerpt carefully. You may want to read the entire excerpt once through before you begin marking. When you do begin to mark the excerpt, remember to underline only parts of sentences and to be sparing with written comments.

D. Recite

Without looking back, write down in note-taking or paragraph form the important points of the excerpt. Then compare the accuracy of your summary with the excerpt.

E. Review

Now review all your material: your underlinings, your marginal comments, and your recite notes. You may now want to organize this material into one or more study maps.

F. Study-Reading Questions

When you have carefully studied the information in the excerpt and in your notes, answer the following questions without looking back at either the article or your notes. Place all answers in the answer box.

1. It has been legally decided that the air and water people use can be considered:
    a.   their property.
    b.   industry's property.
    c.   no one's property.
    d.   permanently damaged.
2. To clean up the pollution it creates, industry invariably:
    a.   loses money on its product.
    b.   increases the price of its product.
    c.   goes to court to prevent having to clean up the pollution it creates.
    d.   hides its pollution.

3. When pollution results from a product being made and sold, it is referred to as a(n):
   a. direct approach.
   b. private cost.
   c. external effect.
   d. bubble plan.

4. When the government forces an industry not to pollute:
   a. the price of the product goes up.
   b. the price of the product goes down.
   c. the industry sues.
   d. demand goes up.

5. Effluent charges seem to be favored by:
   a. businesses.
   b. consumers.
   c. environmentalists.
   d. both *a* and *c*.

6. Environmentalists reject the bubble plan because it:
   a. cannot be enforced.
   b. encourages some individuals to pollute.
   c. is too expensive.
   d. both *b* and *c*.

7. What often results when the government corrects an industrial pollution problem?
   a. Prices go up.
   b. Unemployment goes up.
   c. Unemployment goes down.
   d. Both *a* and *b* occur.

8. The excerpt concludes that antipollution legislation:
   a. discourages industry from growing.
   b. discourages society from growing.
   c. is never popular.
   d. is often difficult to get through Congress.

9. The excerpt suggests that an unregulated economy:
   a. serves society well.
   b. does not serve society well.
   c. serves both society and industry well.
   d. does not serve industry well.

10. Allocative efficiency concerns:
   a. external costs.
   b. social benefit.
   c. the buyer.
   d. both *a* and *b*.

Sel. 3   S-Read
Score _____ %
▶ **80%**
Score = number correct x 10

1. _____
2. _____
3. _____
4. _____
5. _____
6. _____
7. _____
8. _____
9. _____
10. _____

Find answers on p. 337.

G. Questions for Discussion and Writing

1.   How does the physical law of the conservation of matter relate to economic concerns?
2.   In your own words, define private costs and external costs. Then show how they are related to social costs.
3.   In your own words, define the charge-polluters-for-their-pollution approach. Show why businesses favor it and environmentalists do not.
4.   In your own words, define the bubble plan approach. Show why industry favors it and environmentalists do not.
5.   What are social costs, and how do they relate to the overall price of an item?

H. Scanning

Assume that you are writing a research paper on the economy and environmental pollution and you must answer the following five questions before you complete your research.

You should take no more than 3 minutes to scan for the answers. Record your finishing time in the answer box.

1.   What is another name for private costs?
2.   What does *CE* stand for?
3.   What are the social costs of air pollution in Los Angeles?
4.   What are the two variables shown in the figure in this excerpt?
5.   What is another term for a national problem?

Sel. 3   Sc

Time _____ : _____

min   sec

Score _____ %

▶ **100%**

Score = number correct x 20

1. _____

2. _____

3. _____

4. _____

5. _____

Check answers on p. 337.

Self-Evaluation Economics

Answer the following questions by circling yes or no. Your responses will help you assess your study-reading strategies in economics.

1.   yes   no   Was your score in Section F, Study-Reading Questions, below 80 percent?

2.   yes   no   Did you have difficulty remembering the definitions of key terms?

3.   yes   no   Did you have difficulty seeing how the various economic terms related to each other?

4.   yes   no   Did you have difficulty separating cause from effect?

5.   yes   no   Was the figure presented in the excerpt difficult for you to understand?

Scoring: If you answered yes to three or more of these questions, you probably need more practice in reading technical material in the economics field.

Follow-up: To improve your skills in reading economics, follow these suggestions:

1. Realize that economics relies heavily on the cause-effect organizational pattern. Be alert for cause-effect patterns in your reading of economics material and isolate cause from effect in marginal comments.

2. Economics material also relies heavily on the definition pattern. You must know the meanings of economics terms before you can discuss the material intelligently. To learn each term, circle the key parts of the definition and write *def.* in the margins. By your review step, you should be able to define the key economics terms without looking back at the text.

3. Graphs are a significant part of reading economics. To read graphs, you must clearly understand what the horizontal and

vertical lines represent and then determine the relationship between the two factors. While you are study reading, refer to the graph to help explain the concepts that are presented. Often the author can condense several pages of material into one graph. A graph can provide an efficient visual summary of information.

4. In economics, a second careful reading of the material after a day or two will often tie up many of the loose ends from your previous reading. A second reading can help you see more clearly the proper sequence of cause-effect patterns and can give you a better grasp of how various terms relate to one other.

SELECTION 4

"The Environment and Ethical Theories" *by Donald VanDeVeer and Christine Pierce 2,689 words*

Vocabulary

postnatal: referring to events occurring after birth; "normal postnatal human beings have moral standing"

anencephalic: referring to that which is without a brain; "anencephalic or (less but) radically defective infants"

comatose: being in a coma, or unconscious; "irreversibly comatose humans"

divine providence: God's plan; "according to divine providence"

callousness: insensitivity; "humans may learn callousness"

unconditional: without qualification; "because of their unconditional worth"

anthropocentric paradigm: the view that the human being is the center of the universe; "to challenge the anthropocentric paradigm"

sentience: a state in which an organism can perceive through its senses; "mere consciousness or sentience"

correlative: a relationship in which one implies the other; "rights can be correlative to duties"

This excerpt is part of the introduction to an environmental ethics textbook, which discusses philosophical perspectives on environmental pollution. Here, you will consider what philosophers have said about how human beings should use the environment. The bulk of the discussion is structured around two organizational patterns: definition and sequence of events. The authors present the arguments of renowned philosophers such as Aristotle, Thomas Aquinas, and Immanuel Kant. Each philosopher uses specific terminology to explain the environment and carefully sequences his arguments to support a pro- or anti-environmental position.

Reading Strategies.   To successfully read this excerpt, use these strategies:

1.   Circle or highlight the key parts of important definitions. In marginal notes, show how various terms relate to one other.
2.   Read each philosopher's argument carefully; and in marginal or study notes, present the key steps in each argument.
3.   Compare each philosopher's argument and his definitions of related terms. See where these philosophers agree or disagree.
4.   By the end of your reading, you should be able to determine how each philosopher defines a human being, an animal, and an inanimate object.

A. Survey

Take 3 minutes to survey the excerpt. Note the boldface print as well as the words and phrases in italics. If time permits, read the first few and the last few paragraphs in the excerpt.

THE ENVIRONMENT AND ETHICAL THEORIES

by Donald VanDeVeer and Christine Pierce

HUMAN ORGANISMS

1   Talk of environmental ethics, ecological ethics, the preservation of nature calls to mind concerns about protection of individual animals or rare species; preserving clean air, wilderness areas, groves of redwood trees; avoiding the destruction of the wonders of nature such as the Grand Canyon; or the sense of loss when woods and pastures are transformed into concatenations of steel, concrete, plastic, and neon. It is a bit surprising, then, when the suggestion is made that there is a link between some of the basic issues in environmental ethics and certain perplexing issues often classified as matters of biomedical ethics such as abortion. Given our prior discussion, however, the link is more evident. If we agree that normal postnatal human beings have moral standing, whether "all things human" do is a matter of some dispute. Several sorts of entities deserve special consideration: (1) human fetuses, (2) anencephalic or (less but) radically defective infants, (3) irreversibly comatose humans, (4) newly dead human bodies. Let us use *NPH* to stand for these nonparadigmatic humans. Do any or all NPH have moral standing? If so, what sorts of duties are directly owed to NPH? Must we make equally stringent efforts to preserve or protect (or somehow "respect") such beings—as are required in our dealings with normal humans?

2   If the familiar contrast between "man and nature" is to be understood as one between normal neonatal humans and things that cannot be so classified, that is, everything else, then NPH are a part of "nature." As noted, according to one view what is part of nature (other than paradigm humans) can be used as a natural resource, for example, for the benefit of (paradigm) humans. Reasoning rather like this may be behind the view that we ought to put to good use, for example, aborted fetuses, the recently dead (where all respiratory and circulatory functions have irreversibly ceased), or those in a persistent vegetative state (sometimes described as brain-dead). There is a great need for organs for transplantation, a need for blood, for

growth hormone, and so on. Hence, some regard the failure to "mine" NPH (or some subset) as a shameful waste—given the scarcity of resources valuable to paradigmatic humans. Disputes about these matters depend in part on ascertaining the appropriate criterion of moral standing. As we have noted, if by *natural resource* what is meant is "what it is morally permissible to use to benefit those with moral standing," one theoretical (and practical) connection of environmental ethics and biomedical ethics is clear. If we are to reassess or query *What's so important about animals?* Or rare species, jungles, wilderness, mountains, or redwoods? it is not out of place to consider *What's so important about people?*—Or nonparadigmatic humans—as well.

TRADITIONAL ETHICAL THEORIES

Natural Law Morality and Judeo-Christian Morality

3   Traditional morality is often associated with the view that there is a certain natural and morally defensible hierarchy of beings. There is, it is claimed, a natural order according to which inanimate objects are to serve animate ones; further, plants are here for the sake of animals, and animals for the sake of humans. It is, thus, right and proper, for the "higher" to use the "lower," as the former see fit. Throughout history this view has rarely been questioned. It is a view implicit in much (at least) of natural law theory dating back to Aristotle (384–322 B.C.) and in Thomas Aquinas's (1225–1274) theological revision of Aristotelianism. In theological versions, of course, the natural order is seen as part of the divine order—and people are around for the sake of God—and are to function within the constraints laid down by divine purposes.

4   In *The Politics* Aristotle says,

plants exist for the sake of animals. . . . all other animals exist for the sake of man, tame animals for the use he can make of them as well as for the food they provide; and as for wild animals, most though not all of these can be used for food and are useful in other ways;

clothing and instruments can be made out of them. If then we are right in believing that nature makes nothing without some end in view, nothing to no purpose, it must be that nature has made all things specifically for the sake of man.

Elsewhere in *The Politics* Aristotle compares the function of women to that of animals in an effort to explain the low position of each in the hierarchy of being:

As between male and female the former is by nature superior and ruler, the latter inferior and subject. . . . Wherever there is the same wide discrepancy between two sets of human beings as there is between mind and body or between man and beast, then the inferior of the two sets, those whose condition is such that their function is the use of their bodies and nothing better can be expected of them, those, I say, are slaves by nature.

In short, those with less rationality exist to serve the needs, interests, or good of those with more. One's place in the hierarchy of being reflects Aristotle's judgment concerning one's rational abilities.

5   Aquinas, like Aristotle, makes it clear that to kill and otherwise use animals for human purposes is part of the natural order of things. In the *Summa Contra Gentiles*, Aquinas says,

we refute the error of those who claim that it is a sin for man to kill brute animals. For animals are ordered to man's use in the natural course of things, according to divine providence. Consequently, man uses them without any injustice, either by killing them or by employing them in any other way. For this reason, God said to Noe: "As the green herbs, I have delivered all flesh to you." (Genesis 9:3)

6   In Aquinas's view, animals have no independent moral standing or intrinsic goodness. Aquinas thought that we ought not to be cruel to animals, not because animals have an interest in not suffering, but because if such cruelty is allowed, humans may learn callousness and inflict it on their fellow humans:

Man's affections may be either of reason or of sentiment. As regards the former, it is indifferent how one behaves towards animals, since God has given him dominion over all as it is written, 'thou has subjected all things under his feet.' It is in this sense that St. Paul says that God has no care for oxen or other animals. . . . As to affection arising from sentiment, it is operative with regard to animals. . . . And if he is often moved in this way, he is more likely to have compassion for his fellowmen. . . . Therefore, the Lord, in order to stir to compassion the Jewish people, naturally inclined to cruelty, wished to exercise them in pity even to animals by forbidding certain practices savouring of cruelty to them·

7   According to Genesis, God has given human beings dominion over the earth: "Be fruitful and multiply, and replenish the earth, and subdue it; and have dominion over the fish of the sea, and over the fowl of the air, and over every living thing that moveth upon the earth." There is, in the recent literature on animal liberation and environmental ethics, a dispute over the interpretation of the biblical notion of dominion. Some say that (1) dominion permits humans to do whatever they want with animals, plants, rivers, and rocks. Others claim that (2) dominion means stewardship. According to this view God expects us to exercise some responsibility toward the earth. The earth belongs to God and we are commanded to take care of it and the creatures that dwell therein.

8   A stewardship interpretation may be committed to an acceptance of a traditional private property view. That is, humans should not ruthlessly exploit the earth because the earth is God's. If we ought to treat the earth in a responsible and virtuous way, it is not because the earth and its creatures have independent moral standing or intrinsic goodness, but because it is God's property. It is important to note that this result—the lack of independent moral standing on the part of any being except humans—seems to follow from either interpretation of dominion. This is not a surprising outcome. In the history of ethics, Aristotle and Aquinas exemplify what is called *virtue ethics*. In this tradition, for example, if one is not cruel to animals, it is because one believes that cruelty is a vice. It was too early in the history of thought for the notion of a right, that is, for the idea that there

is something about the being or entity toward whom (or which) we act that must be respected, that makes it or them not simply the beneficiaries of our good character.

Natural Rights Theory

9   **The Kantian Argument.**   It is generally accepted that persons are the sorts of being that have rights. Immanuel Kant, a German philosopher (1724–1804), provided the original argument that explains what persons are and why they have rights.

10   Kant explicates what a person is by distinguishing persons from things. Persons are rational, autonomous beings who are capable of formulating and pursuing different conceptions of the good. That is, persons have ends of their own; things or objects in the world do not. For example, suppose I walk into a classroom and decide to break up all the chairs in order to use them for firewood. If I do this, it does not matter to the chairs. Now, there may be many reasons why I should not destroy the chairs. The next class may be planning to sit on them. Presumably, somebody owns the chairs and does not want me to destroy them. However, I cannot give as a reason for refraining from breaking the chairs that it matters to the chairs. It can even be said that it is in the interests of chairs not to be broken (or in the interests of lawnmowers not to be left out in the rain), but this is not the same as claiming that chairs or lawnmowers have interests of their own if we mean by this that chairs or lawnmowers care about how they are treated. Persons care about how they are treated; things do not. According to Kant, things can be used to suit the purposes of persons, but persons are not to be used as if they were mere things, as if they had no ends or purposes of their own. Persons have rights because of their unconditional worth as rational beings, whereas the worth of things is relative to the ends of persons.

11   Conceptually, it is difficult, if not impossible, to extend rights to environmental objects such as rocks and streams on a Kantian analysis of

rights. This is so for the following reason: According to this analysis, rights are designed to protect persons from being treated as things. Rocks and streams are paradigm cases of things or objects; they are incapable of formulating ends. *Thing*, in Kant, is a technical term. Something is a *thing* if it is incapable of autonomy in the Kantian sense which entails self-rule, that is, formulating and following rational principles. Hence, inanimate objects do not have rights in Kant's view. Nonetheless, we may have duties regarding inanimate objects. These duties, Kant maintained, are indirect duties toward human beings, as the following quotation shows:

Destructiveness is immoral; we ought not to destroy things which can still be put to some use. No man ought to mar the beauty of nature; for what he has no use for may still be of use to some one else. He need, of course, pay no heed to the thing itself, but he ought to consider his neighbor.

12   Animals are also considered "things" in Kant's scheme. In his *Lectures on Ethics*, he referred to animals as "man's instruments." Despite Kant's innovative work on the subject of rights, many older notions persist in his philosophy. The idea that animals, like any tool, exist for the use of human beings is one example. Likewise, we find in Kant the idea that our treatment of animals is a matter of our virtue. For example, in the *Lectures*, he says, "A master who turns out his ass or his dog because the animal can no longer earn its keep manifests a small mind."

13   Some human beings are not autonomous, yet Kant accorded them rights. Since Kant defined persons as rational, autonomous beings and not merely as human beings, he had the philosophical ammunition, so to speak, to challenge the anthropocentric paradigm. That is, a little reflection shows that a rational being in the Kantian sense and a human being, that is, a member of the species *Homo sapiens*, are not one and the same. Some human beings are not rational: fetuses, infants, the permanently comatose; some rational beings may not be human beings. For example,

some animals may be autonomous in the Kantian sense, even though Kant denied it. Moreover, as mentioned earlier, there may be extraterrestrial beings, like the movie character E.T., who are rational beings, but not members of our species. Not only did Kant treat *human being* and *rational being* as interchangeable (thereby attributing rights to all and only human beings); he also attributed all the traditional rights (liberty, property, and so on) to rational beings. Although autonomy may be necessary for possession of a right to liberty, one might ask why a being must be autonomous in order to have a right not to be tortured? The failure to take seriously the relevant criteria for the various rights is considered a serious weakness in classical rights theories by many contemporary philosophers.

14   **Taking Qualifications Seriously.**   The new literature on animal liberation and animal rights has caused many to rethink the claim that humans have rights solely because they are human. If we no longer rely on this kind of argument, then right-holders must possess some morally relevant features that may turn out to be shared by humans, animals, and environmental objects alike. The method employed is to identify the morally relevant qualifications for the possession of specific rights in order to determine what rights, if any, a being or entity has. With respect to some rights, a plausible case can be made that certain qualifications are morally relevant. To do this, however, one needs to know the specific purpose of each right. For example, the right not to be tortured protects the basic interest certain beings have in not suffering. The right to liberty protects the interest in directing one's life as one sees fit without unjustified interference from others. If a being is capable of suffering, but not capable of autonomy or self-rule, it can have a right not to be tortured, but not a right to liberty. On this model, the right to life must protect some specific interest or desire. One plausible candidate, suggested by Michael Tooley, is a desire to continue into the future, that is, to continue to live.

15 The desire for continued existence presupposes the capacity to have a concept of oneself as a continuing self—as an entity existing over time. Of course, each right, according to the view we have been developing, presupposes some morally relevant capacity. The right not to be tortured presupposes a capacity for suffering. The right to liberty presupposes a capacity for autonomy. Once we figure out the morally relevant capacity for any given right, only those beings or entities that have the relevant capacity have the right. Thus, only sentient beings have a right not to be tortured, only autonomous beings have a right to liberty, and only self-conscious beings have a right to life. Most adult human beings can meet the self-consciousness requirement, as may some animals. However, as Tooley points out, some adult human beings do not have the requisite capacity, nor do human fetuses or newborn infants. It is worth noting that the self-consciousness requirement is a fairly sophisticated one. According to a view like Tooley's, mere consciousness or sentience may be sufficient for having a right not to be tortured, but not for having a right to life.

16 According to the above approach to rights, many animals fare rather well. Some animals most certainly have a right not to be tortured, and quite possibly a right to life. Environmental objects, such as rocks and plants, however, appear to fare rather badly. For example, it would be absurd to claim that rocks have a right not to be tortured if they are incapable of suffering. If environmental objects are not sentient or conscious, it is hard to see how they would qualify for any rights. Peter Singer claims that plants have no conscious experiences, and thus I do nothing seriously wrong if I pull out weeds from my garden. Nonetheless, some people believe that plants have feelings, and some, like Christopher Stone, think that the entire planet is at some level conscious. So, there are matters of disagreement about who or what has certain capacities, but the important point here is that the challenge to the anthropocentric paradigm has changed the character of the rights debate into one about capacities and the moral relevance of capacities.

17 **Rights and Duties.** Rights can be correlative with duties. For example, correlated with my duty not to kill you is your right not to have me kill you. Some philosophers claim there can be duties toward another without that other's possessing correlative rights; others claim that a being can possess rights without others owing that being duties. Moreover, some philosophers claim that only those who can perform duties or act from a sense of duty can have rights; others claim that beings or entities (such as animals and trees) can have rights even if they cannot act from a sense of duty.

18 It is doubtful that animals can act from a sense of duty. Promise keeping is a paradigm of a duty or obligation. Suppose I say to my cat as I leave in the morning, "I want you to meet me here at 5:00 P.M." Can I seriously expect her to make and keep a promise? Animals kill and eat one another (and occasionally us). As unfortunate as this may be, it does not seem to make sense to say that animals have duties not to do this.

19 In arguments about the correlativity of rights and duties, it is often pointed out that infants and retarded persons may be incapable of duties, yet they may have rights. If this is so, an animal's inability to perform duties does not imply that it cannot have rights. If the only requirement for rights is to be capable of having certain interests, then beings that have those interests have rights whether or not they can meet additional requirements for being able to perform duties. But this is simply to say that rights and duties are two different things. Acting out of a sense of duty presupposes certain rational capacities, whereas possession of the right not to be tortured, for example, presupposes a capacity to suffer.

20 If animals cannot perform duties, it is even less plausible to suggest that the "environment" can be morally responsible for the disasters it causes. Rivers overflow and damage property, forest fires destroy lives, sinkholes swallow up

Porsches. The interest argument, which tenably can allocate rights (or, at least some rights) to animals, cannot do the same, with comparable ease, for environmental objects. Trees and streams not only lack the rational capacity required for duties, they appear to lack interests as well at least in the Kantian sense of caring about how one is treated. If a wilderness is destroyed to make a home for Mickey Mouse, it does not matter to the wilderness.

Donald VanDeVeer and Christine Pierce, *People, Penguins, and Plastic Trees*, pp. 9–13. ©1986 by Wadsworth, Inc. Reprinted by permission of the publisher.

• •

1. This selection presents several excerpts from philosophical works.
   a. true
   b. false

2. Which philosopher is *not* mentioned in this excerpt?
   a. Aristotle
   b. Aquinas
   c. Plato
   d. Kant

3. How are subsections highlighted?
   a. italics
   b. boldface
   c. underlining and capitals
   d. both *a* and *b*

4. This excerpt will likely focus on:
   a. the ethical considerations involved in environmental decisions.
   b. how Aristotle disagreed with Plato.
   c. the nature of the good as it relates to the environment.
   d. the arguments for and against an afterlife.

5. The major philosophical theory that this excerpt treats is:
   a. natural rights theory.
   b. Aristotle's theory.
   c. Aquinas's theory.
   d. the new morality theory.

Sel. 4 Sur	1. _____
Score _____ %	2. _____
▶ **80%**	3. _____
Score = number correct × 20	4. _____
	5. _____
	Check answers with your instructor.

B. Question

Having surveyed the excerpt, draw up five questions that you intend to answer when you study read. Base them on the subtitles and the words and phrases in italics. Write the questions below.

1. _____
2. _____
3. _____
4. _____
5. _____

Ask your instructor for sample questions.

C. Read

With these questions in mind, read the excerpt carefully. You may want to read these pages once through fairly quickly before you begin marking the excerpt. When you do begin to mark the excerpt, remember to underline only parts of sentences and to be sparing with written comments.

D. Recite

After marking the pages, write down in note-taking or paragraph form the important points made in the excerpt. When you have finished your summary, compare its accuracy with the original statements.

E. Review

Now review all your material: your underlinings, your marginal comments, and your recite notes. It would be helpful to organize the information into one or more study maps.

F. Study-Reading Questions

When you have carefully studied the information in this excerpt and in your notes, answer the following ten questions without looking back. Place all answers in the answer box.

1. The excerpt suggests that certain types of human beings can be considered as natural resources to be used for the benefit of others.
   a. true
   b. false
2. Aristotle suggests that animals are:
   a. equal to humans.
   b. to be used by humans as they see fit.
   c. better than humans.
   d. part of God's plan.

3. Aquinas notes that animals:
   a.   may be used by humans for their own needs.
   b.   are considered by God to be superior to humans.
   c.   are considered by God to be inferior to humans.
   d.   both *a* and *c*.

4. Biblical scholars suggest that the Bible:
   a.   allows the human being to dominate and use natural resources.
   b.   requires that the human being respect his or her natural resources.
   c.   both *a* and *b*.
   d.   neither *a* nor *b*.

5. Kant defines a person as:
   a.   being like a thing.
   b.   being unlike a thing.
   c.   being part of God.
   d.   with rights equal to an animal's.

6. Kant believes that rocks have:
   a.   an equal status to human beings.
   b.   a superior status to human beings.
   c.   an inferior status to human beings.
   d.   a spirit within them.

7. Kant defines a thing as an object that:
   a.   does not move.
   b.   thinks.
   c.   cannot make decisions for itself.
   d.   cannot grow.

8. Michael Tooley defines self-consciousness as:
   a.   being aware of the concept of time.
   b.   liking oneself.
   c.   having a brain.
   d.   all of these.

9. The excerpt suggests that animals do not have a sense of:
   a.   being alive.
   b.   being tortured.
   c.   being free.
   d.   duty.

10. The excerpt argues that the wilderness has:
    a.   no moral sense.
    b.   a spiritual and moral sense.
    c.   the same consciousness as an animal.
    d.   the same consciousness as a human being.

Sel. 4 S-Read	1. ____
Score ____ %	2. ____
▶ **80%**	3. ____
Score = number correct x 10	4. ____
	5. ____
	6. ____
	7. ____
	8. ____
	9. ____
	10. ____
	Check answers with your instructor.

G. Questions for Discussion and Writing

1. Reread Aristotle's and Aquinas's arguments in paragraphs 4–8. Summarize their arguments; then show where they differ.
2. Summarize the two biblical interpretations of the use of the earth.
3. In your own words, summarize Kant's argument. How does it differ from Aristotle's and Aquinas's?
4. In your own words, summarize Tooley's argument; then explain why he thinks newborns do not have the same rights as adult humans.
5. In your own words, define rights and duties. Show how rights and duties are similar as concepts and where they differ. Then discuss an animal (of your own choosing) that has rights but not duties.

H. Scanning

Take no more than 3 minutes to scan for the following bits of information from the excerpt. Assume you need to know this information for an examination on environmental ethics.

1. What does *NPH* stand for?
2. When did Thomas Aquinas die?
3. Where do the two excerpts from Aristotle come from?
4. What book from the Bible is quoted?
5. Who believes that the entire earth has a consciousness?

Sel. 4   Sc   1. _____

Time _____ : _____   2. _____

     min   sec   3. _____

Score _____ %   4. _____

  ▶ **100%**   5. _____

Score = number correct x 20

                                Check answers with your instructor.

Self-Evaluation Philosophy

Answer the following questions by circling yes or no. Your responses will help you assess your study-reading strategies in philosophy.

1. yes   no   Was your score in Section F, Study-Reading Questions, below 80 percent?

2. yes   no   Did you have difficulty remembering most of the terms while answering the study-reading questions?

3. yes   no   Did you have difficulty remembering each philosopher's argument as you answered the study-reading questions?

4. yes   no   Did you have difficulty understanding the primary-source excerpts taken from Aristotle, Aquinas, and Kant?

Scoring: If you answered yes to two or more of these questions, you may need more practice in reading philosophy.

Follow-up: To improve your strategies in reading philosophy, follow these suggestions:

1. Read philosophy slowly, and reread passages that you do not at first understand.

2. Realize that to comprehend philosophy, you must understand the definitions. When you come to a definition, underline or circle the main elements.

3. Start seeing how various terms and arguments in philosophy are interrelated. Mark in the margins comments suggesting how terms or arguments are similar.

4. Be sure that you can summarize a philosophical argument accurately, listing all the necessary steps, before you begin reading new material.

. . . .

FOLLOW-UP

Now that you have read four study-reading selections on environmental pollution, you may want to consider how your understanding of this issue has changed. Individually, in small groups, or in large groups, you want to consider the following questions:

1. What scientific evidence do you now have that helps you better understand the environmental problem?
2. In what ways can industry help solve the pollution problem?
3. Do you think people have the right to control nature, or should nature control people?
4. After reading, discussing, and writing about these selections, has your attitude toward environmental pollution changed? If so, how?

Rapid Reading

*C*hapter 4 continues the theme introduced in Chapter 3, Study Reading: A proficient reader must develop different reading techniques and speeds for different reading tasks. In this chapter, the What (materials) and the Why (your purpose for reading them) will be very different from those in Chapter 3. Also, it is the first of two chapters that will teach speeded (time-pressured) reading. Nearly all the Practices and Selections will be timed. So please do not read ahead in this chapter or ignore any of the directions!

You will learn the rationale behind speeded reading, some cautions about it, and a variety of methods to try out. Some of these methods you will eventually adopt as your own.

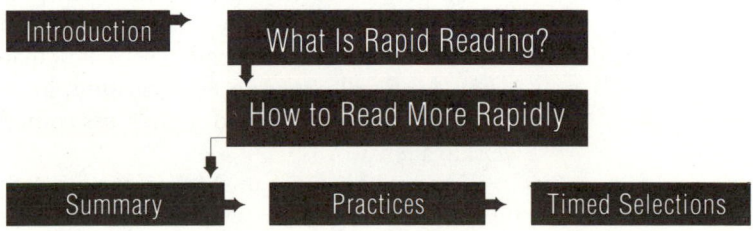

*I*NTRODUCTION TO RAPID READING

. . . .

CHECKLIST OF SYMPTOMS

Do you often:

_____ 1. "hear" every word clearly in your head, even when you read silently?

_____ 2. read everything in the same way, at the same speed (i.e., slowly and carefully) whether you need to or not?

_____ 3. read an article or story so slowly that by the time you reach the end, you can't remember the beginning?

_____ 4. avoid courses in literature or any subject that requires much outside reading?

_____ 5. own several good books you have "never had time to finish" (the ones with bookmarks stuck in them)?

If you checked one or more of these symptoms, you need to learn how to read more rapidly. You have probably mastered the Essential Reading Skills (main idea, support, patterns, inference, summarizing, and previewing) presented in Chapter 1. You can scan quickly and accurately for answers to specific questions, as you did in Chapter 2. You can study read your textbooks well enough after working through Chapter 3. In fact, you may already be an *A* student or have a successful career.

But you are also apparently the typical compulsive reader. You are still reading everything slowly, correctly, "orally," just as you did in grade school. The problem is, nowadays you're supposed to be reading silently, not orally. Also, as an adult your reading tasks vary tremendously, both in *what* you are reading and *why* you are reading it. So it is inappropriate for you to use only one reading style and rate.

The old word-by-word method is especially inefficient for the mass of general reading that you do, or should do (e.g., newspapers, magazines, and light books). These are fairly easy and do not require study reading. You don't have to memorize today's newspaper or take a test on this week's *Time* magazine!

So why do most of us tend to read light materials so slowly? First, because that is how we first learned to read. Second, because it's now a comfortable habit. Third, because we're afraid we'll "miss something" or "lose comprehension" if we skip a few words.

These old habits can slow us down unnecessarily. The paradoxical truth is that *when reading matter is fairly easy, our comprehension actually drops if we read it too slowly*. For one thing, we can miss the flow of the writer's story line or argument. For another, our minds wander if we don't feed them information at an

124

optimum speed; that is, we "lose concentration." Many studies have shown that average readers can often *double* their rate in general reading with no loss of basic comprehension. Many even *increase* their comprehension because they concentrate better at the higher speeds.

However, let us offer just one note of caution. Common sense tells you not to push your speed if you have serious vision or perception problems. You also should not push to increase your rates if you do not already have good basic skills as reviewed in Chapter 1 and at least an average vocabulary and a ninth-grade-level comprehension. Finally, if, at your own slow rate, you are reaching less than 70 percent on the comprehension quizzes given so far in this book, you are not ready for time-pressured reading. You will find it frustrating, and you may even make more errors in comprehension than before.

Now for the good news. If you have none of those problems, you are ready to venture into rapid reading. Just remember these two things:

1. Make sure your *material* (the What) is fairly easy for you. You should know something about the subject matter and have no major problems with the vocabulary, style, or ideas. Don't expect to read *Scientific American* or Spinoza's philosophy rapidly and with full comprehension the first time through, unless you are a scientist or philosopher.

2. Make sure your *purpose* for reading (the Why) is appropriate for rapid reading. Do you need to memorize the contents of the material? Discuss it in detail? Savor the style? Are you aiming at 100 percent understanding of new, difficult principles, as when you study read a textbook? If so, don't expect a fast, once-through reading to be sufficient. Your purpose should not be study, as in Chapter 3, nor analysis, as it will be in Chapter 6. (Although a single rapid reading prior to study or analysis is often very useful.) Your purpose when you decide to rapid read should be general information and enjoyment.

. . . .

WHAT IS RAPID READING?

First, let's take the word *reading*. In this book we use *reading* to mean seeing and processing all, or nearly all, the words on the printed page. Tests prove that human eyes can do this only at rates up to 800 words per minute (wpm). Above that rate, the eyes must skip some words or sentences. So rates over 800 wpm imply *skip-reading* or *skimming*, not reading in the strict sense. You have already practiced two kinds of skip-reading in this book: preview skimming in Chapter 1 and scanning in Chapter 2. If you recall, you learned to read selectively, focusing on the key parts and skipping less important parts.* But when you rapid read, we expect you to read most of the words on every page and to grasp most of the content at rates *under 800 wpm.*

---

*A third kind of skip-reading, overview skimming, is presented in Chapter 5.

Second, look at the word *rapid*. This simply means a reading rate that is faster than normal for the average reader—in other words, speeded or time-pressured reading. The average high school graduate who is not trained in efficient reading reads general material—newspapers, magazines, easy paperbacks—at about 200–300 wpm. To qualify as a "rapid reader" in this chapter, you should aim for at least 400 wpm.

The target rates in this chapter, then, range from 400 to 800 wpm. One side benefit of reading above 400 wpm is that at these speeds, "hearing the words" or subvocalizing tends to drop out. We simply cannot talk, mentally, that fast!

If reading rapidly makes you a little anxious, remember the Why of general reading—no tests, no analysis. In fact, you should never aim for 100 percent comprehension of the literal or surface content. Rather, your goal will be only 70–80 percent! Why shoot so low? First, if you aim for 100 percent comprehension in all your light reading, you will never relax enough to read any faster than you do now. Second, the selections in this chapter, like most of your daily reading, are not so important to your life that you must comprehend and retain 100 percent. After all, it is better to read a great deal and be widely informed, than to be so letter-perfect that you seldom read or finish anything.

In conclusion, most of our daily reading materials are one-dimensional; they require a once-through reading for surface content only. So you should read them as rapidly as possible. A single, slow rate prevents you from dipping into all the great material that is out there awaiting your pleasure.

HOW TO READ MORE RAPIDLY

For best results, don't start right in by forcing yourself to read at 800 wpm, especially if you have been a habitually slow reader. Instead, read the following six tips and do the Practices in order. (Note: Some of the Practices require you to use an easy paperback book, so please have one handy before you start.)

If you have trouble reaching your rate and comprehension goals in the Timed Selections that follow, reread this section.

As you become more fluent at reading easy materials rapidly, you will find that Tips 1, 2, and 3 will become part of your new reading habits. Then you can concentrate on *increasing your rate with no loss of basic literal comprehension*.

TIP 1   *Approach rapid reading with a relaxed, confident mind-set.* First, *forget any 100 percent compulsion you may have built up over the years*. Remind yourself that in the future, no one is going to test you on your leisure reading! Once you leave this book or course, you'll be free to use your new rapid-reading techniques without fear of test scores. Second, *leave the slow rates (100–300 wpm) to talking or reading aloud*. Your eyes can see all the words on a page at speeds up to 800 wpm, and your brain can operate at thousands of words per minute. So feed yourself printed words at a more challenging pace—400–800 wpm.

TIP 2 *Trust your sense of closure.* All adult readers know enough about English words, sentence patterns, and common logic to understand most of the contents of a page even if they do not clearly see every word. ("Function words"—those not essential to literal comprehension—may easily be omitted. "Key words," however, are important to comprehension.) Depending on how concise a writer's style is, we can omit 10–50 percent of the words in ordinary prose without losing any basic literal comprehension.

Turn to Practice 4.1 on page 131, and try reading passages consisting of only key words. (Function words have been deleted.)

TIP 3 *Use your eyes efficiently.* A slow reader tends to fixate (focus) on every single word across the line. Yet the average eye span on the printed page is about 1-1/2 inches. That is, by fixating on one point, we can identify many words above, below, and to the sides of that point. (We are using our peripheral vision.) Fixating less often on a printed line will cause less eyestrain. It also guides us toward that prime goal of faster reading, *reading the ideas* on a page instead of the individual words. To test your own eye span, mark a small x in this paragraph, and draw a circle around it about 1-1/2 inches in diameter. Can you identify most of the words within the circle without moving your eyes off the x?

To increase your eye span, ask your instructor for phrase-reading drills or other materials.

Two popular speed-reading techniques will help you increase your visual efficiency:

a. *Use soft focus as you read.* Don't peer tensely at the words. Relax your eye muscles and face muscles. Let your peripheral vision do more of the work. Look slightly above the line of print, and let your eyes "float" down the page. Try to read the lines, not each letter and word.

b. *Use shortened margins.* That is, don't fixate on the first or the last word on each line. Rather, fixate about a half inch in from each margin, letting your peripheral vision pick up the words to the side. Like the soft-focus technique, this one takes time and practice.

A note of caution: The best eye span and soft focus in the world will not, by themselves, make a good or a fast reader. Ninety-nine percent of all reading takes place in the brain, not in the eyes. As you concentrate on the *ideas* on a page rather than on each word, and as you increase your rate in easy materials, your brain will become more alert and active, and you can forget what your eyes are doing.

Turn to Practice 4.2 on page 132. Using a page in an easy paperback, start practicing soft focus and shortened margins. You may need to mark up many extra pages, or ask your instructor for additional drills, before you feel comfortable with these two visual techniques.

TIP 4 *Use all the Essential Reading Skills,* as presented in Chapter 1. This means that you must first preview skim your material for the main ideas and overall structure. If, as we saw, previewing helps with basic comprehension, scanning, and study reading, it is an absolute necessity in rapid reading. You will never increase your speed if you do not begin with a "map of the territory."

Besides previewing, remember the other essential skills. You will need to pay attention to important transitions and other signals, and notice organizational patterns—all keys to the "writer's path." Even when we read rapidly, our goal is to grasp the writer's message as accurately as possible.

TIP 5   *Use time pressure.* This is an outgrowth of Tip 1. Be confident that your brain can handle print faster than you can talk or read aloud. To rapid read, you should be physically relaxed but mentally active! Most people find that *some* tension, some pressure, helps them concentrate on their reading. In fact, skilled rapid readers are not passive and comfortable. In rapid reading as in scanning, you must be conscious of time passing. So time yourself, or have someone else time you, or work up a little competition with class members.

One tried-and-true way to apply time pressure is to chart your reading rate. As usual, choose a fairly easy book and make sure your purpose is enjoyment. Keeping an objective record (e.g., list, chart, or graph) is important, since we seldom know just how fast we are reading.

Rate charts, whether handmade or commercial, operate the same way: graphic records of your ups-and-downs that will spur you to faster and more consistent speeds. Even a simple time-block record is helpful. With this, you read for a fixed time, then stop, count the pages read, and list or graph the number. Your instructor can provide you with a sample from the Teacher's Manual. For another type of rate chart, see those at the end of this chapter and Chapter 6.

Another easy way to keep your rate over 400 wpm, on your own, is to time your reading of a paperback book page by page. Since the average paperback contains 350 to 450 words per page, your speed will fall into the lower range of "rapid reading" if you can read at least one page per minute. To help maintain a steady, rapid pace, try using your finger as a pacing device down each page.

Turn to Practice 4.3 on page 133 for directions on how to time and pace your reading of light paperback books.

TIP 6   *Use a crutch,* until you can read rapidly without one. If you try the first five tips and still continue to read easy materials at a grade-school rate, the following may help you concentrate and speed up:

a.   *Use your finger as a pacing device.* You can move the finger rapidly from left to right under each line. This technique is effective if you intend to read every line, but it will hold you back if you wish to skip.

Or you can use one or more fingers vertically. Place your finger(s) under the center of the first line of a page, then move your finger straight down the page. (A slight left-right wiggle is permissible.) Keep your finger one or two lines below your eyes. (You may have already tried this in Practice 4.3.)

b.   *Use a speed-reading device or automatic reading film,* set at 400 wpm or higher. Some of these gadgets present their own materials; some may be used on your paperback book. The imposed pacing will force you to keep going, no matter how uncomfortable it is. Also, a good pacing or "shutter" device prevents you from nervously regressing or rereading. Slowly but surely, you will begin to keep up with the machine, comprehending more and more of the content. As soon as a rate feels comfortable, increase it.

c. *Use an index card* as your own portable shutter. Like commercial gadgets, the card prevents you from regressing to previous lines of print. Also, because you use your arm and hand to move the card down the page, you are physically more focused on the reading. Unlike other gadgets, an index card is cheap, is easy to carry with you, and can double as a bookmark! Do not forget to use soft focus and shortened margins as you read.

For more directions on using an index-card pacer, turn to Practice 4.4 on page 134.

All these crutches—finger, machine, card—help keep your attention on the page and pressure you to read faster. Some readers continue to use their favorite crutch for years, especially when they feel distracted. Eventually, though, it's best if you can really change your old habits of unnecessary slow reading, "throw away your crutch," and read general materials at 400–800 wpm, simply by using your eyes and brain. A good slogan to keep in mind: "Read the ideas on the page, not the words."

Turn to Practice 4.4 on page 134 and follow instructions for use of index cards and other aids to reading more rapidly.

SUMMARY

All of us began reading in the primary grades, with a slow, word-by-word, letter-perfect, mainly oral method of reading. This old habit dies hard. But it is not appropriate for the adult's reading tasks, which vary tremendously from easy, light materials to difficult, serious materials. For the former kind of reading—newspapers, magazines, light paperbacks, so-called general reading—we should develop a faster reading rate. We are physically able to see and read words up to 800 or 900 wpm (above that, we are really skipping or skimming). So in rapid reading, we aim to read *all* of the material, but at rates of 400 wpm to 800 wpm. Also, since the materials are not for study or analysis, we aim for 70–80 percent comprehension, not 100 percent.

In rapid reading, besides changing an old habit, we must build confidence in our ability to comprehend light materials at a faster-than-average rate. With practice, most of us discover that we can double our old reading rate with no loss of comprehension. In fact, comprehension often improves because we are reading fast enough to see the material as a whole and to focus on the content. Reading under some time pressure actually helps keep our brains active and interested, rather than allowing them to become passive and bored.

Here in condensed form are the six tips for faster reading of light materials:

1. Have a confident mind-set—forget any 100 percent compulsion and leave the slow rates to talkers and oral readers.
2. Trust your sense of closure—many function words in English may be skipped over.
3. Use your eyes efficiently—use soft focus and avoid fixating on the ends of lines.
4. Use all the Essential Reading (Comprehension) Skills—preview skim, look for transitions and other signals of the writer's organization and emphases.
5. Use time pressure—1-minute pacing in paperback books, keeping a time chart or graph.
6. Use a crutch, at least in the beginning—fingers, reading machines or other gadgets, or an index card as a "shutter."

So learn a few rapid-reading techniques! You'll comprehend and remember better than before. You'll be informed. And best of all, you'll finish those partially read books, and you will read those magazines and newspapers. And that's where a lot of the fun is.

SUMMARY BOX: RAPID READING

What?	Why?	Acceptable Comprehension	Acceptable Rates
Light or general reading—newspapers, magazines, airport reading, doctor's office reading, adventure novels, biographies, mysteries, detective novels, familiar topics, weekend-in-the-mountains reading, best-sellers, supplemental course reading	Enjoyment, escapism, background reading, hobby reading, keeping up with popular reading, entertainment	70–80%	400–800 wpm

PRACTICES: RAPID READING

Answers for these exercises are not provided in the answer key. Answers are available from your instructor.

4.1 PRACTICE FOR TIP 2, "TRUST YOUR SENSE OF CLOSURE"

4.2 PRACTICE FOR TIP 3, "USE YOUR EYES EFFICIENTLY"

4.3 PRACTICE FOR TIP 5, "USE TIME PRESSURE"

4.4 PRACTICE FOR TIP 6, "USE A CRUTCH"—INDEX-CARD PACER

4.1 PRACTICE FOR TIP 2, "TRUST YOUR SENSE OF CLOSURE": KEY-WORD READING—FUNCTION WORDS DELETED

Read through this excerpt quickly. Can you comprehend it?

> *Chapter 4 continues theme Chapter 3: proficient reader develop different techniques, speed, different tasks. This chapter, What Why very different Chapter 3. First of two chapters teaching speeded reading. Practices, Selections timed. Not read ahead, ignore directions. Learn rationale speeded reading, cautions, variety methods. Some, you adopt.*

This paragraph uses only 47 of the original 116 words, yet the content is probably quite clear. The last sentence required only 3 key words of the original 10 words!

Now try key-word reading in an article you have never read before:

> *Xeriscape not mean desertscape, or landscape style. Formal or naturalistic; forest or desert. Limited only by imagination. Nor only grays, beiges. Oak woodland perfect example natural xeriscape, adapted local climate yet green, attractive year-round. Many surprised; typical xeriscape boldly textured, colorful.*

In this tightly written factual article, we have managed to cut the original 83 words down to 41 key words. Again, you probably had little difficulty comprehending the writer's ideas.

Now try key-word marking. On your own, try to read only key words, not function words or those inessential to the main content. Turn back to page 125 in this chapter.

1. Start reading the paragraph beginning "However . . ." as rapidly as you can, underlining only the key words. Don't worry about being precise; be relaxed and confident that your sense of closure is as good as any other English-speaking reader's!
2. Continue for several paragraphs, picking up speed if you can.
3. Then pause, go back, and silently read *only* the marked words.

4. If working with a group, read your version to others to check against serious omissions or distortions. (Minor differences in key words are to be expected and accepted.)

If you managed to delete most of the inessential words, and you or a listener could comprehend the writer's ideas from your key-word version, you have done the exercise correctly.

For best effect on your slow reading rate, do this kind of practice daily and in timed competition with other readers. Remember to emphasize *speed* over 100 percent agreement.

4.2 PRACTICE FOR TIP 3, "USE YOUR EYES EFFICIENTLY": SOFT FOCUS AND SHORTENED MARGINS

For this Practice, you should have an easy-to-moderate paperback book. (You may also substitute earlier pages in this chapter, but please do not use any materials still ahead in the book!)

When you try to soft focus, relax your facial and eye muscles as you read a page of print. Imagine that your eyes are tired or that you're on vacation at the beach; you simply can't peer closely at every word. Yet you're curious about the story, viewpoint, or information before you. Some people find it helpful to look slightly above the line of print (soft focusing on the space above, or "space-reading"). Try letting your eyes drift down a page of this book or a paperback book. Keep in mind that it's okay to miss some words or details.

When you use shortened margins, you are also trying to avoid eyestrain by letting your peripheral vision do some of the work.

1. Bring out your paperbook again—or use an earlier page in this book. With a pencil and ruler (or steady hand), draw a vertical line down both sides of the page, a half inch or less in from the margin.
2. Then begin to read from the top of the page. Consciously relax your facial and eye muscles. Try to soft focus as you read down the page. Try not to fixate (look carefully) outside your two vertical lines. (If you do, simply pull back and read the line again, fixating as often as needed but only between the two lines.) Do try to let your eyes float or drift down the page. Let your mind see the action, get the thoughts. Don't worry about comprehension at this point. It will pick up later, as you become accustomed to reading more rapidly.
3. Read the page several times this way; try to increase your speed, from 1 minute down to half a minute.
4. Move onto the next page—you may have memorized the first one already! Mark the shortened-margin lines, remind yourself to soft focus, and practice again.

Spend at least 5 to 10 minutes in each session. You will find these new eye-use techniques become more comfortable each time you do them. Soon you won't need to draw margin lines; your eyes will handle each line efficiently without conscious direction.

Some readers with good peripheral vision eventually fixate an inch or more inside the margins; they read a page in a relaxed meander or zig-zag down the page, at 600–800 wpm; and they can still recite nearly all the content of the page! Others are happy if they learn to read at 400 wpm without headaches.

4.3 PRACTICE FOR TIP 5, "USE TIME PRESSURE": PAGE-BY-PAGE TIMING

1. Bring out a paperback book again, making sure it is fairly easy fiction or non-fiction. Sit near a watch or clock that has a second hand.
2. Prepare your mind for the "reading mode": If the book is new, read one or two pages carefully without timing. If you are currently reading the book, turn back to a page you have already read.
3. When the second hand is on the minute, start reading from the top of the page. When the minute is up, stop reading.

Did you finish the entire page? If not, start at the top again; read the same page, this time within 1 minute. If you still cannot finish the page, try again, this time reminding yourself to soft focus and shorten the margins. Depending on the density of the print, a 1-minute pace should yield from 350 to 450 wpm, a reasonable goal for beginning rapid readers.

4. Now move to the top of the next page. Repeat the 1-minute timing down the page. Start at the top of a new page whenever the signal is given. Important: If you have not finished the page, do not continue reading to the end after the minute is up! Always skip to the top of the new page. Soon you will be so determined not to miss the ending of a page that you will pressure yourself to reach it in time. Eventually the pace will seem almost normal, and you will comprehend most of what was on the page. In other words, your brain has speeded up to grasp the content; you are now an alert and active reader!

Remember, though, that readers are individuals. Success arrives fairly soon for some readers, for others only after many sessions, discouragements, and encouragements.

Any speed demons who finish before time has sounded must wait for the signal to begin a new page. If this happy state continues, they can switch to half-minute timing—thus doubling their rate to 700 to 900 wpm. Such a rate in light, general reading should be gratifying to anyone.

Suppose, though, that you still have trouble reading one page per minute or keeping your mind on the book.

5. Optional. Try using your finger as a pacing device. When the clock's second hand is on the minute, draw your finger smoothly down the middle of the page. Read the print one or two lines above your finger. To make sure you do not fixate on margins, use very little side motion (a slight wiggle is permissible). Just allow your finger to draw your (soft-focused) eyes down from line to line. Continue reading down the page even if you feel your

comprehension is lagging. Only by repeatedly forcing yourself to read at this pace will you reach the 1-minute-per-page rate.

Always remember that in any pacing or charting program, you must not allow yourself extra time. Without a sense of time pressure, you will simply revert to your old slow, careful, passive habits.

In their rapid-reading practice, some students use several methods at once. That is, they first draw shortened-margin lines down several pages, then go back and time their reading of each page, all the while using a finger to pace steadily down the center. Others preview skim ahead for 5 to 10 pages for general structure, then go back and time each page. Is that cheating? Absolutely not. Whatever works to increase your rate is legal.

One last note: if you want to know your typical words-per-minute rate in your current book, count the number of words printed on three separate, average-looking pages, and then take the average of those three counts.

4.4 PRACTICE FOR TIP 6, "USE A CRUTCH": INDEX CARD

Choose any plain card, preferably no larger than the print portion of your book page. Rest your hand comfortably on it. Starting at the top of a page, draw the card down over your reading; that is, you will be reading below the card. Do not hold the card *under* your reading because you could then regress easily!

You are allowed to pause for a moment to let your thoughts catch up, but never move the card and peek to see what you missed. In fact, you may have to take The Pledge: "I will not lift the card. Anything I have missed is lost forever." The psychological gimmick here is that, if you know you must read under your card, you will move it down at a realistic and steady pace—and will keep your mind on your reading.

As usual, remember to use soft focus (but an alert, aggressive mind!) and shortened margins. Some students draw short lines up from the bottom edge on their cards to correspond with the shortened-margin areas of the page. These little lines continuously remind them not to fixate outside, on the empty margins. Other students prefer to draw the usual lines directly on each page, at least at the beginning. Eventually, you may be among those who do their best and fastest light reading using only their eyes and brains.

Now try the index-card technique on your paperback book. After a few pages, begin to add 1-minute timing per page.

Here are some general points drawn from years of reader experience about any method designed to increase rate:

1. Don't give up easily. It took years for you to develop your present reading methods, and it will take more than a few days to change them.
2. When you practice a new technique, continue the session for at least a half hour to an hour.
3. Practice your new methods frequently—once a day if possible.

4. Practice over several weeks or months. Don't expect a weekend seminar or a short course to change your reading habits for life.
5. Check your reading rate in general materials (magazines, paperback books) once a year. All of us slip downward if we stop pressuring ourselves. But after this book, you will know how to time yourself and apply some pressure and a few tricks, to regain your former speed.
6. Don't worry if you sometimes choose to read slowly, carefully, and most inefficiently! That is your right and, sometimes, your duty. But after this course, you will also know how to vary your technique and your rate if the What and the Why—and the time available to you—are appropriate for rapid reading.

Try all the methods presented here. Some readers end up preferring one, some another. It doesn't matter which method you adopt, as long as you always remember that the hardest part of reading does not take place in the eyes, hand motions, or page turning. It takes place in that complicated "device" of ours—the brain.

TIMED SELECTIONS: RAPID READING

The ten timed selections in this chapter and the ten in Chapter 5, Overview Skimming, may be done in class with an instructor or outside of class on your own. In either case, be sure to follow the step-by-step instructions carefully. Please do not skip any step or change the order.

First, *do not preread any selection.* This is a hard rule to follow, especially for people like us who love to read anything and everything, and the more casually the better! But we are trying to help you change your reading habits, and that means setting up a rigorous pattern for you to follow, from first glance at the material to the last bit of close reading. If you have already read a selection your own way, your methods will not change and your words-per-minute rates and comprehension scores will be meaningless.

Second, *time yourself precisely, to the nearest quarter-minute (fifteen seconds).* We indicate the times required to reach preview-skimming or rapid-reading rates, and you should always try to stay within them. If on a first try your time is less or more than ours, find your wpm rate in the rate table at the back of the book. Knowing your exact rate is essential to building reading speed and proficiency.

Finally, *don't preread the quizzes, and don't refer back to a selection while you answer the questions.* Trust that our questions will not be tricky or ask for more knowledge than can be expected of an average preview, rapid read, or overview skim. (Of course, you are welcome to reread any material afterward, any way you choose.)

Any unusual vocabulary words will be defined at the outset. Target scores to aim for in comprehension quizzes are marked with an arrow ▶. Notice that the preview questions are so reasonable that we expect you to get 100 percent on them! For the reading quizzes, however, a score of 70–80 percent is the accepted sign of success.

Answers to odd-numbered selection quizzes are given on page 338. Answers to even-numbered selection quizzes are not provided; please ask your instructor for those. You may check your preview quiz answers immediately, with the key on page 338. However, most students prefer to wait and check them along with the reading quiz answers.

RAPID READING SELECTIONS

1. "Touring by Model T" 928 words
2. "Just an Overheard Plea" 774 words
3. "Seminarians Live Among the Flock in East L.A." 898 words
4. "Helping Patients Control the Pain" 1,112 words
5. "I Recently Came Across . . ." 939 words
6. "Trapped in a Musical Elevator" 1,343 words

7. "The Memory Puzzle" 952 words
8. "At Your Service" 1,934 words
9. "What If Women Ruled the World" 1,178 words
10. "Ordeal in the Winter Woods" 1,746 words

SELECTION 1

"Touring by Model T" *by Glen G. McNeley 928 words*

Your first timed selection for rapid reading is an easy but enjoyable account of a favorite American pastime. The vocabulary is familiar or is made clear by the context. We have marked some key words and sentences for you with italics. You won't have time to read them all in your preview, but do use them when you return to rapid read.

Follow these steps in reading this article:

1. Preview skim the article.
2. Answer the three-item preview quiz.
3. Read the article rapidly.
4. Answer the five-item reading quiz.

A. Preview Skimming

Preview the article in 30 seconds (= 1,856 wpm). In this short time, get a "map of the territory"—focus on the title, the source, any subtitle, any lead-in, any subheadings within the article, and possibly the ending. If you have time to glance at paragraph beginnings, do that, too. Then take the preview quiz. Remember: Don't look ahead to the questions. Also, when you take the quiz, don't look back at the article.

TOURING BY MODEL T

by Glen G. McNeley

1 *Cousin Hale and I left Des Moines, Iowa, on November 29, 1921 in a Model T Ford. Destination: California.*

2 We chose a *Southern route* for its kinder winter camping weather. There were few motels, and anyway, we weren't well-heeled. We had a few blankets, a makeshift tent, cooking supplies and *four weeks* to make the trip.

3 We traveled mostly by day. The Model T headlights were weak and burned out if we revved the engine. So we soon learned to stop wherever darkness overtook us. It made for some unusual campsites.

4 The *roads through Iowa* weren't bad as dirt roads go. We had, for the most part, left paved roads behind in Des Moines. The little Ford

chugged doggedly up and down the ungraded hills and when conditions were good, we made 10 miles an hour.

5   Somewhere in *Missouri* the rains overtook us and the going got rough. The worst roads were the stretches of "corduroy," logs placed crosswise in the swampiest areas. Some had settled while others had washed away completely, leaving great gaps. The jolting was so bad at times it seemed the Ford would shake apart.

6   But once through the swampy area, Missouri slid by and *Oklahoma loomed ahead*. Two things I remember most about that state were the rich red soil (mighty slippery when wet) and the braided, Stetsoned Indians in their Cadillacs. The oil boom was in full swing and many of the Indians were royally rich. As for the soil, we carried souvenirs of it on our mud spatters all the way to California.

7   It was *in Texas* that we heard our first coyote. We were sleeping in the open and I awoke to what sounded like the yapping of a hundred of them. I reared up, grabbed the hand axe, and waved it over my head shouting. Hale awoke then, too, and we laughed when we realized there was only one. We soon grew accustomed to the coyotes' nightly serenade, and developed a friendly feeling toward them.

8   Near Dallas we found a tourist camp that was the temporary quarters of a traveling vaudeville troupe. We stayed there an extra day because the troupe put on shows at the nightly bonfire.

9   As we traveled through *southern Texas*, the roads grew less traveled. Although called the "Southern National Highway," in places it was merely parallel tread marks with grass growing in between.

10   It got worse *in New Mexico*. The sharp, rocky surfaces chewed up our tires, which were of miserable quality anyway in those days. We carried four or five spares.

11   Discarded tires lined the worst roads and occasionally, too, you'd see an abandoned car. Abandoned cars were considered by passing motorists to be fair game and most of them were stripped bare for spare parts.

12   We passed on *into Arizona* and found some of the roads made by Mother Nature herself. They were simply dry stream beds called arroyos. All man had done was to roll the larger rocks aside. It was down one arroyo and up over its steep bank to another just like it. The road on the flat area in between was often a series of parallel tracks. When one path got full of chuck holes, someone started another alongside.

13   As the terrain grew more barren, we saw more and more wildlife: fat sage hens; jack rabbits with black ears and tails; road runners, those long-legged birds that run with such awkward and startling speed; and of course, the coyote, who flaunted his tail derisively as he ran ahead of us.

14   We also had visits from other human beings. Sometimes our nightly campfires attracted wayfarers, such as the cowboy who stopped for a chat while his horse rested, the carnival barker who showed us how to make gypsy bread in the hot coals and ashes, or the hobo with stories from 20 years on the road.

15   *Finally, three weeks into the trip, we reached the California border*. We crossed the muddy Colorado by cable-drawn ferry to face 100 miles of the dreaded Mojave Desert.

16   We traversed it at night, by moonlight so bright we had no need of headlights. The Mojave belied its reputation and proved easy traveling. The sand was just deep enough so that the winding ruts held the car on course without our steering.

17   On the other side of the desert was the aptly named town of *Mecca and paved roads*. We were back in civilization. That meant an increase in traffic—more passenger cars and our first sight of really big freight trucks, still unknown to Midwest highways. Then we hit San Bernardino and *the California we'd imagined*—orange groves, monkey-tailed palms and fields of grape vines.

18   *The old roads are gone now and the new superhighways are a wonderful convenience*. My young neighbor boasts of speeding across the country

on vacations to California because, he says, *"There's nothing much to see till you get there."*

19   *Well, we didn't find it so.* To us it was the adventure of a lifetime. Once, only recently, traveling one of the new highways, I believe I caught a fleeting glimpse of the old road. You might see it, too, if you look hard enough. To the side of the highway you might see an abandoned two-lane road. If you look beyond that you might see a third road, the old dirt road that wound its natural course through river valleys and over ungraded hills. It's the road that accommodated itself to the natural terrain. *It's our road, the road of adventure and enchantment.*   4:30

Glen G. McNeley, "Touring by Model T," *Modern Maturity*, October–November 1985, p. 8. Reprinted by permission.

• •

1. What are the source and the year? Is the date significant in this case? (Yes or No)
2. Do you think this is a fictional story or a true-life (nonfiction) article? How can you tell?
3. The writer's route stretched from:
   a. coast to coast.
   b. Iowa to California.

Sel. 1 P-Skim	**1. Source:** _____
Time :30 = 1,856 wpm	**Year:** _____
Score _____ %	_____
▶ **100%**	**2.** _____
Score = number correct × 33.	**3.** _____
	Check answers on p. 338, or check answers after the next quiz.

Are you curious about this early trip in a Model T? If so, go back now and read for details. As you probably noticed, the overall organization is strongly spatial-geographic, so try to visualize the route and the varied landscapes. A little American geography would help, too!

B. Rapid Reading

Write your starting time in the next answer box, or wait for the signal to begin reading. When you finish reading, write your finishing time, or ask for your total time. Try to read all of the article in 1-1/2 minutes (= 619 wpm) or in 2 minutes (= 464 wpm). Leave the 2-1/2 minute rate (= 371 wpm) or slower for sissies.

1. This trip was taken in:
    a. 1910.
    b. 1921.
    c. 1931.

2. How long did it take from start to finish?

3. In spite of all the troubles, the old Model T Ford made it all the way.
    a. true
    b. false

4. Which one of the following states is *not* mentioned in the paragraphs of description?
    a. Arkansas
    b. Oklahoma
    c. Texas
    d. Arizona

5. The writer ends his little travelogue with:
    a. praise for modern superhighways.
    b. regret for the old, adventurous road.
    c. praise for modern, air-conditioned cars.

Sel. 1 R-Read   1. _____

Finish _____ : _____   2. _____

Start _____ : _____   3. _____

Time _____ : _____   4. _____

      min   sec   5. _____

Rate _____ wpm   **Check answers to both quizzes**

Find rate on p. 330.   **on p. 338.**

Score _____ %   **Record rate and score on p. 183.**

   ▶ **80%**

Score = number correct x 20.

Did you answer all the preview questions correctly? Did you get at least 80 percent on the reading quiz? Were you able to read the entire article at 400 wpm or faster? If so, congratulations—you are doing very well!

If not, take time out now to practice a few speeded techniques on the article. Push yourself to preview within 30 seconds. Push yourself to read the entire piece in 1-1/2 minutes. Draw half-inch lines in from both margins for shortened margins. Try using, in turn, an index card, your finger, and your hand. Let your eyes float down the lines with soft focus. Repeat the technique until you complete the article within 90 seconds. Don't move to longer and more difficult selections until you are fairly comfortable with the rapid reading rate and method.

C. Questions for Discussion and Writing

The timed selections in Rapid Reading and Overview Skimming will be followed by two to four questions that are neither timed nor based on recall (memory) of the reading. Rather, you should reread the selection or refer back to it as needed. Follow directions carefully, or see your instructor for further guidance.

1. In paragraph 18, McNeley quotes a young neighbor who says, "There's nothing much to see till you get there [California]." Why do you think McNeley includes this remark?

2. Glance over the article. Besides the obvious geographic organization, what is another major pattern throughout?

3. The last two paragraphs have a third kind of organization—compare-contrast—which produces the nostalgic tone of the ending. Jot down (single words or phrases, not sentences) the pluses and minuses of auto travel, 1921 versus the 1980s, as McNeley sees them. How might you organize your four lists?

• •

SELECTION 2

"Just an Overheard Plea" *by Rich Seeley 774 words*

Here is a human-interest story by a staff writer of a local newspaper. It is touching enough to warrant a second, slower reading. However, a rapid reading probably will make the incident more real and dramatic to a reader than a slow reading. In any case, read it rapidly here: Visualize the setting and the action, hear the man's voice, empathize with the listener.

(We have combined some of the very short, newspaper-style paragraphs into longer paragraphs to conform better to the textbook format.)

Follow these steps in rapid reading this selection:

1. Preview skim the story.
2. Answer the three-item preview quiz.
3. Read the story rapidly.
4. Answer the five-item quiz.

A. Preview Skimming

Your first step, as always, is to preview skim. You can probably check the piece for source, length, topic, and writing pattern in 30 seconds (= 1,550 wpm). Do not peek at the questions first!

JUST AN OVERHEARD PLEA

by Rich Seeley

1   The muffled voice in the Santa Monica Library made me look up from the pages of a John Updike story called "The Happiest I've Ever Been."

2   At first I thought I was hearing a dramatic recording turned up too loud. It might have been a tragic movie soundtrack. It was not loud enough to be clear, and yet it was too loud to ignore. It was a man's voice with a terrible sobbing plea in it.

3   I suspect the Santa Monica Public Library is not a place where terrible sobbing pleas are often heard.

4   "Please take me back . . . ," the voice said. "I know I don't deserve it, but please . . . please take me back."

5   I looked around the main reading room and didn't see the person who went with the voice. Other readers were looking around, too. The voice was too muffled to be in the same room with us; it had to be coming from behind a door. I suppose many of us were curious and yet trying to ignore it at the same time.

6   There was no answering voice. Whoever this distraught man was pleading with seemed to be speaking very quietly. Perhaps the other person was trying to calm the man down.

7   There would be silence for a minute or two, and then the man would repeat his plea: "Please, please, please, I'll try to do better. I promise, I promise. I will try, just please . . ."

8   Curiosity got the better of me, and I put John Updike under my arm and got up to search for the voice. I walked in the direction where it got louder. It wasn't far.

9   The voice was coming from a rather large man, speaking into the pay phone near the checkout desk. Through the glass doors that separate the lobby from the main reading room, I could see his face was red, and his cheeks were wet with tears.

10   Here I must let you down.

11   I am not the sort of reporter who can casually eavesdrop on someone's personal crisis. Nor am I the sort of human being who can go to a perfect stranger in trouble and offer words of aid and comfort. So I avoided the situation as the other library visitors avoided the situation.

12   Soon the man hung up the phone, and I did not hear the pleading voice any more.

13   But I was haunted by it. As I walked back through the Santa Monica Mall, I could hear it over and over again. "Please take me back—I know I was wrong . . . I know you don't have to . . . but please, please, please . . ."

14   Walking along, trying to sort through the troubling confusion I felt over the voice in the library, I came to conclusions which did not make me feel any better. I no longer trust conclusions that do make me feel better.

15   In a bad time, Zenobia once wrote me a letter in which she referred to what she called "my determinedly happy life." The phrase stuck in my head because we both knew we had been pretty unhappy children. She had compensated for it by a determination to be happy; I by a determination to be funny. As a result our lives were, by turns, poignant and pathetic. We did our best to deny our pain, and we paid for it with more pain.

16   I don't know if Zenobia is still determined to be happy. But I am no longer determined to be funny.

17   What the pleading voice in the library reminded me was that life is not always happy or funny; too many times it is not happy or funny at all.

18   The expectation of the advertising-dominated society we live in is that we can easily find happiness if we buy the right candy bar, love if we use the right deodorant soap, and friendship if we serve the right wine.

19   People who are smarter than I am know that the television commercials are just lies told to sell candy bars and soap and beer. I had to hear that troubled voice in the library to know that whatever crisis this man faced—the loss of love, the loss of a job—it was beyond the reach of retail products.

20   When we feel most lonely, there is always someone we want to call, someone we want to plead with, some place we want to be taken back to, a place where we can be happy forever.

21   And there is a great emptiness when we realize there is ultimately no one we can call with any reasonable hope of finding happiness.

22   Out of that great emptiness, I am told, some people find faith.

3.00

Rich Seeley, "Just an Overheard Plea," *Evening Outlook*, Santa Monica, Calif., August 27, 1984. Reprinted by permission.

• •

1.   The form of this piece is mainly:
    a.   personal essay.
    b.   informational and factual.

2.   Seeley opens the piece with:
    a.   details of the episode.
    b.   his general theme or main idea.

3.   He overheard the plea:
    a.   in a public library.
    b.   on a college campus.

Sel. 2 P-Skim	**1.** _____
Time :30 = 1,550 wpm	**2.** _____
Score _____ - %	**3.** _____
▶ **100%**	**Check answers after the next**
Score = number correct × 33.	**quiz.**

What questions did the preview raise in your mind? Are you curious about the man and his plea? Are you ready to read the story for a clearer understanding of the main idea and for the details supporting that idea?

B. Rapid Reading

Write your starting time in the next answer box, or wait for the signal to begin your rapid reading. In either case, do not peek at the quiz. Expect to finish reading the entire story in less than 2 minutes, since 2:00 would mean a rate of 388 wpm—not quite up to minimum rapid reading (400 wpm). Try for 1 minute (= 775 wpm), 1:15 (= 620 wpm), or 1:30 (= 517 wpm). Remember to aim for about 80 percent of the content, not 100 percent.

Finally, record the time when you finish reading. Then answer the quiz without looking back at the story.

1. Overhearing the man on the telephone leads Seeley to the basic truth that:
    a. life is often very unhappy.
    b. we can help each other in time of need.

2. He further supports this insight by referring to:
    a. "lies" told by advertising.
    b. his own views of life and those of his friend Zenobia.
    c. both *a* and *b*.

3. The man on the telephone is begging for forgiveness from:
    a. a wife or girlfriend.
    b. an employer.
    c. an unknown person—it is never clear.

4. Seeley still believes, with his friend Zenobia, that a person should try to conquer life's pain by striving to be funny, happy, and so on.
    a. true
    b. false

5. In the very last sentence, Seeley strikes a note of:
    a. pessimism—life is neither happy nor funny.
    b. pessimism—no one is "out there" to make us happy.
    c. guarded optimism—out of this knowledge, some of us find faith.

Sel. 2 R–Read

Finish _____ : _____

Start _____ : _____

Time _____ : _____
         min   sec

Rate _____ wpm

Find rate on page 330.

Score _____ %

▶ **80%**

Score = number correct **×** 20.

1. _____
2. _____
3. _____
4. _____
5. _____

Check answers to both quizzes with your instructor.

Record rate and score on p. 183.

Once again, if you could not finish reading the article in the maximum time for rapid reading (less than 2 minutes), go back and push through it several times until you do finish. Use all of the strategies for faster reading that you learned in the Introduction to this chapter.

C. Questions for Discussion and Writing

1. Quickly reread the first two-thirds of the article (paragraphs 1-14). Then, determine what organizational pattern Seeley was using in this section. What sentence in paragraph 14 signals that Seeley is going to change both pattern and major focus? Can you label the writing pattern he now uses?

2. One of Seeley's insights is that some ways of coping with life's sorrows just don't work. What three approaches does he mention? What is wrong with each one?

3. What steps does Seeley go through in developing insight into the meaning or impact of this "overheard plea"? List the steps chronologically, from his first awareness of the man to the last sentence of the selection. (The number of steps and how they are worded will vary.)
    a. Hears troubled voice on phone in library—is curious
    b.
    c.
    d.
    e.
    f.

. . . .

SELECTION 3

"Seminarians Live Among the Flock in East L.A." *by Elenita Ravicz 898 words*

This is a so-called feature article from a daily newspaper. Unlike straight news stories, the feature's interest is not limited to this day's paper, but, of course, the details are current, to the date of the paper.

By now you are well aware of the short paragraph length common to newspapers—adapted to the narrow columns of print. (Features and editorials, however, may use wider columns and, therefore, longer paragraphs.) Many of these paragraphs are too short to have topic sentences, main ideas, or real development. Except for that oddity, however, newspapers are usually ideal for rapid reading.

Follow these steps in rapid reading this newspaper article:

1. Preview skim the article.
2. Answer the three-item preview quiz.
3. Read the article rapidly.
4. Answer the five-item reading quiz.

A. Preview Skimming

Preview the article in about 20 seconds (= 2,694 wpm).

SEMINARIANS LIVE AMONG THE FLOCK IN EAST L.A.

by Elenita Ravicz

Casa Guadalupe Urges Students to Mingle with the Community

1   As a probation officer, Gerry Leonard-Doblado saw his share of drug dealers. Now that he's living in an East Los Angeles seminary, he sees them daily.

2   As Father Leonard, a priest for more than five years, he says that the pushers are part of the scenery near Casa Guadalupe, the small Catholic seminary he directs.

3   Founded eight years ago, the seminary, which is run by the Society of the Divine Word, a missionary order, was the first to be housed in the barrio area of Los Angeles.

4   It represents an increasingly popular concept in seminaries, encouraging those studying for the priesthood to mix with the community rather than be apart from it.

USUALLY ISOLATED

5   "At traditional seminaries, the students are usually isolated from the community. If they want to get to people, they go away for the weekend," Father Leonard said.

6   "We don't need to do that, the world is outside our door. There are dopers and alcoholics on the corner and, if we need to see the hungry, we can go around the corner.

7   "Living here gives students a more realistic sense of the priesthood. They do volunteer work in nearby elementary schools, at the L. A. County general hospital (County-USC Medical Center) and with Ministry Hall (where juveniles are kept while awaiting trial).

8   "They also go to Cal State L.A. and East L.A. City College to get a secular education and work part time to earn money to pay their way.

9   "When we opened here in 1976, we were the first in the area," Father Leonard added, "but this type of seminary is becoming a trend.

10   "The Maryknollers, Benedictines and others have talked to us about founding projects like ours. In fact, since we opened, five similar programs have moved into this area."

11   Father Leonard explained that the seminary tries to base itself "in the Hispanic culture since that's the type of area we're in, but, two years ago, our order opened a similar seminary in New Orleans with an emphasis on black students."

12   The dropout rate in seminaries is especially high among blacks and Latinos, according to Father Leonard.

13   "This is serious because, of the 60,000 priests in America, only about 600 are Hispanic, and yet they're saying that, by the year 2000, Hispanics will be the largest minority in the Catholic Church," the priest said.

14   "Priests need to be especially sensitive to the cultural needs and realities of the people they serve because everything is becoming multicultural now. Without this adjustment, we will become an ineffective church."

15   Father Leonard says that although Casa Guadalupe has a few Anglo students, the majority are Latino and come from all over America as well as from Chile, Mexico, Nicaragua and El Salvador. There are five to 10 students in residence at a time.

16   Instead of wearing the traditional black robes and collar of a priest, Father Leonard had on dark pants, a matching shirt and a V-necked sweater when interviewed.

17   Housed in two small buildings, Casa Guadalupe's facilities consist of 16 rooms, including an office, kitchen, chapel, laundry room and bedrooms.

18   While the white walls of one house are decorated with a god's-eye (a weaving of colorful

threads over a cross of wood), a small cross and several wooden figures, the other features crowded bookshelves and torn carpeting.

19   He said of the seminary, "I share residency here with another priest, anywhere from five to 10 students a year, the roaches and the 1920s plumbing and wiring."

20   Unlike most traditional seminaries, the students at Casa Guadalupe cook, clean and do maintenance work on their buildings.

130 STUDENTS IN EIGHT YEARS

21   Leonard, who is also chairman of the Firehouse Food Project, said that about 130 students, most of them college-age, have attended the seminary in the last eight years.

22   The students stay at Casa Guadalupe for four years, getting a secular degree from a local college, receiving religious instruction from Leonard and having the responsibility of a ministry—doing community service at a local school, hospital or other institution.

23   After leaving the seminary, the students have another five years of study ahead of them at the order's novitiate in Bay St. Louis, Miss., before they can become priests.

24   Leonard said that Casa Guadalupe, which has a budget of $70,000 a year, gets the money from its order, from what the students earn at their part-time jobs and from donations.

25   "We try to live at the same economic level as the people around us," he said. "We get no funding from the archdiocese although we have their blessing."

26   The seminary also seems to have the blessing of families in the neighborhood.

27   "Casa Guadalupe is the spirit of the community," East Los Angeles native Casimiro Echeverria said. "They sponsor a lot of events and programs that are important to the community.

28   "We go over there often and for the last four years my wife and I have been trying to help them out with food and things."

29   The seminary sponsors numerous community events, including a tree-trimming party before Christmas that attracted more than 300 people last year and an outdoor service to commemorate the Feast of Our Lady of Guadalupe, patron saint of the seminary. Religious classes for the students at Casa Guadalupe are open to the community.

30   Leonard said that the seminary also holds a neighborhood street party every spring featuring mariachi music and food prepared by people in the area.

Elenita Ravicz, "Seminarians Live Among the Flock in East L.A.," *Los Angeles Times*, February 25, 1985. Copyright, 1985, Los Angeles Times. Reprinted by permission of the author.

• •

1.   The article has a title, a lead-in (summary at beginning), and two subheads within the article.
   a.   true
   b.   false

2.   This is a(n):
   a.   feature article.
   b.   straight news story.
   c.   editorial.

3.   In what year was it published? Is the exact date—month and day—important?

Sel. 3 P-Skim	1. _____
Time :20 = 2,694 wpm	2. _____
Score ____ %	3. **Year:** _____
▶ **100%**	_____
Score = number correct x 33.	**Check answers after the next quiz.**

B. Rapid Reading

Now write your starting time in the next box, or wait for the signal to read. You must read all the details in about 2 minutes to qualify for the title of Rapid Reader!

1. The title and lead-in summarize the main idea quite well.
    a. true
    b. false

2. The seminary is small but tasteful, a tiny island of beauty amid the poverty of East Los Angeles.
    a. true
    b. false

3. Seminary students:
    a. attend Catholic colleges in the area.
    b. attend public colleges in the area.
    c. do community service.
    d. get religious instruction from Father Leonard.
    e. all except *a*.

4. The concept of a community-based seminary:
    a. is becoming popular in the Catholic Church.
    b. is unique to Casa Guadalupe.

5. The ending stresses:
    a. the students' next five years at a novitiate.
    b. the seminary's close ties with its neighbors in East Los Angeles.

Sel. 3 R-Read	1. _____
Finish _____ : _____	2. _____
Start _____ : _____	3. _____
Time _____ : _____	4. _____
min sec	5. _____

Rate _____ wpm
Find rate on page 330.
Score _____ %
▶ 80%
Score = number correct × 20.

Check answers to both quizzes
on p. 338.
Record rate and score on p. 183.

C. Questions for Discussion and Writing

1. Reread the article. Then write a paragraph describing Casa Guadalupe. Include who its members are, what its functions are, and how it differs from traditional seminaries. Use specific details from the article, and use your own wording.

2. Two organizational patterns are working in this article: thesis-support and description. What is the thesis of the article? What kinds of details support the thesis? What parts are purely descriptive?

3. Can you tell how the writer feels about Casa Guadalupe? If so, what evidence do you find? If not, what details are missing that would indicate her attitude?

. . . .

SELECTION 4

"Helping Patients Control the Pain" *by Ann Japenga 1,112 words*

This is another feature article. It is about an unpleasant subject we have all had some experience with: pain. And if you have ever had pain while a patient in a hospital, you will really be interested. Don't forget your soft focus and shortened margins—pain or not, you want to finish within the target times!

Follow these steps in reading this selection:

1. Preview skim the article.
2. Take the three-item preview quiz.
3. Read the article rapidly.
4. Take the five-item reading quiz.

A. Preview Skimming

Naturally, you always start with a preview. Take only 45 seconds (= 1,483 wpm) to notice and read the following: title, subtitle (if any), author, source, date, length, and any subheads inserted into the body of the story. Then take the preview quiz without looking back. Don't preview the questions!

HELPING PATIENTS CONTROL THE PAIN

by Ann Japenga

Self-Sedating Device May Become Norm in Hospitals

It is the only thing in my life I can control.
—A 32-year-old cancer patient talking about self-administered pain medication

[1]   Following back surgery in 1977, Dorothee Triest of Menlo Park felt as though she was on a roller coaster as the pain surged and receded. She never got used to the excruciating wait—that gap between the time when she would press the nurse-call buzzer, and the moment when pain medication was injected and finally began to give relief.

[2]   The worst part, the 62-year-old retired social worker said, was that the pain management was out of her hands.

BACK IN HOSPITAL

[3]   Triest was back in Stanford Hospital last week for a total hip replacement. But this time, when she felt the pain approaching an unacceptable level, she simply reached to her bedside for something that resembles a nurse-call cord. Triest would depress a button, and a buzzer would sound to tell her a dose of pain medication was being released directly into her bloodstream through an attached intravenous line.

[4]   "By doing it yourself, you feel somehow a little more in control of the pain," Triest said in a telephone interview from her hospital bed. "It's not something that's being done to you."

[5]   Leaders in anesthesiology predict that the device Triest was using, called a PCA (patient controlled analgesia) unit, will become the norm for managing pain in post-operative and cancer patients within five years.

[6]   The machine has been shown to reduce patient dependency on nurses, to decrease the amount of medication required, and to enhance post-operative pulmonary recovery. But its major benefit, according to Dr. Paul White, assistant professor of anesthesia at the Stanford University School of Medicine in Palo Alto, is that the device "reduces the anxiety surrounding pain" by putting patients in charge of their own medication.

[7]   While PCA is in use mostly at university-affiliated institutions around the nation, Dr. Ronald Katz, chairman of the Department of Anesthesiology at UCLA, argues that PCA "is not a research issue anymore. We have the technology. We should be using it in hospitals."

[8]   Katz invited 25 leaders in anesthesiology from this and other countries to a meeting this past summer in Aspen, Colo., in order to "stir them up" about PCA.

[9]   "Everyone there had heard of PCA, they had read about it and thought it important," Katz said in an interview at his UCLA office. "It works. Doctors like it. Patients like it. Nurses like it. But it's a hassle (to implement)."

[10]   An impediment to use of the device is widespread physician fear that patients could become dangerously oversedated, or even addict themselves to painkillers if they were allowed to regulate their own drug intake.

[11]   "This is a myth taught in medical school," Katz said. "You don't make addicts of patients (by allowing them access to painkillers). I've been at this (pain management) for 25 years and I've never seen it happen."

[12]   To ensure that a patient would not be able to medicate himself or herself to the point of unconsciousness, a timer built into the unit inactivates the device for a period ranging from five to 10 minutes following a dosage release. Theoret-

ically, a patient could get a dose large enough to interfere with breathing if the machine wasn't working properly. But the risk of serious injury or death to a patient using the machine is almost non-existent, Katz said, because of the built-in safety factors and the fact that nurses and doctors monitor patients who are using the device.

STAYING ALERT

[13] A cancer patient at Stanford commented that PCA allows her to stay alert enough to talk with her parents and friends, while at the same time letting her receive adequate pain relief. That is not the case with nurse-administered analgesia, which often leaves patients groggy. According to a report cited by PCA researcher Dr. Richard Bennett, 48% of those post-op patients receiving analgesia by conventional methods are "grossly sedated."

[14] Bennett said that studies routinely document that pain is seriously mismanaged in more than half of the patients studied who were receiving analgesia by traditional intramuscular means. Part of the problem, according to Katz, is that levels of perceived pain vary so greatly among individuals that it's impossible to set a standard of care that works equally well with all patients.

[15] Katz is of the opinion that doctors are undereducated when it comes to pain. He gives the example of a surgeon at UCLA who claimed he was never able to understand why some patients complained so vigorously following surgery. Then this particular surgeon was operated on himself. "Now I know what they're talking about," the surgeon told Katz. "It (the amount of analgesia) wasn't enough."

[16] The surgeon has since directed his residents to talk to Katz about PCA and about pain management in general. UCLA will soon be getting its first PCA unit, Katz said, which it intends to begin using with cancer patients.

[17] Bennett, who is in private practice in Lexington, Ky., became interested in the PCA device when he observed the typical manner in which pain was treated in the hospital. A patient had to communicate his or her need to a nurse, who was often busy with other demands. It might be 15 minutes or more before a nurse responded to a patient summons. Then the nurse had to get the painkiller from a locked cabinet and make a note in the patient's chart, or perhaps consult with a physician.

[18] After the nurse gave the injection, it could be anywhere from 16 to 90 minutes before the drug took effect. Patient Dorothee Triest said she feels some relief 20 seconds after pushing the button on her PCA unit. (It may still take five to 15 minutes for peak effect, White said.)

[19] The first research on the device was done 15 years ago in this country. Interest flagged because the device was not commercially available, and European researchers picked up the topic.

[20] Bennett was the one to renew interest in PCA in this country when he started doing clinical demonstrations with prototypes of the device five years ago at the University of Kentucky College of Medicine. He said he was contacted almost daily by physicians who wanted to use PCA, but there were no units commercially available until last year.

[21] Hospitals that want to offer patients the PCA option must go to the trouble of purchasing the machines (each PCA unit currently costs $2,000 to $3,000), and obtaining approval from various committees. The operation of the device—which is "the easiest thing in the world," according to patient Triest—also must be explained to patients individually, a task that requires about 20 minutes.

[22] With health care becoming more competitive, Bennett said PCA will become standard, despite the added work for hospital personnel, only if patients begin insisting on it. So instead of buzzing for the nurse after the pain hits, Bennett suggests patients request that a PCA unit be waiting back in their hospital room before the surgeon makes the first cut. 4:00

1. What are the source (name of the newspaper) and the date (year) published? Do you think the date is important in this case? (Explain)

2. The story starts out with a headline, a subtitle, and a quote from a patient.
   a. true
   b. false

3. Two subheads are inserted into the article; neither one was very helpful in determining the main ideas.
   a. true
   b. false

Sel. 4 P-Skim **1. Source:** _____

Time :45 = 1,483 wpm **Year:** _____

Rate _____ wpm **Explain:** _____

▶ **100%** _____

Score = number correct × 33. **2.** _____

3. _____

Check answers after the next quiz.

B. Rapid Reading

Now write your starting time in the rapid-reading box, or wait for the signal to begin reading. When you finish reading, write your finishing time, or ask your instructor for elapsed time. Then immediately answer the reading quiz without looking back.

To qualify for rapid reading, you will have to read the story in 2 minutes (= 556 wpm) or less. If you read faster or slower than 2 minutes, find your exact wpm rate in the rate table at the back of the book.

You may want to try finger pacing down the middle of this article if you have not done it before.

1. The main idea is that a new device for hospital patients is gaining wider acceptance.
   a. true
   b. false

2. The acronym (initial letters) PCA stands for:
   a. "personal care agitron."
   b. "passive centered activator."
   c. "patient controlled analgesia."

3. Use of the new device is being pushed mainly by:
   a. two health-care organizations, Blue Cross and Blue Shield.
   b. two doctors who are quoted several times, Drs. Katz and Bennett.
   c. professional nursing associations.

4. While the device mainly improves patient care, it has one drawback: Patients can easily become addicted to their painkillers.
   a. true
   b. false

5. Which one is *not* a feature of the invention?
   a. Each PCA unit costs $2,000–$3,000.
   b. Patients require a short introduction to its use.
   c. PCAs have so far been used only in European hospitals.
   d. It saves nurses time and trouble.

Sel. 4 R-Read		1. _____
Finish _____ : _____		2. _____
Start _____ : _____		3. _____
Time _____ : _____		4. _____
min sec		5. _____
Rate _____ wpm		**Check answers to both quizzes**
Find rate on p. 330.		**with your instructor.**
Score _____ %		**Record rate and score on p. 183.**
▶ **80%**		
Score = number correct x 20.		

Were you able to preview and read within the prescribed times? More important, were your comprehension scores on target? If your answer to anything is no, go back to the article and try the various strategies for faster reading: shortened margins, soft focus, and use of index card, hand, or fingers.

C. Questions for Discussion and Writing

Reread the article for answers to these questions.

1. Which writing pattern(s) has the author relied on in this feature story? Be able to defend your choice by referring back to the story. Choose from description (of what?), compare-contrast (of what two situations?), time sequence, and definition. Remember that all may be used here and there, but we are asking for the dominant, overall pattern(s).

2. In four or five sentences, summarize this selection in your own words. (a) Write a thesis statement (main idea sentence). (b) Describe the positive features of this "self-sedating device." (c) Describe any negative features.

3. Reread the last paragraph. What does Dr. Bennett say must happen before PCA units become common in hospitals?

SELECTION 5

"I Recently Came Across . . ." *by Jack Smith 939 words*

Vocabulary
kaleidoscope: constantly changing set of colors; "kaleidoscopic individuality"
conglomerate: a corporation made up of many different companies that operate in widely diversified fields; "enormous conglomerates"
automaton: one that behaves in an automatic or mechanical way; "they turn into automatons"

Here is another newspaper selection, a personal essay or opinion piece by a staff columnist. We have combined some of the very short paragraphs in order to adapt to book format.

Since this is the fifth of ten timed selections, you should consider it a halfway point in your rapid-reading progress. Preview skim and rapid read this selection without any introduction or help from us. When you have completed the exercises, read the Midway Evaluation (p. 157) to see how you are doing.

A. Preview Skimming

Preview skim briefly, in about 30 seconds (= 1,878 wpm).

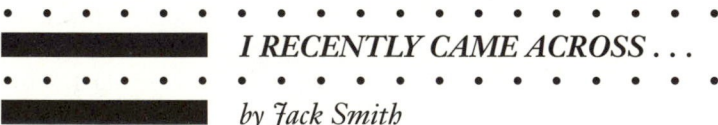

I RECENTLY CAME ACROSS . . .

by Jack Smith

[1]   "I recently came across the following," writes Leslie H. Bennett of Agoura, "and thought you might find it amusing:

[2]   " 'The fearful standardization of this age is making one place so like another that there will be no point soon in leaving home. Architecture, dress and food as prepared by the gigantic hotel combines in their exactly similar restaurants and grill rooms are becoming the same the world over. . . .' "

[3]   What was the source of this complaint, which seems so contemporary? It was in a book called *In Search of Scotland*, written by H. V. Morton and published in 1919. Thus, in a world that I still remember as one of kaleidoscopic individuality, compared with today's, a seasoned traveler was already noticing the creeping disease of our age—standardization.

[4]   Back in the 1920's, long before the low-cost European imports, there were dozens of makes of cars, not merely the Big Three of Detroit. They were so distinctive in design that it was the hobby of most small boys, including me, to know them all by their lines, and to recognize them on sight.

This pastime lightened many a long drive to visit our relatives over the three-lane highways of those days; one called out their names as soon as they came into view. Franklin . . . Grant . . . Essex . . . Hupmobile . . . Chandler . . . Lafayette . . . Peerless . . . Velie . . . Jordan . . . Wills St. Claire . . .

5   We *owned*, that I can remember, a Wills St. Claire, a Franklin, an Oakland, a Graham-Paige, a Terraplane and a Hudson. I myself once owned a Packard.

6   There were hundreds of them. They are all gone now, all but those made by the Big Three and American, and the imports that have come in like the Mediterranean fruit fly.

7   Trying to create the illusion of variety, the Big Three have given us a multitude of names to choose from, with a little face-lifting here and there, but underneath the cosmetics they are pretty much the same car.

8   But people like to believe they have a choice. Remember the outrage a few years ago when people who bought Oldsmobiles found out they had Chevrolet engines in them? Or something like that. I may have the wrong models, but that was the idea. The difference between them was one of image, of memory. People who had been buying Oldsmobiles for generations didn't want to find out that they were really buying Chevrolets, with a slightly different fender line and a different emblem.

9   But the trend has been toward standardization in all things ever since the industrial revolution began. In America it probably began with the Harvey House cafes along the Santa Fe railroad lines. They were familiar, trustworthy oases at the end of a long, dusty ride across the western plains. They offered good food, and pretty waitresses— the famous Harvey Girls—all served and dressed alike. You knew just what to expect. There was even a Harvey House at the Los Angeles Station, an excellent restaurant with a long copper bar that was always crowded three deep during the war. Then came the jet airplane; railroad travel became passé, and the Harvey House closed. It has been defunct for years.

10   What has taken its place? The airport Hiltons, Marriotts, Holiday Inns. They are all over the world, giving the traveler no surprises. One would hardly know whether he is in Los Angeles, Chicago, or London; the service is the same, the lobby is the same, the bill is the same, and you pay with a plastic card.

11   People must like standardization. Everywhere the junk food franchises proliferate. You go to a McDonald's in Torrance, you get exactly the same kind of hamburger you get in Atlantic City, served in exactly the same way. You stand in line, give your order to the cashier, pay and take your order to a table on a tray. Everyone knows how to act. No manners to learn. No tips to leave.

12   A few years ago my wife and I set out to drive to Northern California, taking a leisurely holiday, and attempting to avoid chain motels and restaurants. We found out that you can't do it. They sneak up on you. We went to a restaurant that had once been a favorite of ours, an old-time, independent, individualistic restaurant. I was studying the menu when I noticed down at the bottom that the restaurant now was owned by some giant conglomerate—Coca-Cola, or Gulf Oil, or somebody like that. The changes in its character were subtle, but critical. The old personal touch was gone. The waitresses were homogenized. They said "Enjoy your lunch" and "Have a nice day" with exactly the same distracted inflection as waitresses in Los Angeles.

13   By the time we got to Bakersfield, on our way home, we had given up the game and deliberately went to a Jolly Roger for lunch. At least we knew what to expect.

14   But more and more, every private enterprise is swallowed up by something bigger, and that is swallowed up by something even bigger, until finally everything will be owned by one of a half-dozen enormous conglomerates that are fighting it out for control of the world.

15   It's like in that movie "Invasion of the Body Snatchers," in which these gourds come from space and settle down in a community and one by

one supplant the minds and philosophies of its citizens, so that gradually they turn into automatons, mindlessly repeating the dogmas of the body snatchers. Mindlessly we surrender to the franchises, the chains, the giant conglomerates, which, in the end, tell us where we will sleep, what we will eat, what will entertain us, and how we will look.

Jack Smith, "In a world filled with standardization . . . ," *Los Angeles Times*, March 6, 1985. Copyright, 1985, Los Angeles Times. Reprinted by permission.

• •

1. Title, subtitle, and lead-in—the essay contains only one of those features. Which one is it?

2. What are the source and the year published?

3. What one word is repeated several times and, therefore, is a good clue to the main idea?
    a. change
    b. standardization
    c. game

Sel. 5 P-Skim	1. _____
Time :30 = 1,878 wpm	2. **Source:** _____
Score _____ %	**Year:** _____
▶ **100%**	3. _____
Score = number correct × 33.	**Check answers after the next quiz.**

B. Rapid Reading

Write your starting time in the box, or wait for the signal. Now go back to the article and read rapidly, in 2 minutes (= 470 wpm) or faster. Then take the reading quiz that follows.

1. "Fearful standardization" is the theme not only of Smith's column here but also of a book written in:
    a. about 1920.
    b. about 1940.
    c. about 1960.

2. Which specific set of examples for this theme is *not* used by Smith?
    a. clothing
    b. restaurants
    c. cars

3. Jack Smith lives and writes in Los Angeles, California. Does this fact limit the validity of his thesis?
    a. Yes, it does—he is describing a California phenomenon.
    b. No, it does not—his thesis applies to America as a whole.

4. Smith states that the trend toward standardization is:
   a. fairly recent—it began within the last fifty years.
   b. not so recent—it began in the nineteenth century.

5. According to his last two paragraphs, he thinks the trend:
   a. will be reversed, since people are tiring of so much sameness.
   b. will continue and get worse.

Sel. 5 R-Read   **1.** _____

Finish _____ : _____   **2.** _____

Start _____ : _____   **3.** _____

Time _____ : _____   **4.** _____

        min   sec   **5.** _____

Rate _____ wpm   **Check answers to both quizzes**

Find rate on p. 330.   **on p. 338.**

Score _____ %   **Record rate and score on p. 183.**

  ▶ **80%**

Score = number correct x 20.

C. Midway Evaluation

Time out! Stop and evaluate how well you rapid read this selection. For example, in your preview skim you should have discovered:

1. the source and the date of the article.
2. the title, the lead-in, and the subheads used.
3. the subject matter, the length, and the type of article (news, feature, editorial, humorous column, and so on).

In your rapid reading, you should have determined:

1. Jack Smith's topic or subject.
2. what he means by *standardization* and how he will develop his case (examples).
3. what time period is covered; what many of the examples are.
4. how he ends his piece: with solutions? With hope? With no hope?
5. his style and tone: light? Serious? Scholarly? And so on.

Evaluate how you are doing in general as you read short articles. Do you complete the preview and the reading within the target times? Are your comprehension scores within the target percentages? If you need extra practice before moving on to the rest of the selections, go back to any selection and mark key words, draw shortened margins, and use finger or index card to finish each selection within the time limit but with clear comprehension of the contents.

Selections 6–10 will be somewhat longer, which may help you "hit your stride" more consistently.

D. Questions for Discussion and Writing

1. In your own words, write the main idea or thesis of this selection. Then list four examples that support it.

2. In your own words, write the meaning of the sentence in paragraph 12, "The changes in its character were subtle, but critical." You may have to look up the exact meaning of each word in this context.

3. Reread the ending (the last two paragraphs). Does Smith end on a pessimistic note? Cite details that support your answer.

4. While the dominant pattern is thesis-examples, Smith also includes some compare-contrast—contrasting the past, before the era of galloping standardization, with today. Which paragraphs describe the past? Which paragraph signals the transition from "before" to "after"? (Use paragraph numbers in your answers.)

· · · · · · · · · · · · · · · · · · · ·

SELECTION 6

"Trapped in a Musical Elevator" *by Otto Friedrich 1,343 words*

Vocabulary
metastasis: transmission of disease from an original site to one or more sites elsewhere in the body; "the sound . . . is metastasizing"
omnivorous: eating all kinds of food; "his omnivorous curiosity"

This article says that "Muzak music is not supposed to be consciously heard." Maybe after you read this article, you will listen for it the next time you are in an elevator or a supermarket!

Follow these steps in rapid reading this magazine article:

1. Preview skim the article.
2. Answer the three-item preview quiz.
3. Read the article rapidly.
4. Answer the five-item reading quiz.

A. Preview Skimming

Preview skim this magazine article in 30 seconds (= 2,686 wpm).

TRAPPED IN A MUSICAL ELEVATOR

by Otto Friedrich

1 Yes, this was the year in which Ronald Reagan was re-elected to the White House, but those with a broader historical perspective have other things to commemorate. Like the 400th anniversary of Sir Walter Raleigh's first colony in the New World, the 300th anniversary of the completion of the Hall of Mirrors at Versailles, the 200th anniversary of Mozart's *Marriage of Figaro*, the 100th anniversary of the first volume of the Oxford English Dictionary and the 50th anniversary of Muzak. Muzak? Wouldn't that be like celebrating the first broadcast singing commercial (1924)?

2 The sound of Muzak is, of course, almost everywhere, and metastasizing: in the bank and the supermarket and the office elevator, on the telephone line when the victim has been put on hold. It plays in the White House and the Pentagon; it played during the Olympics; it played in the Apollo XI spaceship that carried Neil Armstrong to the moon. The Muzak Corp., which is now part of Westinghouse, estimates that its recordings are heard by 80 million people every day; they are syndicated in 19 countries; the company and its affiliates take in more than $150 million annually. "Muzak promotes the sharing of meaning," says James Keenan, an industrial psychologist and chairman of the firm's board of scientific advisers, "because it massifies symbolism in which not few but all can participate."

3 But not quite all, Dr. Keenan.

4 "Horrible stuff" was the term once applied by the artist Ben Shahn. "Abominably offensive," said the novelist Vladimir Nabokov. And Philip Glass: "The range of music is truly enormous—opera at the top, Muzak at the bottom." John Cage spoke of composing a piece especially for the tormentors, with no notes in it. "The first step in describing silence is to use silence itself," Cage explained. "Matter of fact, I thought of composing a piece like that. It would be very beautiful, and I would offer it to Muzak." Perhaps Cage had that in mind when he created *4'33"*, which consists of one or more musicians sitting on a stage and not playing their instruments for 4 min. 33 sec.

5 That Muzak should soothe the inhabitants of the Pentagon is fitting, for the whole system was basically the creation of an unusual general, George Owen Squier, a West Pointer ('87) who devoted much of his Army career to science. Assigned to evaluate the military potential in the experiments of the Wright Brothers, he became in 1908 one of the first passengers to fly, for all of nine minutes, in a Wright machine. As a young artilleryman, he invented the polarizing photochronograph to measure the speed of a projectile.

6 On the U.S. entry into World War I, Squier became head of the Signal Corps, and his omnivorous curiosity led to a notable invention: a system for transmitting several messages simultaneously over existing electric power lines. In 1922, nearing retirement, he took his ideas and his patents to the North American Co. utilities combine, which backed him in launching Wired Radio, Inc., a kind of competitor to the booming fad for wireless radio. But not until 1934, the year of his death, did the general think up a catchy new name, combining the sound of music with the sound of the popular camera called the Kodak.

7 The first Muzak recording in 1934 was a medley of *Whispering, Do You Ever Think of Me?* and *Here in My Arms*, performed by Sam Lanin's orchestra. The first customers were householders in the Lakeland section of Cleveland, who were offered, for $1.50 a month, three channels ranging from dance music to news. As a novelty, Muzak might well have gone the way of Sam Lanin's orchestra. But a series of experiments started in the late 1930s provided Muzak with the secret that converted base music into gold.

8   The secret was that music could get more work out of people. Eureka! An early test, conducted at the Stevens Institute of Technology in New Jersey, showed or purported to show that "functional music" in a workplace reduced absenteeism by 88% and early departures by 53%. Other tests produced even richer results. When *The Blue Danube* was piped into a dairy in McKeesport, Pa., the cows gave more milk; recordings inspired chickens to lay more eggs. The coming of World War II made this more than a matter of money: thousands of U.S. factories, arsenals and shipyards were wired for music and increased production by as much as 11%.

9   Muzak is still conducting such tests, and still crowing over the results. At a firm called Precision Small Parts Inc. in Charlottesville, Va., for example, Muzak spent three months last year testing six women who spent their dreary days deburring very small items with dental drills. With Muzak in their ears, they deburred 16.8% more than before. Other tests showed that if music can make people produce more, it can also make them buy more. Sedately paced melodies in a supermarket slowed down customers enough so that they spent 38% more money.

10   Muzak enthusiasts argue that there is a great tradition of music as an accompaniment to work. "It did so in the fields behind the great castles and monasteries of the middle ages," says Keenan. "It did so on shipboard and in the taverns where sailors met to sing their chanteys." Keenan has even unearthed a songbook once issued by a youthful industrial firm, which included a spirited ditty called *Ever Onward Ever Onward*: "Our reputation sparkles like a gem/ We've fought our way through and new/ Fields we're sure to conquer too/ Forever onward IBM."

11   The gentler inspirations that Muzak calls "environmental music" work for several reasons, particularly for people subject to either stress or boredom. Music is soothing. Oddly enough, Muzak even claims that its recordings make workers feel more in control of their environment and more cared for by their employers. Most important, though, is that workers slow down in mid-morning and mid-afternoon, and music can counteract that. Muzak's selections get faster as the workers near those slack periods. The company calls that "stimulus progression."

12   Muzak music is not supposed to be consciously heard. "Once people start listening they stop working," says Muzak's president Tony Hirsh. That is why its songs never have words. But though Muzak has come to seem synonymous with slushy string tones, the company makes a great effort to keep up to date. Its current repertory of 5,000 includes songs by Michael Jackson and the Police, as well as Cyndi Lauper's *All Through the Night*. In fact the company records about 1,000 new hits every year. It makes its selections with the help of a computer and broadcasts the tunes by satellite from Stamford, Conn., to 180 receiving stations around the country.

13   But if Muzak at 50 is so useful and productive and successful and popular (the company says its polls repeatedly show that more than 85% of its customers enjoy what they get), why do some people hate it so passionately? One reason is simply that they believe this system perverts and prostitutes one of life's greatest pleasures, listening to music. And it probably deadens people's ability to enjoy music that they do listen to by choice. And the whole process is coercive. People who did not want to hear radio music pumped into them on Washington buses carried their objections all the way to the Supreme Court, only to have the court rule in 1952 that this invasion of their privacy was not an invasion of their privacy. (Justice William Douglas' dissent reasserted the principle that "the right to be let alone is indeed the beginning of all freedom.") Composer Jacob Druckman is one man who retains a sensitivity to music even when Muzak tells him not to listen. "I grit my teeth whenever I go into an elevator or a restaurant," says he. "With any other medium, you can turn your back or close your eyes, but there's no escape from music."

Otto Friedrich, "Trapped in a Musical Elevator," *Time*, December 10, 1984. Copyright 1984 Time Inc. Reprinted by permission from *Time*. All rights reserved.

1. What are the source and the date (year) of this selection?
2. The title and lead-in tell the reader that the article will cover:
   a. the benefits of Muzak.
   b. the evils of Muzak.
   c. both *a* and *b*.
3. The article was written and published in 1984 because it was Muzak's fiftieth "birthday."
   a. true
   b. false

Sel. 6 P-Skim	**1. Source:** _____
Time :30 = 2,686 wpm	**Date:** _____
Score _____ %	**2.** _____
▶ **100%**	**3.** _____
Score = number correct × 33.	**Check answers after the next quiz.**

Did your preview arouse your interest in Muzak? Do you like or dislike Muzak?

B. Rapid Reading

Write your starting time in the next box, or wait for the signal to begin reading. Then go back to the article and begin reading rapidly. Try to finish in 2-1/2 minutes (= 537 wpm) or less.

1. The overall writing pattern in this article is:
   a. description—of the Muzak system.
   b. compare-contrast—of pre-Muzak to post-Muzak days in the United States.
   c. definition—what is popular music?
2. What percentage of Muzak customers reportedly say they enjoy the selections they are given?
   a. 45 percent
   b. 60 percent
   c. 85 percent
3. Which one group is *not* mentioned as having been soothed by Muzak?
   a. factory workers
   b. cattle and chickens
   c. prison inmates
   d. shoppers
4. It is fitting that Muzak is used in the Pentagon because it was invented by an army private.
   a. true
   b. false

5. Muzak would have faded away as a novelty except for the sudden discovery
    that:
    a. it could be transmitted by wireless radio.
    b. costs could be cut in half.
    c. the music made workers produce more.

Sel. 6 R-Read	1. _____
Finish _____ : _____	2. _____
Start _____ : _____	3. _____
Time _____ : _____	4. _____
min sec	5. _____
Rate _____ wpm	**Check answers to both quizzes**
Find rate on p. 330.	**with your instructor.**
Score _____ %	**Record rate and score on p. 183.**
▶ **80%**	
Score = number correct x 20.	

C. Questions for Discussion and Writing

1. The writer includes both positive and negative features of Muzak. In a well-writ-
    ten sentence, state the main idea of this article. Then scan through the article
    for two details supporting each side. List these details in your own words.

2. As an extension of question 1, do you think the article presents a completely
    even-handed picture—pros and cons—of Muzak? If your answer is yes, reread
    the key position for any argument, the end (the last paragraph). Also reread
    the first sentence of paragraph 2, paying careful attention to every word.

3. Reread paragraphs 6, 7, and 8. What organizational pattern is used in these
    three paragraphs as a unit?

4. Reread the third sentence of the last paragraph. For the best sense of the sen-
    tence, what one word should be emphasized?

• •

SELECTION 7

"The Memory Puzzle" *by Al Cole 952 words*

Vocabulary
Alzheimer's disease: a progressive, degenerative disease characterized by loss of
    memory: "severe disorders such as Alzheimer's disease"

neuroscience: the science of the nervous system; "the Laboratory of Neuroscience"
hypertension: abnormally high blood pressure; "for instance, some hypertension"
congestive heart failure: the failure of the heart to maintain output, resulting in re-
    duced blood flow and congestion to the body; "and congestive heart failure
    drugs"
compensating: to provide an equivalent for; "a way of compensating for"

This is an informative article concerning memory, particularly the types of memory loss experienced by older people. This article tries to dispel myths about aging and memory. Al Cole presents several readable experimental results that examine memory among younger and older subjects. You can most efficiently read this article rapidly by focusing on what these experiments say about memory and age. After you have read this selection rapidly, you may want to reread it to analyze more carefully the details about memory that these experiments present.

Follow these steps in reading the article:

1. Preview skim the article.
2. Answer the three-item preview quiz.
3. Read the article rapidly.
4. Answer the five-item reading quiz.

· · · · · · · · · · · · · · · · · ·

THE MEMORY PUZZLE

· · · · · · · · · · · · · · · · · ·

by Al Cole

[1]   On stage, the nimble fingers of a 75-year-old jazz clarinetist move lightly along his instrument, recalling intricate musical passages learned over a lifetime. Offstage, he can never remember where he put his car keys.

[2]   The puzzle of how someone's memory could perform so well in one situation and so poorly in another baffled earlier generations of researchers. But today's view of this complex mechanism provides a simple answer: The brain uses different processes to store and retrieve different kinds of information.

[3]   This realization has produced new insight into the relationship between aging and memory loss. In fact, while most studies indicate that a decline in many types of memory is to be expected, some aspects of memory, such as vocabulary, actually show improvement well into the 70s.

[4]   Thomas Crook, director of Memory Assessment Clinics, a private research group based in Bethesda, Md., says a better understanding of what is a normal result of aging can greatly reduce the fear common among older people and those close to them: that memory lapses may mean the onset of severe disorders such as Alzheimer's disease.

[5.]   "Older people need to realize that it is perfectly normal for certain types of memory ability to decline with age and that these changes are not generally predictive of a serious problem," he says. In fact, only about 5 percent of those over 65 suffer from acute memory disorders. "The good news is that unless you're a jet fighter pilot, the kinds of memory declines that come with growing older don't matter much and can usually be compensated for."

[6]   Crook says that memory training, reducing distractions, writing things down and keeping

everyday items like eyeglasses and keys in the same place can be helpful strategies.

[7]   Determining precisely how much memory drop-off is due solely to aging is a thorny problem. A University of Colorado experiment illustrates why.

[8]   A group of people age 65 to 87 was shown a black and white map of a room containing 40 common objects. A short time later, they could recall only a handful of items. But when the test was repeated using an actual room with the same items, they were able to recall 25 or more objects. A group of college students did better on the map test than the older participants but no better on the real room test.

[9]   Did the difference in performance occur because of age or because college students were more familiar with the written format? The question is debatable. However, researchers generally agree on a couple of points: Older people have more trouble recalling isolated facts, like names; and the brain's processes for storing and retrieving information slow down over time.

[10]   Here's how it happens. Incoming data in the form of electrical impulses cause transmitters and receivers to branch out from the brain's nerve cells, called neurons, to form electrical circuits with nearby neurons. The transmitters and receivers relay information across the cell junctions, and chemicals called neurotransmitters are produced at the junctions to speed the electrical impulses along. One theory for why a slowdown occurs is that as the brain ages, it produces fewer of these neurotransmitters.

[11]   The riddle of why older people can vividly recall experiences as children and young adults but forget what they had for lunch has no easy solution, says Carol Fuchs, a memory specialist with the Laboratory of Neuroscience, part of the National Institute on Aging. "One way to look at it is that those early memories have been there the longest and have been reinforced over the years. Recent stimuli, on the other hand, must compete for space with a lifetime of accumulated data in

the brain and have only a short time to be encoded."

[12]   Other factors, such as medications and stress, can adversely affect this delicate mechanism.

[13]   The Department of Health and Human Services reports that the average adult over 65 takes 7.5 medications, many of which may cause confusion and memory loss—for instance, some hypertension and congestive heart failure drugs. Stress resulting from fear of having to enter a nursing home or being forced into early retirement can also cause temporary memory failure.

[14]   One way to improve memory performance is to be selective, says Alan S. Brown, author of "How to Improve Your Memory." For instance, he says, it's not essential for most people to remember every person they meet.

[15]   "An enormous amount of information bombards us each day, and most of it is not worth remembering," Brown says. "Make a conscious decision about each new bit of data. If you decide it is important, turn on your attention radar; if not, let it pass right by."

[16]   A National Institute on Aging study seems to indicate that older people may instinctively operate this way, retaining what they consider important and discarding the rest.

[17]   The study involved asking 79 men and women aged 23 to 93 to recall some of their daily activities during a 2-1/2-day stay at a research center. The group was tested again seven to 10 days later by telephone, and 33 of the participants were tested a third time about 18 months later.

[18]   No significant difference was noted in their ability to remember information that would be needed for further action. However, older participants did much worse in recalling incidental items. The study concluded that selective remembering may be a way of compensating for a decline in the ability to recall isolated facts that must be retrieved from among clusters of similar data residing in memory.

[19]   Regardless of just how much memory loss is normal, it usually is not enough to create a

problem for most people, says Denise Park, a psychologist at the University of Georgia. "Although laboratory studies show that there is a decline in long-term memory—for example, in the ability to remember very long lists of words—the differences matter little for everyday life."

Al Cole, "The Memory Puzzle," *AARP Bulletin*, April 1990, p. 2.

• •

1. This selection comes from:
    a. *AARP Bulletin.*
    b. *New York Times.*
    c. *Los Angeles Times.*
    d. *New York Magazine.*

2. The article contains several major subdivisions set off in boldface print.
    a. true
    b. false

3. The author will be addressing the:
    a. recent research on memory.
    b. loss of memory among the old.
    c. loss of memory among the young.
    d. none of these.

Sel. 7 P-Skim	1. _____	
Time 1:00 = 952 wpm	2. _____	
Score _____ %	3. _____	
▶ 100%	**Check answers after the next quiz.**	
Score = number correct x 33.		

B. Rapid Reading

Write your starting time in the next box (or wait for the signal to begin reading). Then go back to the article to begin reading rapidly. Try to finish in 2 minutes (= 476 wpm) or in 2-1/2 minutes (= 381 wpm).

1. The author suggests that as a person ages, all aspects of memory decline.
    a. true
    b. false

2. Older people tend to forget:
    a. names.
    b. isolated facts.
    c. childhood experiences.
    d. both *a* and *b*.

3. Older people tend to have fewer:
    a. neurotransmitters.
    b. brain cells.
    c. occasions to learn.
    d. both *b* and *c*.

4. Medication generally seems to:
    a. make memory loss worse.
    b. improve memory loss.
    c. increase the number of neurotransmitters.
    d. increase brain cell production.

5. Selective memory seems to:
    a. get worse with age.
    b. get better with age.
    c. stay the same throughout life.
    d. none of these

Sel. 7   R-Read   1. _____

Finish _____ : _____   2. _____

Start   _____ : _____   3. _____

Time   _____ : _____   4. _____

        min   sec   5. _____

Rate _____ wpm   **Check answers to both quizzes**

Find rate on p. 330.   **on p. 338.**

Score _____ %   **Record rate and score on p. 183.**

    ▶ **80%**

Score = number correct × 20.

C. Questions for Discussion and Writing

1. Summarize the experimental procedures and conclusions explained in paragraph 8.

2. Summarize the experimental procedures and conclusions explained in paragraphs 17 and 18.

3. Reread the article and list the five most important features of the memory abilities of the elderly.

· ·

SELECTION 8

"At Your Service" *by Leslie Gregory 1,934 words*

Are you rich? Are you poor? Did you ever wonder what it's like to be a servant in a very wealthy household? Or whether the movie, television, and stage butlers were realistic? Did you ever want to be a butler? Have you ever been a butler? We hope at least one of those questions interested you, because this article will give you the latest news of real butlers—yes, they still exist.

Follow the usual steps in reading this article:

1. Preview skim the article.
2. Take the three-item preview quiz.
3. Read the article rapidly.
4. Take the five-item reading quiz.

A. Preview Skimming

Spend about 1 minute (= 1,934 wpm) or 1-1/2 minutes (= 1,289 wpm) previewing the article for any subtitle, lead-in, or headings, and for length and difficulty level. Then answer the preview quiz without referring back to the article.

· ·

AT YOUR SERVICE

by Leslie Gregory

[1]   In a time when millionaires are becoming commonplace, there are still those very few whose net worth stretches nine or 10 digits. These are the people who make an easy million in a matter of weeks or those who were born knowing they would never, ever have to worry about making a dime.

[2]   They are the privileged few who live in mansions at the end of winding driveways hidden behind iron gateways—the mysterious passengers in the back seats of limousines with darkened windows. Seldom glimpsed. Rarely addressed.

[3]   At the heart of many of these households there lives a man whose very purpose is to know everything that goes on, making sure that each need is met, each comfort provided for. He is the butler and, though he is of a rare breed, he still thrives in a modern world that shuns tradition and propriety. And, there at the center of this private world, he knows precisely what is going on behind closed doors.

[4]   Most of us can only fantasize about what it would be like to live among the creme de la creme of society, traveling to the most exotic corners of the world in the lap of luxury, bantering with royalty or witnessing dinner conversations that determine the price of gold or the strange bedfellows among the powerful. For the butler, these privileges are part of daily life and he often grows as familiar with enormous wealth as his employer.

[5]   Anthony Ivory is one of a handful of top butlers on the Westside. Ivory's mother was a cook and his father a butler in a number of fine houses in England. At 16, Ivory left home and went to

sea, serving in the British Merchant Navy and eventually working his way to tending the captain and crew on the Queen Mary. "I've met a lot of people," he says. "I've traveled the world and lived in some of the most beautiful homes on earth."

6   Ivory's most recent position was head butler for a woman whose family amassed a great fortune in the steel industry. Like most in his position, Ivory was careful to protect the woman's name. His duties in that home consisted of supervising the household staff, caring for the silver, choosing the finest wines and generally tending to anything and everything that kept the household in perfect order.

7   "From six in the morning (the house) went like a clock up until when dinner was finished and the alarms were put on. You make sure you don't run out of catsup, caviar or lavatory paper—the very important things," Ivory explains with a mischievous gleam in his eye.

8   Though the butler's position keeps him subtly removed from the family, his duties often involve close interaction with his wealthy employer. "This woman (his previous employer) wouldn't let anybody feed her but me until the day she died," he recalls. "Still you don't feel part of the family. I remember that this is their home."

9   Anthony Beckett, also born and bred in England, agrees, explaining his butler position as intimately close to his employer while keeping his distance as propriety dictates. "The Southern California lifestyle is very relaxed," he says. "But you can't be if you're in a formal household. It's very difficult sometimes. Everyone may be in bathing suits and diving in the pool and you're sweating in your suit thinking, `Oh, I'd love to get in that pool.' But you don't. Quite often they'll say, `Go ahead and have a swim.' But I've found that I can't just change and put on a costume and dive into their pool because it's not my home, even though I'm living there."

10   Matthew Riley, founder of the English Butler Service and an instructor of a course on butlering in the Learning Network, recalls his position as butler for one of the foreign royal families living in Los Angeles. "The Prince's dinner entertainment would last all night long most every night," he says. "The butler is the one who keeps a straight head while everyone else is enjoying themselves. It's the butler's image. You don't let your hair down. Not while you're at work."

11   Most of the best butlers are trained in England, apprenticing in the finer hotels or even Buckingham Palace. They come from a very old tradition that originated in France in the 12th or 13th century, according to Robert Mann of the Sandra Taylor Agency, a Westside placement agency. "They were originally 'buteliers'—trained in the vineyards in wine tasting then passed down from family to family. Today, wherever there is great wealth, there are a few formal households with full domestic staffs."

12   A butler's primary duties involve supervising the household help which, in a few cases, includes up to 30 people—butlers, footmen, ladies' maids, chefs, cleaning staffs and chauffeurs. He makes sure the lady of the house never has to tend to domestic problems. The butler greets guests at the door and answers the telephone. Many employers prefer English butlers because the British accent nicely complements these duties.

13   It is the butler who plans the menu with the chef and the lady of the house and serves the meals with strict adherence to codes of etiquette. When guests arrive, he has made sure the house is stocked with the particular favorites of each guest. Anthony Ivory explains how he makes a mental note of the people who have been to the house before, recalling who prefers lime with their Perrier, which gentleman loves Dunhill cigarettes or which lady is constantly on a diet. "You tend to the one thing that will make each person think, 'Oh, I'm being looked after.'

14   "I have the feeling that when I'm looking after someone they are very lucky that I'm doing it. I do know how people should be looked after. No, I don't feel servile. I think we're all looked after in one way or another."

15   Robert Mann put in one word as the single most important feature in a good butler: "Dis-

cretion." It's a word that surfaces in any conversation on the art of butlering. Ivory agrees. "If I walk in the bedroom in the afternoon and Madam has her gigolo in bed, or say it's the morning and I walk in with the coffee tray. Well, I merely get another cup and saucer and put it down. Perhaps just draw the curtains. You often become the confidant. But I feel the less they know about me, the better. Basically, nobody is really interested in you. So, you don't draw onto them your life or what makes you tick—better to keep that a mystery."

16   Doris Romeo runs her own agency out of Beverly Hills, placing butlers and domestic help from all over the world in the finest homes in the United States. "The butler knows all the household secrets and where the skeletons are buried," she explains. "And I hear all the gossip. Sometimes I know when someone has died even before their families know.

17   "You've got to be the creme de la creme to have a butler," she explains. "Some of these people have a billion dollar net worth."

18   It is a world peopled with events too fantastic for the commoner to comprehend. Anthony Ivory, who is in the process of wrapping up his late employer's household, is in charge of cleaning up many of her domestic affairs. "I just handed over thousands and thousands and thousands of dollars worth of jewels," he says. "Mind boggling jewels. Black pearls like this," he curls his fingers into a circle, leaving a pingpong ball-sized hole, "and blood red rubies the size of pigeon eggs. It was amazing."

19   Anthony Beckett has similar stories of his days working for a notorious English woman who began as a hat sales girl and, through three well-chosen marriages, became a titled Lady. Beckett butlered aboard her 1,000 foot yacht as it sailed the Mediterranean. "We would go to the South of France, Cannes, Monte Carlo, Capri. We'd be out of England for six months of the year. It was great adventure.

20   "In my time off the chauffeur and I went around the South of France in a gold-plated car.

The rest of the staff was afraid of Madam. But I found the inner woman charming and very courteous. I used to dance down the hallway with her. I knew her fairly well. We used to talk sometimes an hour at a time. I always knew when she had gone through the house because of her perfume. If you wanted to know if she was in the lounge, you just went into the hallway to smell her perfume. She wore some beautiful perfumes and she had more than 20 wardrobes."

21   Tending to the lives of the rich and powerful may mean great personal sacrifice for a butler. Live-in help usually has one or two days off a week. When they are working, their job is 24 hours each day. "Personal life? It goes way down," Anthony Beckett stresses. "I find work more demanding in the United States because people often have no idea of what your life should be—only theirs."

22   Still, the butler is recognized as a strategic element in a well-ordered household. "I have seen powerful men—billionaires—leave board meetings to take care of domestic staff matters. Anything to keep the household running smoothly," says Robert Mann. "One director I know in New York stopped everything—he was filming a movie—to meet two new butlers coming in from London."

23   Though a good butler enjoys some status, he rarely receives much personal recognition. "You just blend in with everything," Ivory explains. "Madam (his former employer) used to look up and she'd say, 'Divine.' That meant the food was divine. We had nine chefs in one year. At the other home (where I worked) the prior cook committed suicide. He jumped in the pool. Put heavy stones at the end of ropes on his arms and feet. It was his final statement, I would say."

24   Some butlers are compensated quite well for their work. Doris Romeo mentions one butler who was set up for life when his employers, the owners of a major department store chain, willed him $50,000 a year and an indefinite stay in her mansion following her death.

25   But some might argue that no amount of money could compensate for the butler's personal

sacrifice as he dedicates his lifetime to giving careful attention to the details of an opulent household which does not belong to him. Many have places of their own to retreat to during their minimal free time.

26   Beckett says he has saved his earnings to acquire finery of his own. "I like the best. When you are raised in surroundings with scrub top tables with newspapers for tablecloths, sharing with nine other children, you choose the other world. You do learn to appreciate a lot of things more because you are not able to get them yourself. They are at your fingertips, but they're not actually yours. I always wanted my own Waterford (crystal). I do entertain—with my own china and my Waterford."

27   Anthony Ivory has built a very different kind of home away from his work. His is a retreat where he can go and relax. "My place is very simple, and I would say very chic, because it is so simple. I would say, my place has more warmth and more comfort than the mansion."

28   And who would know more about comfort than a butler?

Leslie Gregory, "At Your Service," *Evening Outlook*, Santa Monica, Calif., June 25, 1985. Reprinted by permission.

• •

1. Several subheads throughout the article help highlight the content.
    a. true
    b. false

2. According to the end note, the writer is the wife of a butler.
    a. true
    b. false

3. The discussion centers on butlers serving great houses in England.
    a. true
    b. false

Sel. 8 P-Skim	**1.** _____	
Time 1:00 = 1,934 wpm	**2.** _____	
Score _____ %	**3.** _____	
▶ **100%**	**Check answers after the next quiz.**	
Score = number correct x 33.		

B. Rapid Reading

Write your starting time in the box, or wait for a signal from the instructor. Take no more than 3 minutes (= 645 wpm) to rapid read this article; in fact, try to read it in 2 or 2-1/2 minutes! Whatever your speed, you can find your wpm in the rate table as usual.

1. The butlers interviewed here were born and bred in England; in fact, most wealthy families prefer English butlers.
    a. true
    b. false

2. According to the writer, the one trait essential in a good butler is:
   a. discretion.
   b. fastidiousness (attention to tiny details).
   c. a good memory.

3. Any household that employs a butler:
   a. must be *very* wealthy.
   b. must be *very* formal.
   c. must have a large staff under the butler's direction.
   d. all of these.

4. A butler's free time is:
   a. limited—one or two days a week.
   b. nonexistent.
   c. fairly good—evenings and weekends.

5. The article implies that butlers:
   a. really enjoy their opulent surroundings.
   b. like to live well in their own homes.
   c. must always know their "place."
   d. all of these.

Sel. 8 R–Read	1. _____
Finish _____ : _____	2. _____
Start _____ : _____	3. _____
Time _____ : _____	4. _____
min sec	5. _____
Rate _____ wpm	**Check answers to both quizzes**
Find rate on p. 330.	**with your instructor.**
Score _____ %	**Record rate and score on p. 183.**
▶ **80%**	
Score = number correct x 20.	

C. Questions for Discussion and Writing

1. What major organizational pattern does this article use?

2. Part of this article talks about the accommodations butlers must make in their behavior and personal life to suit employers' demands. Reread the article and find three or four examples of such accommodations. State each example in a complete sentence, using your own words.

3. Reread the last three paragraphs, which describe the homes of the two butlers, Beckett and Ivory. How are the homes similar? How are they different? Be sure to back your views up with details from these paragraphs.

. . . .

SELECTION 9

"What If Women Ruled the World?" *by Bella Abzug 1,178 words*

Vocabulary
Nordic: Northern Europe or Scandinavia; "the Nordic countries"
renascence: renewal of life; "Since the renascence of the women's movement"
periphery: the external boundary; "on the periphery of decision making"
sanctions: authoritative permissions for an action; "interested in sanctions"
rationalize: to invent explanations for; "to rationalize its own discriminatory practices"
acculturated: to adopt various traits or patterns; "women are acculturated differently"

This selection is from a speech made by Bella Abzug concerning women's rights to power that has been traditionally given to men. It follows the logic of the thesis-support structure, providing ample evidence that women can be effective leaders. Your task in reading this selection is to consider the evidence that Abzug uses to support her thesis.

Follow these steps in reading this selection:

1. Preview skim the article.
2. Answer the three-item preview quiz.
3. Read the entire article rapidly.
4. Answer the five-item reading quiz.

A. Preview Skimming

Preview skim this selection. As you do, you will find that the article presents evidence in an organized fashion. That is, each paragraph provides an additional point to support the major thesis.

Take 1 minute (= 1,178 wpm) or 1-1/2 minutes (= 785 wpm) to preview.

. . . .

WHAT IF WOMEN RULED THE WORLD?

by Bella Abzug

1   I submit to you that those women have as much to contribute to the direction of making this a better world than most of the large numbers of men who occupy the seats. At times like this, it is difficult to figure out whether those who control power really know what they're doing.

2   The question is always raised whether the attainment of greater numbers of women in high positions would make a difference in results. In broad opinion surveys it has been revealed that women's attitudes generally differ significantly from men's. When women have a chance to use power in settings where there is some important commitment to their presence, as in the Nordic countries, government policies are usually noteworthy for their emphasis on equality, development, and peace.

3   Since the general renascence of the women's movement in the 1960s, I think most people believe that women have made significant advances in many phases of US national life, and I believe that to be true. We may debate whether all the advances are permanent or deeply rooted, but there can be no doubt that women's rights to equality, opportunity, and leadership roles have become imbedded in our nation's conscience, and increasingly in practice.

4   But even in the United States, the foremost democracy in the world, we have only 23 women out of 435 in the House of Representatives, and only two women out of 100 in the United States Senate. We have increased the number of women mayors, but only about 15 per cent of state legislators are women. And it's shocking that here, with all the advances and raised consciousness we have about the rights, needs, and potential of individuals, both male and female, in high councils of government, decisions of life and death are made by only one part of the population. I think we suffer from that. Particularly in foreign policy, where with a few notable exceptions, we see that government has remained virtually an all-male preserve, perpetuating the impression that only men are experts on all aspects of war, peace, and foreign policy, and that women, except for the occasional token female presence at an international event, have little or nothing to contribute to the realm of governance.

5   This is contrary to fact. Women have a long, impressive history of involvement in US foreign policy. Individually and organizationally they have worked for world peace and cooperation and have played leading roles in the creation of the World Court, the adoption of the Kellogg-Briand pact, the founding of the United Nations, and so on. But they have been largely on the periphery of decision-making—good citizens acting without formal power or public office. I think we would grant that women have a right to participate in the formulation and conduct of American foreign policy as a matter of equity and social justice, but beyond that, consider the cost to our nation and the world, when the wisdom, scholarship, and experience of women are ignored by government in policy making.

6   The low visibility of women in public debate as well as in government, deprives us of role models of women capable of participating in the highest levels of governance. It seriously restricts the political leadership potential of women, and creates doubts in the mind of the public as to whether women can fill top posts, or even understand the complexities of arms control. A prejudicial viewpoint has been expressed by more than one high administration official suggesting that with respect to the Geneva Conferences, women don't understand throw weights, and with respect to South African policy, that women are interested in their diamonds, and therefore would not be too interested in sanctions.

7   According to the State Department's figures, as of December, 1986, only about 3.6 per cent of senior level foreign service officers and career candidates, are white females.

8   There are no minority women on the top career rung and no women serve as deputy secretaries or under secretaries. Of four women assistant secretaries only one, Rozanne Ridgway, deals with major foreign policy issues as head of the Bureau of European Affairs.

9   Many female foreign officers have not been given the same opportunities as men to serve in political and economic positions in Moslem, African, Latin American, and Asian countries, based on the belief that they're unable to establish and maintain the necessary contacts in male-dominated environments. So the State Department uses the male

supremacy of other nations to rationalize its own discriminatory practices.

10   What would happen if women held foreign policy decision-making positions? I contend that although their views are diverse, as are men's, many would propose needed alternatives to American foreign policy. My experience has been that since women have largely been outside of power, they tend to be less wedded to policies of the past. Since they've had very little to do with developing those policies, they don't feel the necessity to defend them and seem able to look at them much more objectively. I remember when I was in the Congress of the United States, there was much opposition from some of us to the continuation of the war in Vietnam. Many longtime members of Congress, particularly after the revelation of the Pentagon Papers, said, "You think we enjoy having been lied to and that we wouldn't like to join you in your opposition to the war? But we voted for it for all this time, it is something that we're committed to."

11   Women don't own the oil wells, the corporations, the uranium mines, and they're not the arms dealers who have risen to such prominence in the Iran-contra crisis. My experience as a member of Congress, and as one in contact internationally with women in power, is that women, regardless of party, often advocate peaceful, diplomatic solutions to international problems rather than aggressive military actions. I think this is largely the result of the differences in how women and men were brought up. It's clear that men and women are acculturated differently.

12   We can argue at great length about whether women can change the nature of power or power will change the nature of women. I suggest to you that women have indicated they can change the nature of power. I think that women

are created in a different image; we're not an elite obsessed with military supremacy. Some might even question the government's preference for Star Wars over homes for the homeless. Should we use the space up there in the skies for military purposes when we have no space here on earth for people or peace? Birds have the trees, and the fish have the seas, and we have problems adjusting the great democracy, the richest in history, to meet the actual life needs of people.

13   Inevitably, in this discussion, someone mentions Prime Minister Margaret Thatcher of Britain as proof that, given power, women will behave just as so many male leaders do. I think the true answer may come only when there is a critical mass of women, and as many women as men govern and counsel us. Of course, if we proceed in the United States to elect women in the numbers that we've had in the last 20 years, it will take us 410 years to equalize the numbers of men and women in Congress.

14   At a conference in Nairobi in 1985, a woman from Northern Ireland said that "to men security is cruise missiles, to women it is a house and a future for the children; to men development is to conquer territories, to women it's human planning to secure the survival of the planet." I think this is true. The continuation of a whole series of theses and patriarchal values has not created the improvements in present and future lives that I believe we would all like for ourselves, our children, and our children's children. I think a government of, by, and for men and women would be far better than any government we've had before.

Bella Abzug, "What If Women Ruled the World?" *The World*, January–February 1988, pp. 4–7. Reprinted by permission of *The World*. This article is based on an address before the Cambridge Forum.

• •

1.   The article was written in:
   a.   1978.
   b.   1988.
   c.   1989.
   d.   1990.

2. The author seems to clearly favor:
    a. more women in politics.
    b. liberal political causes.
    c. a female-dominated society.
    d. a male-dominated society.
3. This selection focuses on women in:
    a. business.
    b. law.
    c. politics.
    d. medicine.

Sel. 9 P–Skim	**1.** _____	
Time 1:00 = 1,178 wpm	**2.** _____	
1:30 = 785 wpm	**3.** _____	
Score _____ %	**Check answers after the next quiz.**	
▶ **100%**		
Score = number correct ✕ 33.		

B. Rapid Reading

Now read rapidly, filling in the gaps left by your preview. Take no more than 3 minutes (=393 wpm) to read the selection rapidly. Write your starting time in the box, or wait for the signal to begin.

1. The author deplores the fact that there are so few women in the:
    a. House of Representatives.
    b. Senate.
    c. state legislature.
    d. all of these.

2. The author contends that women have been instrumental in the creation of the:
    a. World Court.
    b. United Nations.
    c. space exploration projects.
    d. both *a* and *c*.

3. The author contends that top-level diplomatic positions in Third World countries are denied to women because the State Department feels that these countries:
    a. would jeopardize women's safety.
    b. prefer only married women.
    c. are not used to women in political positions.
    d. would not be respectful toward women.

4. The author believes that women tend to deal with political problems:
   a. peacefully.
   b. aggressively.
   c. as aggressively as men.
   d. emotionally.

5. The author suggests that if women continue to enter politics at the rate they are currently entering, they will:
   a. make up 50 percent of the politicians by the year 2000.
   b. be equal to the number of male politicians in 100 years.
   c. be equal to the number of male politicians in 410 years.
   d. be equal to the number of male politicians in 500 years.

Sel. 9 R-Read	1. _____
Finish _____ : _____	2. _____
Start _____ : _____	3. _____
Time _____ : _____	4. _____
min sec	5. _____
Rate _____ wpm	**Check answers to both quizzes**
Find rate on p. 330.	**on p. 338.**
Score _____ %	**Record rate and score on p. 183.**
▶ **80%**	

C. Questions for Discussion and Writing

1. Reread the article and summarize Bella Abzug's three strongest reasons for women being in politics.
2. Reread paragraph 11 and summarize Abzug's argument concerning women and their response to war. Do you agree?
3. What does Abzug mean when she says in paragraph 14: "To men security is cruise missiles, to women it is a house and a future for the children"?

• •

SELECTION 10

"Ordeal in the Winter Woods" *by Joseph P. Blank 1,746 words*

Vocabulary
precipitated: to hasten the occurrence of; "had not precipitated an avalanche"

odyssey: a series of wanderings that lead to unforgettable experiences; "begun his odyssey"

fervor: great warmth of feeling; "not with the same fervor"

unencumbered: unhindered; "unencumbered upright position"

Some narratives—short stories and nonfictional accounts—lead the reader into other worlds. They are experiences in characters and places and actions and just in the words themselves. The reader needs time to delight in the words, to reread, to pause, to reflect, to wonder. Some narratives, like this nonfictional account of a man's struggles in nature, are fairly easy to understand the first time through.

In previewing this narrative, you need to alter your strategies a bit. Instead of searching for a main idea and details to support it, look for the major characters and the basic story line—the problem the narrator faced and how, or if, it was resolved by the narrative's conclusion.

Follow these steps:

1. Preview skim the short story.
2. Answer the three-item preview quiz.
3. Read the narrative rapidly.
4. Answer the five-item reading quiz.

A. Preview Skimming

Pass through this selection quickly, in about 1 minute (= 1,746 wpm). Find out a little bit about the narrator, the setting, and the problem he faces.

ORDEAL IN THE WINTER WOODS

by Joseph P. Blank

[1] For several weeks Robin Sachs, 31, had been looking forward to a solo cross-country ski trip in the northern mountains of Yosemite National Park in east-central California. He wanted to get away from the hurly-burly of his restaurant on the campus of the Santa Cruz branch of the University of California. Robin was an expert cross-country skier and conducted classes in the sport. He never felt lonely skiing alone. He felt, instead, a spiritual linkage with the mountains, the snow, the silence.

[2] In late April 1986, he spent three days on the Pacific Crest, acclimatizing himself to the 10,000-foot altitude and planning his journey. Using maps, Robin made certain that, in case of emergency, he would never be more than 12 miles from a place where he might encounter other people.

[3] Robin then carefully packed for his 100-mile, ten-day journey. He chose lightweight trail foods and included a first-aid kit, shovel, rope, stove, two quarts of cooking fuel, clothing and sleeping gear. His pack weighed about 70 pounds.

[4] At dawn on April 23, he left the Crest, push-skiing along a snow-covered ridge. At noon he stopped to rest and cook some cereal.

5   As Robin ate he noticed a slightly inclined, snow-free area of large boulders. Below it lay a beautiful stretch of snow that angled downward at about 40 degrees, leading to his destination at Hope Valley. He decided to take this shortcut. He attached his skis and poles to his pack and began backing carefully down the slope.

6   The rocks that had looked dry were in fact covered by a thin skin of melted snow, which Robin had not detected because of the angle of the sun's rays. He tried to climb back to the ridge, but couldn't. Instead he began sliding.

7   Robin had not suffered an accident in more than a dozen years. But now he realized that he was in trouble. He shrugged off his pack, which bounced downhill, scattering his skis and poles. No help! Continuing to slide, he hit a six-foot drop to a second rocky, snow-covered slope. As he gained momentum, his weight forced him into a full backward roll. Finally, after tumbling another 100 feet, he clawed his way to a stop.

DIGGING IN

8   For a few minutes Robin lay quietly, trying to settle his thoughts and feelings. He was fortunate that he had not been knocked unconscious, that his fall had not precipitated an avalanche, but each movement caused intense pain in his lower back. His arms were okay, and he shoved his hands into his snow pants and down his left leg. He could feel a fracture and, worse, a complete dislocation of his left ankle. His foot flopped uselessly.

9   Robin had always believed that God exists within the person who believes in God, that for comfort and support his presence just needs to be felt. In reaching within himself Robin found some peace. To survive, he knew, he had to keep his wits. Fear and impulsiveness could produce disaster.

10   When he tried to stand, his left leg collapsed, dumping him into a sitting position. He felt angry with himself. How, with all his experience, could he have been caught in such a trap?

11   Robin saw his pack about 100 feet below him, his skis and one pole almost 100 feet up the slope. The other pole had vanished. He slowly began climbing up the snow, dragging his useless left leg. He retrieved the skis and pole, grasped them under his right armpit and eased his way down again.

12   By the time he reached his pack, Robin was utterly spent. He lay in the snow to rest and relieve the unrelenting back pain. He reminded himself that to push on, especially with his injuries, he required energy. He cooked cereal on his stove and melted snow to drink. He then pulled the shovel out of his pack and burrowed a hole into a bank of snow. He firmed the snow inside by slapping it with the back of his shovel, and then carved out blocks, which he piled at the entrance as a barrier against the wind.

13   Exhausted, he removed his ski boots and crawled into his sleeping bag. The pain in his back and ankle allowed him to sleep only fitfully. In the morning the swollen ankle prevented him from replacing the left boot.

CONTEMPLATING DEATH

14   At daybreak Robin studied his map and decided to take advantage of terrain that descended about ten miles southwest to Glen Aulin camp. There he hoped to find shelter and someone to help him.

15   The distance facing him was awesome, but he believed that determination and patience would see him through. He could stretch his food to last at least 12 days. Water could keep him alive for another two weeks. But he had to have his pack and skis, and how was he going to move them and himself?

16   Robin had put his pack on the skis to keep them from sliding away as he pondered. Suddenly he saw them move a few inches. That was it! He'd make a toboggan.

17   Using the straps from his pack, he lashed the skis together and tied the pack to this makeshift sled. On his knees, he pushed the pack ahead of him a few feet, then waddled after it. If he encountered several feet of smooth snow he sat on the pack and pushed along with his one pole. That was luxury.

18   When the toboggan bogged down in snow that had been softened by the afternoon sun, he

stopped. He couldn't afford to waste energy by pushing twice as hard. Robin dug another shelter. His legs and feet ached from being dragged along the snow. He was worn out, and decided to allot the third day to rest.

19   He read several pages of a book in his backpack, Hermann Hesse's *Steppenwolf.* The principal character believed that the future held no hope for mankind. Robin didn't buy that.

20   "If death was in 'The Plan,' so be it," he said to himself. "But I won't invite it, accept it or submit to it. If it happens, it will happen only while I am fighting to reach safety."

PUSHING ON, AND ON

21   At dawn on the fourth day, Robin found himself refreshed. The white, untouched snow seemed to be not his enemy but his ally, enabling him to make progress. Birds sang for his pleasure. The sky, steel blue and studded with fleecy clouds, almost hypnotized him with its beauty. He began visualizing the faces of close friends. "I could see them right in front of me, reaching out their hands to help me push on," he recalls. "They wanted me to live."

22   But each day's progress was more tedious, more draining, more painful. Rocks and trees became more numerous, and it took double effort to skirt them. Robin had begun his odyssey by thinking in terms of daily miles, then in terms of city blocks, then in feet. He felt crushingly frustrated, but knew he could not express his frustration in any physical act of defiance. He had to stay calm, "go with the flow."

23   He had improvised a splint from two pieces of branch and bound them with a strip torn from the waterproof pad used under his sleeping bag. It did little good. His leg and ankle kept hurting.

STORM AND SAFETY

24   Early on the afternoon of the tenth day, a Friday, Robin suddenly heard the swish of skis. He saw a cross-country skier on a course that would bring him about 100 feet away. Robin shrieked, "Hello!"

25   The skier was 22-year-old John Steinmetz, a state-parks lifeguard in Santa Cruz. Also a lone skier, he was trying to come to grips with a problem of his own. A few weeks earlier, he and others had failed to resuscitate a drowned swimmer. He was ridden with remorse.

26   Some quality in Robin's shout made John swerve to a halt and pole his way back. "How's it going?" he asked the injured skier.

27   "I have a broken leg and ankle."

28   "How long have you been out here?"

29   "Ten days."

30   "It took me about 45 minutes to get here from McCabe Lake," John said. "Well," Robin answered, "it took me six days."

31   The two men compared maps and agreed on Robin's precise position. It now was nearly 3 p.m. John said he would ski to the ranger cabin at Tuolumne Meadows, telephone ranger headquarters in Yosemite Valley and request help. He left some food and urged Robin to stay put. When he poled away, Robin silently implored John not to rush or be careless.

32   When John phoned ranger headquarters he was told that the park helicopter was being repaired. A commercial helicopter was called in. No specific time could be promised for the rescue.

33   That afternoon, low, thick, scudding clouds blocked out the sky. It began snowing, and Robin burrowed into his small snow cave. The snow fell harder throughout the next day, covering Robin's shelter with a foot-deep layer.

34   Around noon on Sunday, Robin's 12th day, the storm passed. As the sun broke through, Robin heard a helicopter. He furiously waved his red jacket, yelling, "Here! It's me! Down here!" But the helicopter passed him and dipped over the eastern horizon. Robin watched it in despair.

35   Ten minutes later the craft approached again, and again disappeared. Robin kept waving his red jacket, but not with the same fervor. On the fourth pass the helicopter came in very low, and the pilot's and Robin's eyes literally met. The pilot waved, then cruised out of sight.

36   The craft didn't have the winch and cable needed to lower a basket to the victim, and the pilot couldn't chance a landing in the deep snow. He flew

south a half-mile to firm ground, dropped off park medic Chris Jackson and guided him to Robin.

37   Jackson put an inflatable splint on Robin's left leg and a snowshoe on his right foot. For the first time in 12 days, Robin stood erect. He took a few hops, felt dizzy, and was eased to the ground by Jackson, who radioed the helicopter that a toboggan was needed.

38   Within an hour the helicopter flew into sight, and Jackson returned to its landing point. He and a ranger then hauled the toboggan to where Robin lay. About the same time, John Steinmetz appeared. He and Robin grinned at each other and gripped hands. Robin felt an inexpressible gratitude—and so did John, whose whole attitude about himself had been changed by the rescue he put in motion.

39   Over the next three months the pain in Robin's back gradually subsided. He progressed from wheelchair to crutches, then to unencumbered upright movement. Slowly he regained full strength and stamina. Although a stiffness in his left ankle remains, he can walk for hours and bicycle 30 or 40 miles without fatigue.

40   Shortly after recovering, Robin talked to another skier, who told him, "I could never have gone through your ordeal. I would have just lain there and died."

41   Robin shook his head. This skier could not understand that his "ordeal" had actually strengthened him. He had been cruelly tested, and had met the challenge. "It was," he says, "the greatest experience of my life."

Joseph P. Blank, "Ordeal in the Winter Woods," *Reader's Digest*, January 1988, pp. 95–100. Reprinted with permission from the January 1988 *Reader's Digest*. Copyright © 1987 by The Reader's Digest Assoc., Inc.

• •

1. This narrative was published in:
    a. *Time*.
    b. *Newsweek*.
    c. *Reader's Digest*.
    d. *Nature*.

2. The title suggests that this narrative:
    a. will take place in the wilds.
    b. will involve a serious problem.
    c. will involve animals.
    d. both *a* and *b*.

3. The main character is:
    a. a young male skier.
    b. a middle-aged athlete.
    c. a young female skier.
    d. an elderly man.

Sel. 10 P-Skim	**1.** _____
Time 1:00 = 1,746 wpm	**2.** _____
Score _____ %	**3.** _____
▶ **100%**	**Check answers after the next quiz.**
Score = number correct × 33.	

B. Rapid Reading

Take no more than 4 minutes (= 437 wpm) to read the story rapidly. Fill in the details regarding the narrator's ordeal.

1. As a skier, Robin seems to be:
    a. sensible.
    b. reckless.
    c. timid.
    d. an overplanner.

2. Robin's fall was caused by:
    a. an avalanche.
    b. melted snow.
    c. his carelessness.
    d. his friend accidentally pushing him.

3. Robin realized that in order to survive, he needed to:
    a. eat daily.
    b. stay put.
    c. stay calm.
    d. call for help.

4. Robin survives on his own for:
    a. a week.
    b. ten days.
    c. two weeks.
    d. a month.

5. This narrative shows the power of:
    a. cheerfulness and determination in the face of adversity.
    b. physical strength.
    c. the love of family and friends.
    d. nature in determining one's fate.

Sel. 10 R-Read	1. _____
Finish _____ : _____	2. _____
Start _____ : _____	3. _____
Time _____ : _____	4. _____
min sec	5. _____
Rate _____ wpm	**Check answers to both quizzes**
Find rate on p. 330.	**with your instructor.**
Score _____ %	**Record rate and score on p. 183.**
▶ **80%**	
Score = number correct x 20.	

C. Questions for Discussion and Writing

1. Reread the story and find three ingenious ways that Robin finds to survive.
2. Robin realizes that "God exists within the person who believes in God." What is Robin saying here, and how does it relate to his story of survival?
3. Why does Robin conclude that his ordeal was "the greatest experience of my life"? How do you think this experience changed him for the better?

How to Record Your Scores on the Progress Chart

After you have finished a Timed Selection and have entered your time and score in the score box:

1. Find the correct selection number on the top row of the chart. Transfer your rate (wpm) to the chart, under the selection number. Make a dot, **X**, bar, or other mark. (If you know your time only, not your rate, you must first look up your wpm in the Rate Table in the appendix. Then mark that number on the chart.) Note that the acceptable or "target" rates for the featured skill are shaded. Do your rates fall within the target area?
2. Transfer your comprehension score to the top blank on the chart. Note that the acceptable or "target" percentage for that selection is printed underneath the blank. Does your score meet—or surpass—the target percentage?
3. Connect the rate marks with a line, to see your progress clearly. Remember, though, that your scores will not necessarily rise steadily. The different selections contain too many variables—difficulty, your interest in or familiarity with the topic, and so forth.

PROGRESS CHART: RAPID READING

Selection number	1	2	3	4	5	6	7	8	9	10
% Comprehension	%	%	%	%	%	%	%	%	%	%
Target % ▶	80%	80%	80%	80%	80%	80%	80%	80%	84%	80%

Words per minute (wpm = rate)

Target Rates

	1	2	3	4	5	6	7	8	9	10
1000										
950										
900										
850										
800										
750										
700										
650										
600										
550										
500										
450										
400										
350										
300										
250										
200										

Selection number

CHAPTER 5

Overview Skimming

*C*hapter 5 teaches a second kind of speeded (time-pressured) reading: overview skimming for main ideas. The proficient reader will find it just as practical as the rapid reading taught in Chapter 4. Once again, you should make sure your materials (the What) and your purpose (the Why) are proper for this high-speed treatment. Overview skimming is probably the closest thing in this book to the so-called speed-reading of commercial courses. Actually, every reader has skimmed prose often, perhaps without being aware of it. But since you may find it difficult to do in a controlled way at first, we provide an extra measure of Practices—before the Timed Selections.

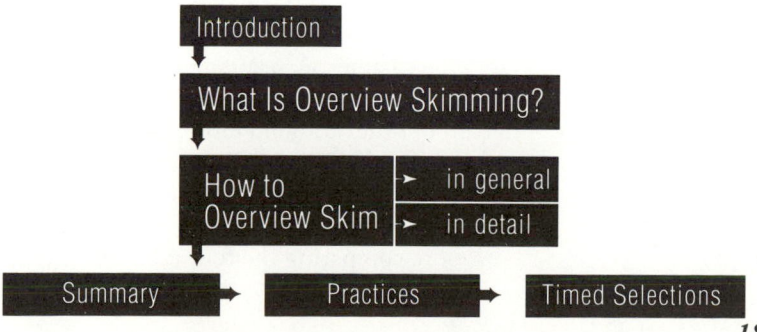

INTRODUCTION TO OVERVIEW SKIMMING

CHECKLIST OF SYMPTOMS

Do you often:

_____ 1. wonder at and secretly envy the speed-reader, who turns a page every ten seconds yet seems to get the gist of the book?

_____ 2. wish that you could grasp the main point of an article, a business letter, a report, or an essay without reading the entire thing?

_____ 3. believe that it's impossible to get the main ideas of a selection without reading all of it?

_____ 4. believe that it *is* possible, but don't know which parts to skip and which to read?

_____ 5. wish you could sometimes process print even faster than you did in Chapter 4, Rapid Reading, where the top speed was 800 wpm?

If you checked one or more of these symptoms, you should be interested in the next reading technique, overview skimming. When you have mastered it, you will be able to skim prose of average difficulty at rates over 800 wpm, yet grasp and retain all the main ideas.

We hope that the Introduction, Practices, and Timed Selections of Chapter 4, Rapid Reading, brought about some behavior changes in you, especially if you began as a typical compulsive reader. For example, did you rid yourself of the 100 percent compulsion, accepting comprehension scores of 70 to 80 percent? Did you manage to let go of occasional words—to infer them through your use of peripheral vision, soft focus, and shortened margins? We hope so, because we will now ask you to settle for only 50 percent comprehension and to let go of entire paragraphs, sections, even pages!

In this book, overview skimming is the fourth reading technique that is time-pressured. The first three, as you recall, were preview skimming of all reading materials (Chapter 1), scanning for answers to specific questions (Chapter 2), and rapid reading of general materials (Chapter 4). Once again you will be timing yourself in order to build efficiency, and once again you will start with the first step, preview skimming. (Remember, we told you to "Preview everything first!") But in some other respects, overview skimming differs from the other three speeded methods.

Before comparing the four methods, though, we should define the term.

WHAT IS OVERVIEW SKIMMING?

First, the word *skimming*. You already know from your study of preview skimming and rapid reading that anything called skimming must take place at high rates, over 800 or 900 wpm. At these rates, the eyes cannot see and "read" all the print on the page, so they must be skipping over some of it. (In fact, some experts call all kinds of skimming skip-reading or selective reading.) This is true of overview skimming. You will be aiming at overall rates of 900 to 1,000 wpm and up, but you will not attempt to read all the print—only certain selected portions of it. Some readers actually learn to overview skim for main ideas at 1,500 wpm or better, which translates into four to five paperback pages per minute (= twelve to fifteen seconds per page).

Second, the word *overview*. An overview is a rather general, holistic view of the content. You aim for only the gist of the reading material—the main idea(s), the core, the outline—plus some of the major supporting details. True, your goal will be to understand and retain all (100 percent) of the main ideas, but you will ignore most of the details. You will not be reading and grasping the entire selection as you did in rapid reading. On average, a skimmer comprehends only about 50 percent of the total content. This selective process takes practice and discipline, since the details often make up the most interesting and accessible parts of an article, news story, or other nonfiction work. But only by skipping them and focusing on the main ideas can you reach the overall high rates that characterize skimming.

How does overview skimming compare with the speeded techniques you have already practiced?

1. Like rapid reading, it is used on one-dimensional prose—easy to moderate difficulty—or where your purpose is not analysis and study but a surface understanding only. As in all comprehension, you must be familiar with basic literal comprehension. You must know the vocabulary, distinguish between main ideas and details, and pay special attention to all the writer's signals: titles, transitions, and key words. Organizational patterns, too, become crucial as you move through prose at high speed, trying to understand the main ideas without reading all the support.

2. Overview skimming is much like preview skimming in that you carefully read the same key parts of the passage: titles, beginnings, and endings. However, while previewing prepares you to go back to the material for a more thorough reading, overviewing is the *only* reading you will do on it. Therefore, you must spend a little more time and read the key parts more thoughtfully than you would if you were only previewing.

What do you learn through overview skimming? How does your comprehension compare with careful reading or rapid reading? First, like a preview, a good overview can tell you whether you want to read the material more carefully.

Second, by itself it can give you the thesis, the main support for the thesis, and the organizational patterns (but not many details). For example, it can tell you what the Supreme Court's latest ruling is (but not how the justices arrived at it). A good overview can tell you the overall style, the main characters, and the plot outline of a novel (but you won't get to enjoy the clever dialogue or beautiful descriptions). It will tell you the main features of your insurance policy (but not whether it will cover that peculiar little accident you had last week). As with rapid reading, overview skimming may not do justice to many a fine piece of writing, but it is better than not reading at all. And for many of your reading purposes and materials, it is a very handy technique.

In fact, you have done this kind of skimming already, many times—whenever you have looked over a page of the daily newspaper, or flipped through an article while waiting in a checkout line, or looked through last year's magazines before throwing them out, or reviewed textbook chapters already studied. In all these situations you were skimming for overview—to get the gist, the main ideas. So now all you must do is learn how and when to use this skill most effectively.

HOW TO OVERVIEW SKIM—IN GENERAL

When you preview skim, you raise questions about the reading material. When you overview skim, you gain answers—about the main points in an argument, the conclusions of a research study, the outcome of a trial, the story line of a novel. How is it possible to find these answers at rates over 800 wpm?

You can do it because, as we said in the beginning of Chapter 1, all writing has a structure, whether obvious or not. All prose writers work from outlines or plans of some sort. When you overview skim, you imagine that you are reading for only the major headings of the outline. For example, a typical essay outline might look like this:

I. The Western movie (1930–1950) as history
  A. Focused on only about 30 years of actual history
  B. Fostered stereotypes: Indians, outlaws, dance-hall women, lawmen
II. The Western movie as myth
  A. Symbolized universal, individual struggle
    1. Against forces of nature
    2. Against "evil"—in self and in others
      Ex.: Gary Cooper in *High Noon*
  B. Symbolized rise of "civilized society"
    1. Church
    2. Schools
    3. Farming
      Ex.: settlers in *Shane* vs. cattlemen
    4. Law, courts, sheriffs

Roman numerals I and II are topics, letters A and B are major details, numbers 1–4 plus the examples are relatively minor details.

If you were overview skimming, you would try to skip over details, examples, repetitions, and filler—the numbered items toward the right side of the outline—and concentrate on the main ideas—the I and II, A and B items—toward the left. (Remember, if your purpose is to enjoy the details, you should elect to do slow reading or rapid reading, not skimming!)

Where does a writer place these headings or main ideas in his or her written work? By now, you know the answer: in the title, the subtitle, the lead-in (explanatory note under the title), subheadings throughout the selection, and all beginnings and endings. A reader who is skimming will slow down and notice beginnings of paragraphs, sections, and chapters, and any summary or concluding part, whether it's one sentence or several pages.

Another thing a good overview skimmer must do is notice writing patterns. As you learned in Chapter 1, organization is always an integral part of content; how something is developed or supported is essential to basic literal comprehension. So patterns are especially important to a skimmer, who is trying to grasp the outline of the ideas, not only accurately but also at high speed. To do this, of course, the skimmer must not miss any transitions or other signals. For example, if the passage seems to follow a strong cause-effect pattern, the skimmer makes sure to grasp all the causes and all the effects and to follow the writer's argument linking the two.

Recognizing the organizational pattern also helps increase your skimming speed, since you can thereby sort essential from nonessential material more easily. For example, if you have grasped a writer's main point and reinforced it by reading one specific example, you can skip the next five *for examples* and *for instances*. Some reading experts think that 60 percent of one's skimming skill lies in the ability to recognize patterns immediately.

Remember that a key transition may be very short—like *but*. Or it may be quite long—entire sentences, even paragraphs.

HOW TO OVERVIEW SKIM—IN DETAIL

Imagine that you have before you a newspaper or magazine article, a chapter of an easy paperback book, a long memo or report, or an editorial. You don't have time to read it slowly—or even rapidly. You want to know the thesis and all the main ideas, with some of the important details (about 50 percent of the total content).

1. Preview skim first. Do a minimal preview, since you don't intend to read as a next step, only to skim. Take only a few seconds to focus your mind on the passage and raise questions. As usual, check out the length, title, subtitle (if any), source and date, author, divisions or subheadings, and difficulty level.

A title may be of little help to your overview. It may not even indicate the topic; for example, "Yesterday" could be about anything. Then again, it may state the topic: "Farm Subsidies" or "Farm Subsidies in the 90s." But if the title reads "Time to Reevaluate Farm Subsidies," you know the topic plus the main idea. The selection will undoubtedly include both pros and cons on the subject. In other words, a good title prepares you for the probable content of a selection; you can anticipate to some extent. Such anticipation is invaluable for better comprehension and (ultimately) speed.

Turn to Practices 5.1–5.4, beginning on page 196. You will try to discriminate at high speed between titles and subtitles that are too broad or vague to help in skimming, and titles and subtitles that are more suggestive. (Of course, your minimal preview would include more than just the title, but not much more.)

2.   Go back and start to read selectively. It is important that you select the key areas intelligently and read them carefully, for (unlike what you do in rapid reading) when you overview skim, you will not return! In some cases you may need to reread a key part or read very slowly in order to fully grasp the main ideas the writer is expressing.

Key parts usually include (after title and subtitle):

a.   Lead-in, if any
b.   All of the first paragraph or introduction
c.   All the beginnings of key paragraphs, as indicated by signal words and phrases, plus one or two important details
d.   All of the last paragraph or conclusion

Like all rules, these are to be used flexibly. You will have to adapt them to fit the subject matter, the length of your material (from one page to an entire book), and the writer's style. For example, unless the selection has a strong time sequence or step-by-step pattern, you may choose not to skim the piece in one direction from beginning to end, but rather to jump around from part to part, constructing the "big picture" from bits and pieces. Or, you may want to read the ending before you read the beginning. Many professional writers save their thesis until the end. So skimming backward in a selection is not as zany as it sounds.

Especially notice any *lead-in*—a short summary by a writer or an editor, often in italics, that follows the title or the subtitle. It is a good indicator of what is to follow, and it sometimes provides a complete summary of the article or report. All you have to do is skim the body for organization and major details.

Always use the typographical aids given you by the writer and the editor. For instance, watch for paragraphing: Our system of indenting is invaluable for a skimmer. Also notice any breaks in the print that indicate new sections. John Hersey used an extra line space in his nonfiction book *Hiroshima* to signal a shift from one of his six interviewees to another. Even fiction writers may employ breaks or spacing in a meaningful way to show shifts in time, place, or point of view.

In long works, such as novels (fiction) or nonfiction books, try reading carefully the beginning and ending of each chapter. You'll be surprised how much these parts tell you about the book. You can often get a broad but quite accurate idea of topics covered, style, place and time settings, where the book starts and where it ends, and major characters.

Of course, there are exceptions to this rule about the importance of endings. Straight news stories do not end with summaries; they stop where the editor chopped them off to fit the available space. However, most plays, short stories, poems, essays, editorials, feature articles, novels, and even sermons save the strongest statement of their message for the very end.

There are even exceptions to the rule that beginnings are important. For example, if the first paragraph of a selection introduces the writer's thesis, you should read it carefully. On the other hand, it may only be a "hook" to entice the stray reader—a personal-interest story or a very minor, colorful detail. How many of us would really want to read—or even skim—an article that began, "Yet another dreary tax-reform package has emanated from Washington today"? But what if it began, "Josepha Smelkington stared down at the two quarters and one dime in her hand. How would she ever pay for the paperback textbook for her new course in welding?" By the time we empathize with Josepha, we are deep into an article on tax reform. Skimmers are in a hurry, however. They learn to skip over the hook and slow down only when they find the true introduction or thesis.

Turn to Practice 5.5 on page 198. Distinguish between the professional writer's sly hooks and true thesis statements.

So much for deciding where the main body of a work begins. You also might ask, "How does a reader know which paragraphs in the body are the key paragraphs?" Often, a paragraph is not essential to the gist of a selection. It may be a bridge (transition) linking one group of paragraphs with another, or a digression, or the umpteenth repetition of an idea. A skimmer of course tries to skip over these paragraphs. The clue is usually found in the opening words. A good writer will indicate through various signals that the paragraph is, or is not, an important one.

Turn to Practices 5.6 and 5.7, beginning on page 199, and try to discriminate among paragraph openings.

3. Time yourself rigorously! If you find yourself reading all the details and all the middles of paragraphs, and if your rate falls below 800 wpm, then you are probably reading everything, not skimming. To ensure that you keep skimming, simply watch the clock. If necessary, reskim a selection over and over until you finish it within the skimming time limit (900 wpm or faster).

   As in every reading task, your mind-set is all-important. Keep reminding yourself that you want only the main ideas, that the details must wait for another kind of reading. Keep aiming for only about 50 percent of the total content. If you discover you are retaining 80–90 percent of the details, you have slipped back from skimming to reading.

4. This next point is often missed by "speed-reading" teachers: Use a highly variable rate within the material itself. When you overview skim correctly, you read key parts carefully (maybe even reread them), race past unimportant material, then slow down and read carefully, and so on. In other words, the high skimming rates do not result from a superfast reading of all the words, as most beginners believe. Rather, they result from what is not read at all.

As you learn to skim, you may find you cannot achieve this fast-slow-fast pace with your eyes alone. The habit of reading at an even pace, whether fast or slow, is hard to break. If this applies to you, then you need a "crutch."

Crutch 1: Use your fingers to point out key passages, such as the beginning of a group of paragraphs. Read carefully. Then run your hand down lines, paragraphs, pages if necessary, and point to the next key passage. Make your eyes and your brain follow your hand. This way, you cannot dally on the interesting trivia. Crutch 2: Read aloud, or at least mumble, the key passages as you point them out. Crutch 3: If you still tend to read it all rather than skim, try highlighting the key passages in a bright color first. Then go back and make sure you read only what is highlighted. You can try these three tips out on the last two Practices, or on the Timed Selections if necessary. Eventually you will be able to skip over, then read, then skip over, at will.

Of course, the real problem when you skim is not where your hand or your eyes go. The problem is to think, to sift through material and locate the gist very rapidly. It takes an alert mind; it also takes repeated timed practice.

Turn to Practice 5.8, beginning on page 200. Here you will practice discriminating among details of support for various topics. In skimming complete works, you would expect to read the relevant details carefully and to skip over the less relevant ones.

5. Use your eyes in the most efficient way for skimming long passages. Of course, key passages must be read carefully and thoroughly. But as you are looking down a page for these passages, try moving your eyes in a slow, wide-ranging spiral down the lines. The soft-focus, floating manner you learned in rapid reading is applicable here, as well as the concept of shortening your margins. The whole idea is to prevent yourself from reading everything, including unessential details, at the same rate.

    Again, if your eyes seem to want to see and read every word on every line, use your hand to direct your vision down the page. Remember to keep alert for topic sentences, key transitions and other signals, breaks, spacing, capital letters, or other essential signs of the main ideas and the structure. Stop immediately and read slowly when you see such elements.

Turn to any timed selection in Chapter 4 and, with your teacher's direction, practice skimming down a page.

6. Use your eyes efficiently when skimming through single key paragraphs. If a paragraph seems important by itself, read to find the topic sentence. Usually (70–90 percent of the time, according to the experts), it will be the first or the second sentence in the paragraph. Read this sentence carefully. Rather than skip over the rest of the paragraph entirely, check it out—use soft focus to pass rapidly through it. Watch for any important detail or signal. You may spiral through or force your eyes through on a slant. This takes only a few seconds, but it can either confirm your first impression of the paragraph's main point or uncover an important shift in or addition to the main point.

Turn to Practice 5.9 on page 201 and see how these eye movements work as you skim one paragraph at a time.

With all this emphasis on speed, you may wonder about other aids, such as a mechanical gadget or a hand-held index card. After all, you recall that these were recommended in Chapter 4 for rapid reading. And students often imagine that if they can keep a card moving over print steadily at a high enough rate— 900–1,500 wpm, for example—they will be overview skimming very effectively. However, a moment's thought will show that this is not the case. The slow-fast-slow, variable rate required for skimming would be greatly hampered by any method that promoted an even rate, even though it might be rapid.

Perhaps we have been overstressing the pitfalls and problems of overview skimming. Actually, in much of the prose you will come across, the "writer's path" is clearly written and carefully constructed, with headings, topic sentences, beginnings, endings, and transitions—all the things that lend themselves to skimming. (Textbook writers pride themselves on this kind of writing!) On the whole, you will find overview skimming a wonderful tool for learning a great deal in a short time, In fact, many business and professional people learn to skim simply to keep up with the flood of memos, reports, and journals that land on their desks.

To see how overview skimming can work for you in typical expository prose, read the following outline of an article, drawn from the first sentences of the paragraphs. Notice how you can get the gist of the article just by reading these selected sentences carefully. They represent about one-fifth of the original article. Remember, don't speed or skip anything—these *are* the key parts! And don't time yourself. The numbers refer to the order in which the paragraphs appeared in the article.

1. (Thesis) In my opinion, students should pay a higher parking fee than they do now.
2. The current fee is fairly low—about one-half the fee at three nearby colleges.
3. We need to develop a fund to pay for construction of a new parking garage.
4. Residents near the college are becoming angrier every year, as they lose all their parking spaces to students.
5. Some residents are threatening to hire an attorney and sue the college.
6. The state will no longer pay half the costs of new parking facilities, as in the past. Where will the money come from?
7. Therefore, I propose doubling the present $30/month fee.

You are probably an expert on this local issue already, just by reading the key sentences!

Turn to Practices 5.10 and 5.11, beginning on page 203. First, try grasping the main ideas of an article by reading only its paragraph beginnings. Then continue into a complete article, marking transitions and key passages and skipping over less important parts.

Once you have finished, you will be ready to overview skim the series of timed selections that follow the Practices.

SUMMARY

Overview skimming is a speeded technique designed to give a reader the gist of a selection or the outline of a selection's main ideas from just one pass-through. Like rapid reading, overview skimming is best used for general reading—that is, easy to moderate nonfiction—but it can give the reader some idea of the content of even difficult material, such as textbooks. It is never a substitute for careful, analytical reading.

Overview skimming is somewhat slower and more thorough than preview skimming, faster and less thorough than rapid reading. The skimmer aims for about 50 percent of the total content—but *all* of the main ideas of a work. Overviewing requires an uneven pace, not a steady one as in most reading. The overall high rate for any given selection—800–1,500 wpm—results from the material that is skipped over. The skimmer continues to read the key parts carefully. The challenge in overviewing is to distinguish, under considerable time pressure, key parts from unimportant parts.

When you skim, you must pay special attention to titles, lead-ins, headings, graphic devices, transitions, patterns of organization, and beginnings and endings—any parts that are likely to contain the thesis and the main ideas. For single paragraphs, you read the topic sentence, if stated, and glance through the rest of the paragraph. In longer works, you may read only beginnings and endings of sections or chapters. You rely on soft focus, shortened margins, and floating on a slant or an S curve as you pass rapidly through less important material.

To skim well, you must be physically and mentally alert. Don't decide to overview skim some books at bedtime or next to a swimming pool! You have to constantly synthesize the writer's ideas from a few sentences and paragraphs, and translate these bits into a meaningful whole without missing key parts or distorting the whole. Skimming is rather hard to do if the material is fiction, if the style is disorganized or indirect (requiring much inference), or if the subject is unfamiliar to you. But you can learn to do it fairly easily if the material (the What) is clearly organized, loaded with signals, and on a familiar topic.

Pragmatically, skimming enables you to get through the morning paper in twenty minutes, an average article in about ten minutes, an entire magazine in an hour, and a paperback in a few hours.

Last, overview skimming requires a certain debonair attitude toward the parts you skip. That attitude will be fully justified the day you return to some work you originally skimmed, read through it slowly, and realize you're gaining little additional content—you had already grasped most of it!

SUMMARY BOX: OVERVIEW SKIMMING

What?	Why?	Acceptable Comprehension	Acceptable Rates
General materials, light-moderate difficulty, familiar topics and fields, supplemental reading, newspapers and magazines, general business mail (prior to discarding it)	For overview, outline, thesis, main idea plus major details, structure; general idea of style; passing acquaintance with best-sellers	50–60% (But *all* the main ideas!)	800–1,500 wpm

PRACTICES: OVERVIEW SKIMMING

These Practices break down the art of skimming into its small elements, from easy to difficult. Please do not skip around; do the Practices in order. Time yourself rigorously—skimming requires pressure!

Answers are not provided in the answer key. Please check your answers with the instructor.

5.1 GOOD (HELPFUL TO SKIMMERS) TITLE VERSUS POOR TITLES

A skilled skimmer begins thinking ahead to possible main ideas, starting from the beginning of a work—that is, from the title (and subtitle, if any). In each of the following items, one title contains strong clues about the content of the article. Read down the list as fast as you can, putting a checkmark (√) by the helpful titles. Be able to explain your choices.

Try to finish the list in 20 seconds.

1. ___√___ Samuel Sorenson, Savior of St. Simeon's Seminary
   _____ St. Simeon's Seminary
   _____ Samuel Sorenson

2. ___√___ Mr. Jones's Matchbook Collection
   ___√___ The Hobby That Became a Hazard

3. _____ Surrogate Motherhood
   ___√___ When Surrogate Mothers Change Their Minds
   _____ A Major Problem with Surrogacy

4. _____ A Discussion About Growth Hormones
   ___√___ Dr. Yule B. Biggar, Advocate of Growth Hormones

5. ___√___ Elvis Disciple Says He Has No Problem with Identity
   ___√___ Interview with Houston's Most Visible Elvis Fan
   _____ Elvis Look-alikes

Time: _____ : 20
Number correct, of 5 __4__
Ask your instructor for answers.

5.2 ANTICIPATING CONTENT FROM GOOD TITLES

Time out! Look back over the titles you correctly checked as helpful. Choose two that interest you. For each title, jot down at least two subheadings that you imagine you would find in the article, if you were to read it. (A good skimmer is an alert, aggressive reader!)

> EXAMPLE: Title: Samuel Sorenson, Savior of St. Simeon's Seminary
> 1. S. prevented a freeway from being built through seminary.
> 2. S. gave $2 million toward remodeling seminary.

1. Title: _____
   Subhead a: _____
   Subhead b: _____

2. Title: _____
   Subhead a: _____
   Subhead b: _____

Check answers with your instructor. Answers will vary.

5.3 MORE GOOD TITLES VERSUS POOR TITLES

Do this exercise the same way you did Practice 5.1, but work faster this time. Aim for 15 seconds.

1. _____ Living with Three Parrots
   __✓__ The Macaw Mafia in Our House
2. __✓__ Latino Groups Not Single Voting Bloc
   _____ Latino Groups in the U.S.
   __✓__ Politics Among Latino Groups
3. _____ Morality and the Arts
   __✓__ Public Funding of the Arts: Whose Morality?
4. __✓__ "U.S. English"—A Hidden Agenda?
   __✓__ The Campaign for English as Our Official Language
5. __✓__ Amtrak
   __✓__ What's Wrong with Amtrak
   __✓__ An Analysis of Amtrak Today

Time _____ : 15
Number correct, of 5 __2__
Check answers with your instructor.

5.4 MORE ANTICIPATING CONTENT FROM GOOD TITLES

Time out! Again, as a skilled skimmer, try to anticipate the "writer's path." Choose two of the titles you correctly identified as helpful. Then jot down at least two subheadings that you imagine you would find in the article, if you were to read it.

1. Title: _____
    Subhead a: _____
    Subhead b: _____

2. Title: _____
    Subhead a: _____
    Subhead b: _____

Check answers with your instructor. Answers will vary.

5.5 DISTINGUISHING THE "HOOK" FROM THE THESIS STATEMENT

Here are typical first sentences of articles, essays, feature stories, and editorials. Read through them quickly, putting a checkmark (√) before paragraphs that probably introduce the writer's thesis or main point. Leave the detailed "hook" or human-interest beginnings blank.

Try to finish in 30 seconds or less.

1. _____ a. Apartment complex manager Al Tyson still remembers only too vividly that hot afternoon in Watts 25 years ago today.
    __√__ b. After 25 years, some people in Watts are better off; but most are not.

2. _____ a. Susan Birch and Margaret Taylor have been neighbors for 16 years, but they have not spoken to each other for the past 8.
    __√__ b. Much of the current controversy over abortion arises over differing views of when a human life actually begins.

3. __√__ a. Can a woman's beauty actually work against her in a business career?
    _____ b. Could it be, she asked herself, that she was being passed over for promotions because she was too pretty?

4. _____ a. We interviewed this group of preteens as they waited for a bus.
    __√__ b. Even among hip urban youth, not all agree that rap music is harmless and should be protected.
    _____ c. One young girl drew out a copy of a letter she had written to the local paper, sharply criticizing rap lyrics.

5. __√__ a. The survey shows that even today, even in the U.S., working moms do more than their share of the housework.
    _____ b. The cartoon strip "Sally Forth" often presents the arguments working couples have over sharing home chores.
    _____ c. Paul Fogarty's wife, Katy, says he probably does 60 percent of the housework, but both parents think they are the exception.

Time _____ : 30

Number correct, of 5 5

Check answers with your instructor.

5.6 RECOGNIZING IMPORTANT PARAGRAPHS: READ THE SIGNALS

Nonfiction prose writers do not always herald their key paragraphs with transition words or signals. But when they do, the skimmer must take notice!

Imagine that the president has decided to send troops to some distant nation. In a regular column, a news analyst critiques the plan, and you want to skim over the main points of his or her argument. Read rapidly through this list of paragraph beginnings, putting a checkmark (√) before those that indicate important paragraphs you must read carefully. Leave the others blank. Try to finish in 15 seconds or less.

_____ a.   There is one major drawback to . . .

_____ b.   On the other hand, the action, if successful, could result in a real gain . . .

_____ c.   It is no doubt too late to consider the alternative, which . . .

_____ d.   One small but interesting bit of history . . .

_____ e.   Two criteria that must be met . . .

_____ f.   The most crucial stage will be . . .

_____ g.   Last year, one senator was overheard to say . . .

_____ h.   To sum up, it is clear that . . .

Time _____ : 20
Number correct, of 8 __5__
Check answers with your instructor.

5.7 RECOGNIZING KEY OR TOPIC SENTENCES

As we learned in Chapter 1, Essential Reading Skills, not all paragraphs have topic sentences. And of those that do, the sentence may be anywhere (although usually it's the first or second sentence). And sometimes only a *part* of a sentence contains the topic! A good skimmer learns to read carefully only the key part and skip the rest.

In fact, writers may distinguish their important ideas from their less important ideas with markers as subtle as a punctuation mark, modifier, or subordinate conjunction. Or you may get a clue from the placement in a sentence or paragraph. (Recall that beginnings and endings are preferred placements for main ideas.)

Underline the *part* of each sentence that indicates the writer's main idea. Discuss your answers.

Example: His truck had hit my Yugo, but *I walked away unhurt.*
I walked away unhurt, but still his truck had hit my Yugo.

Example: Home is where they have to take you in, even when you're broke. Don't live at home, *even if you're broke.*

Now read through these ten sentences rapidly. If the entire item is a topic sentence, write "all." If only a part of the sentence is important for skimming for main ideas, underline that part. Try to finish in less than 30 seconds.

Example: At age 10, James had decided on his career: flute player. (all)
Unlike his brothers, who were all tone-deaf, James had decided on his career—flute player—at age 10.

1. Although margarine has been considered healthful for years, today's medical report states that it is not.
2. The poll showed that, although 8 percent of the people were undecided, 92 percent had strong opinions both pro and con.
3. Ninety-two percent of those polled had strong opinions; however, almost 10 percent had no opinion at all!
4. Weather reports warn of strong winds tonight from Hurricane Mephistopheles.
5. Although weather reports warn of strong winds tonight from Hurricane Mephistopheles, the townspeople remain surprisingly unconcerned.
6. Forest fires in Yellowstone and Yosemite look tragic; but wildfire is just part of the natural cycle.
7. Wildfire may be just part of the natural cycle; but the recent fires in Yellowstone and Yosemite are tragic for our disappearing wilderness. (Notice the position of opposing ideas. Also notice the word choice: *just, are.*)
8. Dr. Barker believes that cosmetic surgery for dogs is justified; other veterinarians think it is silly.
9. Many veterinarians think cosmetic surgery for dogs is silly; Dr. Barker disagrees.
10. The town has banned swearing in all restaurants, but no one expects it to be enforced.

> Time _____ : _____
> Number correct, of 10 _____
> Check answers with your instructor.

5.8 RECOGNIZING IMPORTANT DETAILS OF SUPPORT

You have discriminated among titles, paragraph beginnings, and parts of key (topic) sentences. Now try to discriminate among subtopics included within a selection.

Here are four possible subjects for magazine or newspaper articles. Each one is followed by details of support. As fast as possible, read each subject and keep it clearly in mind as you read the details. Put a checkmark (√) before any detail that provides important support for the topic and therefore should be read if you are overview skimming. If you can afford to skip over a detail, leave it blank.

Try to do each list in 15 seconds or less. Do all four in 1 minute or less.

1. Topic: A dog is a better pet than a cat.
    _____ a. Birds and fish make good pets too.
    _____ b. Cats have more personality than most people realize.
    _____ c. A dog can warn of intruders; did you ever meet a cat who would?
    _____ d. A dog just lies on furniture; he doesn't claw it.
    _____ e. Some dogs attack mail carriers and other friendly strangers.

2. Topic: Smoking should not be banned in public restaurants.
    _____ a. Some people enjoy a cigarette with meals.
    _____ b. Some people ban all smoking from their homes.
    _____ c. Look at what happened in cities that passed such laws.
    _____ d. Restaurants may lose customers as a result.
    _____ e. Smoking can affect nonsmokers who also have a right to eat out.

3. Topic: This city could do more to comply with federal clean-air standards.
    _____ a. Put special vapor-proof nozzles on gasoline pumps.
    _____ b. More people move into the city every year.
    _____ c. Time traffic lights to lessen stop-and-go driving.
    _____ d. Try newer, faster, more frequent bus service.
    _____ e. Industries are already among the cleanest in the state.

4. Topic: Disadvantages of a big family
    _____ a. Both parents may have to work to support children.
    _____ b. In older age, it is nice to have many siblings.
    _____ c. Parents spend less money and attention on each child.
    _____ d. Why contribute to an already overcrowded world?
    _____ e. Siblings are not necessarily similar or close.

Time for all 4 _1_:_00_
Number correct, of 20 _16_

Check answers with your instructor.

Do you now feel as if you could skip over parts of your reading that do not directly pertain to the thesis or main ideas? If so, you have the mind-set necessary for overview skimming at 900 wpm and up!

5.9 USING YOUR EYES EFFICIENTLY WHEN SKIMMING A PARAGRAPH

By now, you realize that you must read certain parts of your material carefully, such as key paragraphs or the topic sentences of other paragraphs. But even if a paragraph is important, you may wish to use the slow-fast method of reading. Practice this on the following sample paragraphs, then try to transfer this style to paragraphs in longer works.

First, read the italicized topic sentence carefully, slowly, and with full comprehension. Then rapidly and easily, skim through the body of the paragraph in a spiral or on a slant. Take only 10 seconds for each paragraph. (You may use your finger or hand on the print for both steps, if it helps.) The skimming will usually verify your first impression of the main idea. But be alert for any shift or contrasting element.

1. *Washington D.C. should be allowed to become a state*—the 51st. Residents feel they live in the last American colony. As it exists now, the District has federal taxation but no representation, and this was what started the American Revolution! Its representative in the House is a nonvoting member, and it has no senator. Residents feel it is unfair that they are the only U.S. citizens who have no federal political power, only local. They say they lose much of their citizenship status when they choose to work in Washington.

2. *Washington D.C. should not become a state.* First, the District belongs to all the American people; it stands for *federal* in our system. Second, it is too small to be a state. Its population is 700,000; fifteen cities are larger. Giving Washington two senators would give it equal power in the Senate with big states like New York (18 million) and California (30 million). Last, residents should not complain about lack of federal programs; the entire city is a federal program. Taxes from all of us go to pay for the existence of the city.

3. *Careful planning and expertise are crucial to a sound business partnership*, according to a partner in an accounting firm. Entering a partnership is very much like getting married. Unless you know the person well, communicate openly, and develop trust, you may end up in court. He says, "You must clearly define what each partner will contribute and the percentage of ownership. It is also important to make arrangements up front as to how the partnership will obtain additional cash if there are operating deficits."*

4. According to recent surveys, the United States ranks low among Western nations for infant mortality. Infant death rates are high largely as a result of low birth weights and premature births. In turn, these factors have always been linked to the physical state of the mother. Now, however, an old wives' tale—the mother's psychological state can cause birth problems—has been vindicated. *It seems to be true that, as our grandmothers believed, emotional shock and stress in the mother can bring about premature labor and birth.*

The last paragraph was different, wasn't it? Did your fast skimming show you the true "topic sentence"? Did you notice an important transition within the paragraph? Luckily for readers, most expository prose paragraphs follow the pattern seen in 1 through 3 rather than the one in 4.

Los Angeles Times, August 17, 1990, p. D3.

5.10 GRASPING THE THESIS FROM A FEW WELL-CHOSEN BEGINNINGS

The following topic sentences are excerpted from a short article in a store newsletter. (The numbers refer to paragraphs.) The writer's style is unusually concise; but even here, we can read about one-quarter of the total words—100 words—and still understand the gist of the article.

Do not time the exercise, since key passages should be read carefully when you overview skim. However, do notice and retain the development, in time sequence, of America's relationship with the metric system. Do not look ahead to the complete article.

Topic sentences, Article A: "Does the U.S. Measure Up?" by Karen E. Debats (*Fedco Reporter*, March 1985, p. 27). Total words in article: 362.

1. Only one holdout remains: The United States.
2. It wasn't supposed to be this way. . . . 1975 . . . experts were predicting a total conversion to metrics in the U.S. by 1985.
3. The American public, however, had other ideas.
4. But this doesn't mean the metric system is dead in the U.S.
5. A 1982 survey revealed that of the Fortune 1000 companies, 16% had suffered some loss of sales because of a failure to use metrics in product design.
6. U.S. metric experts predict that a changeover will take place by the year 2000. . . . If all goes well, the U.S. will indeed measure up—in metrics.

Now compare your understanding of the article with the complete article, reprinted here. If you overview skimmed correctly, there should be no surprises—only some additional details.

DOES THE U.S. MEASURE UP?

by Karen E. Debats

1   When the French invented the metric system in the 1790s, their goal was to replace the British system of feet, gallons, and pounds with something easier to use. Each unit in the new system—centimeters, millimeters, kilometers—was to be 10 times as big as the unit preceding it. Now, nearly 200 years later, most of the world has changed to metrics. Only one holdout remains: The United States.

2   It wasn't supposed to be this way. The Metric Conversion Act, passed by Congress in 1975, legislated a voluntary changeover to the metric system of weights and measures. Within two years, the National Weather Service announced plans to report temperatures in degrees Celsius, barometric pressure in millimeters, and windspeeds in kilometers per hour. Then the Federal Highway Administration decided to add kilometer distances to all highway signs and eventually drop mileage readings altogether. It wasn't long before experts were predicting a total conversion to metrics in the U.S. by 1985.

3   The American public, however, had other ideas. In a 1977 Gallup Poll, Americans opposed

metrics by more than two to one. As a result, both the National Weather Service and the Federal Highway Administration changed their plans.

4   But this doesn't mean the metric system is dead in the U.S. A gradual conversion to metrics has taken place. For example, all wine bottles have been in metric sizes since 1979. Almost all packaged foods are now labeled in both metric and British units.

5   A 1982 survey revealed that of the Fortune 1000 companies, 16% had suffered some loss of sales because of a failure to use metrics in product design. The same survey also found that a majority produced at least one metric-designed prod-

uct, and such products accounted for a third of their total net sales. Today, U.S. companies are even more committed to metric-designed products because of foreign competition.

6   U.S. metric experts predict that a changeover will take place by the year 2000, only if business continues to develop metric-designed products, attention is given to metric education in the nation's schools, and the public is not confronted by sudden change. If all goes well, the U.S. will indeed measure up—in metrics.

Karen E. Debats, "Metric Conversion: Does the U.S. Measure Up?" *Fedco Reporter*, March 1985. Reprinted by permission of the author.

• •

5.11 OVERVIEW SKIMMING A COMPLETE ARTICLE OR OPINION PIECE

This is the last Practice before you begin the Timed Selections in overview skimming. Practice all your previous skills on this short, current article.

First, preview by reading the key excerpts printed here. Since you are at least a rapid reader, we have deleted the function words. But don't skim the excerpts—read them! Take at least 30 seconds.

Please do not look ahead to the complete article—keep it for a timed skimming exercise.

"On the Job" *by Peggy Eastman — 740 words*

1. [Lead-in, in italics—read carefully.] Social Security program aims to get disabled into workplace.*
2. Vacuum, American work force . . .
3. Social Security Administration moving . . .
4. Current system . . .
5. Pilot program assign individual case manager, work personally with beneficiaries on disability.
6. Increasing interest—disabled involved productive work.
7. Social Security initiative comes at time increasing public, private interest getting disabled in productive work. Americans with Disabilities Act . . .
8. Reflects needs of national work force shrinking.
9. But employers, -ees have to drop biases people who "different."
10. "Shouldn't be that piece metal, plastic carry profound implications, invisible barriers, but barriers still exist, socially and economically."

---

*by Peggy Eastman, *AARP Bulletin*, June 1990, pp. 4–6. Reprinted by permission of the author.

You should now have a sense of the thesis and treatment. Next, go on to the complete article. Try to overview skim for main ideas in 30 seconds (= 1,480 wpm). Slower speeds mean you are reading everything, even details that would interest only certain individuals. If you can't finish in 30 seconds, go back and try again until you do. We promise the quiz will be very general, as befits skim reading at this speed!

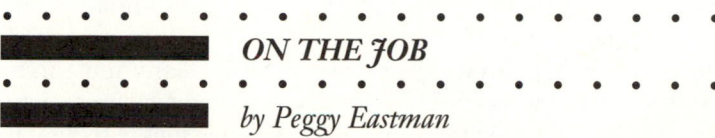

ON THE JOB

by Peggy Eastman

Social Security program aims to get disabled into workplace. (lead-in)

[1] Life was running on cruise control for Stewart Wiggins 18 years ago—good marriage, three nice kids and a solid future as a computer programmer—when suddenly he found himself blind and unable to work. A benign tumor, pressing on the optic nerve, cost him his sight at age 37, and could have ended his career.

[2] But it didn't. Instead, with the support of his family and his employer, the Dupont Co., Wiggins overcame his disability. Today he happily pursues his full-time programmer's job at Dupont's headquarters in Wilmington, Del., using a voice synthesizer and an electro-mechanical device that converts printed letters and numbers to vibrating images that can be felt by a finger.

[3] He's a rarity. There's a vacuum in the American work force that conscientious, skilled workers such as Stewart Wiggins could fill, but government figures show that only 4 percent of the nation's 43 million disabled citizens have full-time jobs, and just 10 percent of them work part time.

[4] Now, the Social Security Administration (SSA) is moving to raise those percentages. Speaking at an AARP-sponsored conference on employment problems faced by disabled Americans, SSA Commissioner Gwendolynd S. King unveiled a two-year pilot program to be launched next fall in the Boston and Dallas areas. The program will test a new way for helping disabled persons, who now receive monthly disability income payments from Social Security totaling $30 billion a year.

[5] The current system, said King, "makes people jump through hoops" to prove eligibility and offers little help to find jobs. Furthermore, she said, it's a system that isn't working, explaining that "less than one-half of 1 percent of the six million disabled persons on SSA's rolls successfully return to work."

[6] The pilot program will assign an individual case manager to work personally with beneficiaries on disability and help them develop individual employment plans. "The manager will make referrals to rehabilitation and employment service providers, will coordinate delivery of services, will monitor beneficiary progress and will arrange for post-placement services," said King. "Essentially," she added, "we are injecting care and compassion into what was an emotionless environment."

[7] The Social Security initiative comes at a time of increasing public and private interest in getting the disabled involved in productive work. An example of that concern is the Americans with Disabilities Act, which would bar discrimination against disabled workers in private sector jobs (discrimination in public employment is already illegal). The bill, which has been endorsed by

President Bush, passed the U.S. Senate, and awaits action by the full House. Also, SSA recently raised the amount that a disability insurance beneficiary may earn without losing those benefits (including Medicare) from $300 a month to $500 a month. That's still "too low," said King, but it's a "first step" in the right direction.

8   Pressure to create opportunities for the disabled reflects the needs of a national work force that is shrinking. Further, as the baby boom generation—80 million strong—moves toward retirement, that labor pool is expected to become even smaller. Compounding the problem, said Judith C. Hushbeck, a labor economist and AARP senior analyst, is a steady decline in the number of workers qualified to fill complex jobs that require growing levels of skill.

9   Emphasis by American public schools on rigorous science and math education that followed the Soviet Union's launching of the Sputnik satellite in 1957 was short-lived, said Hushbeck. Today, 25 percent of young Americans don't graduate from high school. "Productivity growth has been stalled in this country since the 1970s,"

said Hushbeck, and to reverse that trend, "we're going to need the skills, talents and abilities of all our citizens."

10   That may be the case, said Justin Dart, chairman of the President's Committee on Employment of People with Disabilities. But, he added, before disabled Americans can enter the work force fully, employers and employees are going to have to drop their biases toward people who are "different." Said Dart, who contracted polio in 1948 when he was 18 and must use a wheelchair: "Unless we can end massive society-wide discrimination against persons with disabilities, we will never achieve full employment."

11   Commissioner King agreed. "It shouldn't be that a piece of metal or plastic—be it a wheelchair, a brace, an artificial limb or a cane—should carry with it such profound implications and invisible barriers," she said, "but the reality is that those barriers still exist, both socially and economically."

Peggy Eastman, *AARP Bulletin*, June 1990, pp. 4–6.
Reprinted by permission of the author.

• •

Did you notice the writer's hook in the first two paragraphs? We omitted it from the preview; were you able to omit it from your skimming? Of course the individual case is interesting. But it is not essential to understanding the content of the proposed new act.

1.   What is the topic? (phrase is okay) _____

2.   Does the lead-in supply the main idea of the article? _____ If not, state it in a complete sentence of your own.

_____

_____

3.   The writer's dominant pattern in this article is:
    a.   thesis-examples.
    b.   description.
    c.   spatial-geographic.

4. The writer also included a few paragraphs of cause-effect. What were they about? _____

_____

5. Give the name of any person mentioned in the piece.

_____

Time _____ : _____ (= _____ wpm)
Number correct, of 5 _____

Check answers with your instructor. If you skimmed in 30 seconds and got three or four right out of five, you are overview skimming correctly. If you got 100 percent or question 5 correct, you are reading much too carefully! Individual names are not important here. Speed up and miss more details!

TIMED SELECTIONS: OVERVIEW SKIMMING

The ten Timed Selections in this chapter follow much the same format as those in Chapter 4, Rapid Reading. You may do them in class with an instructor or outside of class on your own. In either case, be sure to follow the step-by-step instructions carefully. Please do not skip any step or change the order. Also, exact timing is a must when you are learning to skim. If you allow yourself a minute or two more for a selection, you are not skimming anymore—you are reading too much. So watch the clock, and don't pad your time.

It is important not to preread any selection. We have set up a rigorous procedure for you to follow, from previewing through overview skimming to close reading and scanning. If you have already read a selection on your own, you will find it more difficult to improve your reading habits, and of course you won't be learning how to overview skim new material.

As usual, don't preread the quiz questions, and don't refer back to the selection for answers. If you do, your scores will become meaningless.

You will notice the format differs slightly from that of the Rapid Reading Timed Selections. First, the preview skim will be minimal, since you won't be returning to read the selection—you will only be skimming it. Second, we provide vocabulary help for only one selection (a long one at the end). A skimmer is usually too busy finding the main ideas to slow down for individual definitions, and he or she would not be overview skimming a highly technical article anyway.

Again, answers for odd-numbered selections are listed on page 339. Answers for even-numbered selections are not provided; ask your instructor for them. We expect 100 percent scores for the preview skim quizzes; our questions are mainly designed to keep you previewing correctly.

If your preview and skim times differ from those recommended, use the rate table at the back of the book for your words per minute. Finally, when you have finished the timed part of a selection, record your rate and score on the chart on page 266. The dots and lines should serve to push you on in your drive for reading proficiency!

OVERVIEW SKIMMING SELECTIONS

1. "Talk of Low-Quality Goods Can Be a Low-Quality Argument" 740 words
2. "Zombies: Do They Exist?" 952 words
3. "Together Again" 1,811 words
4. "End of the Dinosaurs" 1,152 words
5. "The Key to Success?" 1,479 words
6. "Artificial Paradise" 2,041 words
7. "For Whom the Bell Tolls" 1,440 words
8. "Probing the Mystery of the Multiple Personality" 2,764 words

9. "Stress on the Job" 3,534 words
10. "Murky Waters" 2,480 words

. . . .

SELECTION 1

"Talk of Low-Quality Goods Can Be a Low-Quality Argument" by *Ellen Goodman 740 words*

Your first Timed Selection for overview skimming is by a popular syndicated columnist. At 740 words, it is shorter than most of the material you will be skimming, but in other ways it makes a good entry: good organization, prominent transitions, and a strong opinion. In fact, if you don't notice the transitions and the organizational patterns, you may rush through and come out with a thesis exactly the opposite of Ms. Goodman's! So you are warned.

To help you avoid that debacle, we have marked key transitions for you. For the rest, remember to vary your rate—slow on the key parts, a glancing or spiral eye motion through the details.

Follow these steps in overview skimming this short selection:

1. Preview skim the article.
2. Answer the three-item preview quiz.
3. Overview skim the article for Ms. Goodman's main ideas.
4. Answer the four-item skimming quiz.

A. Preview Skimming

Remember that when you plan to overview skim, not read a selection, you should spend less time than usual on the preview. So take only 20 seconds (= 2,200 wpm) to do a minimal preview: title, author, source, date, lead-in (if any), length, subheads (if any), and paragraphing. Do not look ahead at the questions. Then take the preview quiz without referring back to the article.

. . . .

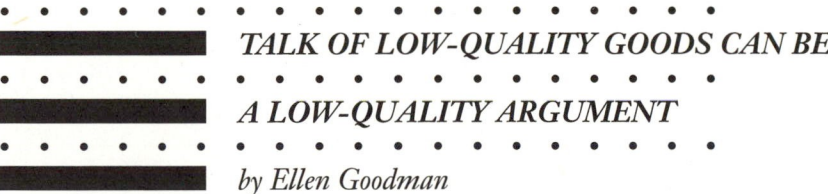

TALK OF LOW-QUALITY GOODS CAN BE

A LOW-QUALITY ARGUMENT

by Ellen Goodman

[1] On top of my desk is a green button. No, not the kind of button you push. The kind of button you normally put through a hole. The hole is still on my sweater. The button, having been used three times, has been cast out of work by the unraveled thread. It is an American sweater.

[2] On the wall of my kitchen is a new clock. Another new clock. The first clock would, from

time to time, start going backward. The next one had a second hand that struggled upward from the number 6 to the number 7 and then collapsed in an exhausted heap back at 6. After 24 hours of this, I replaced it with the third. All three are American clocks.

3   You are now, I am sure, expecting another diatribe on "The Decline of Quality in America," and let me assure you that I can launch one with the best. Give me a minute and I'll gather together my personal exhibits in the case against quality.

4   Step right up! Touch the abominable toaster tray! See the disintegrating book! Taste the inedible tomato!

5   I can also Point with Pride to the products of a simpler and sturdier time. The indomitable oak table of 1900, the unfailing railroad clock of 1860, the unbreakable sewing machine of the 1930's, the unfrayable silk blouse of the 1940's. This is, after all, how we all play the most popular game of the year, "The Rise and Fall of American Quality."

6   *But,* after weeks of listening to the rising ardor of the fans, *forgive me if I use halftime to question the rules.*

7   *I am not a great believer in The Good Old Days.* I think we all tend to idealize the past. A hundred years ago, people were no doubt ruing the decline of quality. I guess I lost my rose-colored retrospectacles in history class.

8   *I also think we tend to compare the worst of now with the best of then.* The products of the past that have survived into the present are almost by definition high-quality. The rotten buildings have fallen, the shabby furniture has been used for firewood, the crummy blouses have long ago disintegrated, the appliances are being used for landfill, the bad movies have been long forgotten.

9   *But it's also worth remembering that some high-quality products often depended on low-quality lives.* It's one thing to miss the delicate handmade lace of another time. It's quite another to miss the long hours at low rates in a desperate cottage industry.

10   It is equally easy to admire the intricate molding on the walls and stairways of another decade. *But it's hard to admire the enormous gap between what the rich could afford and what the working poor were paid.* The high cost of labor is, after all, good for the laborer.

11   We talk about lost quality as if we were the potential buyers rather than the producers. The Chinese always remind foreign visitors that, while the Great Wall was a wonderful achievement, the lives of the people who built it were rotten. Most of us did not live in the mansions of the 19th century, unless we were in the scullery; most of us didn't eat luxurious meals off elegant silver—at best, we made the meals and polished the silver.

12   *In fact, we could make a pretty decent, if unpopular, case that the quality of life has improved in the past century, along with the quality of things such as food and housing.* It seems that the distribution of goods has raised the standards for many (and lowered them for some).

13   Consciously or not, even those who protest most loudly often choose "low-quality" over "high-quality" items, heading for McDonald's instead of the kitchen, and for permanent-press instead of the iron. We often knowingly choose "low quality" over high cost.

14   I'm not trying to defend things that go bonk in the night. I'm as infuriated by sloppy work and saddened by the loss of pride in crafts as the next person. I think we have to blame and cure "bigness," its careless management and alienated anonymous workers—all the rest.

15   *But,* while we are playing the elite, decrying the decline of quality, the erosion of those high standards by mass production and mass standards, it's not bad to remember that we (blush) *are* the masses.

Ellen Goodman, "Talk of Low-Quality Goods Can Be a Low-Quality Argument," © 1981, The Boston Globe Newspaper Company, Washington Post Writers Group. Reprinted with permission.

• •

1. What are the source and the publication date (year only) of this column?

2. The reader can tell this was first printed in a newspaper because of:
   a. the subheads inserted in the text.
   b. the many short paragraphs.

3. There is a helpful lead-in or editor's summary at the very beginning.
   a. true
   b. false

Sel.1 P-Skim	**1. Source:** _____
Time :20 = 2,200 wpm	**Date:** _____
Score _____ %	**2.** _____
▶ **100%**	**3.** _____
Score = number correct × 33.	**Check answers after the next quiz.***

Did you read the long title carefully? It is actually a statement of the thesis.

B. Overview Skimming

Now take 45 seconds at most (= 987 wpm) to overview skim the same column for the thesis, the main supporting details of the argument, and the organizational patterns. If you can do this in 30 seconds (= 1,480 wpm), that's even better. (Of course, a 1-minute rate of 740 wpm is rapid reading, not skimming.) Remember to read the marked portions carefully, and skip over most of the specific examples.

When you're finished, take the quiz without referring to the article. Our skim quizzes are not tricky or detailed; we expect you to know main ideas only. (But, sometime, go back and read the entire column carefully—it's worth it.)

1. The main idea or thesis is that:
   a. things are not made as well as they used to be.
   b. there are a lot of things wrong with the statement in *a*.

2. The dominant writing pattern Ms. Goodman uses for her argument is:
   a. reasons (with some examples).
   b. process (step-by-step).
   c. problem-solution (cheap goods and what to do about them).

3. She even states at one point that the quality of life and food and housing have actually improved, on the whole, since the "good old days."
   a. true
   b. false

---

*You may check your preview quiz answers immediately if you wish. However, it is less distracting to wait until after you have finished the overview, and then correct both quizzes at the same time.

4. Goodman says that the "good old days" complaint ignores several facts:
    a. The junk goods of the past simply haven't survived until today.
    b. The fine things of the good old days were not available to ordinary people like us.
    c. Workers who made those fine things lived in deep poverty.
    d. To be honest, most of us today *choose* to buy cheap things.
    e. All of these.

Sel. 1   O-Skim   1. _____

Time   1:00 = 740 wpm   2. _____

    :45 = 987 wpm   3. _____

    :30 = 1,480 wpm   4. _____

Score _____ %   **Check answers to both quizzes on**

    ▶ 75%   **p. 339.**

Score = number correct x 25.   **Record rate and score on p. 266.**

C. Questions for Discussion and Writing

As in the previous chapter, each Timed Selection in this chapter will be followed by three or four untimed or "power" questions for discussion and writing. These ask you to return to the selection and read more carefully for patterns, inferences, kind of development, special use of words, and so on. You are urged to use a dictionary or mark up the passage as needed. For further directions or for checks on your answers, see your instructor.

Reread Selection 1 for answers to these questions.

1. What paragraphs constitute the introduction to Goodman's thesis? In those paragraphs, is she agreeing or disagreeing with the common gripe that things today are not made as well as they used to be? What little but powerful transition word signals the statement of her thesis?

2. Goodman expresses her position in paragraph 7 with an effective metaphor: "I guess I lost my rose-colored retrospectacles in history class." Put this idea in your own words (use one or more sentences).

3. Another key part is (of course) the last paragraph. It is a long and complicated sentence. Put it into your own words, using one or more sentences.

SELECTION 2

"Zombies: Do They Exist?" *by Claudia Wallis 952 Words*

The next selection is a magazine article aimed at a general audience, yet "scientific" and detailed enough to require a complete reading for total understanding. In fact, even a rapid reading might not be sufficient, except for top readers. So why is it presented here, in overview skimming? Because it begins with a question, it answers the question, and skimming will yield the general components to the answer. If after you skim, you want to know 100 percent—all the details—you can go back and read the article more slowly. For now, however, try to grasp the explanation or the main ideas only.

Again, to help you skim at this early stage of the Timed Selections, we have marked some key passages for you.

Follow these steps in overview skimming this selection:

1. Preview skim the article.
2. Answer the three-item preview quiz.
3. Overview skim the article for main ideas.
4. Answer the four-item skim quiz.

A. Preview Skimming

As in all these overview skimming selections, do not spend much time on the preview. Take 30 seconds (= 1,904 wpm) to do just the minimum: check for title, author, source, date, lead-in (if any), length, subheads (if any). Then take the preview quiz—of course, without looking back at the article! Something harder: Do not preread the quiz questions. Go straight to the article.

ZOMBIES: DO THEY EXIST?

by Claudia Wallis

Yes, says a Harvard scientist, who offers an explanation

1   On a brilliant day in the spring of 1980, a stranger arrived at L'Estère marketplace in Haiti's fertile Artibonite Valley. The man's gait was heavy, his eyes vacant. The peasants watched fearfully as he approached a local woman named Angelina Narcisse. She listened as he introduced himself, then screamed in horror—and recognized him. The man had given the boyhood nickname of her deceased brother Clairvius Narcisse, a name that was known only to family members and had not been used since his funeral in 1962.

2   *This incident and four others in recent years have sparked the most systematic inquiry ever made into the legendary voodoo phenomenon of zombiism. According to Haitian belief, a zombie is an individual who has been "killed" and then raised from*

the dead by malevolent voodoo priests known as "bocors." Though most educated Haitians deny the existence of zombies, Dr. Lamarque *Douyon, Canadian-trained head of the Psychiatric Center in Port-au-Prince*, has been trying for 25 years to establish the truth about the phenomenon, no easy matter in a land where the line between myth and reality is faintly drawn. More recently, Douyon has been joined in his search by *Harvard Botanist E. Wade Davis*. Next month Davis is publishing a paper on his findings in the *Journal of Ethnopharmacology. His startling conclusion: "Zombiism exists and is a societal phenomenon that can be explained logically."*

3   Douyon set the stage for Davis' study by foraying into rural Haiti, where he met with purported zombies and fearsome bocors. At least 15 individuals who had been branded zombies by terrified peasants turned out to be victims of epilepsy, mental retardation, insanity or alcoholism. The case of *Clairvius Narcisse*, however, gave Douyon good evidence. Medical records showed he was declared dead in 1962 at Albert Schweitzer Hospital, an American-run institution in Deschapelles. Yet more than 200 people recognized him after his reappearance.

4   *The best explanation*, Douyon believed, *was that Narcisse had been poisoned in such a way that his vital signs could not be detected.* The psychiatrist obtained a sample of a *coma-inducing toxin* from a bocor. The poison is apparently used to punish individuals who have transgressed the will of their community or family. Narcisse, for example, said that he had been "killed" by his brothers for refusing to go along with their plan to sell the family land. Ti-Femme, a female zombie also under study by Douyon, had been poisoned for refusing to marry the man her family had chosen for her and for bearing another man's child.

5   *Douyon sent a quantity of the zombie potion to the U.S., where it came to Davis' attention.* An expert on tribal uses of plants, Davis flew to Haiti and began collecting his own samples. "The principal ingredients are consistent in three of four localities," he reports in his paper. Several plants con-

taining skin irritants are used, a charred human bone is thrown in just for show, *but the active ingredients are a large New World toad (Bufo marinus) and one or more species of puffer fish. The toad, Davis reports, is a "veritable chemical factory,"* containing hallucinogens, powerful anesthetics and chemicals that affect the heart and nervous system. *The fish is more potent still, containing a deadly nerve poison called tetrodotoxin.*

6   *To learn how these poisons might relate to zombiism, Davis turned to an unlikely source: Japanese medical literature.* Every year a number of Japanese suffer tetrodotoxin poisoning as a result of eating incorrectly prepared puffer fish, the great delicacy *fugu*. Davis found that entire Japanese case histories "read like accounts of zombification." Indeed, nearly every symptom reported by Narcisse and his doctors is described, from the initial difficulty breathing to the final paralysis, glassy-eyed stare and yet the retention of mental faculties. In at least two cases, Japanese victims were declared dead but recovered before they could be buried. Japanese reports confirmed what Davis was told by the bocors: the effect of the poison depends on the dosage; too much will kill "too completely," and resuscitation will be impossible. Even with the correct dose, the bocors said, a zombie must be exhumed within about eight hours or will be lost, presumably to asphyxiation.

7   How zombies are revived from their death-like comas remains a mystery. Both Davis and Douyon heard stories about a graveyard ritual in which the bocor pounds on the earth and awakens the victim, but neither was able to witness it. Davis did learn that *upon reviving, the zombie is force-fed a paste made of sweet potato and datura*, a plant known to Haitians as zombie cucumber. Datura, says Davis, is "one of the most potent hallucinogenic plants known." Thus the zombie is led away in a state of intoxication, usually to work as a slave. Narcisse, who spent several years as a slave on a sugar plantation, reports that zombies do not make very good workers. Says he: "The slightest chore required great effort." He reports that his senses were so dis-

torted that the smallest stream seemed a wide and unfordable sea, as though "my eyes were turned in."

8   *Davis has sent samples of the zombie potion to laboratories in Europe and the U.S., where in one experiment it induced a trancelike state in rats.* Such research in the past led to the discovery of curare, an arrow poison from the Amazon now used to paralyze muscles during surgery. Tetrodotoxin may also one day find its place in the medical ar-

mamentarium. *"People who have lived in the tropics for centuries have learned things about plants and animals that we have not fathomed,"* says Richard Evan Schultes, head of Harvard's renowned Botanical Museum. *"We must not leave any stone unturned, or their secrets will be lost."*

• •

1. How about it—*do* zombies exist?
2. The "explanation" is offered by:
    a. a Harvard scientist.
    b. an African doctor.
    c. the American Medical Association.
3. Two useful subheads are inserted within the body of the article.
    a. true
    b. false

Sel. 2 P-Skim	1. _____
Time :30 = 1,904 wpm	2. _____
Score _____ %	3. _____
▶ **100%**	**Check answers after the next quiz.**
Score = number correct x 33.	

B. Overview Skimming

Take 1 minute (= 952 wpm) or, at most, 1:15 (= 762 wpm) to overview skim this article for the main features of the "explanation" for zombiism. You will want to read the marked portions carefully. Use soft focus and fast eye movement through other portions; actually read only what you have time for. Then answer the skimming quiz without looking back at the article.

1. The setting for zombiism and the research into it is:
    a. South America.
    b. many locations around the world.
    c. several African countries.
    d. Haiti (in the Caribbean).

2. The two men who collaborated on this study are:
   a. an American botanist.
   b. a South American "medicine doctor."
   c. a Haitian psychiatrist.

3. In reality, "zombies" are individuals who:
   a. have been poisoned.
   b. have been put into comas.
   c. have been buried as "dead."
   d. all of these.

4. At the very end, one of the researchers makes the point that:
   a. zombiism is a cruel and dangerous practice.
   b. we have much to learn from other peoples about plants and animals.
   c. zombiism is an important part of local religious practices.

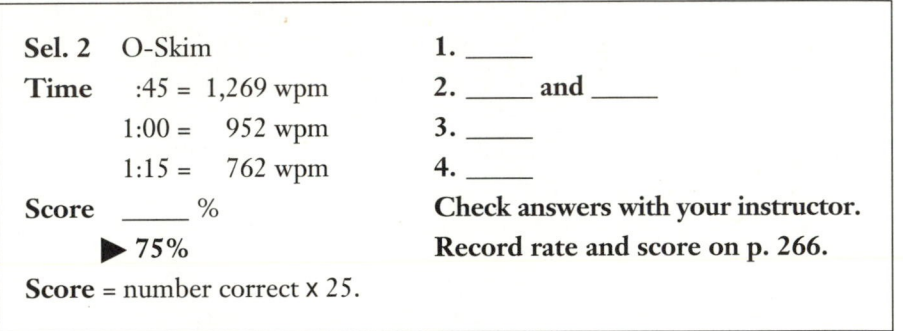

Sel. 2 O-Skim	1. _____
Time :45 = 1,269 wpm	2. _____ and _____
1:00 = 952 wpm	3. _____
1:15 = 762 wpm	4. _____
Score _____ %	**Check answers with your instructor.**
▶ **75%**	**Record rate and score on p. 266.**
Score = number correct × 25.	

Were you able to overview skim within the time limit for skimming? If not or if your quiz score was less than 75 percent, you should now return to the article and once again practice the eye-brain methods described in the Introduction (pp. 192–193). That is, read each marked portion carefully, and quickly pass through unmarked portions in a spiral or on a slant. You might also wish to analyze some paragraphs where the main idea is located in the middle and is indicated by a key transition; paragraph 5 is a good example.

C. Questions for Discussion and Writing

Return to the article for answers to these untimed questions.

1. Paragraph 2 employs two writing patterns. What are they?

2. The main organizational pattern in this article is process—how a person is put into a coma and then awakened to roam as a "zombie." Reread the article and then, in your own words, outline the process step-by-step, including the agents or causes of these changes.

3. Summarize the reasons that botanist Davis believes in the existence of zombies.

• • • • • • • • • • • • • • • • • • •

SELECTION 3

"Together Again" *by Alice Vollmar 1,811 words*

Identical twins: Here we have a subject that everybody finds interesting, whether he or she is a twin or not. It addresses the old question of nature versus nurture—your genes versus your environment. We have included two additional sections (at the end of the article), for your interest; but don't try to skim or read them within the timing period. Just preview and overview the main body of the article. And note: no helpful italics this time.

Follow these steps in overview skimming the selection:

1. Preview skim the article.
2. Answer the three-item quiz.
3. Overview skim the article for main ideas.
4. Answer the four-item quiz.

A. Preview Skimming

Do the usual minimal preview appropriate for overview skimming. In other words, read for title and subtitle, lead-in, source, date, subject matter, and length. Leave the two extra sections for later reading. Take 45 seconds (= 2,415 wpm) to preview for those items.

• • • • • • • • • • • • • • • • • • •
▬▬▬▬▬▬▬▬▬▬   *TOGETHER AGAIN*
• • • • • • • • • • • • • • • • • • •
▬▬▬▬▬▬▬▬▬▬   *by Alice Vollmar*

Twins raised apart offer new insights into heredity and environment

[1] Standing on the sidelines cheering for her son's baseball team, Dianne Cunningham looks like any enthusiastic mother, balancing her pink-bonneted 6-month-old in a back carrier. Only she can't clap, because in her arms she holds a second pink-bonneted 6-month-old.

[2] "Twins?" asks another parent. "May I hold one for you?" Gratefully, Cunningham rests her tired arms. A group gathers around the babies and their mother. "It gets easier," one woman reassures. "Just hang in there. See No. 13 up at bat now? He's one of my twins."

[3] "Twins. What a miracle," murmurs another onlooker. "Yes, well, I'm glad the miracle happened to her and not to me," replies her companion.

[4] Twins draw attention wherever they go. And recently twins have been the center of a different kind of attention: Scientists at the University of Minnesota are studying twins raised apart—and coming up with new insights into what makes human beings tick.

[5] "Everyone is very surprised," says Dr. Nancy Segal, one of about 15 researchers associated with The Minnesota Study of Twins Reared Apart, begun in 1979 by Dr. Thomas J. Bouchard Jr., University of Minnesota psychologist.

6   Long interested in environment's role in shaping human beings, Bouchard read a newspaper story about the reunion of a set of adult twins and saw a rare chance to draw a line between the effects of heredity and environment. What if he could study those 39-year-old twins from Ohio? Since identical twins have the same set of genes, differences between those two individuals reared apart could then be attributed to environment.

7   The enthusiastic university professor located funding, put together a team of scientists and did indeed bring the Ohio twins, Jim Lewis and Jim Springer, to the University of Minnesota. In March 1979, within the modern, red brick walls of Elliott Hall, they began one week of intense testing. Since then, 38 identical and 16 fraternal sets of reared-apart twins have followed in their footsteps, undergoing extensive physical, psychological and intelligence tests, and answering thousands of questions.

8   Bouchard has found long lists of similarities, suggesting that genes and heredity play a far more powerful role in who we are and how we got that way than previously suspected.

9   Lewis and Springer, the first twins studied, turned out to have more in common than just their first names and birthdate:

- Voices and mannerisms were alike.
- Both divorced women named Linda and married second wives named Betty.
- They named their sons James Allan and James Alan, and at one time each owned a dog named Toy.
- Both suffer similar tension-migraine headaches, prefer the same brand of beer and cigarettes, chew their fingernails, drive Chevrolets, vacation on the same beach in Florida and like woodworking.
- Each built a white bench around a tree in his yard.
- Both liked math and disliked spelling in school.
- They have identical blood pressures, pulse rates and sleep patterns, and show similar psychological inventory profiles.

10   Another set of twins shares claustrophobia, timidity about ocean bathing, mistrust of escalators and a habit of compulsive counting.

11   Gregarious British twins Daphne Goodship and Barbara Herbert both have:

- Crooked little fingers.
- The same highly distinctive giggle.
- A penchant for avoiding controversy.
- A taste for coffee cold and black.
- A love of chocolate and liqueurs.
- A habit of pushing up their noses, which each calls "squidging."

12   While scientists may be excited about their findings, the feelings of most identical twins reunited after years of separation can be even stronger. Many are euphoric about finding their "other selves."

13   "It was like two friends meeting, as though we had always known each other," one twin said. Another twin, separated from her sister for 53 years, noted that "you wouldn't normally pick up the phone and speak to someone you'd never seen before for half an hour, non-stop."

14   "We are complete now," said another. In overwhelming numbers, whether they have been reared apart or together, twins are glad to be twins. "We always warn our friends that they will never be 'first.' We are—and always will be—each other's best friend," say Lora Stewart and Linda Longerbone, reared-together identical twins, now co-presidents of the Minnesota Twin Cities Twin Club.

15   Researchers find that twins who have been reared apart are sometimes more similar than those raised together. It seems to be a matter of establishing identity: Twins raised separately have no chance to interact or be compared with one another. Twins growing up together often work to create identities distinct from one another. To cut down on comparisons, they may choose different activities, friends or clothing.

16   A twin admits it can be hard to know who you are when there's another person who is so much like you. Also, most of the world looks at twins and sees a pair—rather than two distinct individuals—and expects them to act and dress alike.

17   "When we were young," recalls Lora Stewart, now 39, "it was easier just to dress alike, because so many people would make comments when we didn't."

18   Thus, twins reunited as adults may have avoided some hassles that go with growing up in the shadow of a twin, and emerge with their natural inclinations more intact.

19   To scientists, the wide-ranging similarities in twins' inclinations—from choices in clothing, food and names to medical, behavioral and intelligence patterns—mean that many of our traits may have more of a genetic tie-in than suspected. The research adds an even subtler insight: Our genes may combine in unique and individual ways to make each of us even less alike than we could have guessed.

20   "Much of what we think of as human individuality—temperament and pace and all the idiosyncrasies that make you different from your friends—may relate a lot more to your particular genetic individuality than we thought," observes research team member Dr. David Lykken, University of Minnesota professor of psychiatry.

21   "A lot of the things that I've assumed to be true about the influence of early experiences are now in doubt," Lykken says. For example, the capacity for happiness seems to be "more strongly [genetically] wired in than I had thought." Lykken works in an office in which all manner of twins peer out of pictures on the walls. Several composite pictures consist solely of sets of twins' eyes and ears—highly hereditary features—creating an unusual and fascinating environment for his work.

22   Lykken's explanation means, for instance, that little Mary's sunny disposition may be part of her genetic makeup, enhanced by—but not the result of—her adoring parents' care. Which, in a way, can be welcome news to parents. Some of those hard days, when smiling is next to impossible, may have little long-term effect on the children.

23   Parents of twins know about "hard days." There are times when sanity comes hard: when both babies are crabby from teething, a mountain of soggy baby laundry looms and there's not been a minute alone to brush your teeth or comb your hair.

24   "I just cry a lot," says Dianne Cunningham, who brought fraternal twins Anna and Rebekah home to four brothers aged 3 through 9. "My recuperation was so much longer because I had one baby naturally and one by Caesarean. When I'd start to do something I'd done in the past with ease, I just couldn't handle it. My older kids probably wonder if a day will come when I won't cry while I'm fixing dinner."

25   What the final result will be of The Minnesota Study of Twins Reared Apart is unknown. Funded by a variety of private and government foundations in addition to the University graduate school's support, the study will test 100 identical and 50 to 70 fraternal twins. No date for completing the study is projected; it will not end until the desired number of sets of twins can be found who will participate.

26   Although it's not always the case in most serious scientific studies, publicity is welcomed, and necessary: Publicity is how new twins are recruited for the study. Twins who've found one another hear about the study and contact Bouchard—or someone will come to him with a possible lead on a twin.

27   How do separated twins find one another? Researcher Segal says it often starts with mistaken identity. Someone says, "Hey, I saw you in Cambridge on Saturday." Only you weren't in Cambridge on that day. Such cases of identity confusion can lead to a search for the look-alike—and to the discovery there is an identical twin.

28   Being able to connect with such reunited pairs is critical to Bouchard's study. But along with publicity comes controversy. Some people doubt the motives behind the study, or the techniques that are involved in the testing.

[29] In a January 1981 article in *Psychology Today*, Dr. Susan Farber wondered if the study was asking the right questions. Peter Watson, in his book, *Twins: An Uncanny Relationship?*, questioned a "methodological flaw" in Bouchard's approach. Repeatedly, Bouchard and associates attest to the open-ended, exploratory nature of their project, and Lykken says the debate over causal forces that shape human beings has "gone on for many years . . . as to which is more important for which characteristics." Inevitably, shaking the old heredity/environment tree brings down both sweet and sour apples.

[30] However, information coming out of the study of those rare, reared-apart twins may have a big impact on how we live with one another—in our families and in society.

[31] "We may need to rethink policies for modifying behavior, prescribing treatment for certain kinds of diseases, identifying persons at risk for certain problems or boosting IQ," Segal speculates. "For instance, Head Start programs [designed to give preschoolers from less-advantaged homes an equal chance in school] have attempted to boost children's IQ, and have done so. But the long-term gains are somewhat in question. It may be we have to reshape those kinds of environmental programs."

[32] Lykken emphatically warns lay people not to jump to improper conclusions: "Of course, you can't become something that your genetic potential will not allow, but you don't know what that is until you try. . . . Most of us do not come close to exploiting our genetic potential in our lifetimes.

[33] "I think we can do a better job of parenting and educating if we realize everybody is starting out with a different deck . . . rather than treating kids as if they all start with the same cards," says Lykken. "We need to adapt our efforts to fit what each kid has to start with."

[34] We have probably all heard parents comment, "Our children are so different; you'd hardly guess they came from the same family." In the light of present findings from Bouchard's study, those parents appear astutely wise.

[35] We may all be more different, one from the other, than any of us ever dreamed.

DID YOU KNOW?

• Twins occur once in every 90 births in the United States.

• The U.S. twinning ratio for blacks is one in every 77 births; for whites, one in 93.

• Women 35 to 40 are more likely to have fraternal twins. Likelihood increases with each pregnancy up to seven. Conception soon after discontinuing birth control pills and the use of fertility drugs predispose to multiple birth.

• Fraternal (dizygotic or two-egg twins) result when two eggs are fertilized by two separate sperms. Technically, fraternals are simply siblings born at the same time. Why more than one egg is released at a particular ovulation remains a matter of speculation.

• Identical (monozygotic or one-egg twins) occur when a fertilized egg divides, forming a replica of itself. No one yet knows what causes an egg to split.

• The identical-twin birth ratio is about four in every 1,000 pregnancies; about one-third of all twins born are identical.

• The term used to identify identical twins in Bouchard's research project is MZA (monozygotic/apart).

• Fraternal or identical? You can't always tell by looking. Hand- and foot-print tests are fairly reliable, but blood tests are most accurate.

REARING TWINS—AND OTHER CHILDREN, TOO

Rearing twins involves some unique problems. Donald Keith, director of the Chicago-based Center for Study of Multiple Birth, and an identical twin himself, recommends some guidelines to encourage the healthy development of both children.

Much of what applies to parenting twins makes sense for child rearing in general. If parents encourage each sibling to "do his own thing," rivalry is decreased and a healthier realization of self-worth is created in all children.

Specialists on rearing twins, as well as scientists with The Minnesota Study of Twins Reared Apart, say being aware of, and nurturing, each family member's differences and talents makes for the soundest parenting approach.

• Don't dress twins alike all the time. Different clothing reinforces distinct identities.

• Treat each child as unique, so he avoids seeing himself as part of a unit. Choose dissimilar names and use each child's name when speaking to twins.

• Separate twins periodically so they learn how to be independent of each other. Take special time alone with each child daily.

• Encourage different friends for each. Let them make separate clothing and hair-style decisions.

• Support their differences in interests and activities, and avoid comparing them with one another.

Alice Vollmar, "Together Again," from *Friendly Exchange*, The Magazine of the Farmers Insurance Group of Companies, Winter 1984, pp. 28–30 © 1984. Reprinted by permission of the author and the publisher.

• •

1. The author is:
   a. a doctor or a psychologist.
   b. a mother and writer.

2. Except for the two sections of extra information, are there divisions or subheadings within the body of this article? (Yes or No)

3. Write the lead-in from memory as accurately as you can.

Sel. 3 P-Skim	1. _____
Time :45 = 2,415 wpm	2. _____
Score _____ %	3. _____
▶ **100%**	_____
Score = number correct × 33.	**Check answers after the next quiz.**

B. Overview Skimming

Take only 1½ minutes (= 1,207 wpm) to overview skim this article for main ideas. Remember, read only what is important to the thesis as stated in the lead-in. What are the "new insights" gained by this study? Which factor do the researchers think is more dominant in our personalities, heredity or environment? Notice that the opening paragraphs are a "hook"; therefore, do not read them carefully. (For other times, look up your wpm in the rate table at the back of the book.) Then take the overview skimming quiz without looking back at the article.

1. The research study reported on here concerns twins who grew up together in one home, as well as twins who had been separated.
   a. true
   b. false

2. When this article was written, the Minnesota study:
   a. was completed—its results were accepted.
   b. was ongoing—the final results were still unknown.

3. The researchers were amazed by:
   a. the great differences between identical twins who had grown up apart from each other.
   b. the great similarities between twins who had grown up apart.

4. Therefore, they concluded that heredity seems to be more powerful than environment in shaping our personalities.
   a. true
   b. false

Sel. 3 O-Skim   1. _____
Time 1:30 = 1,207 wpm   2. _____
Score _____ %   3. _____
        ▶ 75%   4. _____
Score = number correct x 25.   **Check answers to both quizzes on p. 339.**
                                   Record rate and score on p. 266.

C. Questions for Discussion and Writing

1. What, mainly, is the "new insight" mentioned in the lead-in regarding the importance of heredity? State this in a complete sentence, as the thesis of the article.

2. What writing pattern is used to develop this main idea or thesis? List two or more pieces of evidence.

3. Evaluate the evidence given for the dominance of heredity over environment—"nature" over "nurture." Is it convincing, to you? Are there possible dangers in the belief that we are born the way we are and will be? See especially paragraphs 31–35, at the end.

SELECTION 4

"End of the Dinosaurs" *by Richard A. Kerr 1,152 words*

Vocabulary
asteroid: any of thousands of small bodies that revolve around the sun; "a six-mile-wide asteroid"
pummeling: a beating or pounding; "slow but steady pummeling"
crux: basic or decisive point; "the crux of the impact"
paleontologist: one who studies the forms of life that existed in previous geologic times; "Many paleontologists shy away from"
extrapolate: to infer an unknown from something that is known; "statistical techniques to extrapolate"
lethal: causing death; "a lethal one indeed"

This is an interesting scientific article about why dinosaurs disappeared from the earth. Written in a journalistic style, this article is not overly technical, so the layperson can appreciate the general issues concerning the debate about what happened to the dinosaurs. It is also well-organized, carefully presenting various theories.

Follow these steps in overview skimming this excerpt:

1. Preview skim the article.
2. Answer the three-item quiz.
3. Overview skim the article.
4. Answer the four-item quiz.

A. Preview Skimming

Preview the article in 30 seconds (= 2,304 wpm), checking title, subtitle, source and date, subheadings (if any), length, and difficulty level. Then take the preview-skim quiz without looking back.

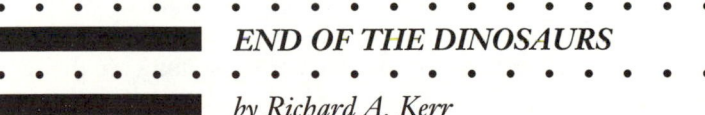

END OF THE DINOSAURS

by Richard A. Kerr

[1] If Earth's close encounter with a half-mile-wide asteroid recently gave you a scare, astronomers and geologists can sympathize. They know only too well what devastation a direct hit can wreak.

[2] Yet ironically, we probably owe our very existence to just such an impact. Scientists have at last concluded a 10-year debate over what caused the global catastrophe that wiped out perhaps two-thirds of all living species 66 million years ago.

3   The event destroyed the last of the dinosaurs, but it also restarted the stalled evolution of our ancestors, the early mammals. The agent of destruction seems to have been a six-mile-wide asteroid or comet striking the Earth at a still undiscovered location at something like 40,000 m.p.h.

4   The public, however, has not gotten the message yet. Leaning over backward to appear evenhanded, the news media portray opposing camps of equally credible scientists still slugging it out over whether the catastrophe was the aftermath of a large impact or solely a huge volcanic eruption.

5   In reality, volcano advocates remain a tiny minority, and the evidence is solidly on the side of an impact.

6   Specialists recognize 120 impact craters around the world, including Meteor Crater in Arizona. (If March's near-miss had been a hit, it would have left a crater the size of the District of Columbia.)

7   Before the Apollo landings began in 1969, the pockmarked face of the moon looked to some geologists like a field of collapsed volcanoes. Now no one questions that they are virtually all impact craters. Space probes have in fact revealed that the entire solar system has been battered.

8   Earth still suffers a slow but steady pummeling. The solar system is aswarm with potentially lethal asteroids and comets that ensure random but inevitable collisions with Earth.

9   Eugene Shoemaker of the U.S. Geological Survey estimates that an object six miles in diameter slams into Earth on average every 100 million years. Traveling at 43,000 m.p.h., such an impact would release 60 million megatons of energy in an instant and create a crater 90 miles wide. The aftermath—including the darkness and cold of a planet-girdling shroud of dust, whole continents in flame and acid rain—might spell doom for life on Earth.

10   Many researchers believe that they have found the debris from such a huge impact at the instant of geologic time that marks the end of the age of the dinosaurs 66 million years ago.

11   The first clue was enhanced concentrations of the element iridium laid down on top of the sediments of the 80-million-year slice of geologic time called the Cretaceous Period (abbreviated K to avoid confusion with other periods starting with C) and beneath those of the 64-million-year Tertiary Period—that is, at the K-T boundary, an instant in geologic time recorded in a fraction of an inch of sediment.

12   Iridium is scarce in crustal rocks but abundant in comets and asteroids. So the original framers of the impact hypothesis (the late Nobel laureate Luis Alvarez, his son Walter of UC Berkeley, and Frank Asaro and Helen Michel of the Lawrence Berkeley Laboratory) assumed that the excess iridium that they had found in 1978 at the K-T boundary came from an asteroid.

13   Evidence of an impact 66 million years ago has since mushroomed. Enhanced iridium at the K-T boundary is found at about 150 sites spread around the world. Other signs of impact are found in the same layer.

14   But the crux of the impact argument has become the presence at the boundary of shocked quartz, grains of the mineral shot through with a regular pattern of thin layers called lamellae in which crystalline quartz has been turned to glass.

15   Such intersecting, multiple-shock lamellae have been found only in minerals from known impact sites, nuclear test sites, laboratory shock experiments and the K-T boundary. No volcano is known to have shocked any minerals that way.

16   Peter Lipman of the U.S. Geological Survey, a volcanologist who had not become involved in the impact-volcano debate, noted at a conference on global catastrophes last fall in Snowbird, Utah, that he had been looking at volcanic minerals for 25 years and "we just don't see this kind of thing. I don't see how you can do it with a volcano."

17   Nonetheless, a small group of scientists contends that a volcano could—in fact, did—generate the shocked quartz found at the K-T boundary. Physicist Alan Rice of the University of Colorado has published a theory for the generation of high

shock pressures within exploding volcanoes, but the idea is roundly rejected by a variety of experts. [18] Shock generation requires a detonation, they argue, similar to dynamite, whereas a volcano decompresses the way a ruptured boiler does. Any mechanism that supposedly creates a volcanic shock, Shoemaker claimed, is "a mythical beast, a unicorn."

[19] Many paleontologists shy away from catastrophism—saying, in effect, "Fine. Kill off all the species you want with an impact, but do not include my favorite. It died out before the boundary." The mass extinction was largely gradual, they say, not catastrophic.

[20] The perceived suddenness of the K-T extinctions would seem to depend at times on the size of the fossil that paleontologists are considering. Pollen of western North America took a sudden drop in abundance at the iridium layer when fern spores suddenly jumped in abundance. [21] That looked pretty catastrophic. But eight years ago paleontologist Leo Hickey of Yale University argued that study of 1,000 leaf fossils revealed no catastrophe at the boundary. The plants did fine if these large fossils were any measure, he claimed. [22] But by last fall's conference, he had reconsidered. Ten thousand newly collected leaf fossils show a dramatic extinction event at the boundary, he and colleague Kirk Johnson said. Likewise, it seems that the extinction of the spiraled, snail-like marine creatures called ammonites occurred near the boundary.

[23] Dinosaurs were a good deal less numerous than leaves, so their remains are far rarer. No dinosaur fossil skeleton has been found closer than about two yards below the K-T boundary. [24] Taken literally, the two-yard gap would mean that the last dinosaur, after its race had ruled for more than 160 million years, died out mere tens of thousands of years before the impact. Consequently, some paleontologists argue that gradual changes, perhaps a retreating sea and a cooling climate, pushed the dinosaurs to extinction geologic moments before any impact.

[25] Others contend the opposite: Because only a tiny fraction of all the buried dinosaur bones has ever been discovered, it is extremely unlikely that the ones found two yards below the K-T boundary were from the very last dinosaur on Earth. [26] But those remains do provide a starting point for pinning down the creatures' disappearance. The late Luis Alvarez, using statistical techniques to extrapolate to the extinction, argued that the observed two-yard gap is just the right size if an impact did in the dinosaurs at the iridium-marked boundary. [27] Could fate be so cruel as to confuse the issue by a near, but totally random, coincidence? Many non-paleontologists think not. Just what proportion of the extinctions near the K-T boundary will finally end up precisely at the boundary is unclear, but there are enough there or heading that way to make the K-T impact a lethal one indeed. [28] Paleontologist Stephen Jay Gould of Harvard University closed the Snowbird conference by providing his view of what role an impact might have played in the evolution of life. Such catastrophic extinctions, he said, would change the rules of Darwinian evolution governing who is most fit to survive and who becomes extinct. [29] If the pattern is not determined by adaptation to a slowly changing environment, he said, "then I think Darwin is in trouble." In a world subject to occasional catastrophes, humans' ancestors—the small, reptile-like mammals—might not have survived the K-T catastrophe because of some commendable adaptation that we carry still. [30] Instead, their saving grace may have been some attribute—such as their small size that could have allowed burrowing out of harm's way—that only became a decisive advantage during the moment of the catastrophe. [31] "The history of life," Gould said, "is enormously more quirky than we imagined."

Richard A. Kerr, "End of the Dinosaurs," *Los Angeles Times*, June 12, 1989. © 1989 The Los Angeles Times. Reprinted by permission.

1. When was this article written?
   a. 1986
   b. 1987
   c. 1988
   d. 1989

2. This article will likely focus on:
   a. how dinosaurs came to be.
   b. how dinosaurs became extinct.
   c. why the dinosaurs took over the world.
   d. information on the largest dinosaurs.

3. This article seems to present few facts and figures.
   a. true
   b. false

Sel. 4   P-Skim   1. _____

Time   :30 = 2,304 wpm   2. _____

Score _____ %   3. _____

  ▶ **100%**   **Check answers after the next quiz.**

Score = number correct x 33.

B. Overview Skimming

Now skim the article for its main ideas. Take 60 seconds (= 1,152 wpm) or 75 seconds (= 922 wpm). Be sure to read the beginnings of the paragraphs that seem important to you, but do not focus on the several numbers that are used as evidence. This is an interesting article that you may want to read carefully after your overview skim.

1. The article suggests that:
   a. dinosaurs died out slowly.
   b. dinosaurs died out quickly.
   c. dinosaurs were taken over by the human being.
   d. both *b* and *c*.

2. One theory concerning the demise of the dinosaur suggests that:
   a. a meteor struck the earth.
   b. dinosaurs no longer needed oxygen.
   c. dinosaurs died off because of their small brains.
   d. dinosaurs were more intelligent than was originally thought.

3. The article suggests that there is no longer any real debate about how the dinosaurs became extinct.
   a. true
   b. false

4. The article ends:
   a. on a note of certainty.
   b. with additional facts and figures.
   c. on a note of uncertainty.
   d. both *b* and *c*.

Sel. 4 O-Skim		1. _____
Time :60 = 1,152 wpm		2. _____
:75 = 922 wpm		3. _____
Score _____ %		4. _____
▶ **75%**		**Check answers to both quizzes**
Score = number correct x 25.		**with your instructor.**
		Record rate and score on p. 266.

C. Questions for Discussion and Writing

Now go back and read this article slowly and pleasurably, and consider the following questions.

1. Discuss the impact theory. Then present the most convincing evidence that the article gives for this theory.

2. Discuss the volcano theory, and cite evidence that the article gives to support it.

3. The article ends with a quote from a scientist: "The history of life is enormously more quirky than we imagined." In light of the evidence from this article, what do you think this quote suggests?

· ·

SELECTION 5

"The Key to Success?" by David G. Savage *1,479 words*

This selection is close to the midpoint of your timed readings in overview skimming, so we won't help you by describing it, marking any key passages, or even announcing the steps to follow. We will only tell you that the subject is something dear to all our hearts: success.

After you finish A and B, you will find C, a short midpoint self-evaluation.

A. Preview Skimming

Do the usual minimal preview: headlines, subheads, length, and so on. Spend no more than 30 seconds on this (= 2,958 wpm). Then take the three-item preview quiz.

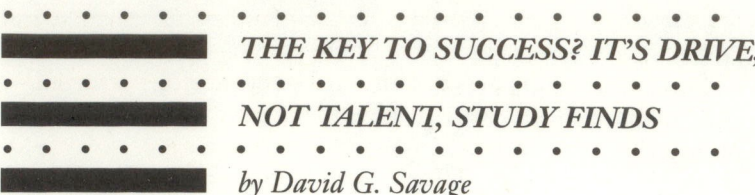

THE KEY TO SUCCESS? IT'S DRIVE, NOT TALENT, STUDY FINDS

by David G. Savage

1   A five-year study of 120 of the nation's top artists, athletes and scholars has concluded that drive and determination, not great natural talent, led to their extraordinary success.

2   "We expected to find tales of great natural gifts," said University of Chicago education professor Benjamin Bloom, who led the team of researchers who studied the careers of America's top performers in six fields: concert pianists, Olympic swimmers, sculptors, tennis players, mathematicians and research neurologists.

3   "We didn't find that at all. Their mothers often said it was their other child who had the greater gift," Bloom said.

4   The most brilliant mathematicians often said they had trouble in school and were rarely the best in their classes. Some world-class tennis players said their coaches viewed them as being too short ever to be outstanding, and the Olympic swimmers said they remember getting regularly "clobbered" in races as 10-year-olds.

ANONYMOUS INTERVIEWS

5   The foundation-supported research team conducted in-depth, anonymous interviews with the top 20 performers in the six fields, as judged by national championships or similar honors.

6   They also interviewed their families and teachers, hoping to learn how these individuals developed into extraordinary performers.

7   Instead, the researchers heard accounts of an extraordinary drive and dedication through which, for example, a child would practice the piano several hours daily for 17 years to attain his goal of becoming a concert pianist. A typical swimmer would tell of getting up at 5:30 every morning to swim two hours before school and then two hours after school to attain his or her goal of making the Olympic team.

8   Bloom, an eminent educational researcher, said his findings "remind me of the old joke about the young man walking down a New York street who stops to ask a little old lady, 'How do I get to Carnegie Hall?' And she looks up and says, 'Practice, young man. Practice.' "

9   Although practice and motivation seemed to explain their success, the top performers, regardless of their field, appeared to follow a similar course of development, the researchers found.

10   In practically every case, the parents played the key role, first by exposing their children at an early age to music, sports or learning. The vast majority of the parents were not themselves outstanding musicians, athletes or scholars. For example, fewer than half of the parents of the distinguished pianists had ever played any musical instrument.

VALUED COMPETITION

11   But the parents of the swimmers and tennis players did enjoy sports and valued competition, Bloom reported. The families of the pianists and sculptors appreciated art and music, while the parents of the research scientists displayed a great love for learning.

12   The parents of the mathematicians and research neurologists reported that their children showed both an unusual curiosity about how things work and an "independent nature" that allowed them to play or work alone for hours.

13   Although it is not uncommon for children to ask repeatedly "why?," "what appears to make the parents of the (scientists) unique is the nature of their response to their children's questions,"

Bloom wrote. "They responded to the questions seriously, often encouraging even more questions."

14   Beyond specific attitudes or interests, the parents also taught their children to value hard work and competition.

15   "These parents placed great stress on achievement, on success and on doing one's best at all times. They were models of the 'work ethic,' believing that work should come before play and that one should always work toward distant goals," Bloom said. The results of the research will be published this week in a book entitled "Developing Talent in Young People."

16   The families said in the interviews that they wanted their sons and daughters to have "normal" childhoods and that they had no inkling that the children would achieve unusual success.

PARENTS ENCOURAGED THEM

17   But once a child displayed an interest and enthusiasm in a particular area, these parents encouraged them at every step and were willing to spend countless hours shuttling them to and from piano, tennis or swimming lessons.

18   "Even in homes where money was tight, no sacrifice was too great in order that the child have whatever he needed to learn to become a musician. 'My parents didn't have nickels to rub together,' Bloom quoted one pianist as saying. 'Those were the bad old days. But there was always money for music.'"

19   Several of the families reported moving to new homes just to get their children in better academic environments or to be closer to a coach or instructor.

20   Bloom's study also found that these extraordinary achievers, all of whom were younger than 40 when interviewed, appeared to have gone through three distinct stages of development, regardless of their field.

21   At first, the parents exposed the children to playing a piano, tinkering with scientific games or hitting a tennis ball, but it was just fun. They played tennis with their families, for example, and developed the habit of regular practice. Usually, the children also had some outside instruction— perhaps a neighbor who gave piano lessons or an uncle who was a good tennis player.

22   Then, at some point, they began to gain recognition for their ability. A 7-year-old would play the piano for a school performance. An 8-year-old would beat all the other children at his local tennis or swimming club.

23   "Within two to five years, most of the individuals in our study began to see themselves in terms of the talent field," Bloom wrote. "They began to see themselves as 'pianists' and 'swimmers' before the age of 11 or 12, and 'mathematicians' before the age of 16 or 17."

24   "Most of our talented individuals had very good experiences with their initial teachers, and many had developed a very comfortable relationship with them," Bloom wrote.

25   At the second stage of development, as a child's rapid progress became apparent, the parents usually sought out a more expert instructor or coach.

26   Typically, the new teachers "were perfectionists who demanded a great deal of practice time for the student and looked for much progress in a relatively short period of time," Bloom wrote. They usually stressed the refining of the child's technique, whether it be their fingers on the keyboard or their strokes in the water or on the tennis court.

27   In the middle years, these young people first tasted extraordinary success. Some set national swimming records as adolescents. The pianists got opportunities to perform with symphony orchestras. The future mathematicians and neurologists were already doing independent research projects and winning science fairs. The tennis players were winning state championships.

GREATER COMMITMENT

28   At this point, their commitment to their field escalated one step further. The subjects said

they began "living" for swimming, or tennis or the piano and devoted hours each day to practice. They also sought out the nation's best coaches or teachers, those who were recognized masters at training the best.

29   Sixteen of the world-class pianists reported having studied at some time with one of five master teachers. The mathematicians and scientists, who often had become attached to a special teacher or gained the attention of a local university professor, gravitated to the nation's top universities in math and science.

30   At this final stage of development, the focus was less on technique than on developing a personal style. The swimmers and tennis players said their master teachers helped them with strategy and psychology. The pianists said they learned about expressing their own interpretation of the music.

31   "During these years the student was completely committed to the talent field. Now most of the motivation was internal and related to their larger goals," Bloom wrote.

32   Few of the talented individuals expressed any regret about devoting so much of their time to pursuing a single goal.

33   "I loved tennis. To me, it was productive," said one former player. "To sit in a (fast-food) parking lot in a car with four or five 16-year-olds

didn't interest me a bit. I never felt I missed that."

34   A few swimmers reported a great feeling of letdown after the Olympics ended and their swimming careers were over. Most of the top achievers, even those who had left their field, said they had retained a feeling of pride in their accomplishments.

35   Bloom said the study convinced him that talent must be carefully nurtured over many years.

36   "The old saw that 'genius will win out' in spite of the circumstances just doesn't hold up," he said.

37   Because natural talent seemed to play such a minor role in the development of these performers, Bloom said he was also convinced that a large number of individuals could achieve at extraordinary levels if given the right encouragement and training.

38   The research "points to the enormous human potential available in each society and the likelihood that only a very small amount of this human potential is ever fully developed," he concluded. "We believe that each society could vastly increase the amount and kinds of talent it develops."

David G. Savage, "The Key to Success? It's Drive, Not Talent," *Los Angeles Times*, February 17, 1985. Copyright, 1985, Los Angeles Times. Reprinted by permission.

• •

1.   The title and lead-in to the news story really sum up the main idea: the results of a research study.
    a.   true
    b.   false

2.   The article concerns individuals who have been successful in the arts, scholarship, and sports.
    a.   true
    b.   false

3.   One inserted subhead is:
    a.   Parents Encouraged Them.
    b.   Money Not a Factor.

```
Sel. 5    P-Skim                          1. _____
Time    :30 = 2,958 wpm                   2. _____
Score    _____ %                          3. _____
         ▶ 100%                           Check answers after the next quiz.
Score = number correct x 33.
```

B. Overview Skimming

Take no more than 1-1/2 minutes (= 986 wpm) to skim this article for main ideas. Of course, if you can skim it in 1 minute (= 1,479 wpm), that's just fine too. (For any faster or slower times, look up your wpm rate on page 329.) Then take the quiz without looking back at the article.

1. The study took 5 years, analyzed 120 people in 6 fields, and was directed by the University of Chicago.
   a. true
   b. false

2. The results of the study seemed to prove that high achievement in various fields resulted from:
   a. great teachers or coaches at a crucial phase of development.
   b. drive, determination, hard work, careful nurturing—all from the start.
   c. unusual natural talents or gifts present at birth.

3. The study also shows that extremely successful people:
   a. shared much the same background and phases of development.
   b. had differing, unique backgrounds and development.
   c. cannot be categorized one way or the other.

4. The article ends with Professor Bloom's conviction that:
   a. "genius will win out," regardless of outside forces.
   b. the human potential for success is enormous and largely untapped.

```
Sel. 5    O-Skim                          1. _____
Time    1:00 = 1,479 wpm                  2. _____
        1:30 =   986 wpm                  3. _____
Score    _____ %                          4. _____
         ▶ 75%                            Check answers to both quizzes
Score = number correct x 25.              on p. 339.
                                          Record rate and score on p. 266.
```

C. Follow-up

Did you preview and overview skim effectively? Were both your scores and your skimming times on target? In the preview, you should have:

1. Noticed the layout—long headlines, inserted subheads—all of which summed up the content

In the overview skim, you should have:

1. Read the beginning (the details of the study) and the end (Bloom's conclusions)
2. Slanted or spiraled your eyes through the many (interesting) details
3. Read as many major details as you had time for

If you had trouble with any of the above, take time out at this point to repeat the skimming of this article from the beginning. If you did well, proceed to a more careful reading and answer the questions that follow.

D. Questions for Discussion and Writing

Reread or refer back to the article as needed.

1. What is the dominant pattern in this article? In the study itself?
2. Do you accept the findings as valid? Why or why not?
3. Outline (in either complete sentences or phrases) the "three distinct stages of development" described as typical of the high achiever.
4. If the conclusions are valid, what significance does this study have for you as an individual? For children growing up in families everywhere?

· ·

SELECTION 6

"Artificial Paradise" *by Bob Sipchen 2,041 words*

Vocabulary
phylogenetic: pertaining to the evolution of a type or kind of animal; "down the phylogenetic spectrum"
savanna: grassy plain, with low scattered trees; "African savannas"
condolences: expression of sympathy to a person in sorrow or pain; "give him my condolences"
dysfunction: malfunctioning of a body or organ; "never caused death, never caused dysfunction"

This is a controversial article regarding the human being's need to use drugs. As with many articles in this section, it is worth a careful reading once you complete your overview skimming. In overview skimming, look for the argument that

Sipchen presents and a few of the significant bits of evidence that he uses to support his thesis. Note that Sipchen is interpreting the findings of the scientist Ronald Siegel.

Follow these steps:

1. Preview skim the article.
2. Answer the three-item quiz.
3. Overview skim the article for main ideas and significant details of support.
4. Answer the four-item quiz.

A. Preview Skimming

Take 1 minute (= 2,041 wpm) to preview this selection, studying the title, date and source, subtitles, and general organization.

ARTIFICIAL PARADISE

by Bob Sipchen

1 Stoned, smashed, bombed, tight, tipsy, tanked, stewed, plastered, looped, blotto, swacked, schnockered, fried, ripped, besotted, blasted, shikker, reeling, soused, soaked, canned, potted, bent, crocked, shellacked, squiffy, jug-bitten, oiled, polluted, raddled, high, lit, loaded, stinko, pie-eyed.

2 There are reportedly more synonyms for intoxication than any word in the English language. For good reason. Catnip-sniffing kittens and alcoholic American presidents alike know that the urge to get high is a strong one.

3 The $6.1 billion the White House Office of Drug Control Policy is likely to spend fighting drugs next year isn't going to change that. Ollie North's anti-drug community service work won't change that. Nor will Nancy Reagan's urging kids to "Just Say No."

4 At least that's the view of UCLA psychopharmacologist Ronald Siegel, whose new book, "Intoxication—Life in Pursuit of Artificial Paradise" (E. P. Dutton) argues that the motivation to achieve an altered state of mood or consciousness is "a fourth drive," as much a part of the human condition—and as important to most other species—as sex, thirst and hunger.

4 "I find it helpful to picture America in a tug-of-war between the laws of the land and the drives of the people," he writes. Siegel doesn't advocate legalizing the drugs society is now battling. But 20 years of research have convinced him that until America comes to grips with the reality of the powerful intoxication drive, the tug-of-war will be a stalemate at best.

6 Siegel looks like a local high school teacher circa 1971. His hair flops over his ears. His eyes shift between intensity and mischievousness as he enthusiastically spins the tale of his life's work.

7 He speculates that his curiosity about altered states of consciousness may have been triggered in boyhood, when a dentist gave him nitrous oxide. "William James, one of my heroes in psychology, had some very interesting experiences and thoughts about psychology as a result of his intoxication on nitrous oxide."

8 Siegel said that his own use of controlled substances since then has been minimal and limited to research. Pressed to discuss that, he

bridled. "That's not important," he said repeatedly. He later explained that he was a research subject in "less than a half dozen" tests more than 10 years ago, although he declined to discuss the substances involved.

9 "I've been really lucky," he said. "I've been able to hire people to take it for me. I've had some very brave volunteers, and there's no lack of drug users out there to study . . ." Until a recent injury knocked him out of the running, Siegel was a marathoner and something of a health nut. "I've always been extremely conservative about my own body. I could probably count on one hand the number of times I've had alcohol in a year."

10 If anything, Siegel appears intoxicated with curiosity; his addiction is to research. "I enjoy poking my fingers in the brains of humans and animals and studying them."

11 Siegel did his undergraduate work in sociology at Brandeis University, and received a Ph.D. in psychology from Dalhousie University in Halifax, Nova Scotia, where he experimented with the effects of LSD, marijuana and other drugs on pigeons and mice. While there, he started consulting to the Canadian government's "Royal Commission of Inquiry Into the Non-Medical Use of Drugs." He then went on to post-doctoral work at Albert Einstein College of Medicine in New York.

12 At Albert Einstein, "a professor made the statement that man is the only animal that intoxicates himself deliberately. I thought, 'Gee, that has to be wrong.'"

13 In 1970, Siegel went to Czechoslovakia to study insects that were eating marijuana plants. Contrary to local folklore, he did not find that stoned grasshoppers were able to make enormous leaps.

14 But later he did find evidence that some insects seemed attracted to some plants such as the opium poppy as an intoxicant as well as a food source. For two decades, Siegel and research associates have been working their way up and down the phylogenetic spectrum and around the world, watching California robins get smashed on

Pyracantha berries and divebomb cats; observing jimson-weed-addled cattle on Maui; hearing tales of tigers in Sumatra that attack children to eat the fermented durian fruit they've gathered, and stories of elephants on the African savannas that get as drunk as Dumbo in the Disney cartoon.

15 "During the Vietnam conflict, our observers found that water buffalo were nibbling opium poppies more often than they naturally do. This was very similar to what our soldiers were doing with heroin," Siegel said. "You can understand that in terms of both animals reacting to stress."

16 Pursuing such connections, Siegel and his research teams also scrutinized primate species, both in the field and in labs and libraries.

17 At UCLA Siegel developed a "psychonaut" program for studying the effects of LSD on humans, and the effects of that hallucinogen and other drugs on chimpanzees and monkeys (although in his book's acknowledgments, he thanks the non-human primates that propelled him "to shift my research out of the lab and into the field, where intoxication is not only natural but right").

18 Sometimes the detective work took odd spins. Armed with a strand of John Keats' hair he acquired from a private 19th Century collection of literary celebrities' locks, Siegel used a process called radioimmunoassay to determine that the poet was an opium user.

19 In fact, lots of important people—maybe most—used some kind of drug, he said, proudly running his hand over folder after folder in the eight file cabinets dominating one room of his homey office suite in a Westwood apartment.

PRESIDENTIAL ADDICTIONS

20 For example, his files contain prescription records, historical accounts, and correspondence on the drug habits of most of this country's presidents. According to Siegel's book, presidential drug preferences ran from cigars to whiskey and beyond.

21 As the book points out, "President Andrew Johnson was said to be rarely sober"; Abraham

Lincoln used chloroform, "a popular recreational drug of the day"; and Ulysses S. Grant was an alcoholic and after retirement wrote his memoirs "sustained by cocaine."

22   "The fact we once had drunks and addicts as presidents is not to say we made a poor choice in our candidates. It's just that they are representative of us," Siegel said, as he sat in his office, indulging in his mind-altering drug of choice: coffee.

23   In all his research, he has yet to find a contemporary or historical culture that hasn't pursued some form of intoxication or consciousness altering. "There may have been pockets but they probably utilized other non-drug methods of intoxicating themselves: Religious ecstasy . . . ritual dancing, drumming, jumping up and down . . .

24   "What I'm saying is, we have always done this. The tobacco industry financed the American Revolution. We were the drug traffickers to the world."

25   During the Colonial period, other countries were as enraged with our tobacco exports as we are with the golden triangle's heroin trade, he said. "Russia had a punishment of slitting the nostrils of tobacco users. In Turkey, they instituted the death penalty. And despite these Draconian measures, tobacco use spread all over the world, and America grew strong because of it."

26   Which is not to say Siegel discounts the tragic consequences of this or any of America's more modern drug habits. Nor does he endorse legalization of outlawed drugs.

27   "My position is that none of these drugs are good," he said. "I'm not advocating the use of any of the drugs we have today. I don't think any of them are healthy or safe. I wish to God we could re-evaluate and reconsider alcohol and let that go through an FDA trial. I don't think it would ever make it."

28   Tobacco may be even more dangerous. "I don't care how many filters you put on it, tobacco is killing 1,000 people a day . . . and there are 125,000 Americans who die every year from pre-scription drug problems. That is more than all the illegal drug deaths put together.

29   "Our use of intoxicants is just getting worse and worse," he said.

30   Cocaine abuse is a good example. "Cocaine tickles the fourth drive and seduces it better than any chemical we have on this planet," he said. "We've never come across our fourth drive as strongly in our history as we have today."

A FUTILE WAR ON DRUGS

31   "That's why we have a war on drugs," he continued. "But it's a war against ourselves. We are fighting against the way we are, against the way in which we're chemically wired."

32   And cocaine use is spreading throughout the world despite measures that have grown so extreme that Peruvian surgeons recently announced a new technique. "They have taken users who refused to say no to cocaine . . . done a procedure known as the bilateral cingulectomy," Siegel said. "Simply put, they've tried to sever some of the pleasurable connections in the brain.

33   "You know, we do the same thing in this culture. We're severing people from their jobs, and their livelihoods and sometimes their freedom on the basis of chemical tests we do on them every day in the workplace. That's a panic reaction too. We're all panicking because we don't know what to do."

34   Which leads to Siegel's unorthodox and controversial conclusion. People use drugs, from caffeine to heroin, for one purpose, he believes. "They're medicating themselves. They're changing their mood. They're changing the way they feel. These are legitimate medical uses.

35   "Our choices of drugs may not always be legal or prudent or safe, but that's what we're doing." The way to clean up our drug problem, he believes, "is to clean up the drugs themselves."

36   In 1979, while digging at an archaeological site in Peru, Siegel unearthed an ancient pottery shard depicting a llama eating a coca leaf as an Indian watched with outstretched arms and an open mouth. Siegel was elated, and not just because he,

too, had been chewing the coca leaf (legally). The shard, he decided, demonstrated his hypothesis that primitive man learned to use drugs safely by observing animals.

[37] "What went wrong?" he asked himself. "There has been not one reported death because of coca leaf chewing in 5,000 years," Siegel said. Indians he researched are disgusted by the idea of snorting purified cocaine. "They think it's a filthy gringo habit."

"MESSING WITH MOTHER NATURE"

[38] Siegel concluded that "we have a drug problem because we have ripped apart these leaves, isolated the chemicals, stripped them down, and injected them directly into our bloodstream, or our nose, or our lungs . . ."

[39] After working with several presidential commissions and the United Nations, Siegel still believes that this misuse of natural intoxicants is the crux of the world's drug dilemma.

[40] "The problem is we're messing around with Mother Nature. We're taking relatively safe medicines, benign intoxicants, and turning them into poisons by concentrating the dose and changing the pattern of use. All the problems that I've seen on this planet . . . are really problems of misusing the dosage and the pattern of use."

[41] If society would invest as much money as it does on the drug war in finding a safe natural drug, or in creating safe synthetic drugs, the war might become unnecessary, Siegel believes.

[42] "What would be wrong if we had a drug that never caused addiction, never caused dependency, never caused death, never caused dysfunction such as driving under the influence, never caused liver problems? What would be wrong if

it were safer than alcohol, safer than caffeine, safer than aspirin, which still kills dozens of people a year in the United States?"

[43] Answering his own question, Siegel said: "I think Americans would say, 'That's morally unacceptable, because we don't need to get high.'"

[44] He gave a slight, professorial shrug. "I'm not taking a moral stand. I'm just saying it is something we do. That's why we have a drug problem. We are medicating ourselves. We have always done this as an animal. Let's learn the reasons for this ancient habit and do it right."

[45] Siegel said he has heard that someone at William J. Bennett's White House Office of Drug Control Policy is reading his book. But official sanctioning of the safe new or natural intoxicating "adaptogens" he proposes will come only far in the future—if at all, he conceded. "Right now we have to start to change our thinking about this."

[46] In the meantime? What would he tell Bennett to do?

[47] "I'd first of all give him my condolences," Siegel said. "I'd say don't abandon any of the efforts you're engaged in now. But I'd advise him to look ahead. And to do that all you have to do is to look back" at how humans and other animals have behaved throughout history.

[48] "It is natural that being chemical organisms, we're going to react with the chemistry around us," Siegel said. "It's too late to take a step back. To 'just say no' is to deny everything that we are and all the things we could be."

Bob Sipchen, "Artificial Paradise," *Los Angeles Times*, August 14, 1989. © 1989 The Los Angeles Times. Reprinted by permission.

• •

1.   This article is from:
   a.   the *New York Times.*
   b.   *Time* magazine.
   c.   the *Los Angeles Times.*
   d.   *The Wall Street Journal.*

2. The "artificial paradise" seems to refer to:
   a. a state of mind induced by drugs.
   b. life after death.
   c. polluting the atmosphere.
   d. food additives.

3. The article seems to be in favor of people using any drug they want.
   a. true
   b. false

Sel. 6   P-Skim   1. _____

Time   1:00 = 2,041 wpm   2. _____

Score _____ %   3. _____

▶ **100%**   **Check answers after the next quiz.**

Score = number correct x 33.

B. Overview Skimming

Now go back and overview skim for main ideas and relevant details in 2 minutes (= 1,021 wpm). Try not to get too involved in this interesting argument. Merely read this time for the kind of evidence that Siegel presents to further his argument.

1. Siegel's research suggests that:
   a. humans crave some sort of high.
   b. even insects want to alter their moods.
   c. processed drugs are just as safe as those found in nature.
   d. both *a* and *b*.

2. Siegel contends that historically powerful and important people:
   a. rarely took drugs.
   b. frequently took some sort of drug.
   c. were often imprisoned for drug use.
   d. did not often know about the power and use of drugs.

3. Siegel targets tobacco as a particularly dangerous drug in use today.
   a. true
   b. false

4. Siegel's conclusion is that people tend to:
   a. overuse drugs.
   b. like prescription drugs.
   c. find great profit in selling drugs.
   d. experiment with drugs because the human being is also made up of chemicals.

Sel. 6   O-Skim   1. _____
Time   2:00 = 1,021 wpm   2. _____
Score _____ %   3. _____
▶ 75%   4. _____
Score = number correct × 25.   **Check answers to both quizzes with your instructor. Record rate and score on p. 266.**

C. Questions for Discussion and Writing

Reread the article slowly and pleasurably. Then consider the following questions.

1. Summarize Siegel's main argument, and cite three reasons he introduces to support it.

2. Reread the paragraphs on animals (13–15). How does this material help further support Siegel's argument?

3. Why does Siegel think Americans today have a drug problem? How does it differ from drug use in primitive cultures? Do you agree with the point he is making here?

. . . .

SELECTION 7

"For Whom the Bell Tolls" *by Patrick Cooke 1,440 words*

This article presents plenty of evidence for its thesis. As usual in overview skimming, you won't have time to do much more than discover what the thesis is, but you can always return to the article and read it for the details, later.

Follow these steps in overview skimming the selection:

1. Preview skim the article.
2. Answer the three-item quiz.
3. Overview skim the article for thesis and main ideas.
4. Answer the four-item quiz.

A. Preview Skimming

Glance through the article in 30 seconds (= 2,880 wpm). Look for the usual features: title and subtitle, subject area, lead-in (if any), subheadings, length, and difficulty.

FOR WHOM THE BELL TOLLS

by Patrick Cooke

1   Boxing lore has it that along the road to becoming a much-feared three-division world title holder, Roberto Duran once knocked out a horse with a single punch on a street corner in his native Panama. Knocked it out cold.

2   Like most professional fighters, Duran can deliver a punch with about 1,000 pounds of force. Just how much physical damage such blows can exact on the human brain has been debated since the Marquess of Queensberry sought in 1867 to civilize the men who, curiously, were to shake hands and come out fighting.

3   Between 1945 and 1982, the "sweet science" killed 349 of them. Eleven have died in the last two years. One victim was Duk Koo Kim, an obscure lightweight who suddenly found himself in line for the big money in 1982. In the 13th round of a contest with Ray "Boom Boom" Mancini at Caesar's Palace, the exhausted Kim took more than 40 punches and then in the 14th received the final shocking blow that sent him sliding to the canvas. Despite emergency surgery, his brain never again showed electrical activity, and he was declared dead.

4   According to Ira Casson, a neurologist at Long Island Jewish-Hillside Medical Center, that last blow was responsible for Kim's death: "It was one hell of a punch." Not only is it force, says Casson, but placement that makes for a killer-punch. "A shot to the temple or the point of the chin are the ones that do the most damage," he says. Because the head more easily moves side to side than front to back, blows that twist the head or tilt it sideways produce the quickest, most violent movement of the head.

5   It is the rapidity of the head's movement that most often causes brain damage—and death. The human brain is suspended in fluid inside the skull. When hit hard, the skull twists and the brain, like a subway rider caught off-guard by a lurching train, whirls and slams against the sides of its hard skeletal casing. Nerve tissue can be bruised, and blood vessels along the surface of the brain can tear and bleed.

6   If jolted hard enough, tissue from deep inside the brain begins to bleed as well. Because the skull is unyielding, pressure quickly crushes the brain against the hard surface intended to protect it. Nerve cells begin to die and the brain stem, control center for vital functions like breathing and heartbeat, is squeezed off from oxygen.

7   Olympic coach Emanuel Steward, whose Kronk Gym in Detroit has produced such champions as Thomas "Hit Man" Hearns and Milt McCrory, says that instinct and conditioning save many boxers from the devastating blow. They learn to literally roll with the punches. "You look at somebody like Ali," he says. "It may have appeared as though he was getting hit hard, but he knew how to move with a punch to soften it."

8   The big problem, says Steward, is that fights are just too long. As a fighter tires in the 13th, 14th, and 15th rounds of a bout, his reflexes become slower and neck muscles become less effective at buffering a powerful punch. "When your body is drained, it's easier to make mistakes. And that's when you get hurt."

9   Equally as tragic as the man killed in the ring are the legions of fighters who retire after years of taking toe-to-toe punches out of a painful belief that, with just a few more bouts, they could have been contenders. "There's a whole spectrum of brain damage," says Casson, "that goes from the staggering punch-drunk guy you can spot at 30 yards right down to the fighter whose problems only show up on neurological tests."

10   According to Casson, more than half of professional boxers will eventually be bested by chronic brain damage. In addition to electronic tests such as the electroencephalogram (EEG)—

which monitors electrical activity of the brain—and sophisticated X rays like the CAT-scan, Casson recently gave a group of active and retired boxers neuropsychological exams. The tests measured the boxers' accuracy recalling simple designs and sentences, connecting dots, and drawing geometric figures. Every boxer showed at least one abnormal sign. What's more, he says, the tests paralleled abnormalities that appeared in the boxers' EEG and CAT-scans.

11   There is no area of a typical professional boxer's brain that escapes at least some injury. The outermost layer, for example, can wear down from repeatedly chafing against the skull. Since this area controls speech, memory, and complex thinking, damage to it can cause slurring, forgetfulness, and mood shifts.

12   The most pronounced damage occurs in the brain's interior, where spinal fluid is stored in hollow spaces called ventricles. As punches shake the skull, tissue around the spaces atrophies, enlarging the ventricles. In severe cases a canal opens up between them. This area of the brain is thought to control the coordination and balance that allows ballet dancers and prizefighters alike to remain on their feet. Once it is impaired, tremors similar to those seen in Parkinson's disease can occur, as well as the unsteady gait that marks the punch-drunk.

13   Coach Steward maintains that while the fighter's trade is no tea dance, the image of the dizzy has-been is much exaggerated. Traditionally, the boxers thought to be most often injured were the "sluggers"—usually heavyweights—and not the artful dodgers. Steward insists that in his 32 years in the profession he's seen only a few men he thought had problems—which, he argues, they may have had before they started in the ring. "Take somebody like Jake LaMotta or Archie Moore," he says. "LaMotta was a slugger and had over 100 fights. They're both very intelligent, articulate men today."

14   But even the man who could float like a butterfly appears to have been stung by a long career in the ring. Muhammad Ali recently underwent diagnostic tests to determine the cause of his sometimes-slurred speech and hand tremors. His doctors said he is suffering from a collection of symptoms loosely called Parkinson's syndrome, similar to Parkinson's disease but much milder. They did not say that boxing was the cause of the syndrome.

15   But others think that Ali's condition was all but inevitable. "They're using semantics to whitewash his condition," says Casson. "I'm not 100 percent sure, but it all fits into the pattern of problems typically suffered by boxers. After all, how many 42-year-olds have Parkinson's disease?"

16   Although Casson would agree that being punch-drunk may not be mentally debilitating—several of the test subjects are now successful businessmen—he cautions that later in life real problems might arise. "Some say it's progressive, some say it stops if you stop fighting—maybe gets a little better. Nobody knows. But everyone over 25 is losing brain cells every day. People who've had injuries like these boxers lose their reserve capacity of cells. When they get older, they won't be able to cover it up."

17   Nearly everybody agrees that there is room for greater safety measures. Besides reducing the number of rounds in a bout, researchers also recommend shorter rounds, more padding in boxing gloves, less emphasis on head blows in scoring, and a mandatory helmet rule. Others say that there should be a fixed retirement age for boxers and a limit to the number of fights in a career. "The syndrome is definitely related to the number of bouts," says Casson. "A boxer who starts at age 25 is going to last longer than one who starts at 15."

18   But because boxing is regulated on a state-by-state basis, these changes may be slow in coming. "In Communist countries things are easier," says Casson. "They just say 'Okay everybody, HEADGEAR!' and suddenly they're all wearing it. Things aren't that simple here."

19   These measures are unlikely to satisfy the American Medical Association, however, which

has called for a ban on the sport for the second time in as many years. In a recent editorial the Journal of the American Medical Association called boxing fans bloodthirsty, promoters greedy, and said that ringside doctors are pressured to keep the "carnage" going.

20 Boxing is so firmly ingrained in the American scene, however, a ban could simply drive the sport to a less visible—and more dangerous—underground existence. But in any incarnation boxing's threat to boxers will not disappear.

21 "People love a good fight," says Casson, an admitted boxing fan. "But there are always going to be injuries and death when people get hit in the head. Some of these new measures will eliminate some of that but not all. Not when these guys hit that hard. Not when one punch can do it."

Patrick Cooke, "For Whom the Bell Tolls," *Science 84*, December, 1984, pp. 88–89. Reprinted by permission of *Science 84* magazine. © 1984 the American Association for the Advancement of Science.

• •

1. Is the source a medical, sports, or general magazine? What are the title and date of the source?

2. Is there a lead-in? If so, quote it or put it in your own words.

3. The title comes from a line in an essay by John Donne. It is also the title of a novel by Hemingway. What is the specific "bell" referred to *here?*

Sel. 7 P-Skim	1. _____
Time :30 = 2,880 wpm	Title: _____
Score _____ %	Date: _____
▶ **100%**	2. _____
Score = number correct × 33.	_____
	3. _____
	Check answers after the next quiz.

B. Overview Skimming

Take either 1 minute (= 1,440 wpm) or 1-1/2 minutes (= 960 wpm) to overview skim the article for thesis and main supporting ideas. As usual, do not preread the quiz. Answer the questions without looking back.

1. Before the writer states his thesis, he begins with a several-paragraph introduction about two fighters, Duran and Kim.
   a. true
   b. false

2. One man is quoted frequently on the issue of brain damage among boxers. He is Ira Casson:
   a. a boxing manager.
   b. a neurologist.
   c. a boxing fan.
   d. both *b* and *c.*

3. According to the experts, about how many professional boxers will eventually prove to have brain damage?
    a. about 10 percent
    b. more than half
    c. nearly all

4. The conclusion of the article stresses that:
    a. this problem could be solved by either banning boxing or regulating it more strictly.
    b. while some measures may help, boxing will always cause brain injuries.

Sel. 7   O–Skim   1. _____

Time   1:00 = 1,440 wpm   2. _____

             1:30 =   960 wpm   3. _____

Score _____ %   4. _____

   ▶ 75%   **Check answers to both quizzes on p. 339.**

Score = number correct x 25.   **Record rate and score on p. 266.**

C. Questions for Discussion and Writing

1. The major task of Patrick Cooke, the writer, is to establish that blows to the head suffered during boxing commonly cause brain injury and even death. What paragraphs are devoted to this argument? (Use paragraph numbers.) Does Cooke answer any opposing views on this cause-effect relationship?

2. The last five paragraphs turn to a different writing pattern. What is it? Which pattern would you say is dominant in the article as a whole?

3. In your own words, make a short outline or sentence summary of the proposals in those last paragraphs and the difficulty with each one.

4. Find the original quotation by John Donne used as a title here. What does it add to the thesis or tone of this article?

· ·

SELECTION 8

"Probing the Mystery of the Multiple Personality"
by Lynn Smith 2,764 words

The following is another feature story by a newspaper staff writer; that is, the subject is of interest over some time, not just for that newsday, but the coverage will include the latest developments. Features are written by journalists for the average reader, so special terms are explained, and personalities or human interest angles are emphasized rather than research and statistics. As with all our overview skimming selections, you may want to return to this feature later and read it carefully. For now, remember the mind-set for skimming: "Just the main ideas, please!"

Follow these steps in skimming this selection:

1. Preview skim the article.
2. Answer the three-item quiz.
3. Overview skim the article.
4. Answer the four-item quiz.

A. Preview Skimming

Preview skim the feature in 45 seconds (= 3,685 wpm). Since this is fairly long for a newspaper article, the writer or the editor has provided subheads at intervals.

PROBING THE MYSTERY OF THE MULTIPLE PERSONALITY

by Lynn Smith

1   Nancy Ross was alone in her kitchen smoking a cigarette. *Go ahead and finish it*, she heard Alice say. *It'll be the last one you'll have.*

2   Ross withdrew as if behind a curtain, she recalled. When she returned, she was standing on a bench with a telephone cord wrapped around her neck.

3   Shocked, she suddenly realized that what her therapist had been telling her must be true. She was sharing her body with someone else.

AN "INNER FAMILY"

4   In fact, Ross, a 40-year-old Redondo Beach resident, said she eventually learned she was living with an "inner family" of 13 personalities, each with a name and a purpose. They included the Actress, a promiscuous flirt; the Nun, a righteous moralist; the Kid, a mischievous 5-year-old; Marsha, who faints under stress; and Richard, the gatekeeper who directs their comings and goings.

5   There was also Alice, a suicidal personality who didn't care that if she killed herself Nancy would die too.

6   Sometimes dramatic and frequently bizarre, stories of selves-within-a-self are not as rare as commonly thought and are increasing, say those who study multiple personalties such as Ross. Of the many professionals who remain skeptical that the phenomenon is real, most have never personally encountered a case, said psychiatrist Frank Putnam, multiple personality researcher with the National Institute of Mental Health in Washington.

7   However, the diagnosis gained respectability four years ago when multiple personality was added to the American Psychiatric Assn.'s list of official diagnoses. Last year nearly 500 professionals attended the first international conference on multiple personality in Chicago, and four professional journals devoted solely to the subject were published.

8   Among believers, there is much debate over the nature of multiple personality disorder, its causes and treatment.

9   To share knowledge and opinions, a multidisciplinary group of mental health professionals called the Multiple Personality Study Group has been meeting once a month for the last seven years at the UC Irvine Medical Center. They have reviewed between 100 and 150 diagnosed cases of multiple personality in Orange County. Based on that figure, group leader Donald Schafer estimates the incidence of multiple personality in the general population to be one per 20,000.

10   While stories like "The Three Faces of Eve" and "Sybil" have fascinated the general public, therapists nationwide are now treating thousands of other multiple personalities from doctors to drifters. The vast majority were physically or sexually abused as children.

11   Most are women. Some speculate the reason is that girls are more often abused.

12   Some say multiples have above-average intelligence; some believe there is a genetic predisposition to develop split personalities. Others disagree.

WALLING OFF CONFLICT

13   It is agreed that creating separate personalities is a type of "dissociative reaction." Ross' therapist, Ted Barnes of Santa Ana, believes it is a sophisticated defense mechanism intelligent children adopt to handle continuous terror or pain. "No one could take it all and remain sane."

14   Their system of walling off conflict reduces stress that otherwise might lead to a mental disorder such as schizophrenia, which Barnes believes is more difficult to treat than multiple personality. Though multiples are commonly confused with schizophrenics, they differ in that the different personalities deal with the real world while schizophrenics create their own separate reality, he said.

15   In general, multiple personalities hold themselves together "with spit and baling wire," unknowingly leading multiple lives for two or three decades until amnesiac blackouts force their separate lives to collide, or flashbacks bring back the past, said Barnes, a licensed counselor, certified hypnotherapist and member of the UCI study group. Barnes, who holds an MS degree in counseling from Cal State Fullerton, is president-elect of the Orange County chapter of the California Assn. of Marriage and Family Therapists and president-elect of the California Society for the Use of Hypnosis in Family Therapy.

16   Like other multiples, Nancy Ross has lost chunks of her own history. She knows there was physical, sexual and emotional abuse. She remembers times in her childhood when she would hear familiar footsteps nearing her bedroom and would lie on the floor hoping to be mistaken for a lump of clothes. She remembers hemorrhaging after a tonsillectomy and hearing her stepfather scream at her to stop bleeding. And she remembers she was repeatedly struck at school by nuns who told her horror stories of what happened to children who didn't believe in God.

PURSUED BY THE ACTRESS

17   At 20, she married to leave home. She has little memory of that five-year marriage. Less than a year after her divorce, she was married again, this time to an abusive alcoholic. Along the way she migrated from New York to California, becoming, for a time, a waitress, a secretary, a cab driver, a house cleaner, a live-in companion and a licensed massage therapist. She lived with another man for 10 years. He lived, she said, with the Kid and Cynthia, an angry, destructive personality who changes age at will.

18   There were other men, pursued by the Actress, she said. But after each conquest, the Actress would retreat, leaving a surprised lover to confront an angry personality in the morning. It was usually Alice, a lesbian.

19   (Usually, said Barnes, the central, overt personality deals with the world normally, and the others come out under stress. Students, for example, have complained of other personalities showing up to take a test for which they studied.)

20 Ross was unaware she had separate groups of friends, unknown to each other. Some would tell her she was strange, or that she sometimes seemed like another person. The inner voices she had heard since childhood were simply a part of her, she said. "I thought everybody was that way," Ross said.

TRAUMATIZED BY A PREGNANCY

21 At 27, she enrolled in junior college, surprising herself with superior grades. Now, she is majoring in theater arts at Cal State Dominguez Hills, where she also works as public relations manager of the theater arts department.

22 Ross dropped her original major, psychology, when she realized she needed therapy herself.

23 Four years ago, she said, she was traumatized by a pregnancy that ended prematurely. "I remember being driven to the hospital by a friend. Marsha came out to handle it. They said I was catatonic, totally disassociated," she recalled.

24 The therapist she saw then, who asked not to be identified, said he did not believe in multiple personalities at the time, but has since changed his mind. He told Ross she was a borderline personality, a mental disorder characterized by radically shifting moods and self-image.

25 Two years later, she made an appointment with Barnes, whom she knew as a teacher, for help with exam phobia and later to help her quit smoking. Barnes said he diagnosed her condition early because she showed so many of the symptoms: history of abuse and failed relationships, selective amnesia, flashbacks and blackouts.

26 After three sessions, other personalities emerged under hypnosis, he said. Her voice and body language would change with each. Ross described the changes as "familiar yet foreign."

27 She resisted the suggestion she might be a multiple, which is also typical of multiples, Barnes said. "Anyone who walks in and says, 'I'm a multiple,' usually isn't," he said. Other symptoms include a history of conflicting diagnoses and attempted suicides or maimings, he said.

INNER VOICES GET STRONGER

28 Meanwhile, Ross said, her inner voices were becoming stronger, telling her she was worthless and ought to kill herself. She began awaking in strange places. She found her house in total disarray after a semi-blackout. Dishes were smashed, and the telephone cord had been slashed. The culprit, she learned under hypnosis later, was previously unknown to the other personalities. In a deep, growling voice he told Barnes his name was Wolf.

29 She said she started to believe the diagnosis.

30 Because most psychiatrists and psychologists are taught that multiple personalities are extremely rare, they frequently misdiagnose the problem as schizophrenia, manic depressive or borderline personality, Barnes said. Since more therapists now know what to look for, more multiple personalities are being diagnosed, he said.

31 The profession has been generally skeptical of multiple personalities. Some have suggested therapists may create the phenomenon through hypnosis. Others believe people may try to fake the condition to gain attention or avoid punishment. Psychiatrists were divided in 1979 when Kenneth Bianchi, the so-called Hillside Strangler, displayed four personalities under hypnosis.

32 "Most psychiatrists know more (about multiple personalities) through the media than their own personal experience. I find they repeatedly express skepticism until they find their first case. Then they are fascinated," Putnam said. The professional journals published last year have provided a rich resource for professionals who believe they have encountered a multiple personality but have no idea how to proceed, he added.

33 Much interest has focused on recent studies by Putnam and others showing that multiples' brain wave patterns change according to the personality that is in control. Through funding from the Intramural Program, a research arm of the National Institute of Mental Health, Putnam is currently studying changes in brain blood flow, immunology, voice and autonomic nervous system in multiples' personalities.

34   Some believe the studies bolster therapists' anecdotal accounts of multiples who, for instance, may have vision problems, cardiac arrhythmia, epilepsy or allergies in one or more personalities but not others.

35   One subject, studied by the UCI Multiple Personality Group, was given anesthesia in preparation for surgery, Schafer said. "The anesthesia worked on a few, but not on the majority of personalities," he said. Not only did the other personalities report feeling pain, but later described the surgery to the amazed surgeon, Schafer said. For a second surgery, the problem was solved by asking the personalities to confer and select one of them to accept the anesthesia for all, he said.

36   Putnam believes future research may well provide a window into understanding how personality affects the body. But he fears that sensationalizing early research may jeopardize funding for further research. "If it's treated as a freak show or a spacy process, it will never get the legitimacy it needs for real support."

37   More enthusiastic is Bennett Braun, director of Chicago's Associated Mental Health Services and organizer of last year's international conference. Topographical maps of varied brain waves in multiples are the first objective studies to show major physiological differences within the same human being, he believes. "Now we see it is something that is real. . . . The study of multiples will teach us an incredible amount about both psychiatry and regular medicine."

VALUABLE INSIGHTS

38   And Barnes thinks the study of multiples offers valuable insight into the healing arts. He is among those who believe that practicing mental techniques such as positive visualization can arrest disease over time; but multiples can produce physical change instantaneously, he noted. "If we had a clue how it works, the implications are mind boggling," said Barnes, who is planning a paper on what the study of multiples can contribute to the healing arts for next October's international conference in Chicago.

39   Barnes had worked as a co-therapist with five multiples through the UCI study group before he started treating Ross alone. Last month, they spoke together at a workshop of the Orange County Mental Health Assn. By going public, Ross said she hopes to prove multiple personality is a real and devastating illness. When more professionals accept that, more multiples will receive help, she said. One such person is a friend Ross has made through letters. The friend is incarcerated on the East Coast for a murder committed by one of her other personalities, she said.

40   Therapists say working with multiples has its hazards. Trying to integrate split personalities has been compared to an attempt to form a united Arab-Israeli nation. Multiples are more violent than the general population, Braun said. But they tend to be less violent when compared with other adults who were abused children, he said.

41   In addition to potential violence, multiples also have an ability to evoke others' interest and sympathy and therapists tend to become overly involved, Braun said. Moreover, since multiples have trouble holding down jobs, few can afford the bills.

A POINT OF DISAGREEMENT

42   Therapists disagree whether they should try to fuse multiple personalities into a single personality or, as one therapist put it, aim for a "functional person, no matter whether it's a corporation, a partnership or a one-owner business."

43   After diagnosis, treatment generally follows the same pattern: discovering the personalities (usually through hypnosis), determining which ones are dangerous, setting up awareness of one another, communication and finally cooperation to achieve mutually agreed upon goals.

44   Long-term treatment involves recovering traumatic memories from the past, much like treating wartime trauma, Putnam said. Though others disagree, he said the process almost always produces new personalities who may have been

formed to deal with a particular trauma and then put to rest. Putnam also believes that as old memories surface, differences between personalities begin to dissolve naturally.

[45] Integration does not mean that different personalities are "killed off," most therapists said. One theory is that the inactive personalities continue to exist much like red and white paint continue to exist after they are mixed into pink.

[46] "They start coming together on their own, usually by stages," Putnam explained. "If you start with 15, they may get themselves down to a collection of five, then the five will become three, then two and the two will merge."

[47] An average multiple patient has 13 personalities and may learn to function well after three to five years of treatment, Putnam said.

[48] Barnes does not aim to "eliminate" any of Ross' other personalities. Not only is it difficult, but many "integrated" multiples—including the real-life Sybil—complain of extreme loneliness and depression without their "inner families," he said.

[49] Under hypnosis, Barnes said, he has practiced "family therapy" with Ross and her other personalities. He said he does not reveal to her anything she cannot recall herself from the hypnosis.

[50] Barnes calls Ross a "recovering multiple," much like a "recovering" alcoholic in that she may never be "cured." However, Barnes does not believe there are regressions once therapeutic progress begins. After two years in therapy, she can call on the others' particular strengths in stressful situations without losing control. She has not experienced "total splitting" (losing consciousness) for six months, he said.

[51] At Barnes' suggestion Ross sent the Nun on permanent retreat. Wolf has received permission to rip up old magazines and newspapers but nothing else. After Alice was told to stay in a closet for a while, she no longer speaks to Barnes, he said. "But Richard said she (Alice) would soon." When Alice seems violent, the others

"gang up on her" and do not let her out, Barnes said.

[52] Ross believes there is no constructive purpose in confronting any of her childhood tormentors. But last Christmas, she returned home for a family visit. "I had to go back to make sure I could," she said. "I needed to see my mother again." Her mother and stepfather are separated now. Both are "born-again" Christians.

[53] However, when she saw the face that belonged to the familiar footsteps, streetwise Richard and a motherly personality, Catherine, came out to help, she said. When the family played Bible Trivia, it was Richard who joined in. "I can't handle religion," she said.

THERAPY HAS BEEN PAINFUL

[54] The difference now, she explained, is that she does not lose consciousness when the others "take the spotlight. It's as though I step aside and look over someone's shoulder," she explained.

[55] Therapy has been painful, said Ross. Not only did detailed memories of childhood incest return, she remembered she was raped in her second marriage. "In the beginning I was always unsettled. My head was fuller for a few days. So full, I thought it would explode. There were times I never thought I'd make it one week to the next. Then this summer, all of a sudden, it clicked and I thought, hey, this is working."

[56] While she believes wholeheartedly she is a multiple personality, she said she is unsure she has accepted it emotionally. She worries some personality will come out at work and jeopardize her job as when the Kid once misspelled words she was arranging on a marquee.

[57] In one way, Ross is grateful to her inner family. "They lived my life for me when I wasn't able to do it," she said. "It was my defense mechanism and it helped me stay alive."

[58] But her new life is a drastic improvement, she said.

[59] "I never thought I could be happy," she said. "But I am."

[60]   To mark her passage from chaos to control, she gave herself a new name that mirrored what she wants to do: Prosper.

[61]   She describes Prosper as outgoing and a good friend. Ross smiled. "I'm getting to like her more."

Lynn Smith, "Probing the Mystery of the Multiple Personality," *Los Angeles Times*, January 29, 1985. Copyright, 1985, Los Angeles Times. Reprinted by permission.

• •

Were all the subheads good indicators of the content? Are you mystified by cases of people with multiple personalities? Now take the preview quiz without looking back.

1. What is the name of the newspaper? In what year was this piece printed?

2. The article does not start out with a subtitle or a lead-in.
   a. true
   b. false

3. It does begin with:
   a. an individual case—Nancy Ross.
   b. a statement describing the disorder.
   c. an individual doctor.

Sel. 8   P-Skim

Time   :45 = 3,685 wpm

Score _____ %

▶ **100%**

Score = number correct × 33.

1. **Name:** _____

   Year: _____

2. _____

3. _____

Check answers after the next quiz.

B. Overview Skimming

Now overview skim for main ideas. We suggest finishing in either 2 minutes (= 1,382 wpm) or 2-1/2 minutes (= 1,105 wpm), although of course you may skim faster if you wish. Just record your exact time to obtain your skimming rate. (For any faster or slower times, look up your wpm in the rate table at the back of the book.)

1. Which statement seems to sum up the thesis best?
   a. Multiple personality is becoming recognized as a real disorder, and treatment by therapists is advancing.
   b. Most therapists still do not believe that the disorder is real.
   c. Multiple personality is accepted by most therapists as real, but so far no effective treatment has been found for it.

2. Which statement best sums up the structure of the article?
   a. A number of individual cases and therapists are given equal treatment.
   b. While various cases and therapists are mentioned, most of the information is illustrated by one individual, Nancy Ross, and her doctor.
   c. The article consists mainly of general descriptions of the disorder and its treatment.

3. There are eight subheads throughout the article; we have copied five. Mark two that you thought were helpful as you searched for the main ideas. Mark one that was not helpful. (Newspaper editors insert these simply to break up blocks of print.) Be able to explain your choice.
   a. An "Inner Family"
   b. Pursued by the Actress
   c. Valuable Insights
   d. A Point of Disagreement
   e. Therapy Has Been Painful

4. The ending is:
   a. upbeat, rather optimistic.
   b. pessimistic, even ominous.
   c. unclear—the editor must have just chopped the story off.

Extra: If you can remember how the article ends, state it in your own words.

Sel. 8 O-Skim	**1.** _____
Time 2:00 = 1,382 wpm	**2.** _____
2:30 = 1,105 wpm	**3. Helpful:** _____ _____
3:00 = 921 wpm	Not helpful: _____
Score _____ %	**4.** _____
▶ **75%**	**Check answers to both quizzes**
Score = number correct x 25.	**with your instructor.**
	Record rate and score on p. 266.

Extra: Stating the ending in your own words

_____

_____

_____

C. Questions for Discussion and Writing

1. Reread the article. Then write a one-sentence definition of the multiple personality. List four characteristics of this personality disorder. (Use your own words.)

2. Reread paragraph 14. What two organizational patterns are being used?

3. Scan through the early part of the article for the relationship between abuse in childhood and the development of a multiple personality. In your own words, summarize the connection.

- -

SELECTION 9

"Stress on the Job" *by Robin Heffler 3,534 words*

This article has been reprinted from a university publication designed for the average college graduate. You will learn some of the latest research findings about this problem that "pervades society and the workplaces that keep it running." If you're headed for a stressful career or your school or work life is already too stressful, you may likely return to the article for a more complete reading.

Since you are an experienced skimmer by now, we will give you little direction or help in this selection. So skim away! And don't forget to use this skill as often as you need to once you leave this book.

Follow these steps in skimming this article:

1. Preview skim the article.
2. Answer the three-item quiz.
3. Overview skim the article for main ideas.
4. Answer the five-item quiz. (There is one extra question, because of the article's length.)

A. Preview Skimming

Take 1 minute (= 3,534 wpm) to preview skim. Note the usual features or any special ones.

- -

STRESS ON THE JOB

by Robin Heffler

1   Stress.

2   Just walking out the front door seems to induce it. Modern city dwellers are barraged by noise, traffic and an array of pollutants. How much greater is the assault when the destination is a large institution where a complex mix of uncertain job expectations and ambiguous rules may await?

3   UCLA researchers say stress pervades society and the workplaces that keep it running,

sometimes with devastating effects on the minds and bodies of workers. Perhaps most disturbing is that they talk about being able to manage the problem, not eliminate it. Their recent work in the fields of psychology, medicine, public health, and business management sheds new light on and reinforces previous discoveries about an elusive topic that has increasingly captured national attention.

4 "It is the common cold of the 80s," says Anthony Reading, a clinical psychologist with UCLA's Center for Health Enhancement. "It's used to cover a multitude of problems and used in such a general sense that it really means different things to different people." Those whom Reading sees in workshops and private therapy sessions seek help because—to use the popular conception of stress—they feel overwhelmed by anxiety, insecurity, and pressure, often in relation to their jobs.

5 Scientists have been exploring the mysteries of stress for nearly 50 years and have yet to reach a consensus about how to define it. The late Dr. Hans Selye, who is considered the father of stress research with his pioneering work in 1936 that described the body's response to stress, defined it as any nonspecific response by the body to a demand made upon it. Stress has also been studied as the psychological response to frustration, threat, or conflict, or the disruption of a social unit.

6 But all agree that some stress is life-enhancing, providing necessary stimulation. "In the workplace," says Reading, "the art is to assure arousal that is high enough to stimulate performance, rather than impede it."

7 Like the person who says he doesn't know much about painting but knows what he likes when he sees it, a worker under stress may not understand it but knows how it makes him feel. A pounding headache, upset stomach and aching back are some of the common symptoms. Workers describe their feelings with phrases like, "I feel uptight"; "I feel like I'm going 90 miles an hour"; or "I feel like walking out and not coming back."

8 More worrisome are those who are not aware that they're under stress or ignore the signals they may be receiving. Some of the more subtle signs include eating and sleeping problems, lack of pleasure in life, and decreased efficiency at work.

9 One view of stress is that it can be addictive. "There is talk of that need for the adrenaline, the rush that gives the energy surge," acknowledged Reading. As with all addictions, though, there is a law of diminishing returns.

10 "Very commonly," Reading explains, "people say, 'If I have one or two things to do, I really can't get them done. However, if I have six or seven, or if I have too much to do, I function very well.' The reason is there's not enough challenge with only a few things to do and the worker tells himself that he can do them later. With many tasks ahead, all of a sudden there's a charge. Then two or three of the most stimulating or appealing tasks are chosen and the pressure gets the arousal curve up to the optimal level.

11 "But if there's always too much to do, there's a sense of never really getting caught up to whatever the individual considers a manageable level. Then the stress is debilitating."

12 One of Reading's private patients who suffers from overload is an eminent UCLA professor. His feelings of being overextended at work are exacerbated by recent relocation to Los Angeles and have fueled marriage problems and alcohol abuse.

13 "His main concern has been a sense of pressure and not having time for himself," says Reading. "I think he is looking at the next 15 years and wondering how he will cope if this continues. In academia it's very hard because there's so much to keep abreast of. It's vague and open-ended no matter what the field, and there's always someone out there producing something else that maybe you should read.

14 "If one is competing for the glittering prizes of academic riches, one's always on a treadmill. This professor is just starting to deal with these things and I don't know that he will

adequately deal with them because of his need to be in that marketplace."

[15]   The example illustrates a widely held principle that being under stress at work is not usually a trauma in itself; one's social support system and personal coping mechanisms must not be working at the same time. "Some people buckle under stress because it's the last straw," says Dr. Fawzy Fawzy, associate professor of psychiatry in the UCLA School of Medicine and a stress researcher. "At another time in their lives they might have handled it better."

[16]   For less eminent academicians, the stress may come from years of striving toward goals like reaching tenure. And, at many levels of the academic chain they face reviews for advancement which hinge on unclear procedures and subjective judgments.

[17]   Dealing with role ambiguity, interpersonal conflicts and most significantly, the lack of control over one's work and position in the hierarchy, are familiar sources of stress to employees of large corporations as well as universities. But they can seem more intense in an academic environment because power struggles are more hidden, according to Charles Leo, a management consultant who teaches stress management courses through UCLA extension and USC, and is on the faculty at Cal State Northridge. Leo, who received a doctorate in applied behavioral sciences from UCLA's Graduate School of Management in 1973, also has 15 years of experience in the corporate business world.

[18]   "The conflicts seem to be more open in the corporation where the financial stakes are greater," he says. "There is also a greater sense of a team concept. The university is a collection of independent producers. Teamwork does not seem to be as much of an organizational objective and maybe that's appropriate in an environment where research and independent publication are supposed to have top priority."

[19]   At the level of support staff, stressful situations are virtually the same in all kinds of settings. Clerical workers often take rather than give direction, feel underpaid, and may perceive little opportunity to move up through the system. Their workloads may be large but unstimulating. As a consequence, they may be "understressed," a form of stress involving lack of challenge.

[20]   Neither boss nor subordinate can claim a greater share of stressful experiences, according to research on monkeys undertaken by Dr. Michael McGuire, professor of psychiatry and biobehavioral sciences. "We find that there's really no difference between the two," he says. "Only when the boss is removed and those remaining are candidates to be the new boss do the indicators of stress (increased blood pressure and other physiological signs) go up for everyone. The new leader has the highest indicators. Everybody's experiencing stress for about 10 weeks after the change."

[21]   Numerous observers of the corporate environment have pointed to middle management as a job area that is vulnerable to high levels of stress. These executives feel burdened by responsibility but may lack the power to act effectively. Or, they may feel caught in the power struggles of superiors.

[22]   Fawzy has researched job dissatisfaction in nurses, a group of professionals in a parallel position to middle management, and one with a high rate of burnout. In a study comparing job satisfaction in five different types of registered nurses at the UCLA Hospital, Fawzy found some surprising results.

[23]   Nurses on units thought to be the most stressful and to have the highest turnover rates, such as those in oncology, expressed the most job satisfaction and in fact did not show excessive rates of departure. He concluded the reason was that these nurses were involved in overall departmental planning and implementation of patient care. They also thought that their skills were being fully utilized, and they felt a bond with co-workers. In short, they had a sense of control over their work.

[24]   On the other hand, general medical nurses showed the lowest job satisfaction. "The main reason was a lack of identification as a significant part-

ner in the health team," Fawzy says. "The identification as a unit was not there because they had to deal with so many areas of medicine as opposed to the more limited areas of oncology or obstetrics."

25   In earlier studies, Fawzy noted that people under stress had a greater susceptibility to ailments such as headaches, flu, stomach aches and back pains. He determined that these were often psychosomatic complaints—physical ailments brought on by the mind as a way of escaping from stress. "Traditionally, it has been more acceptable to have aches and pains," he says. "But recently people have been much more able to talk about problems and seek help."

26   For years, scientists have been studying the relationship of stress to disease and have found increasing evidence of a strong connection between the two. Early research focused on the physiological response to stress, beginning with Selye, who said it consists of three stages.

27   First is alarm, an instinctive response pattern to supply energy. The perceived threat excites the hypothalamus area of the brain to produce substances that stimulate the pituitary gland, discharging hormones into the blood stream. In turn the adrenal glands produce sugar. At the same time, the cardiovascular system increases the heart rate so that blood can be quickly pumped to the muscles in preparation for what is known as "fight or flight." During the resistance period, the body attempts to return to normal, confronting or adapting to the stress. Finally is the exhaustion phase, when adjustment has occurred and adaptive energy has been used up.

28   Later research has focused on how this reaction—essential for primitive people facing short-lived, immediate physical threats—has become dangerous for the modern urbanite. It appears to inflict lasting physical damage when the state of readiness persists for days, weeks or longer. Cancer and heart disease are among the ailments that scientists have linked to hormonal changes during prolonged stress.

29   For Dr. Jacob Zighelboim, associate professor of medicine, the key question about stress is how it may interfere with the immune system, which is believed to play a role in preventing the development of cancer.

30   "It's been known for five years that there is suppressed immune responses under emotional stress," says Zighelboim, an oncologist with a background in immunology. "The question is whether, as we believe, decreased functioning of the immune system makes one more vulnerable to cancer." He has conducted research on changes in the immune system during periods of physical stress, seeking clues to reactions during emotional stress.

31   He found that when healthy people rode a stationary bicycle there were drastic changes in the blood cells that fight infection and cancer. The changes lasted for up to two hours and then the blood composition went back to normal.

32   But cancer patients, who had been free of the disease for six to eight weeks, showed much smaller activations of their immune systems when put under the same physical stress. He said it is not yet known whether the lower immune response led to the disease, or the cancer caused the weak immune reaction. Zighelboim plans future immune system research on individuals who may be at risk of contracting cancer.

33   High blood pressure is another disease that has been increasingly associated with stress. Dr. Walter Greenberg, a postdoctoral fellow in behavioral medicine, studied the combined effects of stress and caffeine on blood pressure in his doctoral dissertation for the UCLA Department of Psychiatry and Biobehavioral Sciences.

34   He used two test groups: one had a family history of high blood pressure; the other did not. He found that both groups had elevated blood pressure readings when performing a stressful mental task while ingesting the equivalent of two cups of coffee in half an hour. But those with a family history scored significantly higher. Normal blood pressure is 120/80. Those with a family tendency toward hypertension recorded an average 16-point increase in the first indicator, rising to 136, while the low-risk subjects increased by an average of 11 points.

35   Hypertension is known as a significant factor in the development of heart disease and artery disease. In recent years it has been sharing this dubious distinction with a stress-related behavior pattern known as Type A. The pattern is characterized by personality traits that include excessive competitive drive, aggressiveness, impatience and a harrying sense of time urgency. In contrast, so-called Type B individuals are more easygoing, less caught up in details and more concerned with the larger picture, and make more time for leisure activities.

36   Physical damage from Type A is believed to occur when emotional reactions cause the secretion of hormones known as catecholamines, which when chronically present, raise the blood's cholesterol level and keep it elevated. Cholesterol clogs the arteries, impairing blood circulation, and ultimately may cause a heart attack.

37   The syndrome has become so widely known that Type A behavior has become something of an office joke. But researchers say the pattern is well-entrenched in the workplace.

38   "Type A's tend to put in longer work weeks, more discretionary hours and travel more days per year," says Judith Siegel, assistant professor of public health, who has been studying various aspects of Type A behavior for more than five years. "Two studies have shown the value of Type A employees. One in Canada showed that if managers of firms are Type A, the company growth rate is higher than that of firms with Type B managers."

39   Siegel's most recent work has focused on development of Type A behavior in children. Building on earlier research findings that Type A boys received fewer positive evaluations and were pushed harder to try than Type B's, Siegel chose to compare the performance of Type A and Type B children when under varying performance expectations.

40   In a 1982 study conducted with Karen Matthews of the University of Pittsburgh, 40 fourth graders, half Type A and half Type B, were asked to list the uses of different objects. Half of each behavior type were told that a "pretty good" performance would be three uses per object. The other half was not given an explicit standard. At the end of the task session, the children were given the opportunity to see the performance score of one other child, ranging from the first-place to the last-place scores.

41   When performance standards were ambiguous, both Type A and Type B children were interested in seeing the highest score. When performance standards were explicit, however, the Type A's were more likely than Type B's to choose the highest score. "In other words," says Siegel, "Type A's were competitive regardless of experimental conditions."

42   In adolescents who displayed Type A behavior, Siegel found in a 1983 study that there was greater blood pressure variability among Type A than among Type B. This is similar to what has been reported for Type A and B adults.

43   McGuire has studied another aspect of chronic stress behavior, adults whom he terms "locked into" stress.

44   The "locked in" theory grew out of a study of a group of women who were chronically stressed and engaged in jobs that were below their potential skill capacity. "They were just not putting it together," he says. "They were not capable of extricating themselves from situations they deplored or that caused them moods they didn't like. They weren't working very hard or taking holidays. They also had fewer social relationships than the control group. Most of them were unmarried. They were highly tense, worried, concerned and ill more often than the average.

45   "What all this suggested to us was that there is a whole package that goes together, that keeps making them knock their heads against the same doors. They didn't realize that they were trying to push open doors that were already open, which is the internalization of the stressful situation. Cognitively they were just incredibly limited with respect to their views of the world. There was no attempt to open up and say 'Gee, maybe there's another way to look at things.' "

46   He also noted more common experiences of being unable to avoid stress. "Let's say you're a college student and you're driven to perform at 'A' level to get into medical school," he says. "Compare that personality to one who might come to college interested in medical school and decides after a year of biology that he's not interested in it and goes off and does something else. The first person is in essence locked in, programmed by genes or environment or whatever.

47   "I think it's becoming increasingly apparent that we're not as free in selecting our environments as our language and our concepts of ourselves would lead us to believe, because some of us are more competitive than others. We all think 'I can quit my job and go live in Montana.' There's not much evidence of that really occurring."

48   For the locked-in individuals there may be little hope of modifying behavior so that stress is reduced. But for others, a flexible attitude is one of several keys to managing or preventing stress, experts say.

49   Fawzy recalled his therapy sessions with a nurse who complained of stress stemming from a lack of support by her superiors. "She said that whenever she approached them with problems, they criticized her," says Fawzy. "When we broke down the problem, she came to understand how they were being educational, not just critical."

50   Group workshops and seminars on stress management seem to take similar approaches. First they identify when one feels stressed and the source of it. Then they discuss ways of coping which usually include three major strategies: changing the stressful situation; changing one's reaction to it; or changing the way one views and interprets the situation.

51   "Stress can be more effectively managed in a group setting because people are sharing and commenting on common problems," says Reading, who directs stress management workshops at the Center for Health Enhancement that are open to the public. "The peer pressure seems to keep people focused on the subject."

52   In the workshops, participants also individually practice deep-muscle relaxation and visual imagery techniques as ways to change their reactions to stressful situations. Other programs emphasize meditation or biofeedback techniques as effective short-term stress reducers.

53   Reading said biofeedback has been useful in the treatment of those with Type A behavior pattern. "Type A's find biofeedback appealing probably because it has some apparatus," he says. "It gives them a sense of control to get external feedback. One woman in therapy has been trained in relaxation, but she wants the external cues to give her some tangible indications of her body's changes from tense to relaxed states and to reinforce and sustain the changes."

54   He acknowledged though, that for individuals whose stress-related behavior is as ingrained as Type A, long-term lifestyle changes are much more difficult to accomplish.

55   Herbert Kindler, Ph.D. '78, an associate professor of management at Loyola Marymount University, examined the effects of meditation and deep relaxation on management problem-solving groups several years ago. The study was his doctoral dissertation at UCLA's Graduate School of Management. He found that a group of management students who engaged in meditation before working on a practice problem solved the problem faster and with fewer steps than those who didn't use meditation.

56   The study was one of the few that apparently have been undertaken on the effectiveness of stress management techniques. Yet corporations and other large institutions seem to be increasingly open to offering their employees help with managing stress, particularly their executives.

57   Stress management has become big business. There are an estimated 300 stress management programs nationwide, with pricetags ranging from hundreds to thousands of dollars. They seem to appeal to employees as part of the general fitness craze that has gripped the country, and as a way to boost work productivity. Employers see them as a way to reduce health insurance costs,

[57] time lost due to stress-related illnesses, and the potential permanent loss of a valuable employee.

[58]   A cure for stress in the workplace seems an unrealistic goal, especially in a society continually faced with new stresses created by ever-accelerating technological changes. But inroads have been made on short-term solutions, primarily, perhaps, in recognition of the problem.

[59]   Says Reading: "People are becoming more aware of health concerns. As stress becomes more widely talked about, people are beginning to recognize it in themselves and recognize the need to do something about it. Much of what we do is help them set priorities and limits in their lives."

Robin Heffler, "Stress on the Job," *The UCLA Monthly*, May–June 1984. Reprinted by permission.

• •

1. The title and lead-in indicate that:
   a. the topic is stress on the job only.
   b. researchers do not expect to eliminate stress.
   c. both *a* and *b* are true.

2. The editor has inserted subheads: key quotes from various individuals who have suffered from severe stress.
   a. true
   b. false

3. The article ends with:
   a. A quote from one of the health professionals.
   b. a dollar estimate of the cost of excessive stress to the nation's economy.

Sel. 9 P-Skim	1. _____
Time 1:00 = 3,534 wpm	2. _____
Score _____ %	3. _____
▶ 100%	**Check answers after the next quiz.**
Score = number correct × 33.	

B. Overview Skimming

Take 3 minutes (= 1,178 wpm) or 2-1/2 minutes (= 1,414 wpm) or 2 minutes (= 1,767 wpm) to skim the article. You already know the thesis from reading the lead-in. Now try to discover what areas of the subject—stress—are covered and what the major results of the research are.

1. The article mentions some past studies done on stress over the last fifty years.
   a. true
   b. false

2. All but one of the following groups were studied; which one was not?
   a. university professors
   b. manual laborers
   c. nurses
   d. children
   e. workers in corporations

3. Doctors working on the subject think that poorly handled stress may be connected to:
   a. heart disease (including hypertension).
   b. cancer.
   c. psychosis.
   d. abused children.
   e. *a* and *b* only.

4. The experts seem to agree that the stressfulness does not reside so much in the job, but rather in:
   a. how much status and salary the worker has.
   b. how much control the worker feels he or she has over the job.
   c. how the worker copes with conditions on the job.
   d. what priorities and limits the worker has set for himself or herself.
   e. whether the worker recognizes he or she is under stress.
   f. all except *a*.

5. Solutions so far include biofeedback, meditation, and group counseling, although "Type A personalities" are difficult to help.
   a. true
   b. false

Sel. 9 O-Skim	1. _____
Time 2:00 = 1,767 wpm	2. _____
2:30 = 1,414 wpm	3. _____
3:00 = 1,178 wpm	4. _____
Score _____ %	5. _____
▶ **80%**	**Check answers to both quizzes**
Score = number correct x 20.	**on p. 339.**
	Record rate and score on p. 266.

C. Questions for Discussion and Writing

1. Reread the article. Then determine how it is organized. Generally, what three questions concerning stress are addressed?

2. Reread paragraph 25. What organizational pattern is used here?

3. Reread the last two paragraphs. Does the writer conclude that stress can be avoided? In your answer, cite specific details in these paragraphs.

. . . .

SELECTION 10

"Murky Waters" *by Maria Goodavage* 2,480 words

Vocabulary
calamitous: pertaining to adversity; "the calamitous *Exxon Valdez* oil spill"
aberration: deviation from what is common; "nightmarish aberrations"
pristine: pertaining to an earlier, purer time; "a more pristine future"
hydrothermal: referring to hot water; "hydrothermal vents"
patently: unmistakenly evident; "patently obvious"
icthyologist: a scientist who studies fish; "an icthyologist with the University of California, Santa Barbara"
eradicate: to completely destroy; "to eradicate their classroom oil spills"
sanctuaries: a place providing refuge; "there are seven sanctuaries"

This is a fairly long selection treating the pollution of our environment. It is well organized with clear and logical subdivisions, so it is an ideal article to overview skim. Locate the subdivisions; then determine the main points the author makes in each selection.

Follow these steps in skimming the article:

1. Preview skim the article.
2. Answer the three-item preview quiz.
3. Overview skim the article.
4. Take the four-item skimming quiz.

A. Preview Skimming

Take no more than 1 minute (= 2,480 wpm) to preview for title and subtitle, author, source, date, subdivisions, as well as beginnings and endings.

. . . .

MURKY WATERS

. . . .

by Maria Goodavage

1   Throughout history humankind has regarded the world's oceans with a reverence usually reserved for the gods. Unfathomable and endlessly bountiful, they have been the most valued resource on Earth.

2   But now the oceans we have loved and exploited seem smaller and less powerful. Perseverance and new technology are allowing us to see them as never before. Recent discoveries have been more fantastic than marine biologists—or even science-fiction writers—could have dreamed.

3   At the same time disaster threatens them.

4 More than 250 dolphins with eerie smiles plastered on their ulcerated mouths washed ashore along the Atlantic Coast during the summer of 1987; coastal sewage laced with industrial toxins is a prime suspect in their deaths. The bodies of aquatic birds with beaks like corkscrews, no eyes, stubs for wings, and high concentrations of selenium are found on segments of California's coastline. In Alaska's Prince William Sound an entire ecosystem was ravaged, perhaps irreparably, by the calamitous *Exxon Valdez* oil spill earlier this year—the worst in U.S. history. All over the globe, nightmarish aberrations are prompting us to ask some fundamental questions:

5 Just how much abuse can the oceans take? Is there still hope for a more pristine future, or is it already too late to reverse the damage we've done?

6 Scientists note that our affections for the sea could paradoxically be one of the major reasons for its present distress: More than 50 percent of the U.S. population lives within 50 miles of a coastline. We generate 150 million tons of solid waste each year, much of it finding a final resting place in the oceans, and much of it a menace to life.

7 Flows of hypodermic needles, sutures and catheter bags onto New York and New Jersey beaches stunned us in 1988. The ugly refuse created a short-term crisis, but it proved to be a powerful warning against using the ocean as a universal waste tank. People who never showed concern about marine pollution suddenly realized that the ocean is not a giant disposal.

8 It's fitting, in an ironic way, that the realization of our neglect coincides with some of our greatest oceanic discoveries.

9 "We've been killing ocean life and trying to find it at the same time," says Kathryn O'Hara, a marine biologist with the Center for Marine Conservation in Washington, D.C. "On one hand, we're destroying our world; on the other, we're just starting to understand it."

LIFE WITHOUT SUN

10 Scientists from Woods Hole Oceanographic Institution expected a desolate black expanse as they cruised just above the Pacific Ocean floor in their deep sea submersible, *Alvin*, in 1977. After all, they were 8,000 feet below the surface, far beyond the reaches of even a faint glimmer of life-giving sunlight.

11 They were amazed to discover a thriving, writhing community of some of the strangest, most colorful creatures ever found in one place. That excursion and subsequent dives brought researchers face to face with dozens of life varieties never before seen by humans. Flowering yellow dandelionlike animals; giant reddish-pink tube worms measuring up to eight feet long; odd variations of old favorites like clams, mussels, snails and crabs: All were part of the bizarre panorama.

12 Life without the sun? The question baffled scientists. But the answer surprised them even more: The exotic animals flourish around vents of water heated by Earth's core. The base of this deep-sea food chain comprises bacteria that thrive on reduced sulfur compounds spewed forth by the vents.

13 These oases of life, which have now been found around many of the world's hydrothermal vents—and cold seeps—need no sun, contrary to the long-held belief that the main source of energy for life is sunlight. It looks as if several of these "new" species haven't changed in millions of years.

14 The vents also help explain the ocean's chemical composition, including its salt content. Water circulating across the sea floor seeps down through the rocks, depositing and picking up chemicals. It is heated, then spewed out at temperatures exceeding 350° Celsius (662° Fahrenheit) through chimneylike vents. The vent system is so large that scientists estimate the ocean circulates all its water through the vents—dissolving and transporting minerals along the way—every 8 million years. That's a relatively short passage of time, geologically speaking.

15 An equally astonishing development in our recent oceanic enlightenment has been rock-hard evidence of plate tectonics, or continental drift. By drilling into the deep-sea crust and bringing

up rock samples, geologists have been able to show how Earth's crust has been ripping apart for eons.

[16]   Scientists say it's no longer speculation that North America used to be part of Europe and Africa. "The development of the plate tectonics theory has provided a revolutionary new way for geologists to understand and explain the origins of geological features," says Richard Rosenblatt, Ph.D., professor of marine biology at Scripps Institution of Oceanography in La Jolla, California.

[17]   These and other discoveries would have been impossible without technological advances like deep-sea submersibles with nimble grasping arms or ships with powerful positioning and drilling systems. But the hero of high-tech ocean exploration never gets wet: the satellite.

[18]   Satellites can reveal data such as water temperatures and the highs and lows of sea level at given locations, gathering information in one sweep around Earth that would take months and countless man-hours to collect from ships.

[19]   Researchers are even using satellites to detect blights caused by man-made pollution—an increasingly frequent task in the past few years. These omniscient eyes float unseen in the heavens, looking upon devastation and reporting our sloth.

DESTROYING THE DEEP

[20]   How could the world's vast oceans, measuring 328 million cubic miles, ever be anything but impervious to our actions? Even marine biologist and writer Rachel Carson, who mobilized environmentalists with her book *Silent Spring* in 1962, couldn't predict the effect humans would have on the expansive seas. "[Man] cannot control or change the ocean as . . . he has subdued and plundered the continents," she once wrote.

[21]   To think we could change the future of something as great as an ocean was to liken ourselves to gods. Impossible, the experts said. But here we stand, approaching a new century, clenching the trident that once belonged to King Neptune.

[22]   How did we acquire this new domain? The oceans fell under our influence because of the same code of ethics applied in many china shops: "You break it, it's yours."

[23]   The oceanic ecosystem is not as hardy as we thought. Until recently we were able to feed the oceans toxic wastes and sewage and notice few, if any, ill effects. Why? Slow reaction time. The oceans, because of their bulk, move lethargically.

[24]   "By the time a problem becomes patently obvious, it may be almost too late to remedy it," says Alfred Ebeling, Ph.D., an icthyologist with the University of California, Santa Barbara. "We have some crises brewing right before our eyes."

POLLUTED HARVESTS

[25]   Jonathan Swift once wrote that "he was a bold man that first eat [sic] an oyster." Swift was referring to the courage it must have taken to be the first to consume the oozy body of the naked mollusk—but in our day his message carries an entirely different meaning.

[26]   Oysters and other shellfish are filter feeders, extracting nutrients, and harmful bacteria and viruses, by pumping sea water through their gills and digestive systems. Pathogens are stored in their tissue and can pose a serious threat to the health of those who eat them. Typhoid, infectious hepatitis and acute gastroenteritis are three maladies humans risk when eating shellfish harvested near grounds where cities dump sewage.

[27]   In 1977 Congress prohibited the Environmental Protection Agency from issuing any permits for dumping sewage sludge after December 31, 1981. New York City, however, went to court and, after a favorable court decision, continued dumping sewage sludge. And during heavy downpours all over our coasts, raw sewage seeps directly into the water because of overflow or equipment failure. "It's scary as hell for business, and for people who value their health," says Clifford Hillman, who owns a shrimp and oyster company on Galveston Bay, Texas. Texas has been closing its shellfish beds about a dozen times a year since 1985.

28 Sewage-dumping is a hotly debated issue. Since sludge typically contains traces of industrial pollutants like zinc, chromium, lead and polychlorinated biphenyls (PCBs), some scientists are working to establish a link between sewage and scourges like the mass deaths of dolphins on the East Coast. Other scientists call such connections absurd, or at least premature.

29 Contamination from toxic wastes is more clear-cut. Around the world's seas, toxic pollution is taking a costly and disturbing toll:

30 • Some 50 beluga whales, already on the federal endangered species list, have washed up on the shores of the St. Lawrence River in the last four years. The whales died of bladder cancer and AIDS-type symptoms. Researchers found high levels of dangerous organic residues in their tissue.

31 • A mysterious epidemic killed more than 7,000 seals in the heavily polluted North Sea in 1988. Biologists say industrial poisons there may have weakened the animals' immune systems.

32 • Most states have issued advisories limiting the consumption of fish caught in certain coastal and recreational waters.

33 The list continues. As toxins travel up the food chain, the contaminants become more concentrated. We're only now realizing that the top of the food chain is not always the safest place to be. But it's not easy at the bottom, either. For phytoplankton—the free-floating microscopic plants that form the basis of our food chain and biosphere—survival is harder than ever.

GRUESOME JUBILEE

34 Scientists are discovering that the growing ozone hole over Antarctica, caused chiefly by extensive use of chlorofluorocarbons in refrigeration and packaging, can reduce phytoplankton productivity. The rate of photosynthesis diminishes as the rate of harmful ultraviolet-B rays penetrating our atmosphere increases. A lack of the food and oxygen these plants provide may lead to the deaths of many creatures, great and small. This almost unnoticeable phytoplankton reduction could result in the demise of our ecosystem.

35 Phytoplankton affects our environment in other, more immediately visible ways. Sewage discharge and fertilizer runoff from farms are common culprits in creating an excess of nutrients in the water. This process, eutrophication, results in explosive blooms of phytoplankton. When the blooms respire and later decay, they rob the water of dissolved oxygen. Creatures in anoxic waters suffocate and wash up on our shores in unappetizing states of decay—sometimes by the hundreds of thousands. . . .

PLASTIC PERILS

36 Rarely, though, do we have cause to feast on the harvest of our neglect. More often the foul bill of goods we've passed along to ocean dwellers is cause for appalled disbelief. Whales and turtles eat floating, shimmering plastic bags and balloons, mistaking them for living morsels. They gradually die of starvation as the plastic blocks their digestive systems. Plastic fishing nets and packing straps drifting through the Bering Sea kill about 40,000 fur seals each year off the Pribilof Islands. The seals play with the plastic, get tangled, and drown, starve or die from the deep gashes created when it tightens around their bodies.

37 Albatross and pelican skeletons hang like ghastly ornaments on trees all over the world, forever entangled on cast-off fishing line. It's nature's reminder that we don't have to shoot an albatross with a crossbow to have it hung around our necks to shame us.

38 Plastic pollution is taking its toll on every form of marine life. In 1975 it was reported that some 26,000 tons of plastic packaging and 150,000 tons of fishing gear were dumped or lost at sea every year by commercial fishing vessels. We litter our beaches with huge amounts of plastics; Los Angeles County beachgoers leave 75 tons of trash—much of it plastic—each summer week. Add to that 690,000 plastic containers jettisoned daily by merchant vessels and we have a weighty affliction. "Plastic litter could be a major killer of large marine life in the world," says Howard Levenson, senior analyst at the Office

of Technology Assessment in Washington, D.C. "The bad news is that it's not going to go away tomorrow or in 100 years unless plastics are made degradable."

39   While scientists are sure of the long life of plastics, they debate the lifespan of oil. Some think the ocean has a greater capacity to break down hydrocarbons than once believed. Others say it lingers longer, citing examples like the 1978 wreak of the *Amoco Cadiz* tanker. Oil from that spill is still interfering with fish reproduction around the coast of Brittany.

40   But no matter how long oil remains a menace to the environment, its immediate effect is ugly and lethal. The wreck of the *Exxon Valdez* tanker in March poured 10 million gallons of oil into Alaskan waters, coating millions of marine creatures with thick, tarry shrouds. "It's the latest tragedy, and the worst, but unless government and industry start acting now, it's far from the last," said Clifton E. Curtis, executive director of the Oceanic Society.

FIGHTING THE DAMAGE

41   Schoolchildren in California, Nevada and Texas are creating oil spills of their own. They're pouring motor oil into basins of water and testing its effect on bird feathers and seal fur. Then they disperse the oil with wind (a fan) and try to clean it up with vacuum suction, cleansing agents and ocean skimmers (straws, detergent and spoons). And though they may fail to eradicate their classroom oil spills, when they travel out to *real* trashed beaches to clear them of garbage they soundly succeed.

42   Education programs like this one run by Project OCEAN of the Oceanic Society's San Francisco Bay chapter will help to determine the long-term health of the oceans. By educating upcoming generations in how to handle the oceans with care, it's possible to hope for the future well-being of our seas.

43   But first we have to get through the next decade or two. "If we don't act now, it will be just that much more difficult to act later," warns

UCSB's Ebeling. The task at hand is perhaps the greatest ever shared by the nations of the world.

44   For inspiration, we can look to the rapidly improving Mediterranean Sea, which long served as a cesspool for the 18 nations bordering it. Ten years ago, one-third of the Mediterranean's beaches were unsafe for bathers. Now, because of a multinational cleanup agreement, only one-fifth are so badly polluted—and the numbers are dropping steadily.

45   The U.S. is also beginning to listen to warnings from the deep. In 1987 we became the 29th country to ratify an amendment to the 1973 MARPOL (Marine pollution) convention that forbids ships and boats to dispose of plastics in oceans around the world. Last year Congress passed and the President signed a law outlawing all ocean dumping by 1992. The effort to protect the marine environment is not new. Legislators have enacted dozens of laws in the past three decades, since environmentalists like Jacques Cousteau raised our consciousness about the oceans. One of the most successful of these is the Marine Sanctuaries Act passed in 1972. Sparked into action by heavy toxic pollution and at that time the biggest United States oil spill ever, Congress moved to provide sanctuaries where natural and historical resources could remain safe. There are seven sanctuaries in American waters today, and their healthy residents are prospering in nearly unblemished habitats.

46   It's going to take time, patience and money to determine what we must do to regain our healthy oceans. "We can't wait for marine animals to die or disappear before we ban a harmful pollutant," says Neylan Vedros, Ph.D., professor of medical microbiology at the University of California, Berkeley. "No price can be too high for such preventive medicine."

47   Research into how pollutants affect the environment will have to be extensive, scientists say. And since we can't realistically banish all ocean dumping, researchers are beginning to

focus attention on how to dispose of wastes more safely.

⁴⁸ Someday, maybe even the most polluted shores will look like today's ocean sanctuaries, or be as untarnished as the deep-sea vent regions. We'll be able to swim at any beach, then dine on our favorite seafood without the fear of becoming ill. The seas will again be Earth's most venerable resource.

⁴⁹ Only then will we have fulfilled our Neptunian duties.

⁵⁰ The following national organizations can help you help the oceans:

American Cetacean Society, PO Box 2639, San Pedro, CA 90731.

Center for Marine Conservation, 1725 De-Sales St NW, Washington, DC 20036.

Environmental Defense Fund–Oceans, 257 Park Ave S, New York, NY 10010.

Environmental Policy Institute, 218 D St SE, Washington, DC 20003.

Maria Goodavage, "Murky Waters," *Modern Maturity*, August–September 1989, pp. 44–50. Reprinted by permission of the author.

• •

1. The title suggests that this article will be treating:
   a. air pollution.
   b. water pollution.
   c. fishing techniques.
   d. both *a* and *b*.

2. The article was written in:
   a. 1987.
   b. 1988.
   c. 1989.
   d. 1990.

3. The article concludes with:
   a. terrifying statistics about pollution.
   b. a list of agencies to contact.
   c. several examples of pollution found throughout the country.
   d. both *a* and *c*.

Sel. 10 P-Skim	1. _____
Time 1:00 = 2,480 wpm	2. _____
Score _____ %	3. _____
▶ **100%**	**Check answers after the next quiz.**
Score = number correct × 33.	

B. Overview Skimming

Take 2 minutes (= 1,240 wpm) or 2-1/2 minutes (= 992 wpm) to overview skim this article for main ideas. Consider each subdivision; then quickly look for the main points that the author is making in these sections.

1. According to the article, some of the material dumped into the sea includes:
   a. needles.
   b. plastic material.
   c. oil.
   d. all of these.

2. The article discusses how the ozone hole affects the production of:
   a. oil.
   b. carbon dioxide.
   c. phytoplankton.
   d. acid rain.

3. One bright area regarding water pollution is the improved condition of the:
   a. Pacific Ocean.
   b. Atlantic Ocean.
   c. Mediterranean Sea.
   d. ozone hole in Antarctica.

4. The article concludes with the warning that all dumping of waste in the ocean must stop.
   a. true
   b. false

Sel. 10 O-Skim	**1.** _____
Time 2:00 = 1,240 wpm	**2.** _____
2:30 = 992 wpm	**3.** _____
Score _____ %	**4.** _____
▶ **80%**	**Check answers to both quizzes**
Score = number correct × 25.	**with your instructor.**
	Record rate and score on p. 266.

C. Questions for Discussion and Writing

1. Reread the subdivision "Gruesome Jubilee." Then summarize how the ozone hole affects phytoplankton.

2. Reread the subdivision "Plastic Perils," and summarize the danger plastic poses to the oceans.

3. Reread the subsection "Fighting the Damage." List the three most effective ways that countries are fighting pollution, and explain what they are doing.

How to record your scores on the Progress Chart

After you have finished a Timed Selection and have entered your time and score in the score box:

1. Find the correct selection number on the top row of the chart. Transfer your rate (wpm) to the chart, under the selection number. Make a dot, X, bar, or other mark. (If you know your time only, not your rate, you must first look up your wpm in the rate table in the appendix. Then mark that number on the chart.) Note that the acceptable or "target" rates for the featured skill are shaded. Do your rates fall within the target area?
2. Transfer your comprehension score to the top blank on the chart. Note that the acceptable or "target" percentage for that selection is printed underneath the blank. Does your score meet—or surpass—the target percent?
3. Connect the rate marks with a line, to see your progress clearly. Remember, though, that your scores will not necessarily rise steadily. The different selections contain too many variables—difficulty, your interest in or familiarity with the topic, and so forth.

• • • • • • • • • • • • • • • • • •

PROGRESS CHART: OVERVIEW SKIMMING

Selection number	1	2	3	4	5	6	7	8	9	10
% Comprehension	%	%	%	%	%	%	%	%	%	%
Target % ▶	75%	75%	75%	75%	75%	75%	75%	75%	80%	80%

Words per minute (wpm = rate) — Target Rates

2000
1900
1800
1700
1600
1500
1400
1300
1200
1100
1000
900
800
700
600
500
400

Selection number: 1 2 3 4 5 6 7 8 9 10

CHAPTER 6

Critical Reading

*T*his chapter may be very challenging for you. You will be mastering the important skills of reading longer sentences, understanding figurative language, and analyzing the logic of particular statements. Compared with your rate in rapid reading and overview skimming, your critical-reading rate will be much slower.

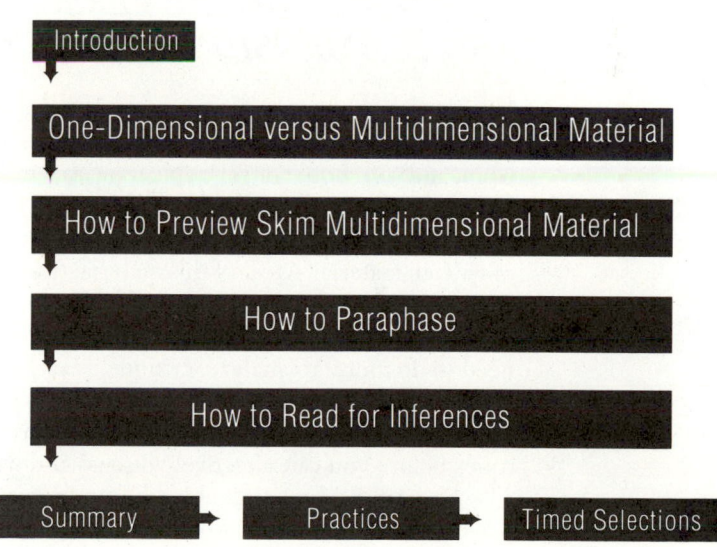

Introduction

One-Dimensional versus Multidimensional Material

How to Preview Skim Multidimensional Material

How to Paraphase

How to Read for Inferences

Summary → Practices → Timed Selections

INTRODUCTION TO CRITICAL READING

CHECKLIST OF SYMPTOMS

Do you often:

_____ 1. try to read difficult material only to give up halfway through?

_____ 2. have trouble getting through long and involved sentences?

_____ 3. feel defeated because your instructor or your classmate explains a particular work to you?

_____ 4. put a story or a poem aside because you can't understand the imagery?

_____ 5. have difficulty articulating a difficult article's thesis?

If you checked one or more of these symptoms, you should read this introduction carefully. Many of your reading questions will be answered, and you will learn strategies to use when you read critically.

ONE-DIMENSIONAL VERSUS MULTIDIMENSIONAL MATERIAL

You have now reached the last stage in your development as an efficient college reader. You have likely established a comfortable rapid-reading rate of at least 400 wpm, and you should now be able to overview skim at rates of 800 wpm and above. In the earlier chapters, your purpose for reading (the Why?) was mainly literal comprehension: to locate main ideas and supporting details as well as the structure of written material. Most of this material (the What?) was *one-dimensional*. That is, you could adequately understand the selections in one reading.

In critical reading, however, your purpose goes beyond surface content. You need to do more: to analyze, critique, react, understand more deeply. This reading material is usually more complex than most of your daily reading. This type of material is *multidimensional*. You may have to read this material two or three times before you can effectively discuss and write about it.

These multidimensional works can be grouped into four types of writing: expository and argumentative on the one hand and descriptive and narrative on the other. The purpose of *expository* writing is to explain a process or concept or to give convincing reasons for an opinion or idea. *Argumentative* writing presents a point of view, not only giving information like expository writing, but also attempting to change the reader's mind about a particular issue. Commentaries in newspapers and magazines are examples of argumentative writing. Often these two types of writing overlap. For example, an article explaining the influence of the environment on criminal behavior is expository in that it is informative, but it is also argumentative because it attempts to show that environment makes a criminal behave antisocially. Most of the critical selections in the chapter both inform and persuade, so you will often see them labeled as *expository-argumentative*.

Descriptive writing differs from expository-argumentative writing in its intent. The purpose of descriptive writing is not to teach or persuade but rather to create or record an experience in sensory and psychological terms. Describing the activities of a fugitive as he attempts to hide from the law or recreating the smell of New York City at 8 A.M. on a summer workday are both examples of description. *Narration*, on the other hand, recounts s series of events, real or imagined. The events leading to the assassination of John F. Kennedy in 1963 (a non-fictional account) or the disintegration of a teenager's life as she takes, then sells, cocaine (a fictional account) are both examples of narration.

Just as exposition and argumentation overlap, so description is almost always part of narration. For example, a novel or a biography will have sections of pure description, even though the overall intent of the work is to tell a story. So you will see in this chapter that the term *description-narration* identifies the overlap that occurs in fiction and nonfiction.

In other words, you can safely divide most critical reading into two types: exposition-argumentation and description-narration. Exposition-argumentation attempts to explain the world; description-narration tries to recreate it or chronicle it.

. . . .

HOW TO PREVIEW SKIM MULTIDIMENSIONAL MATERIAL

To read multidimensional material effectively, you must determine early on whether the material is expository-argumentative or descriptive-narrative and then choose and use an appropriate reading strategy. In both types of writing, a preview skim is essential, just as with one-dimensional material. When you preview skim critical material, your reading is a bit more thorough than a preview skim of rapid-reading material and a bit less thorough than an overview skim of one-dimensional material. When you preview skim critical material, you should read:

1. the title
2. the first paragraph slowly and carefully
3. the first sentence of each of the following paragraphs
4. the final paragraph slowly and carefully

By following these steps, you will determine what the article is about and how difficult it is. After you have preview skimmed exposition-argumentation, you should be able to summarize the selection's thesis in a sentence or two; after a preview skim of fiction or nonfiction, you should be able to accurately identify the setting, the major characters, and the difficulty level of the writing.

Having preview skimmed, you are ready to read the entire work. Unlike rapid reading, you should not critically read under a sense of time pressure. As you read critical material, even for the first time, you will need to reread a particularly difficult or interesting sentence or sentences. So, in some cases, your reading rate of critical material can drop to 150 wpm.

HOW TO PARAPHRASE

Perhaps the most common problem that students face when they read multidimensional material is that they do not understand sentences that are very long or that use difficult words. Instead of trying to understand these sentences before going on, students may continue reading, hoping that their confusion will go away. Instead, the confusion often gets worse.

When faced with such difficult material, a critical reader knows how to *paraphrase*, or how to accurately restate a phrase, a sentence, or sentences in a simpler way. A paraphrase is usually shorter than the original, but it sometimes uses more words. Whether longer or shorter than the original, an effective paraphrase is worded in the reader's voice, using words and phrases that are familiar to the reader. If students copy parts of the difficult passage or merely use synonyms for difficult words, their paraphrases will not help them.

Look at the following passage on criminal behavior and the two paraphrases— one weak and the other acceptable. See how the weak paraphrase merely uses synonyms and omits a few words from the original. The acceptable paraphrase attempts to make the sentence easier to understand without distorting the intent of the original passage.

EXCERPT:
Mr. Samenow believes in a somewhat radical concept of criminal behavior; he contends that if a criminal chooses to engage in criminal activity, he has willfully elected a lifestyle that is antithetical to his society's mores.

WEAK PARAPHRASE:
Samenow believes in a rather controversial idea of criminal activity; he believes that if a criminal decides to get involved in criminal actions, he has chosen on his own to live a life that is opposite to the belief systems of society.

ACCEPTABLE PARAPHRASE:
Samenow's idea about criminals is very different from the one people normally have. He contends that a criminal consciously chooses a lifestyle that goes against everything that society believes in.

In the weak paraphrase, note how the reader has not thought through the passage's ideas, choosing synonyms for *radical* (*controversial*), for *chooses to engage in* (*decides to get involved in*), and for *mores* (*belief systems*). In both passages, the author's intent is still unclear. Note that in the acceptable paraphrase, the vocabulary is simpler, but the point of the passage comes through more easily: Criminals are antisocial, and, further, they choose to be so.

To paraphrase a difficult passage effectively, you should incorporate the following six strategies into your critical reading:

1. Read the difficult passage at least twice. To understand the context of the difficult material, reread difficult sentences that come before and after the passage.
2. If you are still confused after rereading, look up the meanings of any unfamiliar words. A difficult vocabulary often characterizes passages that you need to paraphrase.
3. If understanding the vocabulary does not help you understand the passage, divide the passage up into less complex phrases and clauses, which usually come before commas, dashes, semicolons, and colons.
4. By dividing the passage up into its syntactical parts, you should be able to determine the subject(s) and verb(s). Remember that subjects and verbs form the kernels of any sentence. Notice the relationship that is established between the subject and verb.
5. Then, try to put into your own words what the passage is saying. If you are afraid that reading the passage while you are paraphrasing will encourage you to copy from the passage, put the passage aside and write the paraphrase without looking at the original.
6. Finally, if the paraphrase expresses a key issue in the material that you are reading, write your paraphrase in the margins, next to the original passage.

See how you can use these strategies to paraphrase the previous excerpt on criminal behavior. As you read the passage, you should focus on the meanings of *radical concept, antithetical,* and *society's mores.* You may need to look up the terms *antithetical* and *mores,* so that you can determine early on that Samenow's position is out of the ordinary because he sees the criminal as choosing to be antisocial. Further, you need to see how the two clauses relate; the first up to the semicolon is the more general statement, while the second after the semicolon is more specific. In the first clause, the author establishes that Samenow's position is unique; in the second clause, this uniqueness is explained. These strategies will then help you arrive at an acceptable paraphrase.

As you continue to paraphrase difficult material, you will find this strategy very helpful. It often opens up the meaning of difficult material by encouraging you to reread, to consider new terminology, and to identify the key words in the passage. Paraphrasing often unveils sophisticated ideas that may be new to you. At other times, you may find that a complex style and difficult vocabulary merely mask a simple idea. In either case, paraphrasing can become a valuable tool to use to show how clearly or unclearly a writer thinks.

Turn to Practices 6.1 and 6.2, beginning on p. 280.

• •

HOW TO READ FOR INFERENCES

Along with paraphrasing to understand difficult passages, a reader of multidimensional material can also interpret what is not stated directly. (This strategy is much like the one you learned in Chapter 1: determining the implied main idea.) Reading for inferences is particularly important with multidimensional material because the author's audience is an intelligent reader who is expected to read between the lines.

Critical readers of difficult material use the following strategies to make correct inferences: (1) they analyze the terms of qualification that an author uses; (2) they are sensitive to the connotations of words as well as to metaphors and allusions; (3) they know how to evaluate statements derived from inductive reasoning; and (4) they can analyze the deductions made in critical material.

Terms of Qualification

A *term of qualification* is a word or phrase that modifies the certainty of a writer's statement. Such terms suggest varying degrees of certainty toward a particular topic. A critical reader first identifies the qualifier, then infers the author's attitude from it. Terms of qualification are divided into the following four categories; each category expresses varying degrees of certainty. Study the words and phrases in each category.

1. *Words and phrases that express no doubt:* all, surely, assuredly, there is no doubt, none, conclusively, undoubtedly, without reservation, never, clearly, absolutely, without hesitation, always, unequivocally, constantly, it is a proven fact, certainly, precisely, undeniably, it is undeniable, definitely, plainly, without a doubt, without question
2. *Words and phrases that express little doubt:* most, seldom, there is little doubt, it is believed, mostly, rarely, with little reservation, almost never, usually, slightly, almost always, the consistent pattern, consistently, one can safely say
3. *Words and phrases that express some doubt:* many, ostensibly, it seems, frequently, apparently, one can infer, often, somewhat, one can say with some reservation, may, might, likely, the hypothesis is, can, could, this may (might) mean, it is theorized that, one would assume, the results imply, it is possible that, the assumption is, possibly, it is probable that, one would infer, probably (stronger than possibly), the inference is, at times, it appears, seemingly
4. *Words and phrases that express much doubt:* supposedly, it is guessed that, it is suspected that, it is conjectured that, it is rumored that

Now read the following four statements, each containing a qualifier, to see whether you can determine how the qualifier alters the meaning of the statement. Then read the commentary that follows to see if you agree.

Statement 1: This morning the police department gave the press the following statement regarding the multiple murder case: "There is now no doubt that only one individual was responsible for all five killings."

Statement 2: Recently on a news report, a criminologist noted that teenage criminals are only slightly influenced by their peers.

Statement 3: About his research on psychological therapy for criminals, the criminologist at State University stated, "It is now theorized that making criminals feel vulnerable and guilty for their actions is an effective deterrent for further criminal behavior."

Statement 4: Referring to the personal problems of Senator Good, a recent gossip columnist said, "It is now suspected that Senator Good was involved in the use and sale of heroin."

In statement 1, you should have identified the qualifier as *there is no doubt* and concluded that the police department must now have hard evidence in this case because *no doubt* adds certainty to the statement. In the word *slightly*, statement 2 suggests that teenagers involved in crime are influenced only negligibly by their friends. You should have inferred, though, that friends influence these teenagers in some way, and you would want to look for further information regarding what these minor influences involve. In statement 3, you would have been wrong to infer that making criminals feel guilt stops their criminal behavior. The phrase *it is theorized* places this statement in the theory, not fact, category. Remember that theories are assumptions that have been studied carefully but have not been proven. Finally, you would have been correct in ignoring entirely the validity of statement 4. Conjecture and supposition can never be used as evidence to prove a person's guilt or innocence.

As you can see, by identifying the qualifier in each statement, you can make certain worthwhile inferences. Remember that nowhere in these statements are these suggestions stated directly; you must read between the lines. Often, the inference that you make helps you understand the significance of a statement. For example, you could not have used statement 4 to convict Senator Good, but with the inference that you made in statement 1, you would be correct in telling anyone that the murder case was either solved or close to being solved.

Because of the importance of terms of qualification in critical reading, you should study and become familiar with all of the phrases in the four categories.

Turn to Practice 6.3 on page 284.

Connotations

A critical reader can also draw several valid inferences merely by analyzing how an author uses words. Practically all the words in our language not only have literal meanings but also suggested meanings. The *connotation* of a word is its suggested meaning. A critical reader can infer much about an author's unspoken attitude toward a topic by the connotations of the words he uses. The study of connotations is central to analyzing advertisements, commentaries, and literature.

Many words in our language fall into one of three categories, each of which expresses an implied value: (1) a mildly positive or negative attitude, (2) a positive or negative attitude, or (3) a strongly positive or negative attitude. For example, depending on the extent of a home theft, the owner may feel dismay (a mildly negative emotion), fright (a negative emotion), or terror (a strongly negative emotion). Conversely, a person you know may be your acquaintance (a mildly positive term), your friend (a positive term), or your confidant (a strongly positive term).

A critical reader, therefore, is sensitive to an author's word choice, or *diction*. She is able to determine from the writer's diction positive or negative feelings about a particular topic. Further, a critical reader can identify and analyze peculiar uses of words. If, for example, you read in a short story, "The nephew was perplexed on hearing of the murder of his aunt and uncle," the term *perplexed* should be seen as an unusual word choice. Sadness, grief, or shock—not perplexity! Perplexed is a mildly negative term where a strongly negative term would be more appropriate in this sentence. In using this word, the critical reader would ask, Is the author suggesting that the nephew had bitter feelings toward his aunt and uncle, or was he unable to show appropriate feelings in times of grief? Or are we reading satire or humor? As an analysis of this sentence suggests, the connotation of a single word can be so powerful that it forces you to rethink a character's motivation.

Consider the following sentence from a short story to see how one word reveals a character's feelings: "Mrs. Duncan was irate because the clerk had overcharged her by twenty-five cents." Clearly, being irate over such a small overcharge is strange behavior. A careful reader would analyze the connotations of *irate* and compare them to the context in which the word is used to see how they relate to Mrs. Duncan's character.

Finally, consider the following sentence from a commentary in a newspaper: "These therapists are visionaries who have made many important breakthroughs regarding prisoner rehabilitation." A thoughtful reader knows that *visionaries* suggests farsightedness, imagination, and intelligence. By characterizing these therapists as visionaries, this writer reveals a favorable attitude toward them.

Turn to Practice 6.4 on page 285.

Metaphors

Like connotations, metaphors encourage you to explore the suggestiveness of words. A *metaphor* is a comparison between two objects or ideas that do not at first seem related.

Metaphors are an integral part of the way humans use words, and therefore they are part of the history of many words. Often what we consider a synonym for a word was originally a metaphor for that word. Words like the *blues* (meaning sadness) or *giant* (meaning very large) have their origins in metaphor.

To understand how a metaphor works, you need to establish the suggested equation—that is, identify the two words that are being compared, or the *subject* and the *image*. Place the subject next to the image; then list all the associations that these two words, together, suggest. Consider this sentence: "She is a movie star." See how the following list helps explain the meaning of this now commonly used metaphor:

Subject	Image
she	star
	associations: bright, far above the sky, warm, sparkling, standing out

These were probably the sorts of associations that the person who first compared an actor to a star had in mind.

Advertisements consistently use metaphors to make their products attractive and therefore more salable. The metaphors are often so out of the ordinary that you have to think through the various aspects of the comparison. In an ad for a raincoat, for example, the advertisers describe it as "outdoor makeup." How can a coat be like makeup? Your answer would likely include some of the following associations:

Subject	Image
coat	makeup
	associations: makes you pretty, makes you desired, is feminine, is nice to look at

You can see that all of these associations suggest glamour and femininity. Clearly, the advertiser wants you to consider the coat not only as a protective garment but also as an item that gives glamour and femininity to its user. But is this metaphor an honest one? Is this copywriter creating a false impression? These are the kinds of questions you need to ask as you analyze metaphors that advertisers use.

Metaphors are most consistently used in literature—in poems, in plays, and in fiction. To critically read literature, you need to identify the metaphor and analyze its associations. If you read a metaphor without analyzing its suggestiveness, you will be ignoring one of the most powerful characteristics of literature. You can use the same strategy for analyzing literary metaphors that you used with the previous two metaphors. Consider the title of a William Wordsworth poem, "I Wandered Lonely as a Cloud." How is a person's wanderings like a cloud's movements? A list of associations would uncover the following similarities:

Subject	Image
person wandering	cloud moving
	associations: cloud is in the sky, cloud can be torn apart, cloud is not solid, cloud can change its shape

These associations suggest that the speaker in the poem is likely isolated, moody, and insecure. It is these inferences, suggested in the title alone, that a critical reader of literature brings to this work before reading the first line.

When you read a literary work, several metaphors often work together. In your critical reading of a poem or work of fiction, note the ways that the metaphors often relate to each other. That is, these recurring images, together, create a particular mood, or, what is known in literature, as *tone*.

Turn to Practice 6.5 on page 286.

Allusions

Allusions are often found in multidimensional material. As with metaphors, their power resides in their suggestiveness. *Allusions* are references to people or occurrences in history, politics, or the arts. Unlike metaphors, which often do not require background reading to be understood, allusions test your knowledge of history, literature, art, and music. The more you read in those areas, the better will be your ability to appreciate allusions. If you come across a name from history or the arts that is new to you, look it up in the dictionary or encyclopedia.

Consider the following allusion to the poet John Keats made by a critic of literature talking about modern poetry: "Many modern poets have the Keatsian love for the concrete." Keats was a British poet of the early nineteenth century whose poetry was known for its focus on objects in the world rather than on ideas. He considered these objects from several perspectives and from all the senses—sight, hearing, touch, taste, and smell. Many critics consider him as great a poet as Shakespeare was a dramatist. All of this background knowledge is necessary to appreciate the allusion that this critic is making about modern poetry. In his allusion to Keats, this critic is suggesting that these modern poets also focus on the senses and on objects, rather than on ideas, and may even be considered as great as Keats.

In addition to literature and literary criticism, you will find allusions in film, art, and theater reviews, as well as in historical studies, commentaries in newspapers and magazines, and even in some advertisements. By appreciating the allusions that these writers use, you will derive a more critical understanding of their works.

Inductions

Like metaphors, inductions are naturally used by humans in everyday and academic activities. An *induction* is a general statement derived from specific information. For example, you have had the flu once a year for the past five years. And each time you get sick, aspirin eliminates both the fever and the pain. From your several experiences with using aspirin, you conclude (or make the induction) that aspirin can reduce fever and pain. All inductions are structured in the same process; data is gathered, and from the data a general statement is made.

Inductions have several names, many of which you already know. They are most frequently called *generalizations*. Scientists often call their inductions *conclusions* or *hypotheses*. A hypothesis is a general statement that is derived from careful observation and analysis of data (often in the form of facts and figures). In expository writing, a general statement derived from the process of induction is called an opinion or *thesis*. The data used to support a thesis is referred to as *evidence*, *detail*, or *fact*. In analyzing inductions, you study the specifics to see if they are accurate and if they all relate to the thesis that they generate.

Critical readers need to evaluate the soundness of an induction. A sound generalization must always have convincing details as its basis. Generalizations without sound evidence to support them are known as *sweeping generalizations* or *generalizations derived from insufficient evidence.* To determine whether a generalization is convincing, you must consider whether the details are both accurate and representative. For example, the results of a questionnaire from one American high school would not warrant the generalization that many American teenagers use drugs. The facts gotten from one high school are not representative of the entire nation.

All writers make generalizations of some sort, but you should carefully scrutinize the generalizations made in commentaries and advertisements. For example, you should question an ad that states that "Three out of four doctors recommend Aspirin *X*." Who are these doctors? Do they represent doctors throughout the country, or are they only doctors questioned in one hospital? If the latter is true, you would be correct to call this generalization unsound based on insufficient evidence. Similarly, a commentary about the military budget that states "Military spending is highly wasteful" should include statistics from several branches of the military, showing where the waste is and how the various military branches compare. If you cannot find this evidence in the commentary, you should question the soundness of this generalization.

Critical readers constantly scrutinize a writer's inductions. They study the information to see if it is both accurate and representative. Only if the data are accurate and provide a representative sampling can the critical reader entertain a particular generalization.

Deductions

Like inductions and metaphors, deductions are used by all of us to solve simple, everyday issues as well as complex, abstract problems. A *deduction* is a form of thinking beginning with a general statement, called a *major premise*, followed by a specific concern, called a *minor premise*, and ending with a statement combining both, called a *conclusion*. Deductions are opposite in thinking to inductions. Where inductions begin with a specific statement and end with a general conclusion, deductions begin generally and end with a concluding detail statement.

Here is how deductions work. Suppose you wake up one morning feeling ill and decide to stay home. Your decision to stay home is based on a deductive argument that works this way:

Major Premise: When I wake up sick, I stay home.

Minor Premise: I woke up sick this morning.

Conclusion. I plan to stay home today.

A deduction is valid only if both the major and minor premises are correct. Your task as a critical reader is to analyze each premise to determine its validity, then to determine from these premises whether the conclusion is sound.

Analyzing deductions is difficult when the premises are not stated directly; that is, when you are faced with *hidden assumptions*. If this is the case, you need to infer from the conclusion what the major and minor premises must have been. In an ad for a weight-control center, what is the hidden assumption in this statement:

"Our diet center can cure your cravings"? You can fit this statement into the three parts of a deduction:

Major Premise: People who are sick should try to get cured.

Minor Premise: Overweight people are sick.

Conclusion: Overweight people should try to get cured of their cravings for food.

You probably have no objection to the major premise—sick people should seek medical treatment. But you would likely take issue with the minor premise. Are all overweight people addicted to food? Some overweight people do indeed overeat and, in this sense, have an addiction and a disease, but not all. Some simply gain weight more easily than others. Since the minor premise is not sound, the conclusion that overweight people should seek a cure does not necessarily follow. The writer of this ad purposely does not analyze this conclusion; she hopes that you will accept it without studying the premise that it is based on.

See how the following comment about lawbreakers also uses unstated assumptions: "These picketers and other lawbreakers who surrounded the federal building were mainly young adults." Equating picketing with lawbreaking is based upon the following deduction:

Major Premise: Lawbreakers are people who disobey the law.

Minor Premise: Picketing is against the law.

Conclusion: The young adults who picketed are lawbreakers.

The major premise is valid; however, the minor premise is not. Picketing is a legal act as long as the picketers do not trespass. Since picketing is not a crime, the conclusion that picketers are lawbreakers is invalid.

Writers of commentaries and ads may use false implied assumptions to convince their readers of an invalid conclusion. A critical reader is obliged to carefully analyze the first two parts of the deduction to see if the conclusion follows logically. If one or both premises are unsound, the conclusion is invalid. Such an analysis is sometimes difficult, but it will often provide you with evidence for why an argument is unconvincing.

Turn to Practices 6.6 and 6.7, beginning on p. 289.

· · · · · · · · · · · · · · · · · ·

SUMMARY

You have been presented with a lot of material in this Introduction. You will be using all of these strategies in various ways in the practice exercises and reading selections that follow. When you need to use one of these strategies as you read, you may want to go back to the appropriate section of the Introduction to reread the strategy to use. For now, begin with the premise that critical reading is a multilevel activity that will ask you to reread in order to think through the writer's argument. Moreover, as a critical reader, you will be analyzing the suggested meanings of words and the ways that inductions and deductions are used effectively or ineffectively.

Your goal, then, is a challenging one: to become a proficient reader by going beyond the literal meaning of a work to its suggestions and to its logical framework.

SUMMARY BOX: CRITICAL READING

What?	Why?	Acceptable Comprehension	Acceptable Rates
High-level science and applied science, literature, essays, commentaries, articles in all fields, ads	For inference, mood, and style; thesis, support of thesis, evaluation of the argument and details	80–90%	150–300 wpm

PRACTICES: CRITICAL READING

Answers for these exercises are not provided in the answer key. Please check your answers with your instructor.

6.1 PARAPHRASING

Below is an excerpt on white-collar crime. Read it carefully. Then read the five sentences, taken from the passage, that follow. For each sentence, choose the best paraphrase from the list of four choices and place it in the answer box. Remember that a weak paraphrase often uses synonyms and may sound more confusing than the original sentence. On the other hand, an acceptable paraphrase keeps the intent of the original sentence but uses simpler vocabulary and clarifies any confusing phrases in the original sentence.

SOCIOLOGY: AN INTRODUCTION

by Earl R. Babbie

WHITE-COLLAR CRIME

In reading about the earlier study that showed virtually everyone to have committed punishable crimes, it probably occurred to you that many of those "crimes" were the "little white lies" of law-breaking: technically criminal, but pretty harmless on the whole. Anyone who has ever worked in an office, for example, has probably "stolen" pencils, paper clips, and the like. Even "nice people" like you and me do that.

In 1949, Edwin Sutherland published a book about the crimes "nice people" commit, and the title of his book has become the term associated with the crimes most typical of middle- and upper-class people: **white-collar crime**. As Sutherland and subsequent researchers have pointed out, white-collar crime extends well beyond paper clips and cannot be regarded as harmless.

Embezzlement is probably the most obvious and dramatic example of white-collar crime. In earlier years, this term conjured up images of the trusted bank clerk dipping his or her hand in the till and perhaps shocking the old hometown by running off to South America with a few thousand dollars. This was certainly the image captured by Donald Cressey when he titled his 1953 classic study of embezzlement *Other People's Money*. More in line with the current situation is the *Harvard Business Review's* 1975 "Embezzler's Guide to the Computer." In place of a few thousand dollars stuffed in a satchel, we have the two-*billion*-dollar Equity Funding Corporation fraud and similar capers involving the use of *computers*. With the increasingly complex systems of electronic transfers of funds, sophisticated criminals have become increasingly clever in draining off some for themselves.

Embezzlement is only the beginning, however. White-collar crime—like other forms of deviance—parallels the established agreements of the society. A great many laws define "acceptable" business practices, for example, and they have all been broken. In 1961, many Americans were shocked when a number of high-ranking General Electric and Westinghouse corporate executives were sentenced to prison terms for price fixing and similar violations of antitrust laws. Today's corporate crimes include such offenses as misrepresentation in advertising, manufacturing faulty and even unsafe products, industrial pollution, tax evasion, under-the-table political campaign contributions, bribes, payoffs, and kickbacks.

Big-time white-collar crime is not limited to the business sector, however. Labor unions such as the Teamsters have spawned their own troubles in this respect, and government corruption has become sufficiently widespread as to bring the public regard for politics to an all-time low. The 1972 Watergate scandals of the Nixon administration only dramatized long-standing malpractices in American politics—wiretapping, bribery, slander, and other variations from textbook democracy.

White-collar crime, then, is far more than the harmless filching of paper clips from the office. It is more than an economic concern, but that aspect alone is staggering. The U.S. Chamber of Commerce estimated in 1974 that the loss due to white-collar workers' thefts ran around 40 billion dollars per year.

All this notwithstanding, the more traditional American image of "crime" is inextricably linked to images of "the mob," "the Syndicate," "the Mafia," and with the Al Capones and other figures of organized crime.

Earl R. Babbie, *Sociology: An Introduction*, 2nd ed., pp. 166–167. © 1980 by Wadsworth Publishing Company, Inc. Reprinted by permission of the publisher.

• •

1. "With the increasingly complex systems of electronic transfers of funds, sophisticated criminals have become increasingly clever in draining off some for themselves."
   a. Electronics has made stealing easier.
   b. Criminals are becoming increasingly more sophisticated.
   c. With the continually advanced process of exchanging money electronically, intelligent criminals continue to find ways to pilfer funds.
   d. As money exchange becomes more complicated with the use of electronic equipment, intelligent criminals are finding smart ways to steal money.

2. "White-collar crime—like other forms of deviance—parallels the established agreements of the society."
   a.   White-collar criminals often agree with society's values.
   b.   The crime of the white-collar worker—like other kinds of aberrant behavior—agrees with the society's understandings.
   c.   White-collar crime is a kind of abnormal behavior, yet it works within the social structure.
   d.   White-collar crime is a perverted kind of behavior.

3. "Teamsters have spawned their own troubles in this respect, and government corruption has become sufficiently widespread as to bring the public regard for politics to an all-time low."
   a.   Both the Teamsters and the government have been caught in illegal activities, and the public has lost faith in politics.
   b.   Teamsters and politicians are dishonest and corrupt.
   c.   Teamsters have created their own problems in this respect, and the immorality in the government has expanded so that the public's perspective of politics is extremely negative, more negative than it has ever been.
   d.   Teamsters have caused their own governmental problems.

4. "The 1972 Watergate scandals of the Nixon administration only dramatized long-standing malpractices in American politics . . ."
   a.   In 1972, with the Nixon administration's Watergate problem, people came to realize the continual drama of political wrongdoing.
   b.   With Watergate in 1972, the hidden wrongdoings in American politics came to the surface.
   c.   The scandals of Watergate showed the corruption of Nixon's administration.
   d.   Malpractice in American politics came to be associated with Nixon.

5. "All this notwithstanding, the more traditional image of "crime" is inextricably linked to images of "the mob," . . ."
   a.   Finally, people have come to see crime as synonymous with organized crime.
   b.   Government crime has several friends in the mob.
   c.   Crime is a traditional concern with people in the Mafia.
   d.   All this considered, the more accepted notion of wrongdoing is bound completely to the notion of organized crime.

1. _____
2. _____
3. _____
4. _____
▶ 80%
Check answers with your instructor.

6.2 MORE PARAPHRASING

The following excerpt comes from an analysis of organized crime. In this excerpt, you will find five italicized sentences. In the spaces provided, write paraphrases for these five sentences. Read the entire passage before you begin paraphrasing. Remember that in paraphrasing, you try to make the original sentence simpler without distorting the original meaning.

SOCIOLOGY: AN INTRODUCTION

by Earl R. Babbie

ORGANIZED CRIME

Despite the popular fascination with organized crime and the success of books and movies such as *The Godfather* and, in an earlier generation, *Little Caesar*, there has been a continuing debate over whether any single organization controls a substantial portion of the nation's crime. Although the existence of criminal gangs has long been evident, Estes Kefauver's Senate Crime Investigating Committee shocked many in 1951 by concluding that there was an organization called the "Mafia" that controlled traffic in illegal drugs, gambling, and prostitution across the nation. [1] *It was a national conspiracy, shrouded in secrecy, bound by a fierce loyalty among members, and frighteningly vengeful against any who broke its agreements.* The Mafia was described by the Senate Committee as Sicilian in origin and generally of Italian ancestry in membership, creating a fair amount of anti-Italian hostility and stereotypes among the general public.

In the years following the publication of the Kefauver findings, some began to wonder if reports of crime conspiracies featuring the Mafia, the Cosa Nostra, and the Syndicate had perhaps been exaggerated. [2] *Was the publicity given organized crime merely a romantic successor to the dime novels about Jesse James, Billy the Kid, and other desperadoes of a century ago?*

Donald Cressey, a prominent criminologist and sociologist, had such questions when he was appointed a consultant to the President's Commission on Law Enforcement and Administration of Justice. After an intensive examination of the available evidence, however, Cressey concluded " . . . no rational man could read the evidence that I have read and still come to the conclusion that an organization variously called 'The Mafia,' 'Cosa Nostra,' and 'The Syndicate' does not exist." He went on to report that it was apparently an alliance of two dozen quasi-families active in loan sharking, narcotics, prostitution, extortion, union and government corruption, and deeply involved in legitimate business such as manufacturing, trucking, bars, hotels, and restaurants.

The controversy over the extent of organized crime will undoubtedly continue. [3] *Organized crime is, of course, difficult to study by conventional social science techniques.* Cressey has summed up the situation nicely in saying that we have learned about as much of the organization of organized crime (using bugs, wiretaps, and so on) as we could learn about the organization of the Standard Oil Company by interviewing gas station attendants.

One aspect of organized crime seems generally agreed on: [4] *The backbone of the industry is and has always been profits from goods and services that are desired by a large portion of the society though prohibited by law.* Early in this century, the Al Capones of crime got a shot in the arm with the advent of Prohibition. When the sale of alcohol was later relegalized, Syndicate activity focused on such goods and services as drugs, gambling, and prostitution.

Of course, organized crime is not simply a provider of harmless goods and services. Extortion, murder for hire, car theft, and the like are hardly practices to ignore. [5] *Still it is unlikely that anything resembling a national crime could exist ex-cept for its involvement in what Edwin Schur has called "crimes without victims."*

From Earl R. Babbie, *Sociology: An Introduction*, 2nd ed., pp. 167–168. © 1980 by Wadsworth Publishing Company, Inc. Reprinted by permission of the publisher.

• •

1. Paraphrase of sentence 1: _____
   _____

2. Paraphrase of sentence 2: _____
   _____

3. Paraphrase of sentence 3: _____
   _____

4. Paraphrase of sentence 4: _____
   _____

5. Paraphrase of sentence 5: _____
   _____

Score _____%

▶ 80%

Check answers with your instructor.

6.3 UNDERSTANDING TERMS OF QUALIFICATION

The following ten sentences contain qualifiers that are important to the meaning. Read each one carefully. Then underline the term of qualification. Finally, comment on how the qualifier changes the meaning of the statement, making it either stronger or weaker. Refer to page 272 for the lists of terms of qualification.

Example: The results of the experiment on the monkey <u>could mean</u> that a cure for the virus in humans is near.

Explanation: "Could mean" casts some doubt on the experimental results; that is, a cure for the human virus is not entirely certain.

1. Without question, the burglar committed the seven robberies in the same city within a week.
   Explanation: _____
   _____

2. The university almost never rejects graduates whose combined Scholastic Aptitude Exam scores are 1200 or over.
   Explanation: _____
   _____

3. The laboratory results reveal unequivocally that Tom is not the father of Mary's twins.
   Explanation: _____
   _____

4. The popular country-and-western singer stated in a press release that she may perform a charity concert in New York next fall.
Explanation: _____

_____

5. The president of the state university stated to reporters that the next chancellor to be appointed will undoubtedly be a woman.
Explanation: _____

_____

6. It is theorized that the universe was created after the "big bang" explosion.
Explanation: _____

_____

7. It is possible that all the prisoners of war will be freed within a month.
Explanation: _____

_____

8. The Elizabethan poet in question apparently wrote only six sonnets.
Explanation: _____

_____

9. It is conjectured that the outspoken political activist is being kept in a mental institution against his will.
Explanation: _____

_____

10. The assumption is that the economy will continue to grow over the next three years.
Explanation: _____

_____

Score _____ %

▶ 70%

Check answers with your instructor.

6.4 ANALYZING CONNOTATIONS OF WORDS

Read the following ten sentences, each of which contains an italicized word or words having either a positive or a negative connotation. Determine if the word is (1) mildly positive or negative, (2) positive or negative, or (3) strongly positive or negative. Then substitute another word (just one) that would fit into one of the other two categories. You may refer to a dictionary or a thesaurus for the exact meaning of the italicized word or for a synonym.

Example: I was *outraged* by your behavior.

Explanation: "Outraged" has a strongly negative connotation. "Upset" would have a mildly negative connotation.

1. Sometimes Joan is *unkind*.
   Explanation: _____

   _____

2. My wife was *ecstatic* after she read the telegram.
   Explanation: _____

   _____

3. The discussion ended in a *riot*.
   Explanation: _____

   _____

4. In his law school days, Tom was a *brilliant* student.
   Explanation: _____

   _____

5. But his career as an attorney has been *relatively undistinguished*.
   Explanation: _____

   _____

6. Unfortunately, the party was a *fiasco*.
   Explanation: _____

   _____

   _____

7. To our surprise, the bank staff worked in a *relaxed* manner.
   Explanation: _____

   _____

8. I could tell by her *frown* that she was angry with me.
   Explanation: _____

   _____

9. The host government has accused our diplomat of various *deceptions*.
   Explanation: _____

   _____

10. Your daughter will be sorry for her *indiscretion*.
    Explanation: _____

    _____

Score _____ %

▶ **70%**

Check answers with your instructor.

6.5 ANALYZING METAPHORS

In this exercise you will find ten metaphors used in everyday speech, in advertisements, in poetry, and in drama. Your job is to read each statement to locate the metaphor. Then, make a list of what the image suggests about the subject that it is compared to. Finally, from this list, which should have certain qualities in common, write a sentence explaining the metaphor.

Example: I noticed them sitting there
As orderly as frozen fish
In a package
— From D. C. Berry, "On Reading Poems to a Senior Class at South High" (Note: The "I" is the teacher; the "them" are the students.)

Subject   *Image*
students   orderly frozen fish in a package
associations: organized, cold, cold-blooded, neat, unthinking, dead, impervious

Explanation: By comparing them to frozen fish in a package, the poet is suggesting that the students, though quiet and neat, are passive and unresponsive. Like fish in a package, they are cold and dead.

1. Our text is called *Steps to Reading Proficiency*.
Subject   *Image*

_____   _____

associations: _____

Explanation: _____

_____

_____

2. I am desperate; I have reached the end of my rope.
Subject   *Image*

_____   _____

associations: _____

Explanation: _____

_____

_____

3. The lotion will give your skin a silky texture.
Subject   *Image*

_____   _____

associations: _____

Explanation: _____

_____

_____

4. I feel weak; my feelings are made of glass.
Subject   *Image*

_____   _____

associations: _____

Explanation: _____

_____

_____

5. She presents herself to the world like a cactus.
Subject   *Image*

_____   _____

associations: _____

Explanation: _____

_____

_____

6. "We are such stuff as dreams are made on."
   William Shakespeare, *The Tempest*
   Subject   *Image*

   _____   _____

                   associations: _____
   Explanation: _____

   _____

   _____

7. "Now, therefore, while the youthful hue
   Sits on thy skin like morning dew"
       Andrew Marvell, "To His Coy Mistress"
   Subject   *Image*

   _____   _____

                   associations: _____
   Explanation: _____

   _____

   _____

8. "An aged man is but a paltry thing,
   A tattered coat upon a stick"
       W. B. Yeats, "Sailing to Byzantium"
   Subject   *Image*

   _____   _____

                   associations: _____
   Explanation: _____

   _____

   _____

9. "What happens to a dream deferred?
   Does it dry up
   Like a raisin in the sun?"
       Langston Hughes, "Dream Deferred"
   Subject   *Image*

   _____   _____

                   associations: _____
   Explanation: _____

   _____

   _____

10. "The evening is spread out against the sky
    Like a patient etherized upon a table"
        T. S. Eliot, "The Love Song of J. Alfred Prufrock"
    Subject   *Image*

    _____   _____

                    associations: _____

Explanation: _____
_____
_____

Score _____ %

▶ 70%

Check answers with your instructor.

6.6 DETERMINING IMPLIED ASSUMPTIONS

Each of the following ten statements makes an assumption, based on deductive thinking, that is not stated directly. Your job is to write out this hidden premise as clearly as you can. First, read the statement carefully. Second, write out two of the three parts of the deduction from the information that you have. Third, from the other two statements, infer the missing premise. Finally, write out the hidden premise. After you have identified the hidden premise, you may want to discuss its validity with your instructor.

Example: I won't ask Jane to help me move the couch; after all, she's only a woman.

Deduction: Major Premise:

Minor Premise: Jane is a woman.

Conclusion: I won't ask her to move the couch.

Hidden Premise: Women are physically weaker than men. (major premise of the deduction)

1. The reason I know so much about the arts is that I was raised in San Francisco, a big city.
   Major Premise: _____
   Minor Premise: _____
   Conclusion: _____
   Hidden Premise: _____

2. The only meaningful major in college is one that assures you of a job. That's why I tell students to major in engineering and business, and not in the arts.
   Major Premise: _____
   Minor Premise: _____
   Conclusion: _____
   Hidden Premise: _____

3. Jim, my five-year-old, is a destructive child. I don't worry because he is only doing what is natural.
   Major Premise: _____
   Minor Premise: _____
   Conclusion: _____
   Hidden Premise: _____

4. A student of mine is getting involved with crime lately. I am sure he comes from an economically deprived environment.
   Major Premise: _____

Minor Premise: _____
Conclusion: _____
Hidden Premise: _____

5. My daughter is not a good math student. I am going to push her anyway, because she can do as well as my son, who also needed extra work in math.
   Major Premise: _____
   Minor Premise: _____
   Conclusion: _____
   Hidden Premise: _____

6. We are going to interrupt Mr. Jones when he gives his talk tomorrow. After all, freedom of speech guarantees us this right.
   Major Premise: _____
   Minor Premise: _____
   Conclusion: _____
   Hidden Premise: _____

7. I am a critical thinking person. It's because I had a solid liberal arts education in college.
   Major Premise: _____
   Minor Premise: _____
   Conclusion: _____
   Hidden Premise: _____

8. A moral person does not lie. I'm sad to say that Jim lies constantly.
   Major Premise: _____
   Minor Premise: _____
   Conclusion: _____
   Hidden Premise: _____

9. John was seriously injured in an automobile accident. This is sad, but like everything in life, his accident was meant to happen.
   Major Premise: _____
   Minor Premise: _____
   Conclusion: _____
   Hidden Premise: _____

10. A God of love would not allow evil to exist. Unfortunately, there is much evil in the world.
    Major Premise: _____
    Minor Premise: _____
    Conclusion: _____
    Hidden Premise: _____

Score _____ %

▶ 70%

Check answers with your instructor.

6.7 ANALYZING AN ADVERTISEMENT

Read the following advertisement for an imaginary island in the Mediterranean. Look carefully for the connotations of words, the details, and the hidden assumptions. Then answer the questions that follow.

COME TO MALAMA: AN ENCHANTED ISLAND IN THE MEDITERRANEAN

1. On the scenic island of Malama, you will be dazzled by the beauty everywhere. It has endless miles of sandy beaches and a calm teal-blue sea that tantalizes even the novice swimmer.

2. Hotel accommodations are surprisingly inexpensive; most rooms have beautiful views of the ocean.

3. For those who want to know more about the history of this ancient island, bus tours leave daily for three archaeological sites on the island's north side. Tours may even begin from your hotel.

4. The cuisine is world-famous, and the people are warm and hospitable. Many islanders even speak English.

5. For further information, hurry to see your travel agent. Don't have another forgettable summer. This summer, be sophisticated! Come to the enchanting island of Malama!

1. In paragraph 1, locate five words that have positive connotations.

    _____

2. What specific details are missing in paragraph 2?

    _____

3. What specific information is presented in paragraph 3?

    _____

4. A qualifier is used in the last sentence of paragraph 3. Find it, and determine how it alters the meaning of the sentence.

    _____

5. Locate two words in paragraph 4 with positive connotations.

    _____

6. Would you consider the fact about English-speaking islanders in paragraph 4 a specific detail or a vague detail? Why?

    _____

7. What is the hidden assumption in the statement in paragraph 5: "This summer, be sophisticated"?

    _____

8. What is the hidden assumption in the statement in paragraph 5: "Don't have another forgettable summer"?

    _____

9. Does this ad contain mainly factual details? Or mainly generalizations? Choose two or three examples to support your answer.

    _____

Score _____ %

▶ **80%**

Check answers with your instructor.

TIMED SELECTIONS: CRITICAL READING — ARE CRIMINALS BORN OR MADE?

In the following selections, you will practice your critical-reading skills to determine shades of meaning. As in previous parts, you will preview the material first. Then you will be given strategies for reading this material carefully. Both the preview and critical-reading steps will be timed. Five preview-skimming questions and ten critical-reading questions follow each selection. The latter will include several inference questions (abbreviated *Inf*) and one paraphrase (abbreviated *P*) question. The questions for discussion and writing ask you to read and reread various sections of each selection. Answers for selections 1 and 3 are listed on page 340; your instructor will provide answers to selections 2 and 4.

As in the study-reading selections in Chapter 3, you will be able to evaluate yourself after each excerpt so that you can determine your strengths and weaknesses in reading various kinds of critical material and find ways to read the material more effectively.

You will find that all the articles in this part treat the issue of crime, specifically what motivates criminals and how to treat them. To prepare yourself for critically reading these selections, consider the following questions individually, in small groups, or in class discussion:

1. Do you think that criminals are victims or victimizers of their surroundings?
2. How would you describe the typical criminal?
3. How should criminals be treated once they are caught?
4. Is there more than one type of criminal?

CRITICAL READING SELECTIONS

1. "When the Juvenile System Becomes a Cure that Kills" 1,400 words
2. "The Pathology of Evil" 780 words
3. "The Criminal's Way of Life" 2,630 words
4. From *Brothers and Keepers* 2,444 words

. . . .

SELECTION 1

"When the Juvenile System Becomes a Cure that Kills"   *by John Hurst*
1,400 words

Vocabulary
imperceptibly: in a manner not easily seen; "Jill paused almost imperceptibly"
dubious: doubtful; "I was dubious that such a practice existed"

Bonnie Parker: the wife and partner of Clyde Parker, a famous American gang-
ster in the 1930s; "for being a latter day Bonnie Parker"
brandished: moved or waved; "she once brandished a knife in front of a police station"
rancor: deep spite or malice; "Jill spoke of the Ventura School without rancor"

This commentary concerns the treatment of juveniles in the California Youth
Authority. Instead of supporting his thesis with facts and figures, the writer uses
the narrative mode to get his point across. Like all effective commentaries, this
one has a clear point of view, presented through the details of the inmate's experiences. From this point of view, John Hurst suggests what California's obligation
to juvenile delinquents should be.

Reading Strategies.   To determine what Hurst thinks of the California Youth
Authority and our obligation to juvenile delinquents, use the following strategies:

1. Note the specific ways that Jill is treated. Do these methods seem humane or
    cruel?
2. Consider the section that describes Jill's prison environment. Is it pleasant
    or unpleasant?
3. Underline any words that have strong connotations. Do these words all share
    the same positive or negative connotations? As a group, what do these words
    suggest about the inmate's treatment and environment?
4. From the details concerning Jill's treatment and environment, determine
    Hurst's evaluation of the California Youth Authority. Write this point of
    view in a complete sentence somewhere on the article or on a separate sheet
    of paper.
5. From this point of view, determine whether Hurst is expressing a liberal or
    a conservative approach to the treatment of delinquents in California. A lib-
    eral would contend that delinquents can be rehabilitated if they are treated
    humanely and given proper psychological counseling. A conservative atti-
    tude would maintain that delinquents cannot be cured and that psychologi-
    cal counseling is a waste of taxpayers' money. Make a marginal note indicat-
    ing whether Hurst is presenting a liberal or a conservative point of view.

A. Preview Skimming

Preview skim the following article in 2 minutes (= 700 wpm). By the end of your
preview, you should have some idea of who Jill is, how she is treated, and what
her environment is. You should also have a general sense of Hurst's attitude toward the California Youth Authority.

Remember, in preview skimming a critical article, you should:

1. Read the entire first paragraph.
2. Read the first sentence of the following paragraphs. Some of the paragraphs are
    only one sentence long, so you may want to read only part of these sentences.
3. Read the entire last paragraph.

When you have finished preview skimming, answer the five questions without looking back at the article.

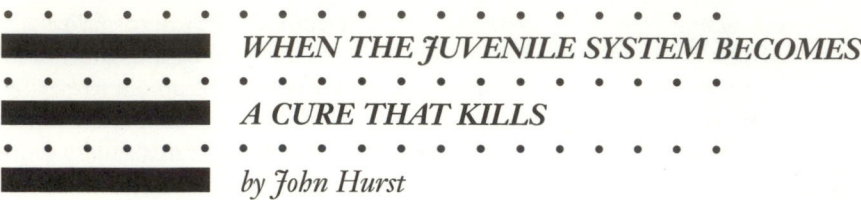

WHEN THE JUVENILE SYSTEM BECOMES

A CURE THAT KILLS

by John Hurst

1   My wife gingerly peeled the Scotch tape from Jill's two little Christmas packages as the security officer watched.

2   "I should have known better," I said.

3   We were standing in the lobby of the Ventura School which is not really a school, but a big California Youth Authority reformatory in Ventura County. We had come to visit Jill, a teenage girl I had written about last summer. We had brought her a couple of rolls of Lifesavers, some gum, a can of nuts and—wrapped in Christmas paper—a little radio and some film for her camera.

4   I should have known better than to bring in wrapped gifts because, as a reporter, I've visited dozens of reformatories, juvenile halls and prisons throughout the state and have become well aware of security concerns.

5   So I was more irritated with myself than with the security officer when he said the gifts would have to be unwrapped for inspection.

6   But then, after the inspection, my wife began to rewrap the packages and the officer asked her not to tape them because they would have to be reinspected later by the night staff.

7   I was bewildered. After all, the man had just inspected the things.

8   "You mean we can't hand these to Jill?"

9   "You can't hand her anything," he responded in a flat tone, without malice, without any emotion at all.

10   The security officer then surveyed the other articles we had brought. He picked up the little can of nuts, peeled back the lid and dumped the contents into a big brown paper bag. With those two quick, bored motions, he had reduced a neat, almost attractive, bit of commercial packaging into what looked like sweepings from a cocktail party.

11   Then he handed my wife the two rolls of Lifesavers. No candy allowed. The gum, though, was ok. But, no, we couldn't give it to Jill ourselves. It would be given to her after we left.

12   We were asked to put the contents of our pockets on a table for a quick inspection. We passed through a metal detection process, put our belongings back in our pockets and, then, were permitted to enter the visiting room to wait with empty hands for Jill.

13   In the visiting room and at patio tables outdoors, inmates sat with their families and ate meals brought in from outside.

14   As we waited for Jill, I puzzled over the rules and the security system. Meals, apparently, could be brought right in, but Lifesavers were excluded and gum had to wait.

15   When Jill arrived, we bought her a can of Dr. Pepper out of a vending machine in the waiting room. She is not allowed to handle money, she said, so I put the change in the machine for her.

16   Jill asked the staff member on duty in the visiting room if she could show her living quarters to my wife and me.

17   "Are they your legal guardians?" asked the staff member.

18   Jill paused almost imperceptibly as she considered lying and then said "No."

19   In that case she could not.

20   Outside on the patio, we looked across the pleasant lawns of Ventura School to the "cottages" where the youngsters live in little 7-foot by 10-foot rooms.

21   We stood in the Sunday morning sunshine and watched inmates, boys and girls, walk to and from chapel services. Most of these youngsters have adjusted to the rules and programs of the California Youth Authority. It is uncertain what that means, because at least 70% of the inmates who pass through the state youth reformatories return to crime.

22   Jill has not adjusted. She is a bright, likable and attractive girl with blond hair and big, clear, blue eyes. She would like to be an airline stewardess, but she is afraid she'll never have enough education.

23   Jill will be 18 this winter. She was born in England and has been in the United States since she was 12 years old. At first she hated California, but now she loves it and doesn't want to live anywhere else.

24   I met Jill through attorneys who told me that she had been hogtied—her wrists chained to her ankles behind her back—on the floor of a cell in the Sacramento Juvenile Hall.

25   I was at first dubious that such a practice existed in California in the 1980s, but I subsequently learned that it is common to chain or tie kids up when they become extremely disruptive in some county juvenile halls and state reformatories throughout California.

26   Jill was not locked up in juvenile hall for being a latter day Bonnie Parker. She got in trouble for things like being drunk in public, and for shoplifting a set of socket wrenches from a K Mart so a boy she knew could fix his car to go cruising. She once brandished a knife in front of a police station, according to a probation report, and she wrote an obscenity on a Porsche belonging to a deputy district attorney. She doesn't like authority.

27   And Jill can't handle being locked up. She pounded on the door of her juvenile hall room in Sacramento, cursed the staff, hit them, kicked them. In response, they locked her in isolation cells and chained her up. When these methods didn't work with her, they did more of the same.

28   Finally, Jill was charged with assaulting a Sacramento County Juvenile Hall staff member—who she says she punched in the chest—and was sentenced to the California Youth Authority. So the teenage girl who, outside of custody, had committed only minor violations, was transported 400 miles from her home and locked up with inmates, some of whom have committed murder.

29   Since she arrived at the reformatory last summer, Jill has been shackled or tied spread-eagled to beds at least 10 times because of disruptive behavior.

30   Near her throat is a long welt-like scratch mark that she got in a fight with another girl at Thanksgiving time.

31   She has tried to escape and she has attempted suicide at least twice. On the inside of her left wrist is a patch of red scabs from self-inflicted cuts.

32   A suicidal youngster at Ventura School is ordered to strip naked, given a gown and blankets and locked in a room monitored by a television camera.

33   "When I am in the camera room," Jill wrote to Youth Law Center attorney Elizabeth Jameson in San Francisco, "I feel more depressed because I feel so lonely and upset and I want somebody to talk to me. Because they have cameras in the room, they feel they don't have to bother with you. But it makes me feel more like killing myself."

34   Two weeks before Christmas, 16-year-old Melissa Pence, a close friend of Jill's, committed suicide at the reformatory. Jill saw her friend hanging by a sheet in a closet. Melissa, who had been on nobody's Most Wanted List—neither the FBI's nor her parents'—was the sixth juvenile to commit suicide in various lockups throughout the state in 1984.

35   During our visit, Jill spoke of the Ventura School without rancor and described her misbehavior with candor and without excuses. Jill says she tries to go along with the reformatory program, but she keeps "going off," as she puts it, losing her temper and self-control.

36   "Some mornings," she said, "I wake up and I can't believe I'm really here."

37   Jill has a year to go on her sentence, but the methods of Ventura School, like those of Sacramento County Juvenile Hall, have not worked with her. So, she is being transferred to Napa State Hospital, the big, violence-ridden mental institution in Northern California, where Jill will be kept in a locked unit.

38   Jill does not consider herself mentally ill, but she is accepting the transfer because it will take her closer to her home and family in Sacramento.

39   Indeed, Jill does not appear to be mentally ill. She probably has some serious emotional problems and needs professional guidance.

40   But should she be locked up? Is a big institution the answer for Jill?

41   I wonder about places that tie kids up, places that put suicidal youngsters in rooms alone and watch them on television sets, places that pour little cans of nuts into great big bags, places that won't let Lifesavers in. I wonder if places like that have any real answers for anybody. . . .

John Hurst, "When the Juvenile System Becomes a Cure that Kills," *Los Angeles Times*, December 30, 1984. Copyright 1984, Los Angeles Times. Reprinted by permission.

• •

1. Jill appears to be in:
    a. an insane asylum.
    b. a reformatory for juveniles.
    c. a private school.
    d. the county jail.

2. Jill seems:
    a. happy.
    b. very happy.
    c. unhappy.
    d. none of these.

3. In this facility, the authorities consider Jill:
    a. uncooperative.
    b. cooperative.
    c. one of their best inmates.
    d. both *b* and *c*.

4. Jill has:
    a. attempted suicide.
    b. been involved in a fight with another girl.
    c. been a counselor for the other inmates.
    d. both *a* and *b*.

5. The author concludes that institutions such as the one Jill is in:
    a. have a positive effect on juveniles.
    b. do not help juveniles.
    c. are overcrowded.
    d. are underutilized.

```
Sel. 1   P-Skim              1. _____
Time    2:00 = 700 wpm       2. _____
Score  _____ %               3. _____
        ▶ 80%                4. _____
Score = number correct x 20. 5. _____
                             Check answers on p. 340.
```

B. Critical Reading

You are now ready to read critically, noting words with strong connotations, analyzing Jill's psychological state, and inferring whether Hurst's position regarding the treatment of juvenile delinquents is liberal or conservative.

Record your beginning and ending times in the answer box only for the time that you took to read the article. Once you have recorded the time, answer the questions without looking back at the selection.

1. From the details presented, it seems as if Jill:
    a. has several freedoms.
    b. has a nice working relationship with the officers.
    c. has had her freedoms severely curtailed.
    d. both *a* and *b*.

2. A television camera is used to watch:
    a. all juveniles in the facility.
    b. suicidal youngsters.
    c. all visitors.
    d. the juveniles at night.

3. Because juvenile hall has not helped Jill, she is going to be sent to:
    a. a foster home.
    b. a halfway house.
    c. a boarding school.
    d. a mental institution.

4. (*Inf*)* The survey officer is described as responding "in a flat tone without malice." This description suggests that the officer is:
    a. angry.
    b. cruel.
    c. apathetic.
    d. confused.

---

*In all selections that follow, *Inf* will indicate an inference question; *P* will indicate a paraphrase question.

5. (*Inf*) A fact mentioned about juveniles who are released suggests that:
   a.   they almost all return to crime.
   b.   they almost all become law-abiding.
   c.   the majority become law-abiding.
   d.   the majority return to crime.

6. (*Inf*) In the following statement from the article, which word has a strongly negative connotation? "I met Jill through attorneys who told me that she had been hogtied . . . on the floor of a cell in the Sacramento Juvenile Hall."
   a.   floor
   b.   cell
   c.   hogtied
   d.   attorney

7. (*Inf*) It seems as if the crimes that Jill committed before being sent to the Ventura School were:
   a.   minor.
   b.   major.
   c.   unnoticed.
   d.   infrequent.

8. (*P*) Choose an effective paraphrase for the following sentence: "During our visit, Jill spoke without rancor and described her misbehavior with candor and without excuses."
   a.   During our visit, Jill showed anger.
   b.   Jill wasn't angry but was dishonest during our visit.
   c.   During our visit, Jill showed no anger about her treatment and was honest and forthright about what she had done.
   d.   During our visit, Jill talked of the Ventura School without anger and defined her crimes with honesty and without rationalizing.

9. (*Inf*) A hidden assumption in the title, "When the Juvenile System Becomes a Cure that Kills," is that:
   a.   juveniles are not sick.
   b.   juvenile delinquents are sick, and juvenile systems should cure their illnesses.
   c.   only doctors can cure juvenile delinquents.
   d.   only psychologists can cure juvenile delinquents.

10. (*Inf*) It seems as if the author presents various details in the narrative regarding Jill to suggest that juvenile facilities in California:
    a.   are highly organized.
    b.   are highly efficient.
    c.   do not attempt to rehabilitate juvenile delinquents.
    d.   are run by too many administrators.

Sel. 1 C-Read

Finish _____ : _____

Start _____ : _____

Time _____ : _____

Rate _____ wpm

Find rate on p. 330.

Score _____ %

▶ **80%**

Score = number correct × 10.

1. _____
2. _____
3. _____
4. _____
5. _____
6. _____
7. _____
8. _____
9. _____
10. _____

Check answers on p. 340.

Record rate and score on p. 327.

C. Questions for Discussion and Writing

1. What does the author think of the California Youth Authority? Choose and discuss specific statements from the article that support your position.

2. Describe Jill's psychological state. Choose and discuss specific details from the article that reveal her character.

3. Reread paragraphs 24, 25, and 29. Find in them three heavily connotative words about how the juveniles are handled. Are these words mildly positive or negative, positive or negative, or strongly positive or negative? What do you think that these words as a group suggest about how juveniles are treated?

4. In paragraph 20, the author refers to the "cottages" that the juveniles live in. Why do you think the word is in quotation marks? What are the traditional connotations of *cottage*? How are the conditions described in the article like or unlike those in a typical cottage?

5. Analyze the meanings suggested by the title, "When the Juvenile System Becomes a Cure that Kills." Choose specific details from the article to support your answer.

Self-Evaluation: Reading Articles of Commentary

Answer the following questions by circling yes or no. These responses will help you understand your critical abilities in reading articles of commentary.

1. yes no Was your score in Section B, Critical Reading, below 80 percent?

2. yes no Were three or more of your answers to the inference questions incorrect?

3.   yes   no   Was your answer to the paraphrasing question incorrect?

4.   yes   no   Did you have difficulty determining the author's point of view?

5.   yes   no   Did you have difficulty locating words with strong negative connotations?

6.   yes   no   Did you have difficulty determining whether the author expressed a liberal or a conservative point of view regarding crime?

Scoring: If you answered yes to three or more of these questions, you probably need more practice in reading commentaries.

Follow-up: To improve your critical skills in reading commentaries, consider the following suggestions:

1. To be sound or valid, opinions must start with facts. A critical reader should notice the proportion of fact to opinion in any opinion piece.

2. Realize that articles of commentary often use language with strong positive or negative connotations. Become more sensitive to the connotations of words in articles of commentary. As you read, ask yourself how certain words suggest a point of view regarding the issue presented.

3. Understand that writers of commentary often make their points through implied assumptions. Become more familiar with the three parts of a deductive argument. Start applying this deductive process to the statements or conclusions that a writer of commentary makes. Determine which assumptions are left out.

4. Most articles of commentary present either a liberal or a conservative point of view. Read more such articles to begin determining for yourself what the common liberal and conservative views are on abortion, gun control, nuclear disarmament, and so on. Then, when you analyze a particular article, you will bring to this article some knowledge about the liberal and conservative positions on that issue.

5. Once you have started reading both liberal and conservative commentaries regularly, you will be able to evaluate the responsible or irresponsible use of words, the validity of the details presented, and the soundness of the assumptions made. In this way, you can agree or disagree more intelligently with a commentator. You will begin to see that articles of commentary in newspapers and magazines are not always perfect compositions; they may demonstrate errors in logic and documentation.

SELECTION 2

"The Pathology of Evil"   *by Rex Julian Beaber   780 words*

Vocabulary

loathsome: disgusting, odious; "the loathsome pit of the county jail"
demeanor: outward behavior; "attempting by my demeanor to look very different"

diabolical: devilish; "transformed into such a diabolical force"
theism: belief in one God; *agnosticism:* the doctrine that God is unknown and un-
knowable; "not since my youthful debates on theism and agnosticism"
inchoate: being only in partial operation; "how apparently orderly systems become
inchoate and disorderly"

This selection is a well-written and moving essay concerning crime—specifically, the reasons for crime. This topic is similar to the one in selection 1. Like
that selection, this commentary begins as a narrative; but in the narrative form of
selection 2, Rex Julian Beaber presents many facts and theories from law, psychology, and physics to support his premise. His vocabulary is somewhat difficult, and his sentences are longer than those in selection 1. By selecting details
from his own experience with criminals or defendants accused of crimes, and by
explaining current and past theories regarding criminal motivation, Beaber reaches
some thought-provoking conclusions about the possible causes of crime.

Reading Strategies. To understand Beaber's conclusions, you need to employ the following strategies:

1. Underline the various words that Beaber uses to describe criminal behavior.
   Look at the connotations of these words, and determine if these connotations, seen together, suggest a particular attitude toward criminal behavior.
   Determine if this attitude is positive or negative.
2. Be sure that you can accurately summarize the Supreme Court ruling mentioned at the beginning of the commentary, as well as the concept of chaos
   discussed toward the end of the article. You may want to write a one-sentence
   summary of each in the margin or on a separate sheet of paper.
3. Be able to summarize the three different theories that Beaber presents regarding the causes of criminal behavior. Write these as one-sentence summaries in the margin or on a separate sheet of paper.
4. Weigh the evidence presented in the article (the details about criminal behavior and the suggestiveness of the words used to describe it) to see if you
   can state in your own words Beaber's conclusion regarding the cause or causes
   of crime. See if you can infer from the details and the language Beaber's attitude toward criminals. Determining his conclusion and his attitude will be
   more difficult than understanding Hurst's point of view in selection 1.

A. Preview Skimming

Preview skim the following article in 1½ minutes (= 520 wpm). In your preview
skim, determine who the speaker is, what his job entails, how he feels about the
confessions that he hears from the defendants, and what he generally thinks causes
people to turn to crime.

When you have finished your preview skim, answer the following five questions without looking back at the editorial.

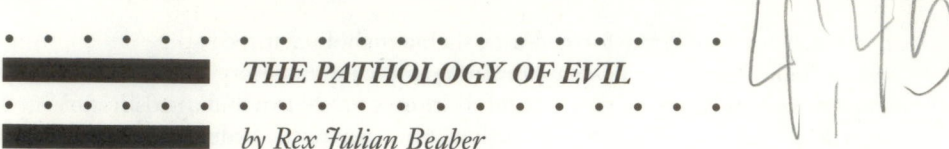

THE PATHOLOGY OF EVIL

by Rex Julian Beaber

1   *Clank!*—the first set of automatic jail doors closed behind me. *Clank clank*—the second and third sets closed as I entered the loathsome pit of the county jail. I paced sternly down the hall, attempting by my demeanor to look very different from the inmates who circled me. I entered the room reserved for visiting doctors and awaited the arrival of the defendant, a convicted capital murderer.

2   My employer, the state and the defense; my mission, to find, if it exists, some aspect of the psychology of the defendant that will convince the jury not to sentence him to death. My method, endless hours of searching interview into the feelings, history and thoughts of the killer.

3   This relatively new approach to sentencing in death-penalty cases came about because the California Supreme Court has ruled that it is wrong to exclude "expert" testimony on the psychology of a killer. Since that ruling, I have interviewed a murderer almost every week.

4   The most potent tool in this psychological exploration is not the skills of scientific psychoanalysis, nor the recent advances in psychiatry, but rather the protective cloak of confidentiality.

5   All psychological interviews are secret from the trial judge, prosecutor and jury. Only if the results are favorable do they see the light of day. Most of my results go unspoken, unwritten and are never presented to the jury. But with the protection of confidentiality, a terrifying confession comes forth. These confessions include undiscovered crimes, the gruesome pleas of the victim before the moment of death, picturesque descriptions of crime scenes that police can only infer, and the callous thoughts of the perpetrator throughout what proves to be a long history of criminal behavior.

6   As I listen to these terrifying tales, I muster all my psychic energy to hide any gestures of disgust, rage and confusion. A single slip and I will lose trust and truth. No matter what the legal issue may be, my curiosity drives me to the ultimate questions: Why and how. Why do people do these horrible things to other people? How can an angelic little boy sucking at a bottle and cuddling his blanket be transformed into such a diabolical force?

7   Yes, it is true that killers are also victims. Their lives are filled with alcoholic parents, physical and sexual abuse, divorce, parental deaths, tough neighborhoods, uninterested teachers and poverty. Some are even victims of biology. Many are born with learning disabilities or low intelligence, which denies them any place in our world of words.

8   But millions upon millions of Americans are born with these handicaps, or worse—and they don't kill. From all those with hard lives, how does fate choose its lustful murderers? Does anyone really believe that people wake up one morning and say to themselves, "I am going to torture, maim and kill. That's my new identity."

9   More often than not, as the jail doors close behind me and I enter the world of fresh air, birds and freedom, I have little idea of the answers to my questions. Late in the evening, in the security of my home, I lie awake as my wife and children sleep, pondering what dark force might be working right now in some other home, to some other man's wife and children.

10   I am forced to ask: Is there evil?

11   Not since my youthful debates on theism and agnosticism have I faced such a basic question. Some teach that such questions are silly and without meaning, but could there be such a thing as evil? Could there be an extra force, a dark force, that works through humans and perpetrates terror? Certainly my subjects appear possessed when they act out their visions of carnage. Might they

literally be possessed? Are they evil, or does an evil force temporarily inhabit their soul?

12   To take such questions seriously is a sin in my profession.

13   A strange answer to my queries recently came in the mail. A prisoner who had been seen in state prison sent me a copy of a scientific article on chaos. Chaos is a new concept in mathematics and physics that attempts to understand how apparently orderly systems become inchoate and disorderly. (The classic example is the way a smooth stream of smoke rising from a cigarette will suddenly become a jumbled mess of particles in mid-air.)

14   The writer, a scientist who has killed, wondered if maybe the regulatory systems of his body entered into chaos before he killed. I wondered whether chaos was the scientific word for evil.

15   Of course, wondering is not knowing, yet as California approaches another decision on the death penalty I wonder whether the prisoners are simply evil—or whether they, too, are victims of chaos.

Rex Julian Beaber, "The Pathology of Evil," *Los Angeles Times*, January 6, 1985. Reprinted by permission.

• •

1. The writer of this article is:
   a. a convict.
   b. a professional person of some sort, probably a psychologist.
   c. a priest.
   d. a judge.

2. The writer's purpose when he visits the prison is to:
   a. administer health examinations to the prisoners.
   b. give the prisoners spiritual advice.
   c. determine if the jailed individuals have psychological problems that caused them to commit such crimes.
   d. write feature articles on the prisoners.

3. Psychological interviews granted the defendants in jail can be shared with any interested party in the court case.
   a. true
   b. false

4. As the writer listens to the stories of the defendants, he:
   a. senses that they are innocent.
   b. is sickened by their terrifying confessions.
   c. sees that they are intelligent.
   d. both *a* and *c*.

5. At the conclusion, the writer is:
   a. sure that evil is the cause of crime.
   b. sure that mental chaos is the cause of crime.
   c. sure that the environment of a criminal is the cause of crime.
   d. unsure whether either mental chaos or evil is the cause of crime.

Sel. 2 P-Skim	**1.** _____
Time 1:30 = 520 wpm	**2.** _____
Score _____ %	**3.** _____
▶ **80%**	**4.** _____
Score = number correct x 20.	**5.** _____
	Check answers with your instructor.

B. Critical Reading

Now go back to read the article critically, filling in the details that you missed in your preview. Look for words with strong connotations, try to understand the various theories that Beaber presents, and try to understand his conclusions.

Record your beginning and ending times in the answer box only for the time that you took to read the article. Once you have calculated the time, answer the questions without looking back at the selection.

1. The author admits that most of the material that he learns in interviewing prisoners:
   a.   is used in the courts.
   b.   is not used in the courts.
   c.   is senseless dialogue.
   d.   shows how prisoners are treated cruelly.

2. The author suspects that:
   a.   evil is a force motivating criminals to commit crime.
   b.   there is no real cause for criminal behavior.
   c.   only poor people commit crimes.
   d.   only uneducated people commit crimes.

3. The concept of chaos suggests that systems in the world:
   a.   become chaotic for no apparent reason.
   b.   only become chaotic when they are ready to die.
   c.   never become chaotic.
   d.   are constantly chaotic.

4. (*Inf*) Which word in the following excerpt from the article has a strong negative connotation? "These confessions include undisclosed crimes, the gruesome pleas of the victims . . .":
   a.   confessions
   b.   undisclosed
   c.   gruesome
   d.   include

5. (*Inf*) The bulk of the words used by the author to describe the defendants accused of crimes:
   a. have violent connotations.
   b. have peaceful connotations.
   c. are neutral terms.
   d. show the intelligence of the defendants.

6. (*Inf*) The author refers to a criminal as "transformed into . . . a diabolical force." By *diabolical*, he implies that:
   a. society causes crime.
   b. devils are part of most religions.
   c. criminals worship the devil.
   d. a devilish force is inside the criminal's mind.

7. (*Inf*) The author refers to the "protective cloak of confidentiality." This metaphor suggests that:
   a. confidentiality is a smothering force.
   b. confidentiality is a guarding force.
   c. cloak and confidentiality have the same meaning.
   d. cloak and confidentiality have opposite meanings.

8. (*Inf*) To consider evil as a force motivating criminals is "a sin in my profession," says the writer. He is implying that:
   a. doctors and psychologists should not believe in God.
   b. sin does not exist.
   c. psychologists and doctors generally believe that criminals can be cured.
   d. psychologists and doctors generally believe that criminals cannot be cured.

9. (*P*) Choose an effective paraphrase for the following excerpt: "The relatively new approach to sentencing in death penalty cases came about because the California Supreme Court has ruled that it is wrong to exclude 'expert' testimony on the psychology of a killer."
   a. This rather novel way of dealing with capital crimes has occurred because the Supreme Court has decided that it is unfair to keep out an expert's findings on the motivations of a murderer.
   b. Experts cannot testify in court.
   c. Because of the new Supreme Court ruling in dealing with the death penalty, testimony from experts can now be used in murder trials.
   d. The Supreme Court has a new attitude in sentencing murderers.

10. (*Inf*) This article presents three different points of view regarding the nature of crime. Which one is *not* mentioned in the article?
    a. Lack of religious training may lead to criminal behavior.
    b. Evil may be the cause of criminal behavior.
    c. Environment may be the cause of criminal behavior.
    d. Mental chaos may be the cause of criminal behavior.

Sel. 2   C-Read   1. _____

Finish _____ : _____   2. _____

Start _____ : _____   3. _____

Time _____ : _____   4. _____

       min   sec   5. _____

Rate _____ wpm   6. _____

Find rate on p. 330.   7. _____

Score _____ %   8. _____

▶ 80%   9. _____

Score = number correct x 10   10. _____

Check answers with your instructor.

Record rate and score on p. 327.

C. Questions for Discussion and Writing

1. The author has an interesting and unusual job. What is his job? In your own words, describe what he does. In this capacity, what does the author find out about the inmates that he observes? Present specific details from the commentary.

2. The author mentions a Supreme Court ruling. Reread paragraphs 3, 4, and 5. Then, summarize this ruling in your own words. Discuss what sorts of evidence can be used in court. Finally, determine whom this decision ultimately favors—the court or the defendant.

3. Reread paragraphs 5, 6, and 8. There are several words used to describe the criminal's behavior. List three or four of these words. As a group, are these words mildly negative or positive? What do these words ultimately suggest about the behavior of criminals, from the author's point of view?

4. If a liberal attitude toward crime contends that criminals are a product of their environment and can be cured, and if a conservative position asserts that little can be done to correct a criminal's behavior, where does Beaber fit into this liberal-conservative spectrum? Choose specific statements from the article to support your point of view, and discuss them.

5. Compare and contrast the statements made about crime and criminals in selection 1 with those made in selection 2. Do these two articles of commentary share any similar ideas? In what ways are the arguments in the two articles different? Choose specific statements from each article to support the comparisons and contrasts that you determine.

Self-Evaluation: Reading Articles of Commentary

Answer the following questions by circling yes or no. These responses will help you understand your critical abilities in reading articles of commentary.

1. yes no Was your score in Section B, Critical Reading, below 80 percent?

2. yes no Were three or more of your answers to the inference questions incorrect?

3. yes no Was your answer to the paraphrasing question incorrect?

4. yes no Did you have difficulty understanding the author's conclusions?

5. yes no Did you have difficulty locating words with strong connotations?

6. yes no Did you have difficulty determining the author's attitude toward criminals and criminal behavior?

Scoring: If you answered yes to three or more of these questions, you most likely need more practice in reading articles of commentary.

Follow-up: To improve your critical skills in reading articles of commentary, consider the following tips:

1. Articles of commentary often use language with strong positive or negative connotations. Become more sensitive to the connotations of the words in articles of commentary. As you read, ask yourself how certain words suggest a point of view regarding the issue discussed.

2. Writers of commentary often make their points through implied assumptions. Become more familiar with the three parts of a deductive argument. Start applying this deductive process to the statements or conclusions that a writer of commentary makes. Determine which assumptions are left out; then analyze these assumptions.

3. Sometimes writers of commentary are unsure about their conclusions or attitudes toward a particular issue, and they may present several possible explanations or points of view. In such cases, you need to be able to separate out, then analyze, each explanation or point of view.

4. After you have read articles of commentary critically for a while, you will be able to start evaluating the responsible or irresponsible use of words, the validity of the details, and the soundness of the assumptions. In this way, you will be able to agree or disagree more intelligently with a particular writer of commentary. You will start seeing that commentaries in newspapers and magazines are sometimes not perfect compositions, that they occasionally demonstrate errors in logic and documentation.

• • • • • • • • • • • • • • • • • • •

SELECTION 3

"The Criminal's Way of Life"   *by Samuel Yochelson and Stanton E.
Samenow 2,630 words*

Vocabulary
criterion: a standard of judgment; "the criterion of responsibility"
exhort: to urge; "to advise, exhort, and persuade"
chronically: recurring frequently; "he is chronically restless"
mundane: ordinary; "to fulfill the mundane requirements of school"
capitulate: to surrender; "until they capitulate"
attrition: a wearing down; "It results in attrition of parental morale"
circumvent: to avoid; "circumvent the behavior"
chagrined: vexed or disappointed; "they are chagrined"
estrangement: a turning away of feeling; "his estrangement from them"
microcosm: a world in miniature; "a microcosm of the child's functioning"

This excerpt is from a full-length study on criminal behavior titled *The Criminal Personality*. Experts in criminology Yochelson and Samenow focus on the similarity of criminal behavior. In this section of the chapter, "The Criminal's Way of Life," the authors treat the typical criminal's childhood. Their conclusions are often surprising and controversial.

Reading Strategies.   To more effectively analyze this excerpt, consider the following reading strategies:

1. Read specifically for how the criminal child is different from the normal child. Highlight these differences in marginal comments.
2. Critique the authors' argument. Include marginal comments that show in what ways you disagree with their conclusions.
3. Determine how Yochelson and Samenow agree or disagree with the comments made by Hurst and Beaber in the previous two articles. You may want to include these comments as marginal notes at the end of your reading.
4. Finally, determine where Yochelson and Samenow fit into the nature-nurture argument? Are criminals products of their environment (nurture), or do they manipulate their environment (nature)? You may want to answer this question in a short marginal comment at the end of the article.

A. Preview Skimming

Preview skim the following excerpt in 2 minutes (= 1,315 wpm). Determine the major subsections of this excerpt and the general conclusions that the authors draw regarding the criminal. When you have finished your preview skim, answer the following five questions without looking back at the article.

THE CRIMINAL'S WAY OF LIFE

by Samuel Yochelson and Stanton E. Samenow

SIBLINGS

1 Most of the brothers and sisters of the criminals in our group are responsible. They have not all achieved highly, but they have functioned quite differently in life from their criminal siblings. Our findings confirm what other studies have noted: that the several offspring from one family may follow very different paths. The communication media have helped to make this a well-known fact. *Time* Magazine (4/24/72), for example, in a story on the Mafia pointed out that only four of twenty-seven fourth-generation Italian-Americans in one Mafia family, are connected with organized crime. Of the remaining twenty-three, one is a university professor and all the rest are doctors, lawyers, and legitimate businessmen. So has it been with the families we have studied, most members of which have been and are responsible. We can cite a criminal whose sister worked her way through college and is now happily married and a criminal whose brother owns a computer programming company. This is not to say that the criterion of responsibility is career advancement; some of our criminals have also reached positions of authority and prestige. What is important here is that most of the siblings are conscientious, loyal workers, and concerned parents and members of the community who have carved out lives within the boundaries of society's laws, manners, and mores.

2 These responsible siblings try to guide their criminal brothers and sisters in the direction of more responsible behavior. They often help their criminal siblings out with money and other resources. In many instances, they take a protective attitude and cover for a criminal when he violates. They may not turn him in when he is a fugitive. Throughout their lives, they attempt to advise, exhort, and persuade the criminal siblings to reform.

3 The criminal has a spectrum of attitudes toward his noncriminal siblings. The attitude varies from time to time, between the extremes of strong sentimentality and bitter hatred. On the one hand, the criminal views his responsible brother's or sister's way of life as "square" or "stupid." On the other hand, there are moments when he envies the sibling for his achievements and for the freedom he enjoys in living responsibly. This occasional envy is usually well concealed, rarely finding its way into verbal expression. The criminal may physically abuse a sibling. If his brother will not lend him his car or give him money, he may turn on his brother and beat him up. Or he may be crassly exploitative.

Ron shielded and protected his criminal brother, C, in every imaginable way. Although not wealthy, through the years Ron spent over $12,000 to bail C out of difficulties. He would cover forged checks that were signed in their father's name. C used Ron time and again. Ron responded as a member of the family who wanted to help, trying to convince C to change. He would not have done the things he did for anyone but a family member.

Here a brother acted in accord with his conscience and idea of family loyalty. The criminal took advantage of it.

4 The criminal distorts his relationship to his siblings when he talks to others. He may say that a brother or sister got more attention, despite the fact that he compelled more attention by the things he did and may, indeed, have been the favorite child initially. Of course, in some instances, the siblings did receive greater attention, if the parents had to protect them from the criminal youngster.

5 Later in life, the criminal stays away from his siblings, just as he avoids close relationships with all who have chosen to be responsible.

However, the criminal is quick to return to a brother or sister when he wants something for himself.

6   There is still another dimension to the relationship of the criminal with his siblings. Although exploitative and vicious, he is at times sentimental toward them and goes out of his way to assist them. We have seen criminals who think that they are their sisters' guardians, to the extent that they will assault anyone who insults a sister. Yet when siblings refuse to be exploited, the criminal discards his protective stance and calls them unfair, inhuman, and disloyal.

7   Seven of our criminals had older siblings who were delinquent, and the criminals admired and emulated them. Particularly at the ages of five, six, and seven, they tagged along, seeking to be "in" on things. They rarely succeeded because the older siblings did not want them along. The younger criminal then used his own resources to find others who wanted to do the forbidden. Invariably, if a criminal has a younger sibling who is delinquent, the criminal is self-righteous and reprimands his parents for not being firmer.

C was amazed to learn from his mother that his two younger brothers, with three other boys, had broken into a store and stolen $80 worth of locks. When his mother told him this, he scolded her for not disciplining his brothers more. She cried when he did this.

The criminal enjoys informing on a younger brother or sister for even the slightest infraction. This takes the focus off him.

THE CRIMINAL CHILD AS DIFFERENT

8   An important commonality among most family members is that they live responsibly. Where there is parental irresponsibility, some children seem determined to be responsible, despite it.

C and Mary had a criminal father. C followed the same path. In contrast, Mary saw her objective in life as being different from her father. She utilized her contempt for what she saw as a stimulus to function differently. The result was that C wound up behind bars, and Mary is responsible and has worked hard in government, gaining several promotions.

9   From a very early age, the criminal-to-be is observed by his parents as "different." His behavior is extreme, either swinging from being an "angel" at five or six to a "hellion" by ten or alternating between the two right along. His energy never seems to be depleted, and he is chronically restless, irritable, and dissatisfied. He seems never to outgrow the period of the brief attention span. He has to have things his way; he will not take "no" for an answer.

C needed a pair of sneakers and wanted a specific type. When his mother bought him another brand, he asked whether he could have them returned for the brand he originally wanted. She said that he would have to wait until these wore out. C promptly cut the soles and heels out of those she had just bought. They were then paper thin and quickly wore out, thus allowing him to achieve his objective.

10   The criminal child seems not to do anything right around the house. His parents constantly tell him to "put your mind on what you are doing," because he has his mind on things far more exciting than the task at hand. Mowing the lawn cannot compete with thoughts about "hanging around with the guys" at the nearest shopping mall and doing some shoplifting! The endless reply to his parents' reprimands is "I forgot." He forgets what his parents told him five minutes earlier, forgets what the teacher told him, forgets what the class did in Sunday school. This is not a learning or memory problem. His mind is on exciting things, and his interests are centered on the forbidden. He does not consider himself obliged to fulfill the mundane requirements of school and home. He thinks others should fall into line with whatever he wants to do. Rather than being appreciative when a parent or someone else gives him something or does him a favor, he generally takes it for granted and expects more the next time. Doing chores, coming in on time for dinner, keeping appointments, running an errand—

the criminal child often reacts to these as though they are serious impositions. He uses any excuse at hand to put off what he is required to do. He usually does what he wants to when he wants to and is remarkably insensitive to others' needs and desires.

11   The criminal child is distressingly different in still another way. His parents find that, unlike most children, he shies away from affection, neither giving it nor receiving it. As one mother sadly said in describing her son as a young child, "He didn't need me." The adult criminal might say that his parents did not love him and that is why he turned out as he did. Actually, he rejected the love that was offered, viewing it as "sissy" or "weak."

12   There is a mantle of secrecy surrounding the criminal child. Parents slowly begin to sense that they do not know their own youngster. They are uneasy, especially those having another child, with whom they can compare him. The secret life is established early. Lying is a major ingredient. The child says he is going one place, but goes another. His accounts of what he does are vague and superficial. He is hard to pin down, with lies of omission being far more frequent than lies of commission. He may even lie when there is seemingly no point to it—for example, saying he is going to the A & P, when he knows he is going to the Grand Union. What seems to matter to him is getting away with things.

13   The criminal child sets himself apart. He does not confide in his family, and he conceals ideas and emotional reactions. Because he lies so often and engages in forbidden activity, he is ever distrustful and suspicious of other family members. This keeping to himself is a self-imposed isolation. He simply does not want other members of the family to be privy to what he is doing. This may take the extreme form of the child's virtually refusing to participate in any family affairs. When he goes to a function with his family, it is likely to be grudgingly. The family may be having fun, but inevitably the criminal child does something to spoil it. At a picnic, he shoves other children. He is the one who plays with the barbecue fire. In playing ball, he starts a fight over an umpire's call. If he attends a family activity or a school function because he is required to, he wanders off, and others do not know where he is. When he is older, he refuses to go at all.

14   With so much lying, sneaking, and concealment, there is clearly a "communication gap" in a home with a criminal child. Usually, the parents are faulted for not understanding the younger generation. But it is the child himself who imposes the secrecy and sets himself apart. He wants to keep his activities secret, so that others will not interfere with him. There is indeed a communication breakdown, but the child has been the determining factor. Sometimes, he pulls away entirely and gives his family the "silent treatment" for months at a time, erecting a barrier that his parents cannot penetrate and becoming even more of a stranger and a mystery to his own family. His more customary mode of operating, however, is to go through the motions of doing what is expected, so that his family will have less reason for suspicion; communication is at best superficial, because the parents think they know more than they do. When the parents become aware that their child has been leading a secret life, it is usually they who frantically search for ways to "restore" communication, which either never existed or existed only when the child was much younger. But the parents cannot establish communication that the criminal child does not want. Of course, if the criminal youngster wants something from his parents, he "communicates" quite well.

15   The criminal child gets his way in one fashion or another. Sometimes it is through secrecy and slickness. Perhaps even more frequently, he engages in constant battles with his parents, wearing them down until they capitulate. The youngster makes a contest out of anything, no matter how minor. He looks for a victory in a dispute about whether he will clean up his room, hang up a wet towel, take out the trash, or be in at a specified hour. Winning the fight overrides the significance of the issue at hand. It results in

attrition of parental morale; eventually, his parents decide to ignore certain behavior. Another technique the child utilizes to get his way is to be "legalistic." He makes so many requests and contests so many things that the parents cannot keep track of them. Inevitably, the child will catch mother or father in a contradiction. In doing this, he may play one off against the other. His memory is adequate, when it comes to reminding a parent of something said earlier. A favorite tactic is to dredge up something said long before and apply it in a different context. It is practically impossible for his parents to avoid being tripped up by his maneuvers. When the criminal child is blocked from doing as he wants, he tries to circumvent the barrier.

When C was 7 years old, he wanted to take a girl to the movies, but his family thought it improper. He went to the corner store and informed the man, with whom the family had credit, that his mother told him to borrow a dollar. With this, he took the girl at 4:30 in the afternoon. It was a double feature, and they got out at 8:30 p.m., only to meet both families waiting outside.

When the parents tighten up their restrictions, the criminal child has to be more ingenious and more careful, or else he becomes sullen, angry, or withdrawn.

16   The criminal child turns on "being good" when it suits his purpose. We have seen more than one set of parents become more hopeful when there was harmony in the house or on a family outing. Some of their fears and pessimism melt away as they point out that "he was so good while we were all in New York; really, we had no trouble at all." Then they are chagrined when they recognize that the reason they had such a good time was that they did everything the youngster wanted and thus avoided any altercations. It is not long until the old patterns are resumed, the first time the parents say "no." When a criminal child seeks a specific privilege or wants his parents to get him something, he can be endearing.

C had created continual turmoil in the family by his neglect of chores, his sullen and sometimes antagonis-

tic attitude toward participating in family activities, and his activities in the community, which included stealing and threatening a girl with a knife. His parents, at a loss as to what to do, took him to a counseling agency. As Christmas approached, C told the counselor he would be "good." For 5 weeks, he did his chores, maintained a pleasant, cooperative attitude around the house, and did not get into trouble. He presented his parents with a list of more than $100 worth of gifts, which he wanted them to purchase. A week after Christmas, he resumed old patterns.

This illustration contains all the essentials of a "con job." Many parents will do almost anything, if they think it is for the good of the child and will contribute to family harmony. They pay for special schools, counseling, gifts, and so on, all to no avail. The criminal child exploits this and "blackmails" his parents to give him what he wants. They know that life will be miserable for them if they do not accommodate their child.

17   The basic stance of the criminal is that he wants to hold on to the comforts of home, as well as do the things he wants to do. The criminal child expects his family to meet his needs. Rarely does he consider anyone else's rights. He thinks that he should be able to do as he wants, but that others should be limited in interfering with him. He plays with a sibling's toys and breaks them, but he beats up a brother whom he finds using something of his without his explicit consent. He invades the privacy of others, but becomes furious when anyone asks him what he is doing. Emotional blackmail is an effective way for the youngster to get what he wants. His presence in the house becomes negotiable. His parents, already alarmed at his estrangement from them, may be fearful of his running away. Only a small minority actually leave the house. However, the criminal may keep running away a live issue to frighten his family into doing what he wants. A more menacing type of coercion occurs when the criminal warns his parents, "If you don't____, you'll be sorry," with an implied threat of retaliation in the form of violation.

C wanted an air rifle, but his family thought it was dangerous. His attitude was that, if they would not give it to him, he would steal $5. After all, it would be "their fault" for not giving it to him. The only way to avoid the theft would be for his parents to give him what he wanted.

The tactics may become extreme, as in the case of the youngster who threatens suicide and inflicts some superficial cuts on himself. When the criminal youngster creates some "emergency," he does his utmost to see that his parents are embarrassed and faulted. For example, if the neighbors find that he is using the family house for drinking, drugs, and sex in the parents' absence, it is seen as a case of parental neglect or permissiveness.

18   The criminal youngster engages in crimes against his family—unauthorized use of the family car, stealing money from mother's purse, misusing parental charge accounts, keeping weapons in the house. The list is endless, but the worst crimes are those which cannot be measured in dollars and cents. The broken hearts and disrupted lives are the most costly of all. His violations frighten his parents, so they curtail their own activities to stay home and supervise him. He does not hesitate to misrepresent his parents and give them a bad name in the community. Because of his conduct, the entire family lives with constant stress and uncertainty. These patterns at home are a microcosm of the child's functioning everywhere. Within them are contained all the essentials of a street crime.

Samuel Yochelson and Stanton E. Samenow, "The Criminal's Way of Life," in *The Criminal Personality*, vol. 1 (Northvale, N.J.: Jason Aronson, 1976), pp. 125–132. Reprinted by permission of Jason Aronson.

• •

1. The main idea of this excerpt seems to be that:
    a. more than one criminal is often produced in a single family.
    b. there are often law-abiding members in a criminal's family.
    c. a criminal often has a criminal for a father.
    d. the environment creates criminals.

2. Criminals, the excerpt suggests, tend to avoid being with responsible people.
    a. true
    b. false

3. Which characteristic does *not* describe a criminal?
    a. unmanageable at home
    b. seen as different by family members
    c. secretive
    d. wants to be loved

4. Criminals seem to be:
    a. aggressive.
    b. domineering.
    c. passive.
    d. both *a* and *b*.

5. The last paragraph suggests that the criminal:
    a. wants to change.
    b. is a forgotten member of the family.
    c. controls the family.
    d. only makes bonds with people outside the family.

Sel. 3   P-Skim   1. _____

Time   2:00 = 1,315 wpm   2. _____

Score   _____ %   3. _____

▶ 80%   4. _____

Score = number correct × 20.   5. _____

Check answers on p. 340.

B. Critical Reading

Now read critically, paying particular attention to the motivation of the child criminal and to the attitude that the authors have toward this child. Record your beginning and ending times in the answer box only for the time you took to read the review. Once you have calculated this time, answer the questions without looking back at the selection.

1. Siblings tend to:
    a.   cover for their criminal sibling.
    b.   ignore their criminal sibling.
    c.   seek professional help to cope with their criminal sibling.
    d.   band together to combat their criminal sibling.

2. When confronted with siblings who are delinquent, criminal siblings:
    a.   cover for them.
    b.   tell on them.
    c.   ignore them.
    d.   beat them.

3. The criminal tends to be:
    a.   slow to act.
    b.   impatient.
    c.   willing to compromise.
    d.   dim-witted.

4. The criminal often lies:
    a.   to protect himself or herself.
    b.   only in childhood.
    c.   only in adulthood.
    d.   when it is unnecessary.

5. With a criminal child, a communication gap exists because:
    a.   parents ignore him.
    b.   she ignores both parents and siblings.
    c.   he ignores parents, but not siblings.
    d.   siblings often do not have time for her.

6. (*Inf*) The authors suggest that the criminal sibling never attempts to be well-behaved.
   a.   true
   b.   false

7. (*Inf*) The excerpt suggests that the criminal is:
   a.   dim-witted.
   b.   overly physical.
   c.   often involved in drugs.
   d.   self-centered.

8. Criminals enjoy:
   a.   taking drugs as an escape.
   b.   blaming parents for their mistakes.
   c.   being sexually promiscuous at an early age.
   d.   saving money they have stolen.

9. (*Inf*) The excerpt suggests that:
   a.   criminals are products of their environment.
   b.   criminals have parents who have a negative attitude toward them.
   c.   criminals manipulate their environment.
   d.   both *b* and *c*.

10. (*P*) Paraphrase the following sentence from paragraph 18: "These patterns at home are a microcosm of the child's functioning everywhere."
    a.   What the child does at home is a small part of his crime.
    b.   The child commits most of her crimes at home.
    c.   The child commits crimes at home that parallel what he does outside the home.
    d.   The child's crimes at home are unlike those she does outside the home.

Sel. 3 C-Read			1. _____
Finish	_____ : _____		2. _____
Start	_____ : _____		3. _____
Time	_____ : _____		4. _____
	min	sec	5. _____
Rate	_____ wpm		6. _____
Find rate on p. 330.			7. _____
Score	_____ %		8. _____
▶ 80%			9. _____
Score = number correct × 10.			10. _____

Check answers on p. 340.

Record rate and score on p. 327.

C. Questions for Discussion and Writing

1.   Reread the excerpt. Then list and discuss the five characteristics that describe a criminal.

2.   Cite five examples from the excerpt that show that environment does not create a criminal.

3.   Discuss sections from the excerpt that show ways in which a criminal is intelligent.

4.   In paragraph 16, the authors discuss emotional blackmail. Reread this paragraph, then cite examples from the excerpt that demonstrate this type of activity.

5.   Do you think that this excerpt describes all young criminals or a type of criminal? What type of criminal is portrayed here? Can you think of other types of people who become criminals? Describe them.

Self-Evaluation: Reading Criminology

Answer the following questions by circling yes or no. These responses will help you understand your critical abilities in reading criminology material.

1.   yes   no   Was your score in Section B, Critical Reading, below 80 percent?

2.   yes   no   Were the answers to two or more of your inference questions incorrect?

3.   yes   no   Was your answer to your paraphrasing question incorrect?

4.   yes   no   Did you have difficulty remembering the characteristics of the child criminal portrayed in the excerpt?

5.   yes   no   Did you have difficulty determining the authors' attitude toward child criminals?

6.   yes   no   Did you have difficulty comparing the attitude toward crime expressed in this selection with the attitudes expressed in the previous two selections?

Scoring: If you answered yes to three or more of these questions, you need more practice in reading criminology material.

Follow-up: To improve your critical strategies in reading criminology material, consider the following suggestions:

1. Determine early on the author's attitude toward the criminal—whether society or the individual is ultimately responsible.

2. Be sure you can easily recall the characteristics that the author considers important in defining the criminal personality.

3. Compare the author's attitudes toward criminals with other authors you have read on the subject. Determine which author seems to most closely agree with your own point of view.

4. Begin to evaluate the evidence that the author uses. Does it explain all criminals or a particular type?

. . . .

SELECTION 4

From *Brothers and Keepers*   by *John Edgar Wideman* *2,444 words*

Vocabulary

hunkered: to squat on one's heels; "where Laramie Lanes hunkered"

talisman: an object supposed to bring good luck; "as if they were a touchstone, a talisman"

incipient: beginning to exist; "they were incipient criminals"

relegated: assigned to a lower position; "had relegated them to the funny papers"

fusillade: a discharge of firearms; "one last fusillade and grin"

manacled: fastened with metal, like handcuffs; "manacled, draped with chains"

ambivalence: uncertainty; "his ambivalence about the Apple"

naïveté: unsophistication or simplicity; "the depths of my naïveté"

This excerpt is from a nonfictional account of two brothers and the lives they choose—one becomes a professor, the other a criminal. This excerpt comes at the beginning of the autobiography when the younger fugitive brother and his friends are in temporary hiding from the police at the older brother's home in Wyoming. This excerpt is a carefully considered character study of both brothers as they react to their lives. Throughout the autobiography, the focus is on the following questions: Why did Robby become a criminal? Why did John choose an academic life?

Your reading goal here is not to determine a thesis and details of support but to focus on the details that depict these two very different brothers.

Reading Strategies.   To more fully appreciate this selection, use these reading strategies:

1. Focus on understanding the two characters: Robby and John. Get a sense for who they are through their actions and statements. Is Robby manipulating and cruel? Is John completely innocent? Write down particular characteristics in the margins as you read and reread the excerpt.

2. Notice how the excerpt's language creates a mood. Determine what this mood is and locate words and phrases that help establish this mood. At the end of the excerpt, write a marginal note summarizing the excerpt's overall tone.

3. Read carefully for Wideman's use of metaphorical language. Study what comparisons are made in each metaphor, and see how this language complements the story's overall mood.

4. Don't expect to appreciate the details of this excerpt entirely the first time through. Good literature, as this is, requires rereading. Just be sure that after your first critical reading, you can describe Robby and John and describe the excerpt's tone.

A. Preview Skimming

Take 3 minutes (= 815 wpm) to preview skim this excerpt. In preview skimming narrative literature, you need to adjust your reading strategies. Read the first and last paragraphs through and the first sentence of any other paragraphs. Instead of searching for a thesis and details, try to keep the general story line in mind, without focusing on any of the details at this time. Merely determine who the two major characters are and what generally happens to them.

When you have finished preview skimming, answer the following five questions without looking back at the selection.

BROTHERS AND KEEPERS

by John Edgar Wideman

1   In Pittsburgh, Pennsylvania, on November 15, 1975, approximately three months before arriving in Laramie, my youngest brother Robert (whom I had named), together with Michael Dukes and Cecil Rice, had robbed a fence. A rented truck allegedly loaded with brand-new Sony color TVs was the bait in a scam designed to catch the fence with a drawer full of money. The plan had seemed simple and foolproof. Dishonor among thieves. A closed circle, crooks stealing from crooks, with the law necessarily excluded. Except a man was killed. Dukes blew him away when the man reached for a gun Dukes believed he had concealed inside his jacket.

2   Stop. Stop, you stupid motherfucker.

3   But the fence broke and ran and kept running deaf and dumb to everything except the pounding of his heart, the burning in his lungs, as he dashed crouching like a halfback the fifty feet from the empty rental truck to an office at one corner of his used-car lot. He'd heard the gun pop and pop again as he stumbled and scrambled to his feet but he kept running, tearing open the fatal shoulder wound he wasn't even aware of yet. Kept running and kept pumping blood and pumping his arms and legs past the plate-glass windows of the office, past a boundary of plastic banners strung above one edge of the lot, out into the street, into traffic, waving his arms to get someone to stop. He made it two blocks up Greys Pond Road, dripping a trail of blood, staggering, stumbling, weaving up the median strip between four lanes of cars. No one wanted anything to do with a guy drunk or crazy enough to be playing in the middle of a busy highway. Only when he pitched face first and lay crumpled on the curb did a motorist pull over and come to his aid.

4   Meanwhile, at the rear of the rental truck, a handful of money, coins, and wadded bills the dying man had flung down before he ran, lay on the asphalt between two groups of angry, frightened men. Black men. White men. No one in control. That little handful of chump change on the ground, not enough to buy two new Sonys at K Mart, a measure of the fence's deception, proof of the game he intended to run on the black men, just as they'd planned their trick for him. There had to be more money somewhere, and somebody would have to pay for this mess, this bloody double double-cross; and the men stared across the money at each other too choked with rage and fear to speak.

5   By Tuesday when Robby called, the chinook wind that had melted Sunday's snow no longer warmed and softened the air. "Chinook" means "snow-eater," and in the high plains

country—Laramie sits on a plateau seven thousand feet above sea level—wind and sun can gobble up a foot of fresh snow from the ground in a matter of hours. The chinook had brought spring for a day, but just as rapidly as it appeared, the mellow wind had swept away, drawing in its wake arctic breezes and thick low-lying clouds. The clouds which had darkened the sky above the row of tacky, temporary-looking storefronts at the dying end of Third Street where Laramie Lanes hunkered.

6   Hey, Big Bruh.

7   Years since we'd spoken on the phone, but I had recognized Robby's voice immediately. He'd been with me when I was writing Sunday, so my brother's voice was both a shock and no surprise at all.

8   Big Brother was not something Robby usually called me. But he'd chimed the words as if they went way back, as if they were a touchstone, a talisman, a tongue-in-cheek greeting we'd been exchanging for ages. The way Robby said "Big Bruh" didn't sound phony, but it didn't strike me as natural either. What I'd felt was regret, an instant, devastating sadness because the greeting possessed no magic. If there'd ever been a special language we shared, I'd forgotten it. Robby had been pretending. Making up a magic formula on the spot. *Big Bruh*. But that had been okay. I was grateful. Anything was better than dwelling on the sadness, the absence, better than allowing the distance between us to stretch further. . . .

9   On my way to the bowling alley I began to ask questions I hadn't considered till the phone rang. I tried to anticipate what I'd see outside Laramie Lanes. Would I recognize anyone? Would they look like killers? What had caused them to kill? If they were killers, were they dangerous? Had crime changed my brother into someone I shouldn't bring near my house? I recalled Robby and his friends playing records, loud talking, giggling and signifying in the living room of the house on Marchand Street in Pittsburgh. Rob's buddies had names like Poochie, Dulamite, Hanky, and Bubba. Just kids messing around, but

already secretive, suspicious of strangers. And I had been a stranger, a student, foreign to the rhythms of their lives, their talk as I sat, home from college, in the kitchen talking to Robby's mother. I'd have to yell into the living room sometimes. Ask them to keep the noise down so I could hear myself think. If I walked through the room, they'd fall suddenly silent. Squirm and look at each other and avoid my eyes. Stare at their own hands and feet mute as little speak-no-evil monkeys. Any question might get at best a nod or grunt in reply. If five or six kids were hanging out in the little living room they made it seem dark. *Do wop, do wop* forty-fives on the record player, the boys' silence and lowered eyes conjuring up night no matter what time of the day I passed through the room.

10   My father had called them thugs. Robby and his little thugs. The same word he'd used for me and my cut buddies when we were coming up, loafing around the house on Copeland Street, into playing records and bullshucking about girls, and saying nothing to nobody not part of our gang. Calling Rob's friends thugs was my father's private joke. Thugs not because they were incipient criminals or particularly bad kids, but because in their hip walks and stylized speech and caps pulled down on their foreheads they were declaring themselves on the lam, underground, in flight from the daylight world of nice, respectable adults.

11   My father liked to read the Sunday funnies. In the "Nancy" comic strip was a character named Sluggo, and I believe that's who my father had in mind when he called them thugs. That self-proclaimed little tough guy, snub-nosed, bristle-haired, knuckleheaded Sluggo. Funny, because like Sluggo they were dead serious about the role they were playing. Dead serious and fooling nobody. So my father had relegated them to the funny papers.

12   Road grime caked the windows of the battered sedan parked outside the bowling alley. I couldn't tell if anyone was inside. I let my motor run, talked to the ghost of my brother the way I'd

talked that Sunday, waiting for a flesh-and-blood version to appear.

13 Robby was a fugitive. My little brother was wanted for murder. For three months Robby had been running and hiding from the police. Now he was in Laramie, on my doorstep. Robbery. Murder. Flight. I had pushed them out of my mind. I hadn't allowed myself to dwell on my brother's predicament. I had been angry, hurt and afraid, but I'd had plenty of practice cutting myself off from those sorts of feelings. Denying disruptive emotions was a survival mechanism I'd been forced to learn early in life. Robby's troubles could drive me crazy if I let them. It had been better to keep my feelings at a distance. Let the miles and years protect me. Robby was my brother, but that was once upon a time, in another country. My life was relatively comfortable, pleasant, safe. I'd come west to escape the demons Robby personified. I didn't need outlaw brothers reminding me how much had been lost, how much compromised, how terribly the world still raged beyond the charmed circle of my life on the Laramie plains.

14 In my Volvo, peering across the street, searching for a sign of life in the filthy car or the doorway of Laramie Lanes, pieces of my life rushed at me, as fleeting, as unpredictable as the clusters of cloud scudding across the darkening sky.

15 Rob. Hey, Rob. Do you remember the time we were living on the third floor of Grandma's house on Copeland Street and we were playing and Daddy came scooting in from behind the curtain where he and Mommy slept, dropping a trail of farts, blip, blip, blip, and flew out the door and down the steps faster than anybody'd ever made it before? I don't know what he was doing or what we were doing before he came farting through the room, but I do remember the stunned silence afterward, the five of us kids looking at one another like we'd seen the Lone Ranger and wondering what the hell was that. Was that really Daddy? Were those sounds actual blipping farts from the actual behind of our actual father?

Well, we sat on the floor, staring at each other, a couple seconds; then Tish laughed or I laughed. Somebody had to start it. A choked-back, closed-mouth, almost-swallowed, one-syllable laugh. And then another and another. As irresistible then as the farts blipping in a train from Daddy's pursed behind. The first laugh sneaks out then it's all hell bursting loose, it's one pop after another, and mize well let it all hang out. We crack up and start to dance. Each one of us takes a turn being Edgar Wideman, big daddy, scooting like he did across the floor, fast but sneakylike till the first blip escapes and blows him into overdrive. Bip. Blap. Bippidy-bip. And every change and permutation of fart we can manufacture with our mouths, or our wet lips on the back of our hands, or a hand cupped in armpit with elbow pumping. A Babel of squeaky farts and bass farts and treble and juicy and atom-bomb and trip-hammer, machine-gun, suede, firecracker, slithery, bubble-gum-cracking, knuckle-popping, gone-with-the-wind menagerie of every kind of fart we can imagine. Till Mommy pokes her head from behind the curtain and says, That's enough youall. But she can't help grinning her ownself cause she had to hear it too. Daddy trailing that wedding-car tin-can tail of farts and skidding down the steps to the bathroom on the second floor where he slammed the door behind himself before the door on the third floor had time to swing shut. Mom's smiling so we sputter one last fusillade and grin and giggle at each other one more time while she says again, That's enough now, that's enough youall.

16 Robby crossed Third Street alone, leaving his friends behind in the muddy car. I remember how glad I was to see him. How ordinary it seemed to be meeting him in this place he'd never been before. Here was my brother miraculously appearing from God-knows-where, a slim, bedraggled figure, looking very much like a man who's been on the road for days, nothing like an outlaw or killer, my brother striding across the street to greet me. What was alien, unreal was not the man but the town, the circum-

stances that had brought him to this juncture. By the time Robby had reached my car and leaned down smiling into the open window, Laramie, robbery, murder, flight, my litany of misgivings had all disappeared.

17   Rob rode with me from the bowling alley to the Harney Street house. Dukes and Johnny-Boy followed in the Olds. Rob told me Cecil Rice had split back to Pittsburgh to face the music. Johnny-Boy was somebody Robby and Mike had picked up in Utah.

18   Robby and his two companions stayed overnight. There was eating, drinking, a lot of talk. Next day I taught my classes at the university and before I returned home in the afternoon, Robby and his crew had headed for Denver. My brother's last free night was spent in Laramie, Wyoming, February 11, 1976, the day following their visit, Robby, Mike, and Johnny were arrested in Fort Collins, Colorado. The Oldsmobile they'd been driving had stolen plates. Car they'd borrowed in Utah turned out to be stolen too, bringing the FBI into the case because the vehicle and plates had been transported across state lines. The Colorado cops didn't know the size of the fish in their net until they checked the FBI wire and suddenly realized they had some "bad dudes" in their lockup. "Niggers wanted for Murder One back East" was how one detective described the captives to a group of curious bystanders later, when Robby and Michael were being led, manacled, draped with chains, through the gleaming corridor of a Colorado courthouse.

19   I can recall only a few details about Robby's last night of freedom. Kentucky Fried Chicken for dinner. Nobody as hungry as I thought they should be. Michael narrating a tale about a basketball scholarship he won to NYU, his homesickness, his ambivalence about the Apple, a coach he didn't like whose name he couldn't remember.

20   Johnny-Boy wasn't from Pittsburgh. Small, dark, greasy, he was an outsider who knew he didn't fit, ill at ease in a middle-class house, the meandering conversations that had nothing to do with anyplace he'd been, anything he understood or cared to learn. Johnny-Boy had trouble talking, trouble staying awake. When he spoke at all, he stuttered riffs of barely comprehensible ghetto slang. While the rest of us were talking, he'd nod off. I didn't like the way his heavy-lidded, bubble eyes blinked open and searched the room when he thought no one was watching him. Perhaps sleeping with one eye open was a habit forced upon him by the violent circumstances of his life, but what I saw when he peered from "sleep," taking the measure of his surroundings, of my wife, my kids, me, were a stranger's eyes, a stranger's eyes with nothing in them I could trust.

21   I should have understood why the evening was fragmentary, why I have difficulty recalling it now. Why Mike's story was full of inconsistencies, nearly incoherent. Why Robby was shakier than I'd ever seen him. Why he was tense, weary, confused about what his next move should be. I'm tired, man, he kept saying. I'm tired. . . . You don't know what it's like, man. Running . . . running. Never no peace. Certain signs were clear at the time but they passed right by me. I thought I was giving my guests a few hours' rest from danger, but they knew I was turning my house into a dangerous place. I believed I was providing a respite from pursuit. They knew they were leaving a trail, complicating the chase by stopping with me and my family. A few "safe" hours in my house weren't long enough to come down from the booze, dope, and adrenaline high that fueled their flight. At any moment my front door could be smashed down. A gunfire fight begin. I thought they had stopped, but they were still on the road. I hadn't begun to explore the depths of my naiveté, my bewilderment.

John Edgar Wideman, *Brothers and Keepers*, Penguin, 1984, pp. 8–14. © 1984 by John Edgar Wideman. Reprinted by permission of Henry Holt and Company, Inc.

1. Early on, we discover that Robby:
    a. was involved in a robbery.
    b. murdered a man.
    c. raped a woman.
    d. was unjustly convicted of murder.

2. The narrator is Robby's:
    a. friend.
    b. father.
    c. younger brother.
    d. big brother.

3. Robby seems:
    a. cold and calculating.
    b. frightened.
    c. exhausted.
    d. both *b* and *c*.

4. This excerpt is seen from whose point of view?
    a. the big brother's
    b. Robby's
    c. the father's
    d. the mother's

5. The big brother seems to:
    a. be a criminal as well.
    b. be law-abiding.
    c. want to turn his brother in to the police.
    d. dislike his brother.

Sel. 4   P-Skim   **1.** _____

Time   3:00 = 815 wpm   **2.** _____

Score _____ %   **3.** _____

   ▶ **80%**   **4.** _____

Score = number correct × 20. **5.** _____

Check answers with your instructor.

B. Critical Reading

Now read critically, making comments in the margins about the main characters' actions and statements and about the suggestiveness of the language used by the author. Record your beginning and ending times in the answer box only for the time that you took to read the excerpt. Calculate your reading time. Then answer the questions without looking back at the selection.

1. (*Inf*) The narrator seems to:
   a. be very close to his brother.
   b. have forgotten much about his brother.
   c. have a strong dislike for his brother.
   d. both *b* and *c*.

2. The narrator recalls his young brother:
   a. playing records with his friends.
   b. talking too loudly with his friends.
   c. stealing money from him.
   d. both *a* and *b*.

3. When they were younger, Robby's father thought that Robby and his friends were dangerous criminals.
   a. true
   b. false

4. (*Inf*) When the older brother refers to his father's assessment of Robby and his friends, he comments: "So my father had relegated them to the funny papers." What does he suggest here?
   a. The father does not take them seriously.
   b. These boys are playful and amusing.
   c. These boys are worthless.
   d. both *a* and *b*.

5. (*P*) The narrator (the older brother) says: "Denying disruptive emotions was a survival mechanism I'd been forced to learn early in life." What is the best paraphrase for this statement?
   a. The narrator cannot take disruptions.
   b. To create his own life, the narrator needs to ignore chaotic feelings.
   c. The narrator only wants to survive.
   d. Dealing with harsh emotions allows one to survive.

6. Robby's presence reminds the narrator of:
   a. how different the narrator's life is from his younger brother's.
   b. his father.
   c. how similar he is to his brother.
   d. the hostile family they came from.

7. (*Inf*) What does the metaphor in the following statement made by the narrator suggest: ". . . pieces of my life rushed at me, as fleeting, as unpredictable, as the clusters of clouds scudding across the darkening sky"? The clouds are like the narrator's emotions in that they:
   a. portend doom or bad weather.
   b. are incomplete and changeable.
   c. are all part of the natural world.
   d. both *a* and *b*.

8. Which person does the narrator mistrust the most?
   a. Robby
   b. Dukes
   c. Johnny-Boy
   d. Cecil

9. (*Inf*) The narrator sees Robby as:
   a. a terrified victim.
   b. a hateful criminal.
   c. a con man.
   d. a disgrace to his family.

10. (*Inf*) One can infer that the narrator:
   a. has a clear sense regarding why his younger brother turned to crime.
   b. finds his experience with his brother painful.
   c. finds his experience with his brother confusing.
   d. both *b* and *c*.

Sel. 4 C-Read	1. _____
Finish _____ : _____	2. _____
Start _____ : _____	3. _____
Time _____ : _____	4. _____
min sec	5. _____
Rate _____ wpm	6. _____
Find rate on p. 330.	7. _____
Score _____ %	8. _____
▶ **80%**	9. _____
Score = number correct × 10.	10. _____
	Check answers with your instructor.
	Record rate and score on p. 327.

C. Questions for Discussion and Writing

1. Review the excerpt and choose three details from the story that best describe Robby. What do these details suggest about him?

2. Review the excerpt and choose three details from the story that best describe the older brother or narrator. What do these details suggest about him?

3. Compare Robbie to Jill, who was described in the first selection. Cite details from both selections that reveal how they are similar and how they differ.

4. Reread paragraph 20 describing Johnny-Boy. What descriptive words describe him in a negative way? Analyze how these words are used in portraying him negatively.

5. What do you think the narrator means at the end of the story when he says; "I hadn't begun to explore the depths of my naïveté, my bewilderment"?

Self-Evaluation: Reading Narratives

Answer the following questions by circling yes or no. Your responses will help you assess your critical abilities in reading narratives.

1. yes   no   Was your score in Section B, Critical Reading, below 80 percent?

2. yes   no   Were the answers to two or more of your inference questions incorrect?

3. yes   no   Was the answer to your paraphrasing question incorrect?

4. yes   no   Did you have difficulty understanding the characters' feelings and motivations?

5. yes   no   Did you have difficulty understanding the overall mood of the narrative?

6. yes   no   Did you have difficulty analyzing the metaphors that Wideman used?

Scoring: If you answered yes to three or more of these questions, you need more practice in reading narratives.

Follow-up: To improve your critical strategies in reading narratives, consider the following suggestions:

1. Understand that successful writers of narratives ask their readers to make inferences as they read. When reading a narrative, make marginal comments about what a character's statements and actions suggest.

2. If a writer uses metaphors, try to visualize them. Make marginal comments about what these metaphors suggest to you.

3. See if the metaphors and allusions of the narrative—taken together—suggest a consistent mood or theme. Write comments at the end of the story describing this mood.

4. Don't expect to understand a narrative the same way you understand the thesis and examples of an expository article. A successful narrative can be read on several levels, and each level can be appreciated in a separate reading. In one reading, you may enjoy the plot, setting, and action; you may also read for the characters' motivations the first time through. In a second reading, you may want to focus on the story's tone, while in a third reading, you may want to study the complexity of certain metaphors or metaphorical patterns. So do not feel frustrated if the narrative is not clear to you on all these levels at once.

Follow-up

Now that you have read four selections on crime, you may have changed some of your original notions regarding crime and criminal behavior. You may want to answer the following questions singly or in small or large groups.

1. What factors do you now think help create a criminal? Society? The individual? Or a combination of factors?

2. Do you think that there is a particular character profile that criminals share? If not, why not?

3. How do you think criminals should be rehabilitated? Or do you think that criminals can ever be rehabilitated?

4. In what ways do prisons serve society? In what ways do they serve the criminals?

How to Record Your Scores on the Progress Chart

After you have finished a Timed Selection and have entered your time and score in the score box:

1. Find the correct selection number on the top row of the chart. Transfer your rate (wpm) to the chart, under the selection number. Make a dot, X, bar, or other mark. (If you know your time only, not your rate, you must first look up your wpm in the Rate Table in the appendix. Then mark that number on the chart.) Note that the acceptable or "target" rates for the featured skill are shaded. Do your rates fall within the target area?

2. Transfer your comprehension score to the top blank on the chart. Note that the acceptable or "target" percentage for that selection is printed underneath the blank. Does your score meet—or surpass—the target percentage?

3. Connect the rate marks with a line, to see your progress clearly. Remember, though, that your scores will not necessarily rise steadily. The different selections contain too many variables—difficulty, your interest in or familiarity with the topic, and so forth.

PROGRESS CHART: CRITICAL READING

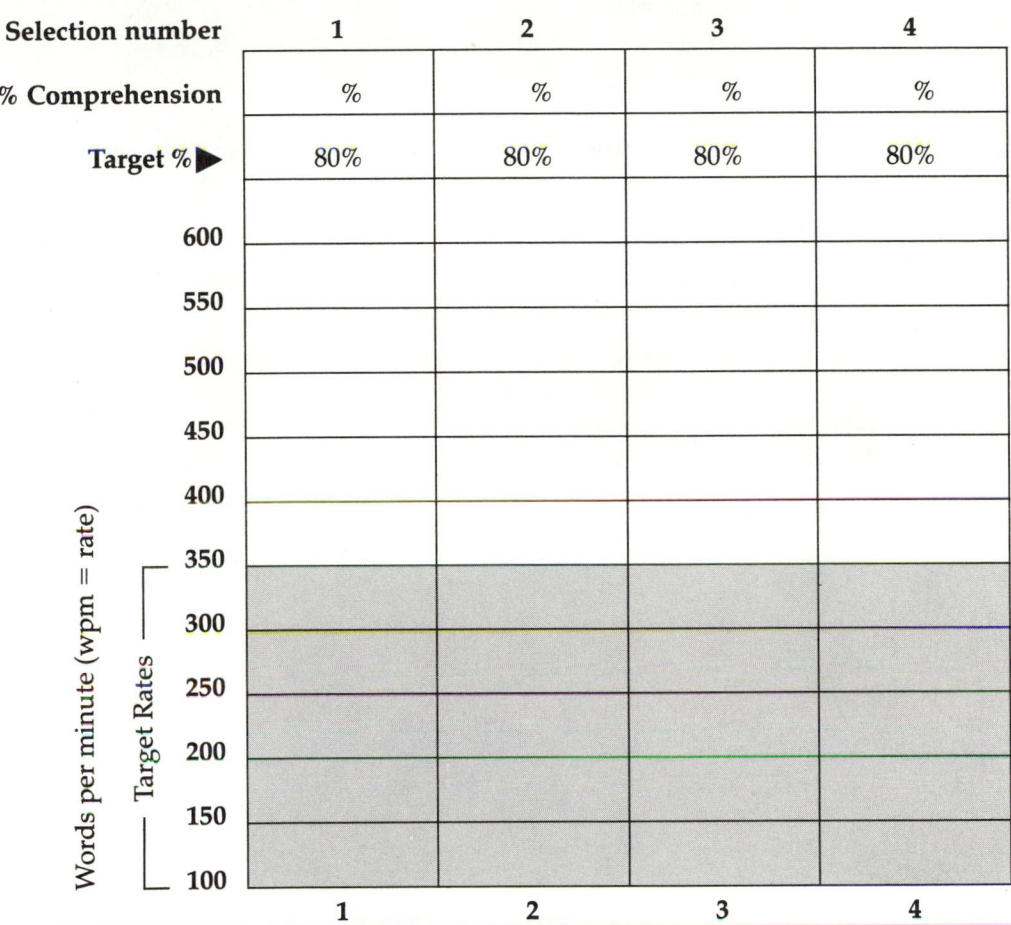

Selection number	1	2	3	4
% Comprehension	%	%	%	%
Target % ▶	80%	80%	80%	80%

Words per minute (wpm = rate) — Target Rates

600
550
500
450
400
350
300
250
200
150
100

Selection number: 1 2 3 4

Selection number

Rate Table and Answer Key

How to Figure Your Rate (Words per Minute) Using the Rate Table

The rate table will yield your words per minute for any timed selection in Chapters 4 through 6. You may already know your wpm if you read according to one of the recommended times. If, however, your time was different, you should have recorded it to the nearest 15 seconds (:30, 4:15, etc.).

1. *Recall the length (number of words) of the selection* you just read. This number is given just after the selection title. It will range from about 700 words to about 3,600 words.
2. *Locate that length (number of words), to the nearest 100 words,* in the column on the left-hand side of the rate table (3,600 down to 700 words).
3. *Locate your reading time at the top of the rate table.* (From 8 minutes on, please find your time to the nearest half-minute.) Run your finger down the column until you come to the line across from the length. This meeting point is your rate—words per minute.

   Example: Timed Selection 3, in Chapter 4, has 898 words. If you read it in 2-1/2 minutes (2:30), your rate was 360 wpm—900 words intersects 2:30 at 360.

Remember to record this rate on your Progress Chart.

RATE TABLE FOR FIGURING YOUR WORDS PER MINUTE (WPM)

No. of words in selection	TIME									
	:30	:45	1:00	1:15	1:30	1:45	2:00	2:15	2:30	2:45
3600	7200	4800	3600	2880	2400	2057	1800	1600	1440	1309
3500	7000	4667	3500	2800	2333	2000	1750	1556	1400	1273
3400	6800	4533	3400	2720	2267	1943	1700	1511	1360	1236
3300	6600	4400	3300	2640	2200	1886	1650	1467	1320	1200
3200	6400	4267	3200	2560	2133	1829	1600	1422	1280	1164
3100	6200	4133	3100	2480	2067	1771	1550	1378	1240	1127
3000	6000	4000	3000	2400	2000	1714	1500	1333	1200	1091
2900	5800	3867	2900	2320	1933	1657	1450	1289	1160	1055
2800	5600	3733	2800	2240	1867	1600	1400	1244	1120	1018
2700	5400	3600	2700	2160	1800	1543	1350	1200	1080	982
2600	5200	3467	2600	2080	1733	1486	1300	1156	1040	945
2500	5000	3333	2500	2000	1667	1429	1250	1111	1000	909
2400	4800	3200	2400	1920	1600	1371	1200	1067	960	873
2300	4600	3067	2300	1840	1533	1314	1150	1022	920	836
2200	4400	2933	2200	1760	1467	1257	1100	978	880	800
2100	4200	2800	2100	1680	1400	1200	1050	933	840	764
2000	4000	2667	2000	1600	1333	1143	1000	889	800	727
1900	3800	2533	1900	1520	1267	1086	950	844	760	691
1800	3600	2400	1800	1440	1200	1029	900	800	720	655
1700	3400	2267	1700	1360	1133	971	850	756	680	618
1600	3200	2133	1600	1280	1067	914	800	711	640	582
1500	3000	2000	1500	1200	1000	857	750	667	600	545
1400	2800	1867	1400	1120	933	800	700	622	560	509
1300	2600	1733	1300	1040	867	743	650	578	520	473
1200	2400	1600	1200	960	800	686	600	533	480	436
1100	2200	1467	1100	880	733	629	550	489	440	400
1000	2000	1333	1000	800	667	571	500	444	400	364
900	1800	1200	900	720	600	514	450	400	360	327
800	1600	1067	800	640	533	457	400	356	320	291
700	1400	933	700	560	467	400	350	311	280	255

No. of words in selection	TIME 3:00	3:15	3:30	3:45	4:00	4:15	4:30	4:45	5:00	5:15
3600	1200	1108	1029	960	900	847	800	758	720	686
3500	1167	1077	1000	933	875	824	778	737	700	667
3400	1133	1046	971	907	850	800	756	716	680	648
3300	1100	1015	943	880	825	776	733	695	660	629
3200	1067	985	914	853	800	753	711	674	640	610
3100	1033	954	886	827	775	729	689	653	620	590
3000	1000	923	857	800	750	706	667	632	600	571
2900	967	892	829	773	725	682	644	611	580	552
2800	933	862	800	747	700	659	622	589	560	533
2700	900	831	771	720	675	635	600	568	540	514
2600	867	800	743	693	650	612	578	547	520	495
2500	833	769	714	667	625	588	556	526	500	476
2400	800	738	686	640	600	565	533	505	480	457
2300	767	708	657	613	575	541	511	484	460	438
2200	733	677	629	587	550	518	489	463	440	419
2100	700	646	600	560	525	494	467	442	420	400
2000	667	615	571	533	500	471	444	421	400	381
1900	633	585	543	507	475	447	422	400	380	362
1800	600	554	514	480	450	424	400	379	360	343
1700	567	523	486	453	425	400	378	358	340	324
1600	533	492	457	427	400	376	356	337	320	305
1500	500	462	429	400	375	353	333	316	300	286
1400	467	431	400	373	350	329	311	295	280	267
1300	433	400	371	347	325	306	289	274	260	248
1200	400	369	343	320	300	282	267	253	240	229
1100	367	338	314	293	275	259	244	232	220	210
1000	333	308	286	267	250	235	222	211	200	190
900	300	277	257	240	225	212	200	189	180	171
800	267	246	229	213	200	188	178	168	160	152
700	233	215	200	187	175	165	156	147	140	133

No. of words in selection	TIME									
	5:30	5:45	6:00	6:15	6:30	6:45	7:00	7:15	7:30	7:45
3600	655	626	600	576	554	533	514	497	480	465
3500	636	609	583	560	538	519	500	483	467	452
3400	618	591	567	544	523	504	486	469	453	439
3300	600	574	550	528	508	489	471	455	440	426
3200	582	557	533	512	492	474	457	441	427	413
3100	564	539	517	496	477	459	443	428	413	400
3000	545	522	500	480	462	444	429	414	400	387
2900	527	504	483	464	446	430	414	400	387	374
2800	509	487	467	448	431	415	400	386	373	361
2700	491	470	450	432	415	400	386	372	360	348
2600	473	452	433	416	400	385	371	359	347	335
2500	455	435	417	400	385	370	357	345	333	323
2400	436	417	400	384	369	356	343	331	320	310
2300	418	400	383	368	354	341	329	317	307	297
2200	400	383	367	352	338	326	314	303	293	284
2100	382	365	350	336	323	311	300	290	280	271
2000	364	348	333	320	308	296	286	276	267	258
1900	345	330	317	304	292	281	271	262	253	245
1800	327	313	300	288	277	267	257	248	240	232
1700	309	296	283	272	262	252	243	234	227	219
1600	291	278	267	256	246	237	229	221	213	206
1500	273	261	250	240	231	222	214	207	200	194
1400	255	243	233	224	215	207	200	193	187	181
1300	236	226	217	208	200	193	186	179	173	168
1200	218	209	200	192	185	178	171	166	160	155
1100	200	191	183	176	169	163	157	152	147	142
1000	182	174	167	160	154	148	143	138	133	129
900	164	157	150	144	138	133	129	124	120	116
800	145	139	133	128	123	119	114	110	107	103
700	127	122	117	112	108	104	100	97	93	90

No. of words in selection	8:00	8:30	9:00	9:30	10:00	10:30	11:00	11:30	12:00	12:30
					TIME					
3600	450	424	400	379	360	343	327	313	300	288
3500	438	412	389	368	350	333	318	304	292	280
3400	425	400	378	358	340	324	309	296	283	272
3300	413	388	367	347	330	314	300	287	275	264
3200	400	376	356	337	320	305	291	278	267	256
3100	388	365	344	326	310	295	282	270	258	248
3000	375	353	333	316	300	286	273	261	250	240
2900	363	341	322	305	290	276	264	252	242	232
2800	350	329	311	295	280	267	255	243	233	224
2700	338	318	300	284	270	257	245	235	225	216
2600	325	306	289	274	260	248	236	226	217	208
2500	313	294	278	263	250	238	227	217	208	200
2400	300	282	267	253	240	229	218	209	200	192
2300	288	271	256	242	230	219	209	200	192	184
2200	275	259	244	232	220	210	200	191	183	176
2100	263	247	233	221	210	200	191	183	175	168
2000	250	235	222	211	200	190	182	174	167	160
1900	238	224	211	200	190	181	173	165	158	152
1800	225	212	200	189	180	171	164	157	150	144
1700	213	200	189	179	170	162	155	148	142	136
1600	200	188	178	168	160	152	145	139	133	128
1500	188	176	167	158	150	143	136	130	125	120
1400	175	165	156	147	140	133	127	122	117	112
1300	163	153	144	137	130	124	118	113	108	104
1200	150	141	133	126	120	114	109	104	100	96
1100	138	129	122	116	110	105	100	96	92	88
1000	125	118	111	105	100	95	91	87	83	80
900	113	106	100	95	90	86	82	78	75	72
800	100	94	89	84	80	76	73	70	67	64
700	88	82	78	74	70	67	64	61	58	56

ANSWER KEY FOR ODD-NUMBERED SELECTIONS

The following answers are only for odd-numbered practices, in Chapters 1 and 2 and odd-numbered selections in Chapters 3, 4, 5, and 6. For answers to even-numbered practices and selections, and to all practices in Chapters 3–6, please see your instructor.

CHAPTER 1, ESSENTIAL READING SKILLS: PRACTICES

Practice 1.1 (p. 18)

1. Sanitation problems in our parks
2. Divorce (or more narrowly, effect of divorce on children)
3. Jury duty (or more narrowly, interesting side of jury duty)
4. Siamese cats (or, Siamese cats vs. dogs)
5. The old Sunset Pier (or, a history of the old Sunset Pier)

Practice 1.3 (p. 21)

1. Topic: cause of the landslide
   Main idea stated in sentences 2–3, also 6
2. Topic: how the Night Killer was captured
   Main idea stated in sentences 1 and 14 (and 11?)
3. Topic: importance of reading beginnings and endings of paragraphs (or, why we should read paragraph beginnings)
   Main idea stated in sentences 1, 3, and 6
4. Topic: high literary quality of today's popular science
   Main idea stated in part of sentence 1, also sentence 2 and 9
5. Topic: return visit to old school
   Main idea stated in part of sentence 2 and in sentences 3 and 10

Practice 1.5 (p. 24)

In Practice 1.3:

Paragraph 1 has 2 or 3 details supporting the main idea: water from cesspools and landscaping, seepage into unstable cliff.

Paragraph 2 has 3 supporting details: storeowner, husband, and passersby all help to capture killer.

Paragraph 3 has 2 or 3 supporting details: speed-reading technique, studies of prose style, and experts' advice.

Paragraph 4 has 3 main supporting details: 3 quotations or excerpts from article to prove writer's point.

Paragraph 5 has about 3 main supporting details: the school's entrance, the principal's office, and the general similarities in the last sentence.

Practice 1.5 (p. 24)

In Practice 1.4:

Paragraph 1 has 4 main supporting details: Hispanics, Koreans, central business area, Europeans.

Paragraph 2 has 3 main supporting details: the family's memories, an old-timer's information, an old man's memories.

Paragraph 3 has 4 main supporting details: the Whiners, the Sunshine Kids, the Innocents Abroad, the Knowitalls.

Paragraph 4 has 4 or more details—but they are tongue-in-cheek. How would *you* answer this question?

Paragraph 5 has 4 supporting details: members of organized religions, those who follow clear principles, those who believe in a great spirit, and those who respect nature and higher values.

Practice 1.7 (p. 25)

1. a, b, d
2. a, b, c
3. a, c
4. a, b, c
5. a, b, c
6. a, c, d, e, g
7. a, b, c?, d, f, g
8. a, b, c, e, g

Practice 1.9 (p. 28)

Paragraph 1: spatial-geographic
Paragraph 2: description (also examples)
Paragraph 3: classification
Paragraph 4: process (also how-to) (humorous)
Paragraph 5: definition (also examples)

Practice 1.9 (p. 29)

Paragraph 1, "Anyone who has used": examples
Paragraph 2, "Divorce always has": cause-effect
Paragraph 3, "Serving on a jury": description, cause-effect
Paragraph 4, "Siamese cat": compare-contrast (also examples)
Paragraph 5, "old Sunset Pier": chronological

Practice 1.11 (p. 30)

Paragraph 1 Topic: the barge industry in Ohio
Main idea: sentence 1
Pattern: cause-effect (reasons)

Paragraph 2 Topic: U.S. geothermal energy (or, location of geothermal resources)
Main idea: sentence 1
Pattern: reasons (cause-effect) (examples)

Paragraph 3 Topic: argument in favor of geothermal power
Main idea: sentence 1 (and 4?)
Pattern: reasons (cause-effect) (examples)

Paragraph 4 Topic: effects of geothermal energy
Main idea: not stated. Geothermal energy does have some drawbacks.
Pattern: examples (cause-effect)

Paragraph 5 Topic: why we should support geothermal energy
Main idea: sentence 1
Pattern: reasons (sentence 2 or 3)

Paragraph 6 Topic: cancer-causing substances
Main idea: sentence 4
Pattern: cause-effect (some contrast also)

Paragraph 7 Topic: a permanent home for the Olympics
Main idea: sentence 1
Pattern: reasons (cause-effect)

Paragraph 8 Topic: possible overpopulation
Main idea: sentence 1
Pattern: reason (cause-effect)

Paragraph 9 Topic: difference between a fact and a value
Main idea: sentence 1
Pattern: definition (contrast) (examples)

Paragraph 10 Topic: human values (or, how human values arise)
Main idea: sentence 5
Pattern: reasons (cause-effect)

CHAPTER 2, SCANNING: PRACTICES

Practice 2.1 (p. 47)

Answers to scanning questions 1–10 will vary, depending on the dictionary used. Suggested time: 4–5 minutes. Suggested accuracy: 90–100%.

Practice 2.3 (p. 49)

Note: A page number must be given for every answer. (See instructions for this Practice.) Be careful to count as wrong any answer that indicates the student has misread the question. For example, question 1 asks for an informal or slang definition of "to beef," so a standard-English definition is wrong. Also, all abbreviations must be spelled out in full.

1. To complain   From Latin, *bos beeves*
2. (Answers will vary—keep noun and verb definitions separate)
3. Greek   long-haired (star)
4. Latin   pile 1: *pila*, pillar
   pile 2: *pilum*, spear pile 3: *pilus*, hair
5. Britain (England) Molasses
   Cloying speech or sentiment
6. gräts
7. 7 words
8. 6 (capital or uppercase X only)
9. his brother Cain
10. 480 B.C.
       Time, 1–10 5–6 minutes
       Accuracy 90–100%
11. German playwright—died 1956
12. 3
13. No To treat as a celebrity
14. j nineteenth-century gunsmith
15. adjective definition no. 9—Music
       Time, 11–15 3 minutes (total, 8–9 min.)
       Accuracy 100%

Practice 2.5 (p. 52)

1. Chapter 2
2. Chapter 5
3. even-numbered items, Chapters 1-6
4. no
5. Introduction
6. 5

7. all (6 Chapters)
8. 3 Progress Charts
9. Chapter 6
10. p. 330
       Time 2–3 minutes
       Accuracy 100%

Practice 2.7 (p. 53)

1. Selection 3 Clue word is seminarians in Selection 3 Beginning on p. 330.
2. Selection 4 Clue words are patients, pain In Selection 4 beginning on p. 149.
3. 3 titles   Selections 5, 8, 9
4. Selection 10   "Murky Waters"
5. Selection 4
6. Selection 3
7. Selection 2
8. Selection 1
9. Selection 2
10. Chapter 4 Selection 1 Title: "Touring by Model T"
       Time 3–4 minutes
       Accuracy 100%

Practice 2.9 (p. 55)

1. a
2. b
3. c
4. h
5. k
6. f (a)
7. j (h)
8. a
9. i
10. c
       Time 1 minute
       Accuracy 100%

Complex Scanning

Practice 2.11 (p. 57)

1. Literal comprehension and preview skimming
2. Golf
3. Example 1 (news story of food poisoning)
4. Paragraph 3
5. From simple to complex

6. Page 45 Yes (last rule applies to complex scanning)
7. Page 43 They disagree; for evidence, see their statement that one "common error" is the "uncritical acceptance of the printed word."

8. Page 43 Complex scanning
9. Page 41 Paragraph 7
10. Page 45 Tolerant, accepting, etc.
    Time 6–8 minutes
    Accuracy 90–100%

CHAPTER 3, STUDY READING: TIMED SELECTIONS

Selection 1 (p. 81)

A. Survey
1. d
2. a
3. a
4. d
5. b

B. Question
1. What are the major causes of pollution?
2. What are the two types of over-population?
3. How is technology involved in the pollution problem?
4. What does the four-factor model suggest?
5. Who are the neo-Malthusians and the cornucopians?

F. Study-Reading Questions
1. a
2. d
3. a
4. a
5. d
6. c
7. b
8. b
9. c
10. b

H. Scanning
1. 3
2. 12–20 million
3. 5–10%
4. Clergyman-economist
5. Entire earth system

Selection 3 (p. 101)

A. Survey
1. c
2. c
3. d
4. c
5. d

B. Question
1. What is the property-rights basis for pollution control?
2. What is the direct approach for pollution control?
3. What is the charging-polluters-for-their-pollution approach?
4. What is the bubble-plan approach?
5. What is the ideal allocation of resources?

F. Study-Reading Questions
1. a
2. b
3. c
4. a
5. a
6. b
7. d
8. a
9. b
10. d

H. Scanning
1. Internal costs
2. The vertical distance between supply curves
3. $10,000 per ton
4. Quantity of steel/price per ton
5. Macro problem

CHAPTER 4, RAPID READING: TIMED SELECTIONS

Selection 1 (pp. 139–143)

A. Preview Skimming

1. *Modern Maturity*, 1985. Publication date not significant, since writer is reminiscing about an event in 1921.
2. True-life (nonfiction) — first person narrative, style is plain and factual.
3. b

B. Rapid Reading

1. b
2. 4 weeks
3. a (true)
4. a
5. b

Selection 3 (pp. 147–151)

A. Preview Skimming

1. a (true)
2. a
3. 1985 (exact date not important— feature has an ongoing interest)

B. Rapid Reading

1. a (true)
2. b (false)
3. e
4. a
5. b

Selection 5 (pp. 156–159)

A. Preview Skimming

1. Title (sort of)
2. *Los Angeles Times*, 1985
3. b

B. Rapid Reading

1. a
2. a
3. b
4. b
5. b

Selection 7 (pp. 164–168)

A. Preview Skimming

1. a
2. b
3. a

B. Rapid Reading

1. b
2. d
3. a
4. a
5. c

Selection 9 (pp. 174–178)

A. Preview Skimming

1. b
2. a
3. c

B. Rapid Reading

1. d
2. d
3. c
4. a
5. c

CHAPTER 5, OVERVIEW SKIMMING: TIMED SELECTIONS

Selection 1 (pp. 211–214)

A. Preview Skimming

1. The Boston Globe Newspaper Company/Washington Post Writers Group, 1981
2. b
3. b (false)

B. Overview Skimming

1. b
2. a
3. a (true)
4. e

Selection 3 (pp. 219–224)

A. Preview Skimming

1. b
2. No
3. Wording may differ. Substance: "Twins reared apart offer new insights into heredity and environment."

B. Overview Skimming

1. b (false)
2. b
3. b
4. a (true)

Selection 5 (pp. 229–233)

A. Preview Skimming

1. a (true)
2. a (true)
3. a

B. Overview Skimming

1. a (true)
2. b
3. a
4. b

Selection 7 (pp. 240–244)

A. Preview Skimming

1. *Science 84* — general (popular) science
2. No lead-in
3. The bell that signals the end of a round

B. Overview Skimming

1. a (true)
2. d
3. b
4. b

Selection 9 (pp. 252–259)

A. Preview Skimming

1. c
2. b (false)
3. a

B. Overview Skimming

1. a (true)
2. b (although the title says "on the *job*," several paragraphs are devoted to children and adolescents!)
3. e
4. f
5. a (true)

CHAPTER 6, CRITICAL READING: TIMED SELECTIONS

Selection 1 (pp. 295–301)

A.   Preview Skimming

1. b
2. c
3. a
4. d
5. b

B.   Critical Reading

1. c
2. b
3. d
4. c
5. d
6. c
7. a
8. c
9. b
10. c

Selection 3 (pp. 301–317)

A.   Preview Skimming

1. b
2. a
3. d
4. d
5. c

B.   Critical Reading

1. a
2. b
3. b
4. d
5. b
6. b
7. d
8. b
9. c
10. c